AN ILLUSTRATED ENCYCLOPEDIA OF

UNIFORMS OF WORLD WAR II

Insterburg
Köln
DEUTSCHLAND
ERWACHE
DEUTSCHLAND
DEUTSCHLAND
ERWACHE
Straubing
DEUTSCHLAND

AN ILLUSTRATED ENCYCLOPEDIA OF

UNIFORMS OF WORLD WAR II

An expert guide to the uniforms of Britain, America, Germany, USSR and Japan, together with other Axis and Allied forces

JONATHAN NORTH • CONSULTANT: JEREMY BLACK

LORENZ BOOKS

CONTENTS

INTRODUCTION 6
COMING OF WAR 8
WAR IN THE WEST 10
WAR IN THE EAST 12
THE AFTERMATH 14
TIMELINE 1922–1945 16

THE BRITISH EMPIRE 18
BRITAIN AT WAR 20
BRITAIN'S ARMED FORCES 22
GENERALS AND STAFF 24
INFANTRY 26
CAVALRY 36
ARTILLERY AND TECHNICAL TROOPS 38
ARMOURED TROOPS 40
COMMANDOS AND SPECIAL FORCES 42
PARATROOPS 44
THE ROYAL AIR FORCE 46
FOREIGN VOLUNTEERS 48
CANADIAN TROOPS 50
AUSTRALIAN AND NEW ZEALAND TROOPS 52
AFRICAN TROOPS 54
INDIAN TROOPS 56

THE UNITED STATES 58
AMERICA PREPARES FOR CONFLICT 60
THE US ENTERS A GLOBAL WAR 62
GENERALS AND STAFF 64
INFANTRY 66
CAVALRY 80
ARTILLERY 82
ENGINEERS AND TECHNICAL TROOPS 84
ARMOURED TROOPS 86
RANGERS AND SPECIAL FORCES 88
MARINES 90
PARATROOPS 94
AIR FORCE 96

GERMANY 98
THE NAZIS AND THE ARMY 100
FROM VICTORY TO DEFEAT 102
GENERALS AND STAFF 104
INFANTRY 106
AFRICA CORPS 114
THE SS 116
SS FOREIGN VOLUNTEERS 120
FOREIGN ARMY VOLUNTEERS 122
CAVALRY 124
ARTILLERY AND ENGINEERS 126

PANZER TROOPS 128
MOUNTAIN TROOPS 130
PARATROOPS 132
LUFTWAFFE FIELD DIVISIONS 134
THE LUFTWAFFE 136

THE SOVIET UNION 138

THE RED ARMY 140
HARD LESSONS 142
GENERALS 144
NKVD 146
INFANTRY 148
FOREIGN TROOPS 160
CAVALRY 162
COSSACKS 164
ARTILLERY 166
ENGINEERS 168
ARMOURED TROOPS 170
MARINE INFANTRY 172
PARATROOPS 174
AIR FORCE 176

OTHER ALLIED POWERS 178

ALLIES, GREAT AND SMALL 180
BELGIUM 182
CHINA 184
DENMARK 188
FRANCE 190
GREECE 202
NETHERLANDS 204
NORWAY 206
POLAND 208
YUGOSLAVIA 214

OTHER AXIS POWERS 216

GERMANY'S ALLIES 218
BULGARIA 220
CROATIA 222
FINLAND 224
FRANCE – VICHY 226
HUNGARY 228
ITALY 232
JAPAN 240
ROMANIA 248
SLOVAKIA 250

GLOSSARY 252
INDEX 253
ACKNOWLEDGEMENTS 256

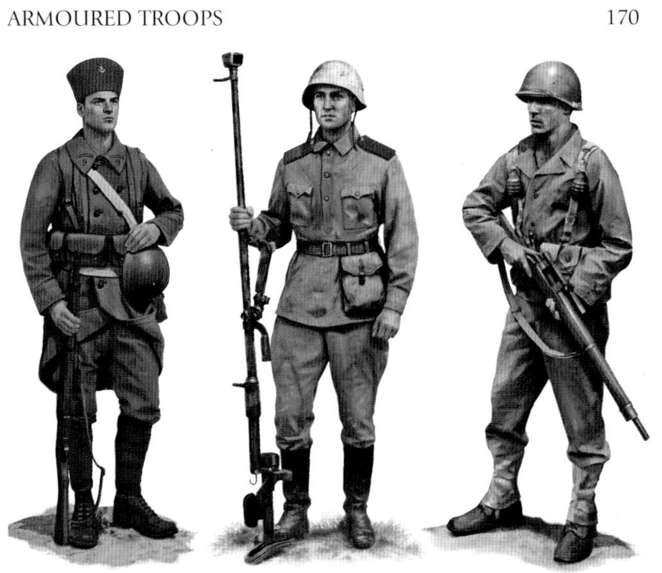

INTRODUCTION

The war fought between 1939 and 1945 has left deep scars on the modern world. It saw a level of atrocity, murder and horror unseen for centuries, and the sheer scale of the death and destruction was unprecedented. Waves of ethnic cleansing, countless murderous campaigns and the savagery of aerial bombardment were rounded off with the detonation of the world's first atomic bombs.

The war has been characterized as a conflict of good versus evil, but its nature was more complex than that. Even our traditional notion of when the war began cannot hold up to scrutiny. The Japanese had invaded Chinese territory well before 1939. The Spanish had fought each other, with both sides being supported by ideological allies. The Germans had annexed Austria, seized Czech lands (then dissolved Czechoslovakia) and taken the city of Memel from Lithuania. Italy had invaded Ethiopia and then conquered Albania, and all this before that fateful broadcast by British prime minister Neville Chamberlain on 3 September 1939 'that consequently this country is at war with Germany'.

The giving of ultimata, annexations, occupations and aggression in the years leading up to 1939 suggest that the war might be seen as a continuation of the First World War. This is perhaps true, even if the nations involved had changed and membership of alliances had shifted. Many countries became involved to right the wrongs, real and perceived, of the treaties that had concluded the first war. However, the second conflict certainly took on a character of its own: it escalated, merged with wars on other continents and lasted much longer than the conflict of 1914–18; it was more global than the first war; and the way in which the fighting – often exacerbated by ethnic, racial and ideological hatreds – pulled civilians into the conflict meant that the damage went deep and was lasting.

▼ *May 1945. Soviet officers stand in the ruins of Berlin after the Red Army took a city that had been devastated by Allied bombing.*

▲ *The unmistakeable 'mushroom' cloud of a nuclear bomb. This one, dropped on Hiroshima, Japan, on 6 August 1945, instantly killed 80,000 people and effectively ended the war with Japan.*

Weapons technology

Bomber and fighter planes had made their mark on World War I and tanks had given the Allies some tactical success. Improved versions had dropped bombs on Spanish cities in the 1930s, strafed refugees in Ethiopia or fought on the plains of Manchuria in 1939. The weapons of war in 1940 were still being perfected, but they were not new. They had been modernized, adapted and tested.

Military uniforms

Uniforms had not developed significantly since 1918. They would change during the conflict, but the infantryman of 1939 was still recognizably similar to his counterpart from 1918. In many countries the same helmet was in use (with minor modifications to strengthen the design or make manufacturing easier), and the same standard rifle. The cut of the cloth was also very similar and khaki continued to predominate – even the French, so proud of their horizon blue, opted for the colour of earth in their only significant inter-war uniform

▲ *A US Bofors 40mm gun, one of the most popular medium-weight anti-aircraft systems during the war, in France, November 1944.*

reforms. The Germans, however, held out for their grey. The nature of the new conflict led to some hasty changes a the beginning of the war. For although the study of uniforms is rather academic, the colour and shape of a uniform in action can make the difference between living and dying, staying healthy or succumbing to disease, being seen or remaining hidden. Metal buttons were subdued, colourful patches were initially kept hidden – as much for secrecy as for denying a sniper a target – and headgear was adapted so that soldiers could comfortably fire from the prone position (there was to be little trench warfare). As the war progressed, economies were made but uniforms also became less tightly fitting, more practical and more comfortable. Tradition persisted, but practicality definitely triumphed over smartness.

This book is designed to examine the uniforms of the powers that were heavily involved in the conflict. It has its limitations. Whole volumes·have been dedicated to some of the details of the dress worn by participants so this book is, in essence, a broad and general survey. It leaves out a number of participants. It does not cover the armies of those states occupied and annexed before 1939: the Czechoslovak armed forces, the Albanians and the armies of independent Estonia, Latvia and Lithuania are not included. There are also some geographic limitations. The Thai army is not described, even though it fought a war with France, and the Brazilian expeditionary force is not featured in any detail, even though a case might have been made for including them as they contributed to victory in Italy.

Although some mention is made of air forces, material on the navies of the participating powers has had to be left out. This is for reasons of space and because the emphasis is very much on land warfare – many air forces were branches of the army, and were dressed in ways that reflected the styles worn by land forces. That's not to say that German sailors did not fight bravely on land in 1945, or that many nations did not have sailors onshore guarding installations or securing ports or islands. Some mention is made of marines as these units were established to conduct amphibious assaults and, consequently, to spend their time fighting on land.

Finally, there has not been space to cover the partisans, guerrillas and irregulars who fought across occupied Europe and Asia. This not to belittle them, for they achieved a great deal against enormous odds and at great cost. Nor is it an attempt to dismiss the military importance of their role, or their bravery. The partisans of the Soviet Union, Poland, Yugoslavia, Greece, Italy and elsewhere deserve a book of their own.

▼ *Some uniforms, such as those worn by these Australian troops in London, had hardly changed since World War I.*

COMING OF WAR

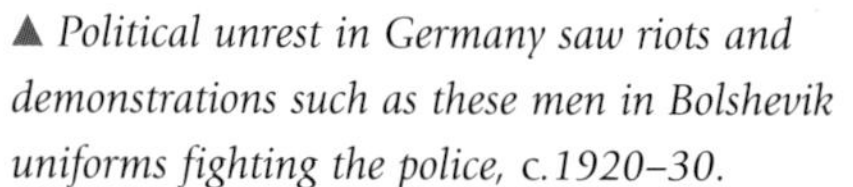

▲ *Political unrest in Germany saw riots and demonstrations such as these men in Bolshevik uniforms fighting the police, c.1920–30.*

Germany had been defeated in 1918 and then made to carry the blame for aggression and forced to deal with the consequences of world war. Faced with a ruined economy, social disorder and sizeable minorities of Germans now beyond her frontiers, she found herself nursing vengeance. Other nations also had reasons to be angry with the peace of 1919. Self-determination had been acceptable for those peoples who had supported the Allies (but even then not for their imperial subjects), but it was a tool used against those who were perceived to have been complicit with German aims. Hungary had been stripped of territory, Bulgaria had lost out, Austrians and Croats found themselves living in alien states.

The peace terms had also left the Bolsheviks in Russia feeling excluded. They had fought their way to power from amongst the debris of the world war, but were treated with suspicion, undermined at every opportunity and kept out of the community of nations. Other states, nominally winners in the war, had been bankrupted by conflict, while their populations had been disenchanted and radicalized by war. Italy stressed that she had not been sufficiently rewarded for her sacrifice. Japan had flexed her muscles and decided that she could be a regional power, now that the European empires were exhausted.

▼ *Japanese troops wave Japanese flags for the camera as they leave Tokyo on a train bound for Manchuria.*

A failed peace

The peace of 1919 planted the seeds of the next war. The status quo that was established was too fragile, and too much resented, to last. The previous war had whipped up hatreds and bitterness and fuelled the rise of aggressive ideologies on the left and on the right, and also exhausted and undermined those powers that might have stood for stability. Italy turned Fascist in the 1920s; Germany turned to Nazism in the 1930s; Spain took a similar path, following a bitter civil war. The forces of the right triumphed in eastern Europe. Such ideologies had militarism at their core and the slights and wrongs of the peace gave them ample opportunity for focused and aggressive nationalism. By 1934 it was clear that Europe was on a road to conflict, although it was not yet clear whether the threat could be contained. In Asia, too, Japan sensed that aggression brought its own rewards. Coaxed into fighting the Bolsheviks in the 1920s, and aware that China was isolated and weak, Japan annexed Manchuria and then prepared to launch a war of conquest against China itself.

Events in Europe demonstrated that the initiative was with the new ideology. Many of the European elites sympathized with movements that emphasized social control and anti-Bolshevism. Others felt that events in faraway lands were irrelevant, or that their own peace should not be troubled by developments abroad. The United States, which had embarked on a course of isolation, stood aside. German leader Adolf Hitler, ever the opportunist, and having settled his domestic affairs to his own satisfaction, took advantage of European indecision and exhaustion. In 1935 the Saarland rejoined Germany, and in 1936 the Rhineland was reoccupied. Germany and Italy supported the Fascists in Spain in 1936 (the British and French prevented the republicans from receiving supplies, even though thousands of volunteers made their way to the peninsula to fight for the republican cause), and Germany annexed Austria in 1938.

The French and British then hesitated about drawing a line in the sand, and watched warily as the next stage in the crisis began to emerge. It was focused on Czechoslovakia, a new democracy that had been founded on lands from the former Austro-Hungarian empire. It contained 3 million German-speakers, the Sudeten Germans, a minority whose leaders resented their status in the country and who were open to offers of influence from across the border. The Germans began to meddle, and to draw up military plans. The British and the French, aware that their militaries and their peoples were not ready for war, baulked at confrontation. They agreed that the Czechoslovaks should hand over the Sudetenland to Germany (in the so-called Munich agreement of September 1938), even though the Czechs were prepared to resist and had solicited some support from Soviet leader Joseph Stalin. However, at Munich the Germans got their way, occupied the Sudetenland and then reached out in March 1939 and dissolved the rest of Czechoslovakia (and took part of Lithuania).

The French and British, realizing that German revisionism had taken on a new momentum, nevertheless took a fatal step by rejecting offers of an alliance with the Soviet Union, a state that was aware of Germany's ambitions in the east. Instead, British prime minister Neville Chamberlain and French prime minister Edouard Daladier cast around for friends, offering an alliance to Greece and Romania before concluding a pact with Poland. Poland, isolated, friendless and hostile to the Soviet Union, relied on its non-aggression pact with Germany (signed in 1934) as a guarantee for peace but welcomed the offer of support. Even so, following on from success against the Czechs, Hitler was confident that the Poles would be unable to stand in his way and undermined them by concluding an agreement with the Soviet Union (which wished to claim back territories lost to Poland in 1920). Hitler felt himself strong enough to launch an invasion force and, early in the morning of 1 September 1939, the Germans marched into Poland.

▲ *A German battalion marches to the Polish front in September 1939. By the end of the month Poland was in German hands.*

▼ *German troops land with their equipment at the port of Memel in Lithuania, 1 May 1939, after taking the country.*

WAR IN THE WEST

The Germans invaded Poland from East Prussia and from the west, bombarding the Polish coast and bombing Warsaw. Polish defences were overcome and the Polish air force brushed aside. In an attempt to aid the Poles, France launched a small attack into the Saar but it was not carried out with any determination. On 17 September 1939 Soviet forces entered Poland from the east and the German assault on Warsaw intensified. By the end of September, with Warsaw occupied, Poland prepared to capitulate. Many thousands of Poles crossed the border into Romania or fled to France and Britain.

The Polish campaign was over in five weeks, and Poland's allies had done little to coordinate assistance to the country or relieve the pressure on the Poles. For Hitler, the campaign had demonstrated the effectiveness of his armed forces and the Allies' predilection for inactivity. Bizarrely, the French and British did more to support Finland when it was attacked by the Soviet Union that November.

The next major development was also in Scandinavia, with Germany's invasion of first Denmark and then Norway. Here the Allies responded, sending an expedition to counter the German attack and fighting fiercely for control of Norwegian ports. The Germans, however, would eventually emerge victorious and recognition of this fact triggered the fall of Neville Chamberlain; Winston Churchill was appointed prime minister in his place.

The day that Churchill assumed office saw the start of the German invasion of the neutral Netherlands, Belgium and Luxembourg. Coordinating an aerial assault with a concentrated ground offensive, the invaders overwhelmed the Dutch, who surrendered after their major towns suffered aerial bombardment. Belgium followed, with the German offensive forcing the retreat of British and French troops who had been coming to the assistance of the Belgians. The Germans then attacked through the Ardennes, skirting around the French Maginot Line (a series of defensive fortifications) and winning battles around Sedan.

The fall of Paris

The Germans then turned northwards, pushing for the English Channel ports and attempting to cut off British, Belgian and French forces in Picardy. The Allies began to evacuate troops

▼ *In late 1938, with Germany in control of Austria and Sudeten, Hitler's attention moved on to the problem of the Polish Corridor.*

▲ *The German Army entered Paris on 14 June 1940, and are seen here parading through the Arc de Triomphe and down the Champs-Elysees.*

towards the end of May, mostly from Dunkirk, with the German air force and navy failing to intervene decisively. The German army turned towards Paris, launching an offensive that broke a badly coordinated defence and burst into Paris in mid-June. A week later, France sued for peace; and to prevent her ships falling into German hands the British scuttled the French navy on 27 November 1942. The Germans occupied the Channel Islands and intensified air operations against the British mainland, eventually targeting London and major cities in the so-called Blitz.

The war had expanded in June 1940 when Italy entered the conflict and launched attacks against French and British positions in the Mediterranean and in Africa. Italy also launched an attack on Greece, but the campaign stalled just as British and British empire forces regained the initiative in Africa. This forced Germany to intervene to assist Italy by sending the Africa Corps to North Africa and by invading Yugoslavia in April 1941 and then continuing the assault into Greece (chasing out British forces and forcing Greek surrender). Two months later, the Germans invaded the Soviet Union, and at the end of 1941 Germany, optimistic about defeating the Soviets, declared war on the United States.

The character of the war in the west then changed. The British concentrated on a bombing campaign against Germany and on naval operations to defeat German submarines and impose a blockade on Germany. Occupied Europe saw the start of intensive partisan war and resistance movements that would trouble German and Italian occupiers and their allies for the rest of the conflict. The mass execution of anyone deemed undesirable, primarily Europe's Jews, continued apace. In North Africa the Allies slowly overcame German and Italian resistance and, in July 1943, were able to launch an assault against Sicily. From there, they moved into Calabria, triggering the fall of Mussolini (later installed by the Germans as ruler of a puppet regime in north Italy) and Italian surrender.

Allied triumphs

This significant development, which forced the Germans to prop up their southern defences, was followed in June 1944 by the ambitious Allied D-Day offensive, launched across the Channel and into Normandy. This was followed, shortly afterwards, by Allied landings in southern France. By the end of August 1944 Paris had been liberated and, that autumn, Allied troops were entering the Netherlands and German territory. A hard winter followed, with a German counter-attack in the Ardennes, which forced an Allied crossing of the Rhine. This was achieved with difficulty, but coupled with enormous Soviet successes in the east, made victory for the Allies now seem inevitable.

The post-war peace was settled by a conference at Yalta in the Crimea in February 1945. That April, Soviet and American forces met at Torgau, north-eastern Germany, and the Americans isolated and destroyed pockets of German resistance in Bavaria, Austria and western Bohemia while the British drove towards the Danish border. Hitler committed suicide in Berlin and, for a week, Germany was governed by Admiral Doenitz until the final surrender was signed on 7 May 1945.

▼ *American troops in landing craft go ashore on one of four beaches in Normandy, France on D-Day, 6 June 1944.*

WAR IN THE EAST

The war in the east began and ended with Japan. In 1931 the Japanese, who had been the preeminent power in Asia for the previous decade, took control of Manchuria and set about securing it by undermining a China then preoccupied with trying to assert central control. The Japanese attacked before this process could be completed, and quickly overran northern China (coming off worse in clashes with the Red Army along the Soviet border). They defeated China's relatively small army, but atrocities and a pitiless occupation regime meant that resistance became stubborn.

Attack on Pearl Harbor

Tiring of this conflict, Japan picked a quarrel with the United States, attacking Pearl Harbor, Hawaii, in late 1941, and then launched a successful offensive through southern Asia and towards Australia. Optimism had clouded the decision-making process but, in the short term, Japan was still winning. The British territories of Hong Kong, the Philippines and Malaya were overwhelmed. Singapore surrendered in February 1942, Churchill's words; 'There must at this stage be no thought of saving the troops or sparing the population. The battle must be fought to the bitter end at all costs ... Commanders and senior officers should die with their troops,' having fallen on deaf ears. Setbacks at sea and in the air dented Japanese progress but, even so, the Japanese were able to launch major offensives against Burma, and to defend the high-water mark of their gains in the Pacific.

Allies on the offensive

The tables began to turn in late 1942, with Allied raids on the Japanese mainland intensifying and troops recapturing islands that had been under Japanese control. The Japanese were now very much on the defensive, and the Allies, having destroyed the Japanese navy and won mastery of the air, were able to take position after position. In early 1945 the Americans launched an assault against Iwo Jima, hoping to capture the airfields there to intensify pressure on Japan (which was now being firebombed).

The Soviets agreed to join in the war following the conclusion of the war in Europe: they launched an attack on Manchuria on 9 August 1945. Hesitant about landing on the Japanese mainland, as the Pacific islands had been stubbornly defended, the United States opted to drop atomic bombs on Japan on 6 and 9 August. Japan surrendered a week later.

The conflict had been marred by a supreme disregard for human lives (on both sides). Civilian populations had

▼ *The territories of the Pacific region, 1941, as Japan prepared to launch a blitzkrieg against the Western colonies of southern Asia.*

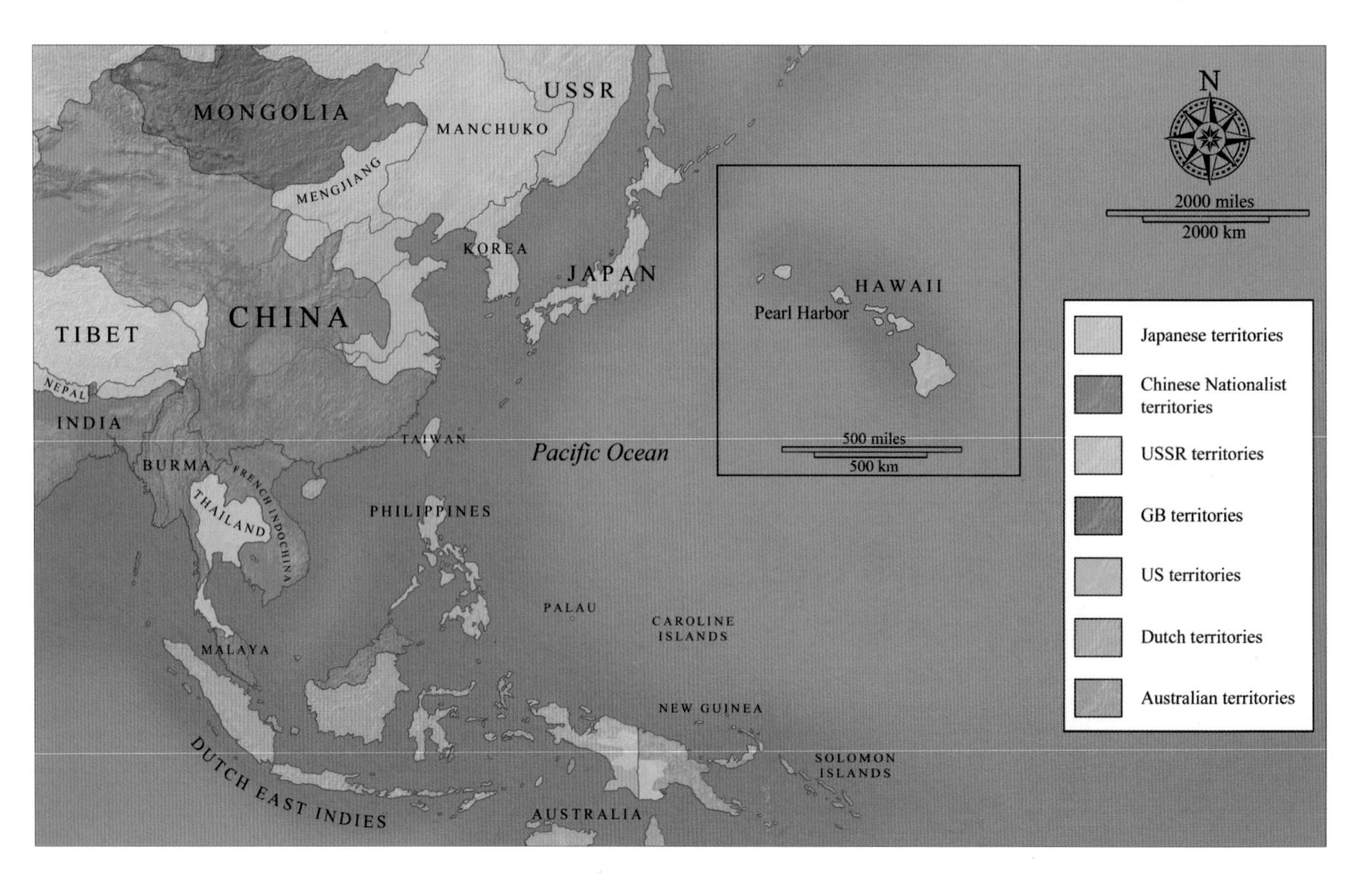

▲ *A photograph of the attack on Pearl Harbor, taken from a Japanese cockpit, as the torpedo hits* USS Oklahoma.

been enslaved, prisoners of war abused and mistreated and intensive bombing campaigns had been launched against civilian targets.

Germany's Eastern Front

The only other campaign to rival the brutality and terror of this conflict was Hitler's war against the Soviet Union. The Germans had briefly occupied the Ukraine in 1918. It had proved an abundant source of grain and raw materials for a Germany blockaded by Allied shipping for four years. The concept of acquiring such territory, and this time settling it with Germans, became central to Nazi plans at a very early stage. The vile proposal that Slavs were subhuman, and could be starved or enslaved, bolstered the idea and the German regime was openly talking about conquest in the mid-1930s. A marriage of convenience between Hitler's Germany and Stalin's Soviet Union meant that both sides avoided a war on two fronts in 1939 – the Soviet Union was at that time fighting the Japanese in Manchuria. But the quick conquest of western Europe, and Soviet difficulties in Finland, gave the Germans the confidence to attack the Soviet Union in June 1941. The initial onslaught was catastrophic for the Soviets. The Germans, supported by Romanians, Hungarians, Finns, Slovaks and assorted volunteers and allies, overran the Baltic territories (occupied by the Soviet Union the year before), burst into Belorussia and soon occupied the Ukraine. Entire Soviet armies were defeated and, by the autumn of 1941, the Germans were approaching Moscow and had blockaded Leningrad, which was to endure an epic siege. A savage occupation policy led to the death of millions of Soviet prisoners of war and the starvation of hundreds of thousands of civilians, a process that fuelled a spike in partisan warfare (and savage reprisals).

The Soviets launched a counter-attack against the Germans in the autumn and winter of 1941, driving them back and inflicting heavy casualties. The Germans, brought to a standstill in the centre, then switched their attention to the south: having taken the Crimea and Rostov-on-Don, they drove into the Caucasus but found themselves unable to engineer a breakthrough. Instead, they became bogged down around Stalingrad until a Soviet counter-attack surrounded the bulk of the German forces and forced their surrender in early 1943.

▼ *German cycle troops advance to the Eastern Front in 1942.*

The Soviets embarked on a series of attacks that wrested the initiative from the Germans and saw them win a crucial victory at Kursk. They built on this success in 1944 by launching Operation Bagration, which swept the Germans from the Soviet Union and into Poland, running out of steam at Warsaw. Offensives into Slovakia, Romania, Bulgaria and Yugoslavia were energetically pursued later that year and the Soviets launched their final assaults (against Berlin, Vienna and Budapest) in the spring of 1945.

The conquest of Berlin on 23 April 1945 triggered Hitler's suicide a week later, and, finally, German surrender, which took place on 8 May (9 May Moscow time). The Soviets then participated in the attack on Japanese forces in August 1945.

THE AFTERMATH

The Germans surrendered to the western Allies at Reims on 7 May 1945, and signed a universal surrender the next day in Berlin. Europe lay in ruins.

The total number of casualties can never be completely assessed. The Soviet Union lost more than 25 million people out of a June 1941 population of 196 million. Of these 9 million were military personnel, out of a total of 35 million mobilized. China had suffered similar losses in eight years of war, and would continue to suffer as world war blended into civil war. It was a heavy reckoning. Poland had been crushed by the war, the heaviest toll taken from its civilian population (6 million including those killed in the camps), almost a fifth of the population. Yugoslavia, torn apart by a vicious war, was also devastated.

Germany had lost 9 million dead, the majority being military personnel but also 3.8 million civilians killed by Allied bombing and in the final months of war, occupation and defeat. Japan, firebombed and blitzed, then pulverized by atomic ordnance, lost 2 million dead. Italy, Britain and the United States suffered casualties in the 400,000s. The Holocaust claimed 5.8 million victims, mostly Jewish citizens of Poland and the USSR. In addition, a similar number of individuals died or were executed in German camps, most of these (3.5 million) being Soviet prisoners of war – the first gassings at Auschwitz concentration camp in Nazi-occupied Poland were experiments on such prisoners.

In all some 60 million people lost their lives. The war also brought economic ruin for many countries, an infrastructure that had been torn apart and civilian populations that had been traumatized, dispersed or severely weakened. The United States' Marshall Plan was launched in western Europe in April 1948, designed to rebuild Europe's economies and put a halt to any post-war political swing to the left.

▲ *One of the millions of graves in the many war cemeteries around the world.*

▼ *Europe was full of refugees or displaced persons; this group was accommodated in a camp in Wiesbaden on their way home.*

Divide and rule

The defeated had been broken but punishment was still to be levied against the perpetrators. Germany was to be demilitarized (also losing its merchant fleet) and split into zones of occupation. Berlin was within the Soviet zone but, similarly, was divided into Soviet, French, British and American zones. Germany was to pay reparations, submit to denazification (a programme in which all remnants of Nazi ideology would be eliminated in Germany and Austria) and allow the settlement of Germans expelled from the east. Austria, too, was divided into zones of influence, but reunited in 1955 when the occupying powers withdrew peacefully. Japan was also to lose its military, and was to be reformed as a democracy (although it kept its imperial family). A peace treaty was signed in Paris in 1947 that allowed the minor Axis nations – Hungary, Romania, Bulgaria, Italy and Finland – back into the community of

▲ *Berlin, in 1946, divided between the Allies, was a symbol of the growing political split between the east and the west in Europe.*

nations, granting them the right to join the United Nations (Germany, East and West, were not granted this privilege until 1973); this was even though most of these countries had surrendered and changed sides in 1943 and 1944. War reparations were to be made (Italy was to pay the most, Bulgaria the least); Italy was to lose its colonial empire and borders were to be adjusted.

This redrawing of borders was significant. Italy lost territory to Greece and Yugoslavia. The Soviet Union absorbed Estonia, Latvia and Lithuania, and kept Bessarabia and parts of Ruthenia. It also established an enclave around Königsberg (renaming the capital of East Prussia Kaliningrad). Germany was split into two by 1949. Perhaps the most significant change concerned Poland. The Allies agreed that the Polish-Soviet border should be along the Curzon Line that had established a border before the Bolshevik-Polish War of 1919. This would have reduced Poland in size but to compensate her she was given Danzig, much of Prussia, the resource-rich parts of Saxony and even Stettin; this Oder-Neisse line forms the current Polish-German border.

Cold War

The new border arrangements were overshadowed by a more significant divide. The conduct of the war had been scattered with examples of mistrust between the big three Allies, and this difficult situation came to a head in 1945. There would be a new balance of power in the world, but, with the Axis defeated, the west saw the Soviet Union as the next ideological enemy, a feeling that was reciprocated. The Yalta Conference had actually set out what would happen in Europe but the situation reverted to the mistrust and hostility of the inter-war period. The west did what it could to undermine the Soviet Union, and the Soviet Union did its best to weaken the west and strengthen its position in eastern Europe.

The situation in the west was complicated by the fact that many of the liberation movements that had fought the Axis were left-wing and pro-Soviet. These would be suppressed (brutally) in Greece, undermined in Italy and marginalized in France. They flourished, however, in Asia and were soon in conflict with the imperial powers in Korea, Vietnam and China.

Collapse of empire

Within the shadow of the new ideological divide, and having being stirred to life by conflict, another process was gaining strength. Europe's colonies had gained a measure of self-governance, and been granted rights and responsibilities. With Europe exhausted, it was only a matter of time before imperial possessions became independent states in their own right. Jordan was the first (and Israel and Syria would emerge from mandated territories); India (and Pakistan) was a more significant step. This momentum continued in Asia in the 1950s and in Africa in the 1960s. A new world order emerged from the ruins of the old.

TIMELINE 1922–1945

1922
27 October. The march on Rome begins, leading to Mussolini and the Fascist Party seizing power in Italy

1931
18 September. Japan occupies Mukden, sparking a clash with China

1933
30 January. Hitler is appointed Chancellor of Germany

1934
26 January. Germany and Poland sign a non-aggression pact
5 May. The Polish-Soviet non-aggression pact is renewed

1935
18 June. The Anglo-German naval agreement fixes the size of fleets

1936
7 March. Rhineland is remilitarized
18 July. The Spanish Civil War begins
25 November. Germany and Japan sign Anti-Comintern Pact against USSR

1937
7 July. Japan and China are at war
6 November. Italy joins the Anti-Comintern Pact
12 November. Shanghai is captured by the Japanese Expeditionary Force
13 December. Nanking falls to Japanese forces

1938
12 March. German troops occupy Austria
20 September. USSR declares it will assist the Czechs if the French also support them
21 September. Britain and France insist the Czechs hand over the Sudetenland
29 September. The Munich conference discusses Czech situation
1 October. The Germans occupy Sudetenland
2 October. Polish troops seize Teschen in Czechoslovakia

1939
14 March. Slovakia declares independence from Germany, and Germany occupies Czech lands
22 March. Germany takes the province of Memel from Lithuania
30 March. Poland accepts the British offer of guarantee
7 April. Italy seizes Albania
13 April. France also offers Poland guarantees
17 April. USSR requests a pact with France and Britain
28 May. Japan and USSR clash in Manchuria
9 June. Germany signs a non-aggression pact with Estonia and Latvia
24 July. USSR's foreign minister meets with western powers to discuss German aggression
5 August. Britain and France send a delegation to USSR by ship
17 August. The Soviet offer of a pact is finally rejected by London and Paris
17 August. Soviets ask Germany for a treaty of non-aggression
23 August. German-Soviet Non-Aggression Pact is signed in Moscow; France and Britain are informed of the agreement to divide Poland
25 August. Britain and Poland sign a mutual-assistance alliance
1 September. Germany and Poland are now at war with each other
3 September. Britain declares war on Germany
17 September. Soviet troops enter eastern Poland
30 November. The Soviet war against Finland begins – the Winter War

1940
19 January. French and British draw up plans to send troops to support Finland, but by March, Finland and USSR have agreed to terms

▼ Hitler, in 1933, newly appointed German Chancellor, with members of the Nazi party.

▼ Italian troops occupying Albania, 3,000 of whom were transported into action by air.

▼ Efficient Finnish ski troops, known as 'ghost troops', were camouflaged in white smocks.

▲ *Volunteer firemen fighting a blazing London warehouse after a German air raid, 1940.*

▲ *Soviet soldiers at the Siege of Leningrad, 1943, just before the Germans lifted the siege.*

▲ *Survivors of the Auschwitz concentration camp peer through the wire fence, 1945.*

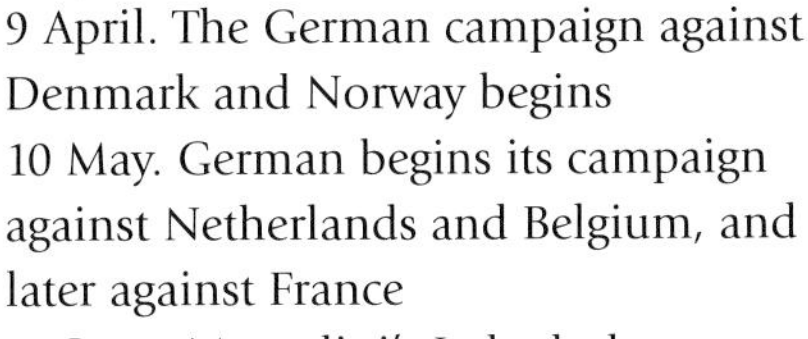

9 April. The German campaign against Denmark and Norway begins
10 May. German begins its campaign against Netherlands and Belgium, and later against France
10 June. Mussolini's Italy declares war on France and Britain
15 June. USSR begins the occupation of Estonia, Latvia and Lithuania
22 June. France surrenders to Germany
13 September. Italy begins a campaign against Egypt
27 September. Germany, Italy and Japan sign the Tripartite Pact
28 October. Italy invades Greece

1941
6 April. Germany is at war with Yugoslavia, the offensive will continue into Greece
27 April. Athens falls to the Germans
22 June. German invades USSR
19 September. Kiev falls to Germany
5 December. German offensive against Moscow is halted
7 December. Japanese planes attack the US base at Pearl Harbor, which results in America declaring war on Japan
8 December. Britain declares war on Japan after attacks on Pacific holdings
11 December. Germany and Italy declare war on the United States

1942
15 February. Supposedly 'impregnable' British territory of Singapore falls to the Japanese
6 May. The Philippines surrenders to Japanese forces
23 October. Axis forces are defeated at El Alamein in north Africa
11 November. Southern France is occupied by Italians and Germans
19 November. The Soviets launch an offensive to surround Germans troops in Stalingrad

1943
31 January. The Germans surrender at Stalingrad
12 May. Axis forces in Africa surrender
5 July. German offensive is defeated at Kursk by Soviet forces
10 July. Allied troops land in Sicily
26 July. Mussolini resigns and is replaced by Marshal Badoglio
25 August. Lord Mountbatten assumes command in south-east Asia and prepares to attack Burma
3 September. Italy surrenders to the US
23 September. Germany establishes Italian Socialist Republic in north Italy
6 November. USSR recaptures Kiev

1944
6 January. Soviet troops enter Poland (crossing 1939 border)
22 January. Allies are in unsuccessful operation at Anzio, behind Axis lines
27 January. Siege of Leningrad broken
7 March. The Japanese unleash offensive against the British in Burma
23 March. Germans occupy Hungary and establish pro-German government
17 May. British launch Burma campaign
4 June. Rome is captured by the Allies
6 June. D-Day landings in Normandy
22 June. The Soviets launch their Operation Bagration offensive
20 July. An attempt by German officers on Hitler's life is unsuccessful
15 August. Allied forces land in southern France
25 August. The Allies liberate Paris
31 August. USSR captures Bucharest
16 September. Soviets capture Sofia
19 October. Finland signs an armistice with the USSR
20 October. Belgrade is liberated
16 December. Germans counter-attack through Ardennes

1945
2 January. 90 per cent of Nuremberg is destroyed in an Allied air raid
17 January. Warsaw captured by Soviets
26 January. The concentration camp at Auschwitz is liberated by Soviets
3 February. The Americans begin the battle to retake Manila
4 February. Start of Yalta Conference to determine post-war peace
13 February. The city of Budapest surrenders to the Soviets
19 February. Iwo Jima battle begins
13 April. The Soviets liberate Vienna
23 April. Soviet troops enter Berlin
28 April. Mussolini is captured by partisans and executed
30 April. Hitler commits suicide
8 May. Germany surrenders
17 July. Potsdam conference begins
6 August. The Americans drop the first-ever atomic bomb on Hiroshima, three days later one is dropped on Nagasaki
8 August. Soviets declare war on Japan
14 August. Japan surrenders

THE BRITISH EMPIRE

Britain was the master of a global empire. In the lean years of the 1930s this had proved both a millstone and a blessing. The empire was difficult to police and it was a challenge to maintain the grip of British rule in the face of rising movements for home rule, but at the same time Britain had easy access to the resources of distant continents. The war would continue this paradox. The empire had to be defended, whether it was Malta or the Malay archipelago – and this imposed a tremendous strain on British resources in 1939 and 1940. However, when the empire began to mobilize, Britain could draw on vast amounts of manpower and war materials. By 1941 this bounty was crucial in stemming the tide of Axis victory, and turning the tables. Germany had gambled on a quick victory; but Britain, so long as the home islands held out, was capable of drawing the conflict out long term, until total victory could be achieved.

▲ Anthony Eden, the Secretary of State for the Dominions, carries out an inspection of Indian troops at their Egyptian camp near the Pyramids, 1 February 1940.

◀ British troops marching through the streets of Aden, a strategic port and outpost of empire that helped control vital shipping lanes flowing towards Suez. The incongruous dark socks, khaki shorts and sun helmets make for an unusual appearance in this early-war image.

BRITAIN AT WAR

Britain was correct to consider itself under-prepared for war in 1939. Years of underinvestment, together with a long-standing emphasis on diplomacy and a reliance on French numerical superiority over Germany, meant that Britain's armed forces were not in a state of readiness.

The German annexation of Austria and subsequent grab for Czechoslovak lands in 1938 hastened the introduction of measures to boost Britain's armed forces. In March 1939, with the Germans taking over the rest of Czechoslovakia, the Territorial Army was effectively doubled in size and following that, in April 1939, a very limited form of conscription was introduced, even though Britain was not yet at war. The regular Army had been augmented by some 212,000 territorials by the summer of 1939.

Initial plans called for the despatch of an expeditionary force to France to assist in the defence of the eastern frontiers, much as had been done in 1914. These troops, the British Expeditionary Force (BEF), would consist of some of the best units available, with some of the most advanced equipment, and its defeat in 1940 led to severe losses and an impairment of Britain's offensive capabilities for some time.

▲ *The defeat of the BEF, and the desperate evacuation of troops from the beaches of Dunkirk, was a severe blow to the British.*

▼ *Soldiers of the British Expeditionary Force on board a ship departing for France, at the very start of the war.*

In addition to the problems posed by equipping a force for service with the French, the entry of Italy into the war in June 1940 caused severe problems for Britain because the theatre of operations was suddenly enlarged to include the Mediterranean and Africa (East Africa and Libya contained Italian colonies). This meant that in a short space of time Britain's armed forces suddenly found themselves stretched by Axis offensives into Greece (threatening Egypt), French surrender and Vichy regime hostility in North Africa and Syria, German intrigue in Iraq and Italian offensives in Africa – all while Britain was being bombed and western France made available to U-boat bases and German raiders. Then Japan joined the fray. The strain began to show and, inevitably, the means required to continue the fight began to run short.

Supplies and manpower

Britain turned to the United States for supplies and for help to fund the war effort, and to its Dominions for manpower. Various measures were put in place to win American support, such as placing large orders with American suppliers, and Britain also leased territories in the Caribbean in return for 50 rather worn-out US Navy destroyers. Then, in March 1941, America approved the Lend-Lease Bill that would enable Britain to be supplied with material in enormous quantities (three times more than was supplied in the US's more famous Lend-Lease scheme supporting the Soviet Union). The cost was high, with much of the expense written off when Britain took an enormous loan from the US in 1946 – Britain only finally repaid this loan in 2006. The Dominions also contributed to funding, with the Canadians making gifts and offering supplies including clothing and food.

Manpower was the other part of the problem. It is commonly asserted that Britain stood alone, but this is very far from the truth; it relied on its Dominions and colonies for support.

Canada

The first Dominion to act was Canada, sending divisions to Britain, calling up personnel for service in Canada in early 1940 and allowing volunteers to enlist for service abroad. The response was enormous, with hundreds of thousands of Canadians taking up arms and enlisting in units destined for service overseas. Even so, demand soon outstripped supply. Therefore in April 1942 the government attempted to introduce universal conscription, which would also mean service abroad. Quebec resisted and political infighting scuppered these plans, although service abroad was eventually enacted in November 1944. Some 13,000 conscripts were finally sent to serve outside Canada, a small proportion of the total number of Canadian personnel involved in the conflict: 800,000 served in the Army during the war, 370,000 of them in Europe, and there were 83,000 casualties.

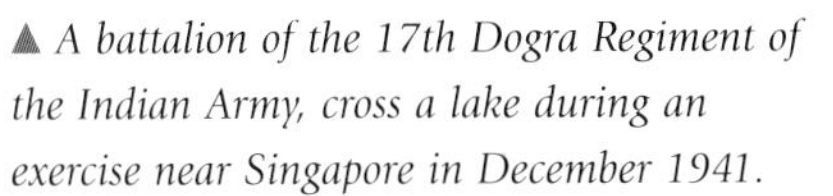

▲ *A battalion of the 17th Dogra Regiment of the Indian Army, cross a lake during an exercise near Singapore in December 1941.*

Australia, New Zealand and South Africa

The situation was similar in Australia, with conscripts serving at home and units composed of volunteers serving overseas. The Australian government was a little more crafty in its use of domestic conscripts, for in 1943 Papua New Guinea was defined as an Australian territory, thus permitting the use of conscripts in those and neighbouring islands. New Zealand initially had similar rules, with volunteers serving abroad and conscripts kept at home, but in June 1942 rules came into force under which conscripts over the age of 21 could fight overseas.

South Africa, which declared war on Germany on 5 September 1939, had more complicated domestic politics to overcome. The tiny army of 3,300 regulars – supported by reservists – was insufficient, but large numbers of volunteers stepped forward to fill units earmarked for service in the north; only whites were considered for front-line formations. The oath taken by these volunteers was amended in March 1940 to allow such service.

▼ *Around 10,000 British children were evacuated to British Dominions; this group are boarding a ship bound for Canada.*

India

Another significant contribution was made by India. The Indian Army, largely officered by Europeans, had performed a vital role in the previous conflict and now in 1939 this army of volunteers began to be shipped overseas for service in Egypt, East Africa and Asia. The Indian Army would remain a voluntary army, but the proportion of European officers would drop significantly over the course of the conflict. This was in part through necessity, but it was also made possible by a policy adopted in the 1920s of training Indian officers. The so-called Eight Unit Scheme of Indianization had established a precedent (staffing selected regiments with Indian officers) that was to be fulfilled on a greater scale after 1939.

BRITAIN'S ARMED FORCES

It was almost as though victory in 1918 led to a negative reaction from Britain's military hierarchy. Nearly all the major innovations that had contributed to the German defeat – and all the essential attributes of modern warfare – were seemingly swept under the carpet, while what little money was available was spent on propping up tradition or the Royal Navy.

This was inevitable, perhaps, because the inter-war Army was completely dominated by a caste whose members viewed themselves as officers and gentlemen. They had gone to private schools, followed by a stint at Oxford or Cambridge university, and belonged to a web of well-connected families (many of which had provided officer material for a hundred years). Labour MP Hastings Lees-Smith caused some commotion in the House of Commons in March 1938 when he said; 'The Army has now become a vast technical mechanism, and one of its most acute problems is not only to find the right number of officers – that may be solved – but to find officers of the mechanical and scientific type of mind which a motorized force requires. There is one source from which thousands of young men of the right scientific and mechanical type are being turned out every year. I refer to the secondary schools.'

▼ *These RAF bomber personnel are shown in high-altitude kit, clutching machine guns and parachutes, in 1940.*

Stagnation

This rigid system, reinforced by a lack of money and reluctance to change, caused stagnation. Air defence was relegated to a minor branch of the War Office, and given cast-off equipment; armoured forces were reduced – and by 1931 were utterly marginalized.

Many in the military thought that the next war would be fought overseas, probably for colonial possessions – and that lightly armed infantry, transported and protected by naval forces, would prove sufficient. Few thought that a large-scale conflict involving Britain would occur in Europe so soon after the last bloodletting. When it became clear that just such a conflict might happen, investment in the air force and navy was prioritized so that defence of the home islands would be secured.

▲ *Chief of the Imperial General Staff, Sir William Edmund Ironside, hurries along London's Downing Street in 1939.*

Modernization

The first significant step towards modernizing the armed forces came in 1932, with the abandonment of the Ten Year Rule – under which levels of spending were governed by the assumption that there would be no major conflict. Abandoning the rule allowed the armed forces to rectify deficiencies in defence spending, mostly by spending borrowed money. Funds were lavished on the Royal Navy so that it could maintain superiority over other navies, and the Royal Air Force was given financial support so that it could achieve parity with the German air force – even if training of required personnel was neglected. Indeed, achieving parity became an obsession in itself rather than providing the core of a carefully reasoned policy.

The Army initially emerged with a less generous programme. This meant that, even as late as 1938, there were only really two well-equipped divisions available for service on the Continent. The German move into the Rhineland and doubts about the Maginot Line had raised concerns, but the Munich Crisis and the German occupation of

Czechoslovakia forced the British to expand – and to promise the French as many divisions as the defeat of the Czechs had lost to the Allies. That meant 32 divisions ready for service within the first year of any conflict.

Throwing money at the problem did not necessarily mean an improved Army. For example, in 1938 it became apparent that a force would be required to match Hitler's panzers and it was decided to mechanize the cavalry at considerable cost. A swathe of units lost their horses in the spring of 1938, but did not actually receive motor vehicles until mid-1939. Officers protested at mechanization, then succumbed, but even then insisting that their units retain traditional names, badges and the cavalry's own officer caste, and only reluctantly consenting to be trained by the Royal Tank Corps. During one such session, on poor vehicles, one officer wrote that his men 'were grateful to Lord Nuffield (the British motor manufacturer, founder of Morris Motors) for the slowness and poor acceleration of his machines', because these failings made driving less dangerous. Most cavalry were issued with the Vickers light tank, a vehicle so erratic and poorly constructed that it constantly broke down.

▼ *Training for the new tanks was vitally important; here officers are instructed on how to change a tread in 1941.*

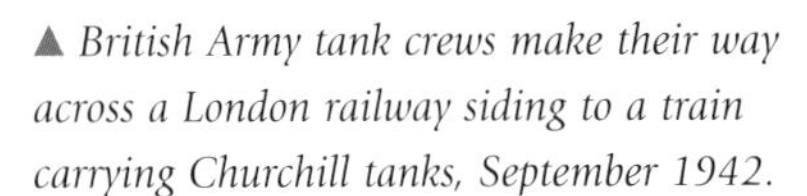
▲ *British Army tank crews make their way across a London railway siding to a train carrying Churchill tanks, September 1942.*

The situation with supply vehicles was even worse and there were severe shortages of lorries and trucks to keep the fighting troops supplied with food, clothing and ammunition. Requisitioning from local civilian sources only solved part of the problem, and created a logistical nightmare when it came to finding spare or replacement parts.

Badly equipped and supported forces such as these were pulled together to form the expeditionary force sent over to France in 1939. Britain was perhaps fortunate that the campaign did not open until the early summer of 1940, giving the troops time to train, yet the Army was aware that even its full-strength, professional divisions were small, badly equipped and lacking a cohesive training – as well as the doctrine that would add spine to such training.

GENERALS AND STAFF

British generals have often been characterized as slaves to tradition, but in fact their dress frequently expressed individuality and a certain level of contempt for regulations.

Rank and functions

Specific ranks related to specific functions. Field marshals commanded an army group, being responsible for operations in a particular theatre. Generals commanded an army, lieutenant generals commanded a corps, major generals commanded divisions and brigadiers commanded brigades. The rank of brigadier had only been introduced in 1928 and before that the appropriate rank had been colonel commandant.

On the surface, British generals and their staff were still uniformed in the same style as 1918. The service dress tunic was privately tailored, had gilt buttons and four pockets with scalloped flaps above and rectangular flaps at the waist. Sam Browne belts, breeches and cavalry boots were worn.

However, the early years of conflict brought about considerable choice, mostly because general officers felt comfortable enough to adapt standard issue dress to local conditions and to expressing a certain amount of eccentricity as they did so – while often encouraging such eccentricity in order to build morale and forge an identity for troops under their command. This meant that the service dress tunic was frequently set aside and rank insignia was worn on the battledress. This was often privately tailored, and in either the European or lighter Middle East style, but never the economy versions of khaki drill tunic or shirt, flannel shirt or woollen pullover. In Asia bush jackets, green shirts, khaki drill tunics and shirts all received the same treatment. Formal breeches or jodhpurs of the 1930s, with the rather old-fashioned emphasis of the thigh, and the brief vogue for golf trousers at the end of the decade, gradually gave way to more practical items of dress: battledress trousers, khaki drill trousers or shorts. Short greatcoats for mounted officers, and

◀ **Major General, 1940** *Very little had changed since 1918 and not necessarily just in terms of the uniform. The buttons on the gorget patches and the shoulder straps both bore the crossed baton and sword device, the latter being a curved light cavalry sabre.*

▶ **Brigadier, 1941** *Brigadiers were entitled to wear gorget patches on their shirt (slightly smaller versions were produced specifically for the collars of shirts and lapels), but it was just as common for the collar to be worn free of insignia and to indicate rank through shoulder strap insignia only.*

▲ *General Sir Bernard L. Montgomery, at the British Eighth Army battle headquarters, in Tripoli, July 1943.*

the traditional British Warm coats – a kind of short double-breasted greatcoat – were also worn.

Headgear

Service dress caps with red bands were very common. The badge worn consisted of a lion above a golden crown with red cloth cap for brigadiers, or lion above sword and baton, and this was universally applied regardless of command. There were variants: generals in Asia adopted the slouch hat, while generals in Europe preferred a service cap with stiffeners removed or the coloured side cap of their original unit or branch of service. Generals in charge of units of a particular nationality adopted the headdress of those troops, whether the Scottish Tam O'Shanter or bonnet, the Polish square-topped cap or the Gurkha slouch hat. Generals in India began the war wearing the domed sun helmet.

Insignia

Rank insignia was shown chiefly on the shoulder strap. Field marshals had an elegant badge on scarlet backing of a crown in gold bullion thread (the King's or Imperial crown with red cloth cap), with a wreath below encircling crossed marshals' batons (of reduced size in order to fit within the wreath). Generals had the same crown, and below it a star with crossed light cavalry sabre and baton (longer than that worn by the field marshal) at the end of the shoulder strap. Lieutenant generals had the crossed sword and baton with crown above, major generals had the same but replaced the crown with the star. Brigadiers had a crown over three stars.

Gorget patches were also worn (smaller versions were used on the battledress or on shirts). These had a button with royal cipher and a line of gimp braid on a background that varied according to branch of service. This was scarlet for most generals and staff officers, although engineers had blue, medical corps commanders had cherry red and ordnance corps had dark blue (until 1941, thereafter red). Aides-de-camp attached the royal cipher in gold thread to their shoulder straps. Generals of the reserve added an 'R' to their shoulder straps.

Formation signs were generally worn. These were either patches for General Headquarters (GHQ India and Middle East also existed), joint Allied commands, home commands, overseas command, Army and Army group commands, Army corps headquarters or divisional patches.

Officers from the Dominions, or commanding troops from exiled nationalities, sometimes wore the coloured shoulder arc titles of their respective nationality. These usually called for the national name to be embroidered in white on a coloured background and general officers used silver bullion thread for the lettering. French, Polish and Czech officers retained national rank insignia.

Intelligence

Staff officers had bright red as their distinguishing colour, and officers would have this colour as the backing for their rank insignia on the shoulder strap. A strip in branch-of-service colours was not generally worn by such officers. The personnel of the Intelligence Corps did wear a green branch-of-service strip and had green backing to their rank insignia on the shoulder. Intelligence was also provided by the Reconnaissance Corps and the GHQ Liaison Regiment (Phantom), which wore a white P on a black patch until it became part of the Royal Armoured Corps in 1944.

▼ **STAFF SERGEANT, INTELLIGENCE CORPS, 1943** *This NCO wears the 1940-pattern battledress that was not fly-fronted but was easier and cheaper to manufacture. Metal shoulder titles (bearing the unit designation 'INT CORPS') had been worn before the cloth title was introduced.*

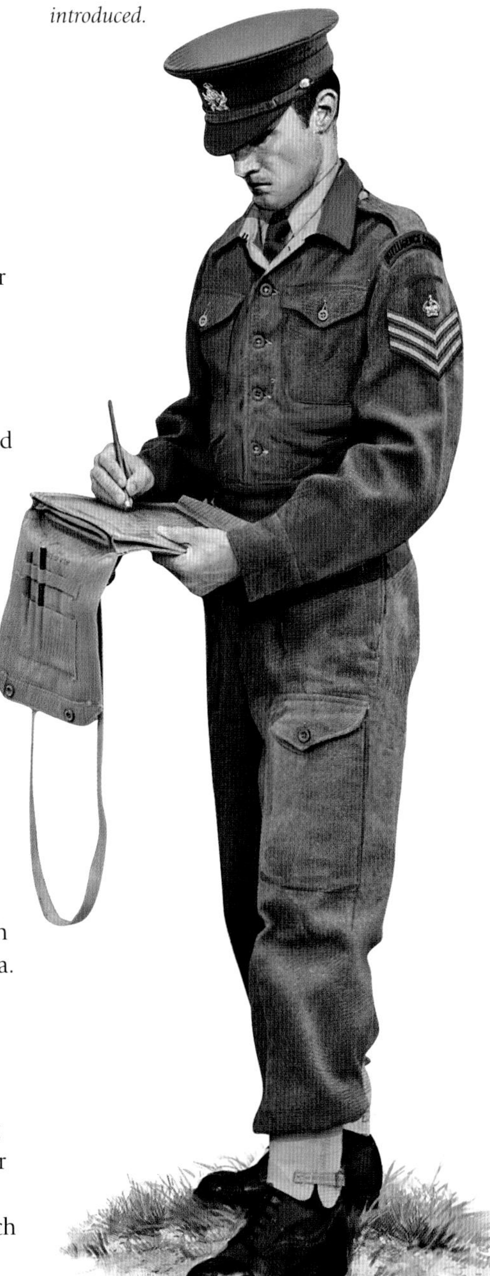

INFANTRY

When the war began in 1939 British infantry seemed, at least superficially, to be dressed in a way that resembled the men of 1918. However, such a view disguises the developments made in attempting to introduce military dress and equipment that was economical, if not always comfortable or elegant.

Even though there were different types of infantry, all fought in more or less the same role. Designations of Guard, Light, Highland or Territorial made very little difference to the role the infantry was expected to play, but inevitably there were some variations in dress, insignia and morale among such units.

Given that British units could serve in Europe, Africa, the Mediterranean and the Far East, there was a great variety of dress – and this was adapted, modified or cannibalized throughout the conflict. Despite being a pre-eminent industrial power, Britain also relied on material supplied by her colonies, Dominions and allies (from American war aid to Canadian battledress and Indian bush shirts).

Battledress

The most significant item in the British infantryman's uniform was the battledress. This ill-fitting, rough garment was smelly because it was impregnated with chemical agents, but proved itself to be remarkably popular: it won acceptance and eventually imitators – France ordered 100,000 Canadian examples in 1944 and late in the war Germany issued a similar tunic.

Discussion began in 1932, with various models of tunic being considered along with khaki golf trousers. It was only in 1937, however, that the preferred option was fixed upon; it went into production in 1938. Given the pressure on resources, it was inevitable that many units went without in 1939 – relying instead on their service dress tunics. These were recognizably the tunics worn in the previous war, with a stand-and-fall collar, four pockets (the two breast pockets pleated, and all with rectangular flaps) and fastened down

◀ **Private, 4th Battalion, Border Regiment, 1940** *Early-war infantry went into action carrying an anti-mask cap on the top of their pack (held in place with the white straps over the shoulder) as well as a gas mask, or respirator, in its canvas bag. From this chest position, the Mark IV respirator could then be quickly taken out in case of attack.*

▶ **Private, 2nd Battalion, King's Royal Rifle Corps, 1940** *British rifle regiments still thought of themselves as an elite and wore a number of distinctions, including blackened buttons. This rifleman carries the rare leather 1939-pattern equipment, which was issued as a stopgap measure or used for troops undergoing training.*

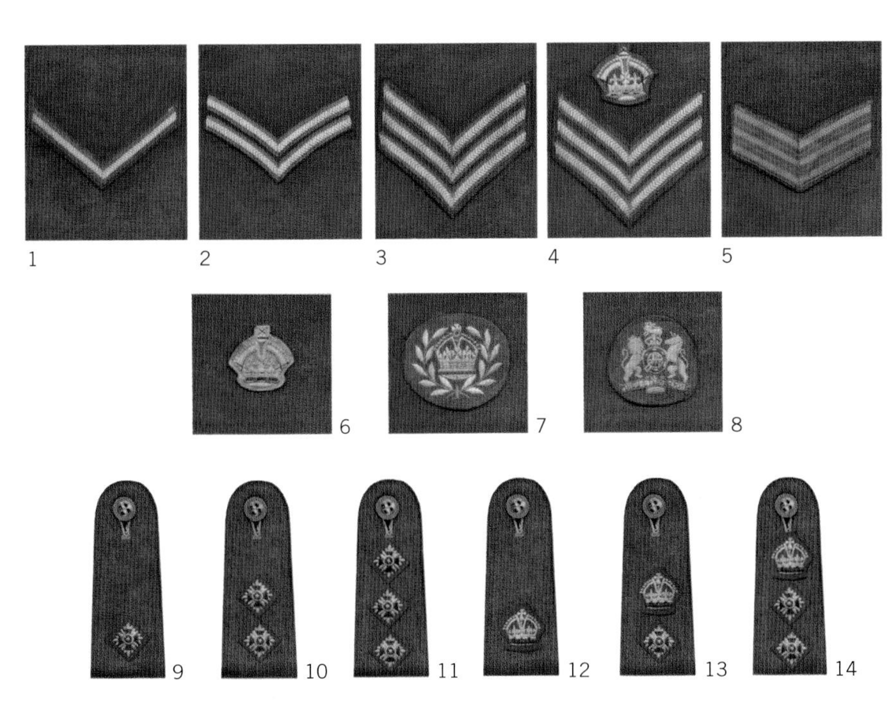

▲ INFANTRY RANK BADGES *1 Lance Corporal, 2 Corporal, 3 Sergeant, 4 Staff Sergeant, 5 Sergeant (1945), 6 Warrant Officer Class II, 7 Warrant Officer Class II, 8 Warrant Officer Class I, 9 2nd Lieutenant (infantry), 10 Lieutenant, 11 Captain, 12 Major, 13 Lieutenant Colonel, 14 Colonel.*

► CAPTAIN, EAST KENT REGIMENT, 1940 *Officers had the choice of purchasing ready-to-wear uniforms or having a uniform made up by a private tailor. In both cases, the fabrics used were superior to those worn by other ranks. Officers generally carried the Webley revolver and had it in a Mills webbing holster. This was generally blancoed or worn in an olive-green shade of khaki.*

the front with five metal buttons. The service dress tunics usually had regimental buttons, regimental badges on the collar and metal shoulder titles (the name or initials of the unit).

The battledress was different. It was short, saving on material – initially serge of good quality. It was supposed to be worn largely unadorned by insignia, had five concealed buttons down the fly front and had a plain collar (closed with two hooks) and straps with plain buttons. There were two breast pockets with pleats and scalloped flaps (with concealed buttons) and there was an interior pocket on the wearer's left. The garment was reinforced at the waist, down the fly and at the elbow.

A severe shortage of cloth meant that the battledress underwent some modifications as wartime restrictions began to bite. The Economy Issue garment, first specified in 1940 but rarely issued before 1942, was no longer in serge but now in woollen fabric and, for ease of manufacture, was no longer fly-fronted or fitted with concealed buttons on the pocket flaps. Most buttons were now plastic.

The United States manufactured examples of battledress in olive drab fabric, of good quality, and these were mainly issued to troops in Italy. They had plain pockets and a fly front. Some Canadian-manufactured items were also used. These were in a greener-coloured material, were generally of better quality, and had more pointed pocket flaps.

Officers wore a similar design of battledress, but usually open at the collar to reveal a green or khaki shirt and tie and the lining of the garment turned back, almost forming lapels (these faded to an off-white). These garments were often privately tailored and were in superior cloth. Officers' service dress was also a common sight in the early years of the war and followed a design largely unchanged since 1902.

Insignia

Battledress had been issued on the understanding that it was to be worn as a plain and rather sober garment. The brass shoulder titles distinguishing particular regiments were not really authorized for the garment but many units went ahead and encouraged their transfer from the SD tunic to the battledress. Failing this, slip-on shoulder titles were worn instead. These worsted titles were simplifications of the metal shoulder titles, usually on a rectangle of khaki or brown cloth. The slip-on titles were largely rendered superfluous on the battledress when coloured cloth titles were introduced, mostly in the form of a red arc of cloth bearing white lettering – the Hampshire Regiment managed yellow lettering on black. The Guards had been among the first to introduce such embroidered titles, but other infantry units followed and by 1943 the practice received official sanction and printed titles were issued.

In September 1940, in an attempt to relieve drab blandness or restore some arm-of-service solidarity, branch-of-service strips were introduced. These thin bars of cloth were to be worn on the upper arm and on each sleeve of the battledress and greatcoat. The colour selected for the infantry was red, although the rifle regiments were given green. Various specialists were given different combinations: the Pay Corps got yellow; the Education Corps, light blue; the Army Physical Training Corps had black/red/black; the pioneers, red/green; and the Catering Corps, grey/yellow. Although infantry had red stripes, they had the unique distinction of having one strip if belonging to the first brigade, two for the middle brigade and three for the more junior brigade.

Divisional insignia, so common in the last war, quickly made a comeback in 1940. Initially divisional signs had been restricted to vehicles, but troops sent over to France quickly adopted the habit of stitching regimental flashes or divisional symbolism to their shoulders. Divisional signs seemed popular – as evidenced by memos in April 1940 forbidding the practice. Five months later there was a change of heart, when the desire to boost morale trumped concerns over camouflage, and divisional (or army, corps and so on) signs were authorized. Such signs were worn on the battledress, positioned above the branch-of-service stripe, with some units adding a regimental flash below the stripe. The insignia was more common in northern Europe after 1941.

Troops deployed in the Mediterranean theatre and Asia adopted a different style for use with khaki drill dress. Troops in Italy seem to have only rarely followed the system in use in northern Europe.

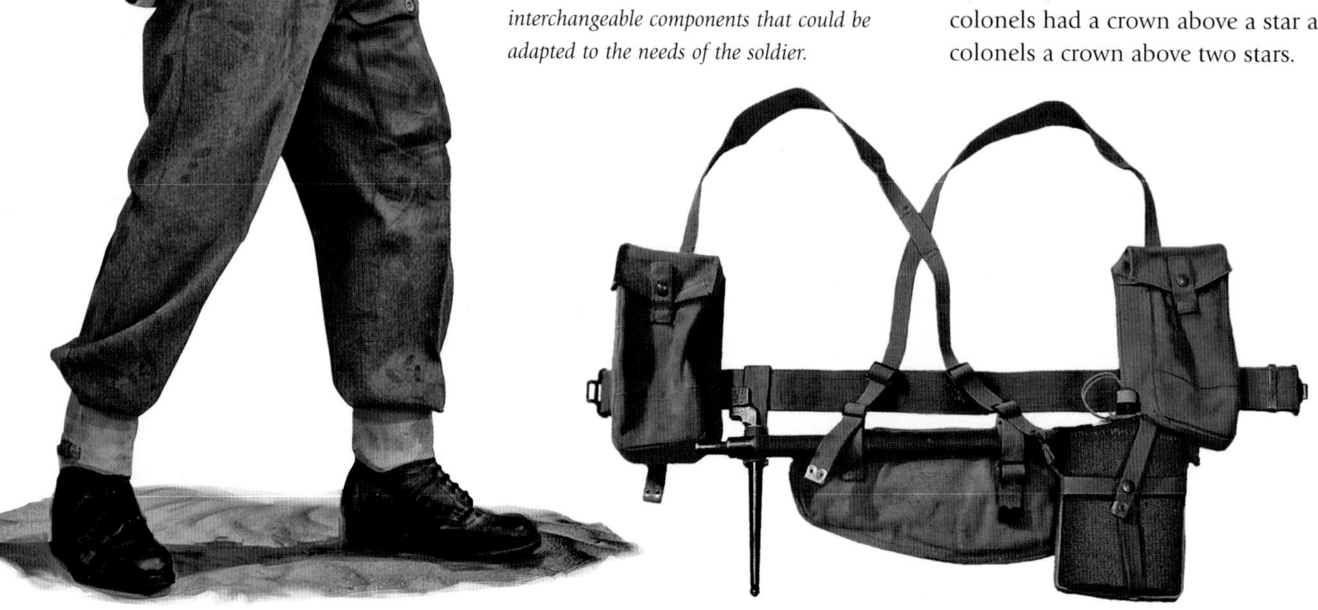

◀ SERGEANT, ROYAL ULSTER RIFLES (2ND BATTALION), 1944 *The two bars on the sleeve show that this Rifle regiment belonged to the second brigade and the 3rd Division, as shown by the triangle-within-triangle formation sign. The brown tab at the end of the shoulder strap shows this NCO belonged to B Company serving in the 2nd Battalion.*

▼ INFANTRY KIT *The load-carrying Pattern-37 webbing equipment was introduced in 1937 and could not only carry significantly more ammunition than its predecessor, it also had interchangeable components that could be adapted to the needs of the soldier.*

Rank

Officers – aside from wearing distinctive and better-tailored items of dress – displayed their rank on shoulder straps. Rank insignia consisted of cloth stars and, for more senior officers, a combination of stars and a crown. These were derived from the metallic badges worn in peacetime. The stars, wrongly called pips, were the Order of the Bath (Maltese crosses in a khaki cloth set on a lighter-coloured sunburst). Second lieutenants had one star, lieutenants had two and captains three. Majors had a crown, lieutenant colonels had a crown above a star and colonels a crown above two stars.

◀ LIEUTENANT, SOMERSET LIGHT INFANTRY, 1944 *The stars on the shoulder are backed in red rather than green. Although the regiment was originally a light regiment, it was not classed as a Rifle regiment and so was not entitled to the green Rifle distinctions.*

▶ PRIVATE, NORTH STAFFORDSHIRE REGIMENT (6TH BATTALION), 1943 *Battledress was impregnated with chemicals to combat mustard gas. This Anti-Vesciant treatment (the garment was stamped with an 'AV' once impregnated) was often mistakenly referred to as Anti-Vermin.*

In late 1939 the use of branch-of-service colours as backing for officers' insignia was discussed – and this became accepted from September 1940. Infantry wore scarlet (Rifles preferring green), pioneers were given red after 1943 and the Military Provost Staff Corps also wore red after 1944. Warrant officers were not authorized backing for their insignia (coat of arms on sleeve for I Class, crown in wreath on sleeve for II Class and crown on sleeve for II Class). NCOs wore worsted cloth chevrons on their sleeves above the elbow. Staff sergeants added a crown above the three chevrons of the sergeant, corporals had two chevrons and lance corporals one. These chevrons were sometimes simplified for use on shirts, and by 1945 were sewn on as a more subdued, single block.

Light infantry

A number of Rifle regiments carried on the tradition of using green as a distinguishing colour. These chiefly were the Cameronians, the King's Royal Rifle Corps, the Royal Ulster Rifles, the Rifle Brigade and, after some debate, the Buckinghamshire Battalion in the Oxfordshire & Buckinghamshire Light Infantry.

These light infantry regiments had darkened badges, green branch-of-service distinctions (one, two or three strips) and green shoulder titles (with black or red lettering); officers had green-backed rank insignia (with dark centres), with NCOs having black chevrons on red. In addition, such regiments fought long and hard to retain the distinction of wearing black buttons. Officers were granted the privilege in 1943, and many other ranks seem to have followed suit (contrary to orders).

Scots and Irish

Battledress did away with many traditional features of Highland and Lowland regiments. The cutaway service dress and kilt were relegated to formal occasions. However, in the realm of headgear, the Scots managed to retain a distinctive appearance. This was especially true of officers because they had almost entirely rejected the pre-war peaked caps.

The Glengarry cap was rare, as was the Atholl bonnet (still worn by the Lovat Scouts and some territorial formations), but the Tam O'Shanter was popular – the Black Watch sported a plumed version – as was the Balmoral. These caps were often worn with a distinctive tartan patch behind the regimental badge: the Gordon Highlanders had Gordon tartan; the Cameronians, Douglas tartan. The Seaforth Highlanders were more complicated: the 5th Battalion (Territorials) had Sutherland tartan,

◀ **Private, 5th Battalion, Coldstream Guards, Armoured Division, 1944** *The 5th Battalion wore the Roman numeral for five below the armoured branch-of-service strip. Infantry attached to armoured divisions generally followed this style, although there were exceptions. The badge below is the ever-open eye of the Guards Armoured Division, which had been raised in 1941.*

▶ **Corporal, Highland Light Infantry, 1944** *The distinctive and rather large cap badge bore the inscription 'Assaye' (a victory in India in 1803) over an elephant. The regiment was entitled to wear tartan trews rather than kilts for formal occasions and many officers elected to wear these garments off duty as an unusual distinction.*

while the other battalions sported Mackenzie. Every opportunity to wear a kilt and white gaiters, or trews for many officers, was taken by the Scottish troops.

With Ireland now independent and neutral, only a few regiments in the British Army maintained Irish traditions and distinctions. The London Irish had adopted the caubeen bonnet in 1937 (sometimes worn with a blue hackle), but it became popular in Italy in 1943 and was there adopted by the Royal Inniskillings (grey hackles) and the Royal Irish Fusiliers (green hackles).

Guards

The guards units had been among the first to wear coloured arc-shaped shoulder titles, the idea having been authorized in 1936 for service dress; these sometimes made their way onto battledress. The Coldstream and Grenadier Guards had white lettering on red, the Irish Guards had white on green, the Scots Guards yellow on blue and the Welsh white on black. Failing that, the Guards wore metal titles – for example, 'SG' and a thistle for the Scots Guards, 'WG' and a leek for the Welsh – or stencilled slip-ons. Guard officers had the right to have distinctive rank insignia on the shoulder: the Household Cavalry, Grenadier Guards, Coldstream Guards and Welsh Guards used the star of the Order of the Garter; the Scots Guards, the Order of the Thistle; and the Irish Guards, the Order of St Patrick. The Coldstream Guards continued the tradition of bearing their battalion number in roman numerals on their battledress sleeve, and the Guards Armoured Division modified the Guards' divisional sign from the previous war.

Helmets

The Mark I helmet, with its distinctive round shape, had been the mainstay of the British Army in the previous conflict. It had proved easy to manufacture, gave suitable protection, at least during trench warfare, and had been issued universally in large numbers. A modified version, the Mark II, appeared in the late 1930s (especially from June 1939) and became the most common headgear for frontline troops throughout the conflict, with 12 million examples being produced.

The helmet had a compressed card and cloth interior, with a band in Indian rubber to provide padding for the head. The interior was screwed to the top of the helmet shell with a screw and pin, although this meant that the liner would sometimes swivel within the helmet (a tendency put right in 1940). The initial fabric chinstrap was attached to the helmet by lugs, an elasticated strap appearing shortly afterwards. Bakelite versions were produced for civil defence.

Although it was issued in large numbers, the helmet had its defects and tests were undertaken to improve the design in order to address the problems made apparent by experience. In the autumn of 1940 the Medical Research Council began working with the War Department to establish a new design and had already issued a prototype by April 1941. However, the discussion was extended when use of the American helmet was suggested. This idea was rejected when the helmet was criticized for being too heavy and for allowing the rain to trickle down the back of the neck – an important consideration in Britain.

The Mark III was the product of these discussions and tests. It had a swept-back design to better protect the sides of the head and the neck and was most usually painted in a matt green-grey for improved camouflage; the shape meant that it was baptized the turtle helmet. The helmet was heavier, designed to allow the use of radio equipment and, after a small adjustment, could be worn with the interior of the Mark II. It began to be issued in numbers from November 1943, initially to the 21st Army Group. A Mark IV was also produced very late in the conflict.

There was no consistent rule, but some divisions had helmets sporting the divisional badge on the front with various emblems or, in the case of Highland units, patches of tartan on the sides. This habit became less common as such devices were sported on the sleeves. Paint could include a granite anti-glare coating but camouflage paint was only rarely applied. Many helmets were issued with netting.

Caps

The field service cap was to be worn with the battledress and was a practical, if rather dull, item of headgear. It was a simple side cap, with two buttons (initially of metal, later of plastic) to the fore and, usually, a regimental badge on the front left. The cap was normally tilted over the right ear. It was intended to replace the peaked service dress cap but this

◀ **Private, York and Lancaster Regiment, 1943** *In the Italian theatre of operations, the khaki drill uniform used in North Africa met the thicker and warmer styles of dress used in northern Europe. This soldier has the wool battledress with sand-coloured khaki trousers and has the insignia of the 46th Infantry Brigade (middle brigade, in this case the 138th Infantry).*

▶ **Captain, Gordon Highlanders, 1944** *One of the complaints levied against the battledress was that it swept away with traditional distinctions of dress. Many of the Highland regiments quickly tried to overcome this restriction by adding patches of tartan to the sleeve and by retaining traditional forms of headgear.*

old-fashioned item could still be seen, complete with regimental badge and leather chinstrap, late in the war. The field service cap was not especially popular with officers and the coloured service cap, of a similar shape but in traditional regimental colours, was often worn instead – even though it had been specified for ceremonial use.

The field service cap was supposed to be replaced in 1943 by the new serge general service cap. This flat cap was normally pulled to the right to give space on the left for a badge or patch and so as not to interfere with the rifle, carried on the left shoulder, although the Royal Ulster Rifles had the cap pulled to the left. It was based on the popular Scottish Tam O'Shanter.

Trousers

The trousers issued with the 1937-designed battledress were straight, long and distinguished by a large (and rather impractical) pocket on the upper left leg; there was a smaller pocket, meant for a field dressing, on the right waist and two vertical pockets on each side. Officers wore breeches – with reinforced inner sections, a throwback to when such garments were used for riding – or, more rarely, plus fours or golfing trousers. These had been popular in the 1930s but had largely died out by 1940.

The trousers could be worn with braces or with a belt. The end of each leg had a cloth strap that helped secure the gaiters that were supposed to be worn with this garment. These gaiters (Anklet, Web) were made of stiffened cotton (webbing) and were fastened with cloth or leather straps. The gaiter's interior was edged in leather to reduce wear and tear and the trouser leg was supposed to billow out over the top of the anklet. The gaiters were worn with ankle boots of various kinds.

Boots were initially of very good quality, with 25 hobnails on the sole (eventually reduced to 13). Officers generally wore superior-quality items; those in Rifle regiments continued the tradition of wearing blackened ankle boots rather than brown leather boots.

◀ **Sergeant, 1st Battalion Irish Guards, 1943** *Although battledress would be produced for the Mediterranean theatre, the most common uniform worn in the hot south was the khaki drill shirt. While this was not especially smart, it was at least comfortable. Rank insignia was stitched to the sleeve, as was the regimental shoulder arc. The divisional insignia, in this case the white triangle of the 1st Infantry Division, was worn on a slide on the shoulder strap although it was later moved down and stitched to the upper sleeve.*

▶ **Private, Lancashire Fusiliers (2nd Battalion), 1943** *This gunner carries a Bren gun, which provided much-needed supporting fire, while infantry Bren sections played an important role in any infantry battalion. The gun's ammunition was loaded into the basic pouch with two magazines fitting into each pouch. The magazine itself was designed for 30 rounds and fitted snugly, although Sten gun magazines were found to be too long.*

▲ *Members of the British Expeditionary Force clad in sheepskin coats prepare for their departure to Norway, April 1940.*

Greatcoats

A practical double-breasted khaki greatcoat was issued to the infantry in 1939 but it did not entirely replace the older-style single-breasted version. The new coat had two rows of four buttons and could be fastened close to the collar for comfort. The coat was lined at the shoulders and sleeves and had a buttoned pleat to the rear. There were two side pockets. The greatcoat usually bore, as appropriate, officers' rank insignia on the straps, NCO chevrons on the sleeve and the branch-of-service strip on the upper arm. Economies were made to the buttons in 1940 and in the cloth that was used to manufacture the coats.

Officers could wear the regulation greatcoat or the finer British Warm, a heavy double-breasted coat in khaki that was the same length as the cavalry greatcoat. Trenchcoats (in beige or khaki) or raincoats were also popular among officers and the long sheepskin coat with matching cap with ear flaps was much used by troops stationed in Norway and by sentries everywhere.

These garments were supplemented by the ubiquitous leather jerkin, a popular item among the infantry – a smaller cotton assault jerkin was issued late in the war. It was sleeveless and fastened with four buttons. The anti-gas cape was often worn as a poncho, despite being prone to tearing. A more robust cape was issued in some theatres later in the conflict.

Cold-weather clothing also included the practical windproof smock (manufactured from denim from 1941 onwards; there was also a snow-camouflaged version), a balaclava or cap comforter, overtrousers in waterproof material and the popular heavy-wool jersey. Denim overalls were also issued for fatigue duties.

▶ **Lieutenant, Durham Light Infantry, 1942** *The only indication as to the unit of this officer is the Durham Light Infantry bugle horn badge. The bugle horn was decorative with strings and ribbons above, all under the King's crown. The letters 'DLI' were positioned just above the horn and below the crown. Badges were often blackened when on campaign.*

Equipment

The British struggled to update the infantryman's personal equipment following victory in 1918. Throughout the 1930s, the 1908 pattern was still in use. A 1919 version was issued in limited numbers, but the initiative was largely stillborn due to cost. A 1925 system of web equipment was also developed (the Canadians purchasing quantities) with narrow braces and modified cartridge carriers. However, various systems were trialled in the mid-1930s and the result, the 1937 pattern of web infantry equipment, was adopted in 1938 and produced in huge numbers thereafter.

The haversack was now much larger to accommodate water bottle and mess tins (plus jersey, spoon, fork and toiletry bag), although older packs were still common. The waist belt of belted webbing had a hook and loop buckle and supported the basic pouch (one on each side) containing ammunition. These pouches were sometimes extended to carry ammunition for the Sten gun. Braces were worn over the shoulder (crossing in the middle of the back) to provide additional support for this load. An entrenching tool and bayonet hung from the belt and the water bottle (sometimes carried in the haversack) hung over the entrenching tool head.

The gas mask was carried in a canvas bag on the chest but, from 1942 onwards, this practice was less common: the new pattern light respirator entered general service and this was generally carried in a cotton bag suspended from the rear of the belt. The mask was still important and

◀ **Private, 2nd Battalion, Scots Guards, 1939** *British forces were sent to Palestine and Egypt in the run-up to war and generally wore the tried and tested tropical sun helmet, which was valued for keeping the head cool. The Scots added Royal Stuart tartan dicing to both sides of the helmet and would have worn side caps off duty – although these were unpopular as they tended to fall off during drill.*

one of the reasons why the American helmet was rejected for British use was that the gas mask could not be worn with the American headgear.

Officers carried less. There was a web equipment binocular case, a pouch for pistol ammunition and a rather inelegant pistol holster (or, later, a pistol case with leg strap). Some officers were issued with a pack or haversack and most carried a leather or canvas map case. The older Sam Browne equipment also remained popular. Bergen rucksacks were issued to some troops in Norway, and later saw service with the Commandos.

Battle order generally consisted of just the belt and braces, pouches, water bottle, entrenching tool and bayonet. The haversack was worn with waterproof tent canvas wrapped around the top or, for motorized infantry, largely discarded.

North Africa

Khaki drill service tunics were a common sight in Egypt and Palestine in 1939 but, by 1941, it was more usual to see British troops dressed in khaki drill or flannel shirts (with rolled-up sleeves) and shorts (often with the incongruous green puttees and ankle boots). A lighter cotton form of battledress was issued to troops in the Middle East (known as Middle East-pattern) and this fly-fronted garment was used in Italy from 1943.

Italy also saw extensive use of the American-manufactured battledress in olive drab. It was also fly-fronted, had two practical breast pockets and could be tightened at the waist. It came with olive drab trousers. American-manufactured herringbone twill shirts and bush jackets were also worn in North Africa from 1942 and in Italy from 1943.

Insignia in North Africa and the Middle East was frequently relegated to the shoulder straps, where divisional and regimental flashes were sewn on or placed as slip-ons. In Italy the situation was more complex, with some units decorating their sleeves with extensive rows of insignia and others maintaining the more understated North African tradition.

Asia

British armies had had considerable experience of the gruelling conditions of fighting in Asia. Throughout the 1930s, the Wolseley helmet dominated as headgear and this was worn with khaki drill service tunics or long-sleeved shirts. The service dress tunic resembled that worn in Europe, with its tight stand-and-fall collar, five metal buttons and plated breast pockets (no lower pockets). Shorts were preferred (including the long Bombay bloomers), and these were generally worn with puttees or gaiters together with ankle boots.

This attire was perhaps suitable for parts of India, but was impractical when it came to fighting in the jungles of Burma or Malaya. The khaki tunic was no longer manufactured after 1941, although stocks were worn until exhausted. The bush jacket proved itself more popular, with long sleeves to protect against insect bites (the sleeves could be rolled up and kept in place with a flap). It was produced in Aertex cloth in khaki drill and then of a greenish shade; a six-buttoned jungle shirt was also popular. A jungle-green battledress blouse was eventually issued and was relatively common after

▼ *British troops photographed in action during manoeuvres in the western desert of North Africa.*

1943. It had five buttons and two breast pockets. Metal buttons generally disappeared as various plastic, rubber or synthetic versions came into use. In addition, there was a profusion of different kinds of shirt, often of American manufacture (usually coming under the denomination of war aid), or else made in India (produced by small manufacturers and in varying styles and quality) or Australia (denim shirts, for example). Shorts fell out of favour in the jungle and long, baggy trousers in khaki cotton drill or jungle battledress green were favoured. Soldiers wore rain capes rather than greatcoats. In terms of headgear, the domed sun helmet soon fell out of favour. Slouch hats, or felt hats, were eagerly adopted. This was not an innovation, as such hats had been in use for 50 years, but it was a practical improvement.

Divisional insignia was worn on the hat band rather than on the sleeve of the tunic or shirt – although this practice can also be seen in period photographs. Divisional insignia was often that of Indian divisions, because these contained a number of European units as well as units raised on the subcontinent. In addition to these round slouch hats, a jungle-green version of the general service cap appeared after 1943. This resembled the one worn in Europe but was made in robust cotton.

Regimental cap badges continued to be worn (either in metal, plastic or as stencils) on the various kinds of caps, bush hats and slouch hats; divisional badges were really only worn on slouch hats or sun helmets. Helmets were also worn in Asia but they were less popular, given the heat. The most common was the Mark II helmet painted in green and frequently worn with netting for camouflage purposes. Some Indian divisions made use of South African-manufactured helmets painted sand-brown.

Equipment differed marginally from that in use in Europe, often because the official patterns were copied and locally produced with local materials. The ubiquitous machete was usually worn slung from the waist.

Some units were issued tropical clothing before setting out for postings overseas, others were issued with the appropriate dress upon arrival. Most items were worn until they fell apart.

◀ **Private, Gloucestershire Regiment, 1944** *British uniforms in the Far East were pragmatic. The Glosters were noted for their cap badge worn on the back of their caps – won as a distinction in the wars against Revolutionary France. The insignia of the 36th Division gets prominence on the side of the slouch hat instead.*

▶ **Captain, 7th Battalion, Worcestershire Regiment, 1944** *This officer was serving with the 10th Battalion and wears the popular slouch hat. Short sleeves generally posed a problem when it came to insect bites; for warrant officers they were even more difficult as their rank insignia was worn at the base of the arm. Some adopted wristbands bearing their badges of rank to overcome this problem.*

CAVALRY

British cavalry had been subjected to mechanization just before World War II began. Even so, mounted personnel were to play a role in some theatres.

Mechanization

The traditional distinction between the regular cavalry and the yeomanry (derived from mounted militia) had already disappeared when mounted units gave up their horses for armoured vehicles. In a sense, this shift had begun in 1930 when yeomanry regiments were used to staff the Tank Corps. After much hesitation, the process was largely completed by 1938, and The North Irish Horse was one of the last units to be transformed, becoming an Armoured Car Regiment in 1939.

This is not the whole picture, however, for mounted troops were still deemed useful in the Middle East: the two units there retained their mounts. In addition, in October 1939 the 1st Cavalry Division was organized and soon sent over to Egypt, where it served before operating in Palestine, Jordan and Iraq (and also against the Vichy French in Syria in 1941). By 1942 only a few of the division's nine regiments were still mounted; the Cheshire Yeomanry were discouraged to find that they had been made into a signals unit. The British were supported by some locally raised and recruited formations, in particular the Trans-Jordanian Frontier Force (and the more famous Arab Legion).

Dress

The uniforms worn by the cavalry had, in Britain, consisted of the battledress with regimental titles worn as slip-ons on the straps. This was not always done logically. The metal 'RWY' became the stencilled 'Y over R. Wilts' for the Royal Wiltshire Yeomanry, for example. Caps had mostly consisted of the peaked service dress cap with regimental badge, although the coloured

◄ **Trooper, Warwickshire Yeomanry, 1940** *The solar topee worn here was an elegant enough piece of headgear, and it kept the head cool, but it offered no ballistic protection at all. The helmet that was worn by the Warwickshire Yeomanry bore a blue-over-white diamond with a central red horizontal line. A flash showing a white horse on green backing material was later adopted and worn on the sleeve.*

► **Sergeant, Trans Jordanian Frontier Force, 1941** *The black colpack (often made of astrakhan lambswool) was a sign of authority shared by many units raised in French and British mandated territory in the Middle East and this unit had a scarlet bag (the material on the top of the headgear). The colour was also shown on the waist sash and on lanyards. The paramilitary Palestine Police, which also had a smattering of European NCOs, wore the same headgear but with a blue bag on the crown.*

service cap would be increasingly popular (and it came in a multitude of colours for cavalry units). Greatcoats were of the shorter cavalry-pattern type dating from 1917. This coat was deliberately shorter for mounted (and mechanized) troops, was double-breasted and had straight rather than angled pockets.

Upon transfer to the Middle East, khaki drill uniforms were worn. Mostly this consisted of the khaki shirt plus riding breeches. Although riding boots were common for officers, most other ranks preferred the more flexible buckled gaiters in natural leather (and some even wore ankle boots and puttees). Headgear consisted of the tropical helmet, solar topee or Wolseley helmet, which had been extensively used in the previous war. The sun helmet usually bore a regimental lozenge on the wearer's left and officers had the habit of affixing the regimental badge to the front of their helmets. The 1st Division did not initially have a divisional patch, although it seems that a device showing a fox's head made an appearance in 1941 and a device showing a white horse on a green patch also seems to have been used.

Local cavalry operating in Jordan and Palestine usually wore the black colpack in astrakhan wool. This had been the mark of authority in the Ottoman Empire (which had ruled the region only 20 years before) and was retained. The Trans-Jordanian Frontier Force had a red and yellow bag on the crown and distinctive badge on the front. The uniform followed the style of the British cavalry regiments.

Cavalry units now using armoured vehicles fought hard to retain traditional items of dress. The 11th Hussars kept its brown beret with crimson band. Those of the 8th Hussars liked to sport the traditional white over red plume at every opportunity. But, in essence, the cavalry adopted the dress of the Royal Armoured Corps and wore the yellow and red service strip of the RAC, with officers having that formation's yellow backing to their shoulder insignia.

Equipment

The equipment of the troops sent out to the Middle East was initially that used in the previous conflict; saddles, which were long lasting, often pre-dated the conflict. First and foremost on the list of personal equipment was the leather 50-round bandolier dating from 1903 (or the 1905 pattern with simplified buckle). However, the British had been working on a new system, and some examples of web equipment had been sold to other countries. The new design, Web Equipment, Cavalry, Patt. 40, was issued too late for use by the 1st Cavalry Division but some examples were sent over to the Middle East and arrived late in 1940 and saw service in Syria in 1941.

Examples were also seen in India. The equipment consisted of wide belt supporting canvas cartridge pouches (one over two on each side) and braces that went over the shoulder and held the water bottle and haversack in place on the wearer's back. These could be accessed by loosening the stud and slot system, sliding the items forward, and sliding them back, all while mounted in the saddle. Alternatively, the water bottle and haversack could be strapped below the belt when the individual was on foot. It was an effective and versatile equipment system but came rather too late in the day.

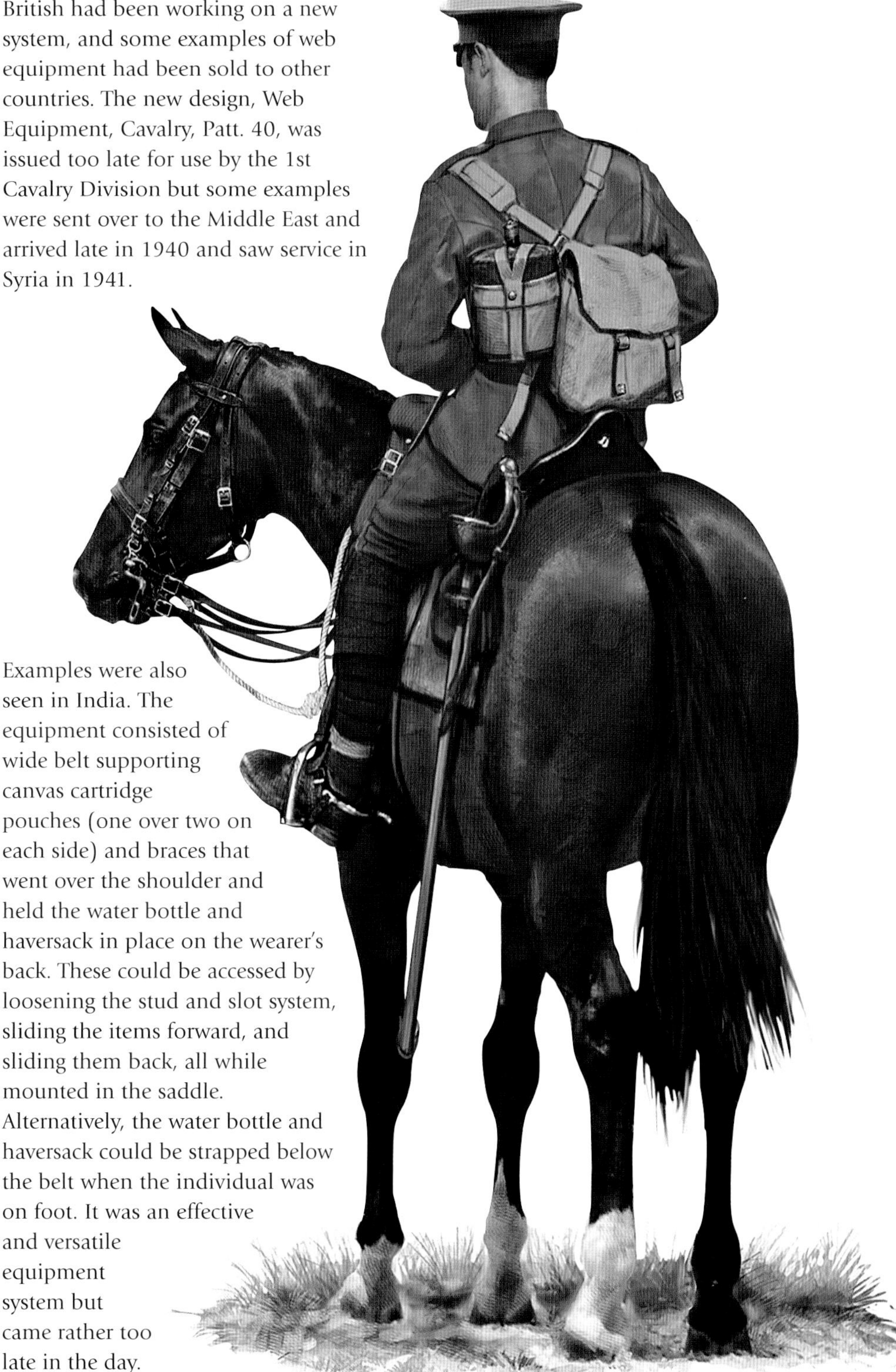

▼ **Trooper, Household Cavalry, 1940**
The Household Cavalry Composite Regiment was formed in 1939, and most of the regiment was sent to the Middle East. This individual, serving at home, wears the new 1940-pattern cavalry equipment to demonstrate the practical and comfortable placing of the haversack and water bottle when mounted on horseback.

ARTILLERY AND TECHNICAL TROOPS

Britain's artillery had strong traditions and had played a key role in the victory of 1918. It was subjected to economies and reforms in the 1930s, but rapidly expanded in 1939 to emerge as a modernized force.

The Royal Field Artillery and Royal Garrison Artillery (which had included coastal artillery) had merged in 1924 and the Royal Artillery was now composed of field and horse brigades. In 1938 a new reorganization occurred and the brigades were transformed into regiments. The bulk of these regiments were field regiments, although horse artillery was retained and there were also anti-tank regiments, light and heavy anti-aircraft regiments, medium regiments and heavy regiments (and three super heavy regiments with three additional batteries, the latter lost in France in 1940). Plus there were the units of Air Defence Great Britain.

Royal Artillery

The Royal Artillery were dressed as for the infantry and adapted their style of address according to the theatre of operations – khaki drill in Asia or battledress in northern Europe. Artillery personnel wore the distinctive cap badge (in bronze for officers) and the 'RA' or 'Royal Artillery' shoulder title – the cloth shoulder arc would be blue with red lettering after 1943. Royal Artillery personnel had red/blue branch-of-service strips and officers had red backing to their shoulder rank insignia. Some artillery regiments wore distinctive cloth regimental badges on the sleeve, usually below the branch-of-service strip. Others, especially later in the war, had a square cloth tactical sign in red and blue showing a regiment number in white.

Artillery ranks included master gunners (first and second class), who wore an embroidered gun device below the warrant officer badge; master gunners (third class) and battery sergeants wore warrant officer II class badges, the former with the gun device. Sergeants added the gun device over their chevrons and although bombardiers existed in place of the infantry's corporals, they had identical insignia. There were some distinctive badges, including the fist clenching lightning bolts for radio operators (only introduced in 1944), the crossed flags of the signaller and the wheel for drivers. Artillery personnel also had the right to wear a white lanyard on the right shoulder.

▲ **Gunner, 80th Field Regiment, 1944**
A gunner of the 52nd (Lowland) Division serves a 25-pounder gun (the Mark 2), shown left. This effective artillery piece first appeared in April 1940 and saw initial service in Norway in that year. The insignia is worn on the sleeve. This Lowland unit was, ironically, trained in mountain warfare before being deployed in the mudflats around the Scheldt estuary in late 1944.

Air defence

Britain's air defence had been grouped under Anti-Aircraft Command but, at a critical juncture, was reorganized in November 1940 into three corps with their own badges, the divisions within them also had their own badges (worn on the battledress sleeve) – if not belonging to a division, they wore their corps device. A new insignia, of a black arm with bow and arrow on a red background, was used by all anti-aircraft units after 1943. Units were supplemented by personnel from the Auxiliary Territorial Service (ATS), female auxiliary personnel who wore service dress with skirt or with battledress and trousers. The peaked ATS cap was also worn, bearing 'ATS' within a wreath badge. Yellow shoulder titles with brown lettering were issued later.

Technical troops

Generally, the style of dress adopted by the artillery was also worn by these formations, although these units did have their own distinctive cap badges and insignia – and, at least initially, buttons bearing unit devices. The Royal Engineers followed the artillery style given above, but with the engineers' badge and 'RE' shoulder titles in metal or as cloth slip-ons. The shoulder title, when introduced, was red and had dark blue lettering. Engineers would have blue/red branch-of-service strips, with officers having blue backing to their shoulder rank insignia. Rank followed artillery pattern, but with a bursting grenade replacing the gun insignia above the sergeants' chevrons.

The Royal Corps of Signals was a relatively junior service, having been formed in 1920. It had blue/white branch-of-service strips and officers wore blue backing to their shoulder rank insignia. The shoulder title had been 'R. Signals' in metal, and a dark blue cloth arc with white lettering (and the full corps title) from 1943.

The Royal Army Ordnance Corps (RAOC) were issued (in September 1940) with dark blue branch-of-service strips, changed to red/blue/red in December 1941, and officers had dark blue backing to their shoulder rank insignia – changed to scarlet in December 1941. It had a red shoulder title with 'RAOC' in blue lettering from 1943 onwards; before that it had been 'RAOC' metal titles or cloth slip-ons. The Royal Electrical and Mechanical Engineers had red/yellow/blue branch-of-service strips and, in 1943, were granted dark blue as the backing colour for officers' insignia. Shoulder titles had been 'REME' in metal or cloth slip-ons before 1943 but, thereafter, dark blue arcs with 'REME' in yellow were used.

◀ **Gunner, 10th Field Regiment, 1942** *Royal Artillery units in the Far East generally showed their status by the flash on the side of the slouch hat (in traditional red and blue colours). The 'RA' shoulder title, worn on a khaki patch of material sewn to the shoulder strap, was also a popular insignia.*

▶ **Major, Royal Electrical and Mechanical Engineers, 1944** *The REME was created in 1942 in order to service, repair and maintain the military's vastly increasing range of motor vehicles. It began to serve from 1943 and was issued with a cap badge showing the initials on four shields linked by a wreath, all below a crown. This badge was unpopular and replaced after the war with a horse device.*

ARMOURED TROOPS

Britain's armoured troops were rapidly expanded as war became inevitable. An emphasis on fielding large numbers of tanks, regardless of vehicle capabilities and the standard of equipment issued to the troops, led to problems and a painful learning curve.

In 1923 the Tank Corps became the Royal Tank Corps, but by 1938 there were only eight battalions – with 12 more added in 1939, mostly from infantry personnel. The Royal Tank Corps became the Royal Tank Regiment in April 1939 and joined with the mechanized cavalry – then busy adapting to their new vehicles, although eight yeomanry regiments had already received armoured cars – to form the Royal Armoured Corps (RAC).

The Reconnaissance Corps began forming in early 1941 and was composed of regiments attached to divisions plus the General Headquarters Liaison, or Phantom Regiment. The corps finally transferred to the RAC in January 1944.

Insignia

The battledress was initially largely devoid of insignia, although branch-of-service strips were introduced in late 1940, worn on the sleeve below any divisional sign; these strips were largely worn only on the battledress. The RAC had a yellow/red strip, the reconnaissance units had a green/yellow version. Officers of the RAC had yellow backing to their rank stars on the shoulder straps.

◄ TANKER, 8TH HUSSARS, 1941 *Obtaining supplies from the US came with its own problems. Stuart tanks, supplied to the British, generally came with US radio equipment. This meant that US tankers' helmets were worn until the equipment could be converted to British radio equipment – and British tankers' helmets, which worked with British receivers, could be used.*

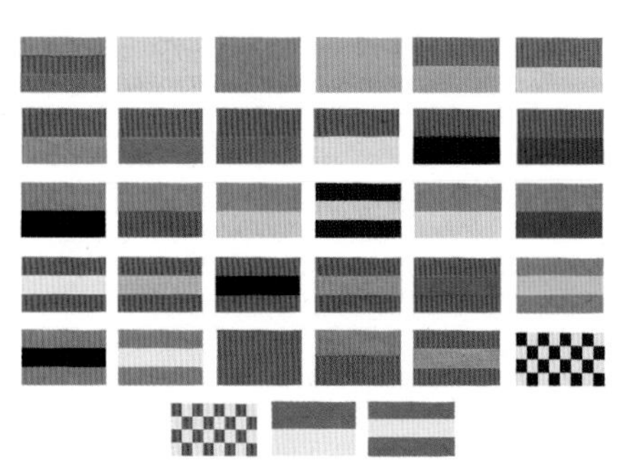

▲ TANK REGIMENT BADGES *The 1st Regiment wore a lanyard rather than a coloured tab on their shoulder straps.*

At this stage there were a number of differences to distinguish personnel of the Royal Tank Regiment (RTR) from the rest of the RAC. The RTR retained the badge of the Royal Tank Corps (a heavy tank in a wreath below a crown, all over the 'Fear naught' motto), while other RAC units had the cap badge of 'RAC' in a wreath below a crown. The tank regiment also wore a distinctive cloth tank badge on the right sleeve and tank battalions had coloured strips added to the end of their shoulder straps to denote particular battalions – the 1st had red; the 2nd, yellow; the 3rd, green and so on. Brass shoulder titles were sometimes worn ('RAC' or 'RTR'), as were slip-on cloth titles, but the RAC had to wait until 1943 to receive its own cloth shoulder arc in yellow with red lettering (not generally worn by the tank regiment). Tank brigades often adopted the Diablo (double triangle) sign below their service stripe.

Headgear

The RAC generally wore the black beret accorded to the tank corps in 1923. A significant piece of equipment was the tankers' helmet. Leather helmets had first been issued in 1916, but the early design too closely resembled that of the German steel helmet and was withdrawn.

The growth in interest in establishing armoured units in the 1930s triggered a fresh attempt to give tankers practical head protection. In 1934 the company Helmets Limited – based in the village of Wheathampstead, Hertfordshire, south-eastern England – began testing a domed helmet made from black-painted canvas and lined with cloth. It was to be issued from April 1936 and was christened the Helmet, Crash, Royal Tank Corps (or Royal Tank

◀ **Tanker, 7th Royal Tank Regiment, 1940** *Tank officers wore the minimum of equipment, generally storing kit within the vehicle. The webbing equipment generally consisted of a waist belt with a holster for the standard (Enfield) revolver, which was worn at the thigh, a water bottle in khaki cover and a respirator in a canvas bag.*

Regiment). The helmet had generous ear flaps that could house radio equipment (or the flaps could be tied up if headsets were being used), reinforced padding at the front of the helmet and a leather chinstrap that could be buckled under the chin. Some modifications were made in 1939, the chinstrap now being made from canvas, and the helmet continued to be manufactured until 1944.

Even so, there were insufficient helmets for the newly enlarged armoured formations. A more domed round hat, meant originally for miners, was modified for use within the vehicle, and a rubber helmet (very much like the one issued to motorcyclists) appeared in small numbers in 1941. Experience soon showed that something more substantial was required. Tests began in 1941 and in 1942 the Helmet, Steel, Royal Armoured Corps, appeared. It was based on the infantry helmet but with improved fastening and interior padding. This early helmet, inspired by the helmet designed for airborne troops, went to the newly formed Polish brigades, reconnaissance units and the 6th Armoured Division.

Modifications followed, the Mark I being manufactured with a metal rim and with an improved strap and the Mark II, issued from April 1945, had a lift the dot liner that meant it could double as a water container.

Overalls

Made from denim, overalls were worn over shirts in the summer and over battledress in winter. From late 1943, armoured personnel could make use of the padded Tank Oversuit ('Pixie suit') in cream-coloured, waterproof material; it had 13 buttons and zipped around the neck. However, a major design fault was that the colouring made individuals stand out and so vulnerable to enemy fire. Denim suits also became available in mid-1944 and were also approved for engineers operating with armoured vehicles. These were usually worn without insignia, although the 13/18 Hussars seem to be an exception.

Reconnaissance

The Reconnaissance Corps briefly had 'Reconnaissance Corps' arcs of yellow lettering on green before becoming merely 'Reconnaissance' and later adopting the 'RAC' title in 1944. Personnel also had a distinctive khaki beret with badge (lightning bolts with spear) before adopting the black beret of the RAC. Reconnaissance unit officers had green backing to their rank stars on the shoulder.

▶ **Corporal, 107th Regiment, Royal Armoured Corps, 1945** *This corporal wears the insignia of the 2nd Army and the 34th Armoured Brigade (the famous silver gauntlet and mace) and would have crewed a Churchill tank. He also has the improved tankers' helmet that was worn by tank crews, but also by infantry acting as drivers and operating Bren carriers.*

COMMANDOS AND SPECIAL FORCES

Winston Churchill was keen to see specialist units raised and equipped to offset what was perceived as German superiority. In mid-1940 a number of commando units were raised from volunteers, then formed into special service companies for the Norway campaign In October 1940 these were reorganized into the Special Service Brigade which in February 1941 were transformed into commando units (the short name, SS battalions, had not proved popular).

Commandos

Initially commandos wore service caps with their original regimental badge. It seems that personnel in 1 Commando elected to wear a green beret rather than the black side cap initially proposed, and this was first seen in late 1942. The green beret quickly became the recognizable emblem of commando units and was worn with cap badges from the wearer's original unit, with some exceptions: No. 6 Commando, No. 9 Commando and No. 11 Commando favoured the Scottish Balmoral bonnet (No. 9 with black hackle). No. 5 Commando wore a yellow hackle in their beret in late 1942, but it was later discarded.

Insignia

Commando units initially developed their own badges and shoulder titles. Some semblance of order was imposed when shoulder title arcs were brought in, but even here the early designs lacked unity: Roman numerals were used or the text was in white or red, or the 'No.' was omitted. Eventually, however, the system was rationalized in early 1943 – so that the design became, for instance, 'No. 7 Commando' in red lettering on a black arc. Middle East Commando had a shoulder title in yellow lettering on black ('ME Commando').

The other significant badge was the circular combined operations badge on the sleeve. It bore a red anchor, sub-machine gun and eagle in flight on a black disc and was therefore supposed to represent sea, land and air forces. The eagle looked

◄ **Private 9 Commando, 1944** *There was some initial confusion on how commando insignia was presented. In this instance, the lettering in the shoulder title is switched from white to red and there is no cap insignia other than the black plume.*

► **Captain, Long Range Desert Group, 1941** *He wears the cap badge of his original unit. The scorpion badge (sometimes known as the scarab badge because the scorpion was deemed to be too fat) was only issued in small quantities and was initially produced, with varying degrees of success, by local manufacturers.*

distinctly American, a gesture towards US personnel serving under Combined Operations Command. A qualification badge, of a red dagger on black patch, was also sometimes worn.

No. 10 Commando was an inter-Allied formation formed by European volunteers organized into the appropriate Troop: 1 (French), 2 (Dutch), 3 (German-speakers), 4 (Belgian), 5 (Norwegian), 6 (Polish), 7 (Yugoslav) and 8 (French). While personnel wore the No. 10 Commando (red on dark blue) shoulder title, national badges were also worn on the sleeve. These tended to follow the style adopted by other groups of that nationality, with the Poles having the 'Poland' shoulder title above the 'Commando' title, the Dutch having the Nederland and lion patch below the Commando title, the French the cross of Lorraine and so on.

Cap badges also reflected national styles – the Belgian lion or Polish eagle, for example. Czechs in 3 Troop bore the Bohemian lion and a crossed-swords cap badge. Three troops of 4 Commando were formed from French marines who sported their naval bonnet and the 'France' shoulder title.

Commandos used specialist equipment, including rucksacks and the ever-present commando knife.

Special Air Service (SAS)

The SAS had a distinctive dagger over their motto badge. It was initially worn on a sand-coloured beret – although a white beret was also briefly worn. In March 1944 the maroon beret of the airborne forces was authorized, but many SAS veterans preferred to retain the sand-coloured version.

SAS shoulder titles were initially 'Special Air Service' in light blue on maroon arcs. SAS parachute wings were worn on the breast. Belgians, volunteers from the Belgian Independent Parachute Company, dropped their lion cap badge and adopted SAS insignia with light blue wording on maroon shoulder titles.

LRDG

The Long Range Desert Group (LRDG) was formed to raid behind enemy lines in North Africa. It had 'LRDG' shoulder tabs (mostly red lettering on black). Silver scorpion-in-wheel cap badges were sometimes worn, as were the more common brass pattern, but many personnel continued to wear their unit of origin's cap badge. Dominion volunteers added national titles below their shoulder insignia.

Chindits

In Asia Wingate's Chindits – volunteers drawn from different units to operate as commandos against the Japanese – played the role of raiders. They wore uniforms largely free of insignia although the round Burmese yellow lion Chindit (lion) badge was sometimes worn on the upper sleeve.

◀ **Private, 1st SAS Regiment, 1944** *The maroon beret had been adopted by this time, but many veterans continued to sport the sand-coloured version to differentiate themselves from other airborne units.*

▶ **Sergeant, Lancashire Fusiliers, Chindits, 1944** *The Chindit badge was sometimes worn on the right sleeve of the jungle shirt and could be worn with regimental or battalion insignia (here the Lancashire Fusiliers bursting grenade badge is in evidence).*

PARATROOPS

German success with airborne troops acted as a spur to the establishment and the development of airborne forces in Britain. An additional incentive was the fact that airborne forces were ideal for attack on Fortress Europe at multiple points while maintaining the element of surprise.

Early years

It took a while for plans to bear fruit, and despite prime minister Winston Churchill's call for airborne troops in June 1940, it was only in 1941 that a battalion was formed. This became a regiment in August 1942, rapidly expanded to a division (followed by another in 1943). Airborne troops not only included paratroopers but also, from 1942, personnel of the Glider Pilot Regiment, all under the command of the Army Air Corps; the SAS would join later. In addition, infantry battalions would be assigned an air-landing role, and these battalions usually retained their unit cap badges but adopted the airborne beret, equipment and airborne badges.

Battledress was the standard uniform for airborne forces and was initially worn with battledress trousers. The famous Denison smock was first issued in grey in 1941 but a camouflaged version appeared in 1942 and this was worn over battledress. The smock had four large pockets and a strip of cloth that hung from the back and could be buttoned to the front, passing between the legs; it was always worn under the equipment. Some smocks had buttonable Raglan cuffs and there were other variants. An oversmock was sometimes worn as a jump suit. This was fastened with a slip and was designed to cover equipment so that it would not become snagged in the parachute when landing.

◀ **PRIVATE, 11TH PARACHUTE BATTALION, 1944** *Paratroopers were armed with fighting knives (usually strapped to the right thigh), rifles or Sten guns, revolvers and various kinds of grenades (defensive, offensive, plastic). As with the infantry some sections were designated to operate Bren guns.*

WITH KIT *The Welbike was initially developed for use by Special Operations Executive (SOE); this small motorbike was used for liaison and reconnaissance.*

More practical trousers were also introduced in 1942. These had a large, padded pocket on the left and a system on the right that allowed the dagger to be carried along the length of the thigh. Field dressings were carried in the rear pockets.

Equipment generally followed that of the infantry, although there was a rather unusual leg bag. In addition, paratroopers carried rations for 24 hours and additional ammunition. Survival gear included a compass, torch and, for many officers, whistles (to gather the scattered paratroopers).

Insignia

The Parachute Regiment had a cloth shoulder title by 1943. It was Cambridge blue and bore the unit name. Branch-of-service strips were generally not worn, but the Airborne band was worn below the divisional badge (although this Airborne badge was sometimes absent). This was usually the celebrated representation of Bellerophon on the winged horse Pegasus designed by Major Seago and issued in May 1942. Pegasus and rider were light blue and were presented on a square of maroon cloth.

Winged parachute badges were also sometimes worn above the Pegasus badge, at least on the battledress. To designate different battalions, coloured cord was placed at the end of the shoulder strap when service dress was worn: the 7th had green; the 8th, blue; the 9th, brick red; the 12th, light blue; and the 13th, black. Generally, only rank insignia and parachute badges were worn on the Denison smock.

The Glider Pilot Regiment followed the same principles as above but with a 'Glider Pilot Regt.' shoulder title and wings above the left breast pocket. Glider-borne infantry kept their unit's shoulder title but added a light blue glider in a disk of khaki cloth badge to the lower sleeve and wore the Pegasus badge and the Airborne band.

◄ **Paratroop Insignia** *Top row, left to right, pilots' wings, glider troops' badge and glider pilots' wings. Middle two rows, regimental cap badges worn on the beret of airborne forces. Bottom row, left to right, sleeve insignia for Glider Pilot Regiment, Parachute Regiment, RASC Air Despatch.*

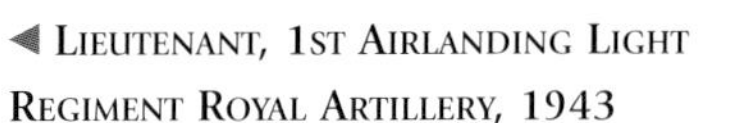

◄ **Lieutenant, 1st Airlanding Light Regiment Royal Artillery, 1943** *Officers' insignia was worn on the shoulder straps of the battledress or even the Denison smock. Members of the Army Air Corps, the umbrella formation for most airborne personnel, were entitled to have Cambridge blue backing to their shoulder insignia.*

► **Staff Sergeant, Glider Pilot Regiment, 1944** *The unit became operational in 1942, taking part in operations against German installations in Norway, and also formed part of the Army Air Corps (the Cambridge blue colour of the corps can be seen in the regimental shoulder arc). The airborne troops' helmet offered a very snug fit as well as stability and protection.*

Headgear

In 1942 the parachute brigades adopted a maroon beret with, initially, the Army Air Corps (AAC) badge (bird in flight in round wreath below a crown) or with the badge of the soldier's original regiment. The 5th Battalion, however, wore the Balmoral bonnet with a tartan patch under the badge. Although the AAC badge continued to be worn by the Glider Pilot's Regiment, the Parachute Regiment's badge was later issued to most personnel.

A blue beret had been considered, but the maroon beret was immensely popular. It was first seen in action in November 1942 during operations in North Africa. In May 1943 a new badge was issued for the regiment – a parachute and wings, with a lion and crown above. Some battalions attempted to retain unit traditions, such as the beret ribbons worn by men from the Royal Welch Fusiliers.

The Mark II helmet was simply impractical for airborne troops to use, so work soon began on more suitable head protection; in the meantime, crash helmets and Royal Air Force (RAF) flying helmets were used, and the so-called bungee helmet was developed for training jumps. This would have to be robust but compact to avoid snagging. The first prototype, Type P, was issued in late 1941, but it was still too bulky and the modified helmet (Mark I) appeared in 1942. The chinstrap was initially of leather, but later of webbing and it was fixed to the helmet at three points for additional stability.

THE ROYAL AIR FORCE

The RAF was an essential service for the island fortress of Britain in 1940, and went on to dominate the skies over occupied Europe.

The RAF was formed in April 1918 from the Royal Flying Corps, the Army's air arm in World War I. After a period of economy and restructuring, the British began to take German rearmament seriously and increased the size of the RAF from 1935 onwards. In 1936 the RAF had four commands: Bomber, Fighter, Coastal and Training. A fifth, Balloon Command was added in 1938. There were 135 squadrons and 19 auxiliary squadrons by 1939, the year the Women's Auxiliary Air Force (WAAF) was formed.

▲ *Royal Air Force pilots, dressed and kitted for action, wait in the pilots' flying room on an aircraft carrier in May 1942.*

◀ SERGEANT, NO. 1 SQUADRON RAF, 1940
The Royal Air Force indulged its pilots, allowing a degree of latitude in dress and behaviour. The tie, for example, was not normally worn when in flight, many pilots preferring to wear the shirt open or with a neckerchief or cravat.

Dress

The RAF was uniformed in dark blue. The most common form of dress on the ground was the service tunic with its open collar. It was worn with a light blue shirt and a black tie, a distinction accorded to all ranks by 1939. Blue battledress was also worn by pilots and ground crew, but this only really came into use after 1942. It had the usual fly front and scalloped pocket flaps over pleated pockets. Some economy versions seem to have been produced later, and usually ended up being worn by observers rather than pilots.

Trousers were also in blue, had flaps at the ankle that could be tightened to stop the trouser riding up, and a small pocket on the left for a field dressing. WAAF personnel wore skirts in a colour to match their service dress tunics.

Headgear consisted of the peaked service dress cap (either the stiff version, or the slouch version) with badge. The dress cap had a black peak and chinstrap. Senior officers had leather peaks with embroidery. Officers had the crown eagle badge, others had to make do with the RAF badge in a wreath. A blue side cap was also worn with the appropriate badge. Cadets added a white stripe around the cap band. Helmets, when worn, were painted dark grey. The WAAF had its own cap with a soft peak, capacious crown and WAAF badge.

The RAF Regiment, charged with guarding installations, wore shoulder titles and usually wore the Army's battledress along with a grey beret.

Insignia

Non-commissioned officers (NCOs) generally wore light khaki chevrons on blue on their upper arms; there was an inverted chevron on the lower arm of personnel awarded this badge of good conduct. Flight sergeants added a crown above the chevron. An albatross

◀ **SERGEANT, WAAF, 1940** *This section leader in the WAAF would have become a sergeant in January 1940. She wears a soft-topped peak cap of a type common to female personnel in the British armed forces, but in air force blue.*

▶ **SQUADRON LEADER, NO. 102 SQUADRON, 1942** *Britain was surrounded by cold water and so a specific kind of survival suit was designed to help the wearer survive in freezing water. The Taylor suit, with its thick lining, helped downed pilots to keep visible, float and keep warm – some models had electric heating.*

badge was worn at the top of the sleeve, usually on a patch of black, dark blue or grey-blue material.

Officers' rank was shown on the cap and by bands of lace around the cuff. This lace was in broad, common and narrow bands. A pilot officer would have one narrow band, a squadron leader two common and one narrow.

Roles within an aircrew were shown by half-wings above the left pocket. These bore initials for the role: 'AG' for air gunner, 'N' for navigator and 'E' for flight engineer. The 'RO' designation was an odd one: officially it stood for radio operator, but the individual was actually tasked with using the then secret radar equipment. It was abandoned as a badge in 1942. 'WAG' was brought out in 1944 and was worn by wireless operators who were also gunners. Pilots wore full wings over their breast pockets, pathfinders briefly had their own gilt eagle and observers had their own distinctive style of half wing brevet, a tradition dating back to the previous war.

Flying equipment

This consisted of a leather flying helmet, goggles (of many kinds), a lifejacket (really only standardized in 1941), a parachute and gloves or gauntlets. Many pilots added oxygen masks (usually Type D, with a microphone incorporated). Most pilots wore leather (Irvin) flying jackets lined with wool (and with matching trousers), or padded flotation suits in light yellow. Boots were usually the 1940-pattern flying boot, which were also well lined and were usually fastened with a zip at the front.

Volunteers

In addition to the RAF, were the air force volunteers of New Zealand (RNZAF), India (IAF, with 'Royal' added in 1945, making RIAF), Canada (RCAF), Australia (RAAF), South Africa (SAAF) and Rhodesia (SRAF). These were mostly distinguished by wings bearing the initials of the service, although shoulder titles were also in use (especially for volunteers without their own national air service, such as Ceylon and the West Indies). Foreign volunteers manned a number of units for the RAF. Initially they continued with their original cap badges and items of dress, but they were gradually standardized – up to a point. The Dutch retained their own badge throughout, as did the Poles, Yugoslavs (the rather enormous double-headed crowned eagle), Greeks and Norwegians. The Poles made use of national shoulder titles, along with the French, and rank was standardized to RAF use, or else the nation's own system was retained.

FOREIGN VOLUNTEERS

It is not true – as is often asserted – that Britain stood alone in 1940. Hundreds of thousands of foreign volunteers, exiled from their occupied homelands, flocked to the British Isles and dependent territories to join the fight. The formation of units of foreign volunteers began in a haphazard way in 1940. Even before then, volunteers had enlisted in British units in small numbers – but by 1940 there were enough to constitute entire units. This process gathered pace with the fall of France in June 1940 and continued until after 1945 when the Czechs and Poles were disbanded.

Belgians

The Belgian troops wore battledress, lion badges on their caps, the 'Belgium' shoulder title and, after 1942, a distinctive lion beneath a crown metal badge on the breast pocket. The Belgians were the only exiles to adopt British rank insignia, although regimental sergeant majors bore a heraldic device on the sleeve that incorporated the Belgian coat of arms. There was a proliferation of unit badges, the most striking being the skull on a shield beneath the tricolour of the fusiliers. The most significant formation was the 1st (known as the Piron) Brigade, formed in 1943; its badge was the yellow lion's head on black triangle with red border.

Czechs

The Czechs were scattered across Europe and the Middle East in 1939. The defeat of France meant that a small Czech Independent Brigade could form, since the Czechs had been in French service. Initially they wore French uniform with Czech badges of rank and then British battledress with the shoulder title 'Czechoslovakia' in red lettering on khaki arcs (sometimes seen in blue). Some personnel had piping on the strap (yellow for infantry, red for artillery). The Czech Independent Brigade became the Czechoslovak Armoured Brigade in 1943 and bore a sleeve badge with red and blue diced shield with white Bohemian lion.

◀ **Captain, Czech Infantry Battalion No 11, 1941** *The Czechoslovak battalion was formed into a battalion in Palestine, moved to Egypt and then used against the French in Syria. Officers had Czech rank insignia on their shoulder straps and also the national shoulder arc. In addition, they attached a Czechoslovak flag flash to the right side of their tropical helmet; this was then transferred to the steel helmet, although a round version was also used.*

▶ **Trooper, 10th Polish Dragoons, 1944** *Polish troops in British service clung on to Polish traditions and much of the insignia worn by the Polish Army in 1939. The only unusual feature was that they painted Polish eagles onto their helmets in yellow rather than the traditional white.*

Czechs who escaped to Cyprus were organized into a battalion in khaki drill with Czech sleeve titles. Czechs retained their rank insignia.

French

Those Frenchmen who escaped German occupation initially had French uniforms and equipment. In late 1940 British battledress began to be issued to French troops bearing the shoulder title 'France' in white lettering on a khaki arc. It was difficult to prise French headgear from these troops, and French Adrian helmets continued in use for some time. In the absence of helmets, side caps, berets and the sailors' cap with pompom (worn by the Fusiliers Marins) proliferated, often with French branch-of-service badges. The French, and Belgians, developed a distinctive badge (a winged sword, later replaced by the cross of Lorraine). Rank was worn on the shoulder straps but the French system was retained. The Free French in the colonies generally retained their old uniforms, gradually replacing items with British or American gear, with the addition of the cross of Lorraine badge.

▶ **Private, 1st Battalion, Fusilier-Marin, 1944** *Following French tradition, the beret was sometimes worn badgeless and pulled to the left of the head rather than the more usual right (seen here) because French drill called for carrying the rifle on the other shoulder. The beret replaced the traditional French sailor's cap.*

Greeks and Yugoslavs

The Greeks formed two brigades for British service; a third was created from remnants of the first in 1944. The Greek Sacred Regiment, formed by officers, was also raised. This unit, used for commando raids, wore British uniforms with a distinctive Spartan sword in wreath cap badge (also worn on the tunic). The Greek brigades wore British uniforms in North Africa and Italy, with Greek badges of rank and, sporadically, a shoulder patch representing the Greek symbol of a white cross on a blue square. Yugoslavs formed a number of battalions for service in North Africa and they wore Yugoslav caps with eagle badges and British uniforms.

Other Volunteers

Dutch exiles (and volunteers from the US and South Africa) adopted British battledress in 1940, but retained the lion cap badge; officers retained orange lanyards. Dutch rank insignia was retained and worn on the collar as was, to a certain extent, branch-of-service colour often worn as piping on caps: blue for infantry, black for artillery. A sleeve insignia with the Nassau lion and 'Nederland' title was introduced. Most Dutch forces were organized into the Prinses Irene Brigade.

The majority of Polish volunteers arrived in Britain in French uniform. This was retained until battledress could be issued with the white-lettered shoulder title 'Poland' on red arc. Polish rank was retained on the shoulder strap and Polish decorative devices were also transferred to the collar: so, for example, armoured personnel often retained the black over orange lance pennon device and those of the 1st Armoured Division retained a black shoulder strap in commemoration of their pre-war traditions. Standard British helmets were introduced, and these usually bore the Polish eagle device in white or yellow – or on a red disk in the Middle East. Polish tankers enthusiastically copied the black beret, while Polish airborne adopted steel-grey berets to match yellow-piped grey collar tabs.

◀ **Private, Prinses Irene Independent Brigade Group, 1944** *Dutch volunteers, along with personnel of Dutch origin from overseas (many of them South African), were formed into this small unit that fought alongside Belgian volunteers. The brigade had the distinctive Nassau lion as a shoulder insignia.*

CANADIAN TROOPS

The Canadian Active Service Force (CASF) was quickly mobilized in 1939 and a division was sent to Britain that December. A second followed eight months later and they formed a corps in 1941. A second corps was formed in 1943. Canadians from the I Corps fought in Italy before rejoining the bulk of Canadian forces in the Low Countries in early 1945.

Canadian dress generally followed the patterns adopted by the British (although Canadian battledress was greener in tone and of better quality, retaining – for example – metal rather than plastic buttons), as did officers' rank insignia. After 1943 a slightly modified battledress was introduced fastened at the collar with a cloth strap rather than hook. Equipment followed the British model but, again, items of Canadian manufacture were slightly different, Canadian cotton being slightly yellower.

Canada was short of helmets and the first wave of Canadians sent over to Europe mostly wore the old Mark I helmet. The Canadians began producing the Mark II helmet in January 1940 and began to fit remaining stocks of the Mark I with more suitable interiors to make up any shortfall. Canadians in the Normandy campaign of 1944 were issued with the new Mark III helmet and a brown General Service Beret after 1943.

Insignia

Canadians serving in the CASF wore the 'Canada' worsted sleeve title at the shoulder; orders in November 1939 specified that this was not to be worn on the greatcoat.

Divisional patches were also worn. The 1st Division had a red rectangle; the 2nd, dark blue; the 3rd, light blue; the 4th (Armoured), green; the 5th (Armoured), maroon; the 6th, red over blue (diagonal); the 7th, light blue over green (diagonal); and the 8th, green over maroon (diagonal). The two main armoured brigades had a black diamond with yellow maple leaf over red or blue central strips respectively. Canadians in I Corps initially wore a red diamond and II Corps adopted a blue diamond, leading to some confusion among support services. Support troops had their branch initials superimposed over the diamond or divisional patch, a practice sometimes followed by a few regiments, or wore a unit shoulder title and plain corps or divisional

▲ *Men of the Canadian Pictou Highlanders iron their uniforms while waiting to ship out from America to Europe in 1944.*

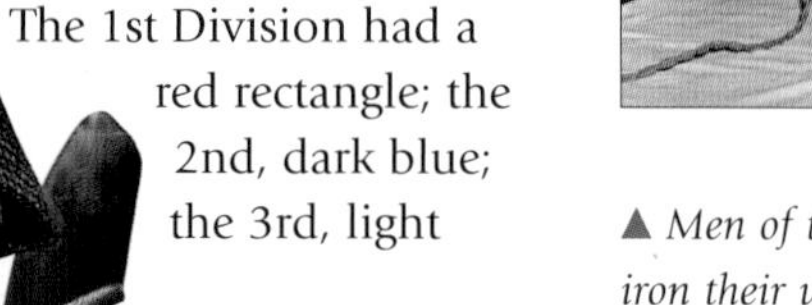

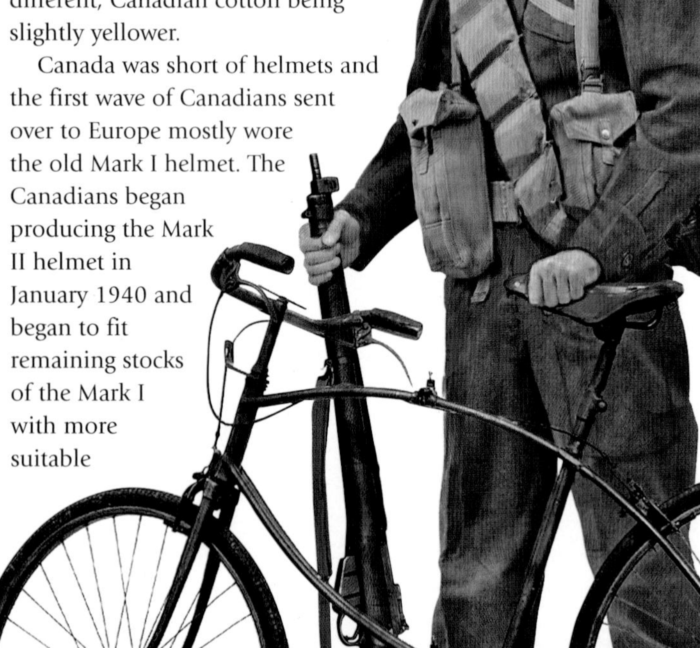

◀ **Private, Nova Scotia Highlanders, 1944** *Canadians going ashore in 1944 wore the black Canadian ankle boot (known as the ammunition boot) without toecaps. These were worn with canvas anklets (usually blancoed). A taller boot, known as the 3rd Division boot, seems to have been issued to this unit as late as September 1944.*

▲ SERGEANT, ROYAL 22ND RÉGIMENT, 1943 *This Canadian unit was known as the Van Doos (a play on the French for 22, 'vingt-deux') and was a francophone unit recruited around Quebec, with a regimental title in French on the colourful shoulder arc (blue over yellow over red). The red rectangle is the divisional patch of the 1st Division.*

patch. The 2nd Division had initially continued the tradition of different battalions sporting different geometric shapes above their divisional patches, but this was dropped in 1943.

Colourful regimental titles became something of a Canadian speciality. They had originally been worn by the Governor General's Foot Guards, Canadian Grenadier Guards, Princess Patricia's Canadian Light Infantry and the Canadian Provost Corps, but were extended to the vast majority of Canadian regiments in late 1940 and were a common sight from 1941.

Artillery and Tankers

The Royal Canadian Artillery had shoulder titles bearing 'RCA' in red on dark blue cloth. By 1943 the regimental number was being added for field regiments along with smaller initials for specialist units – for example, '2AT RCA' for the 2nd Anti-Tank Regiment, with the 'AT' in small letters; or '6LAA RCA' for the 6th Light Anti-Aircraft Regiment.

Canada's armoured personnel followed British styles, even adopting the traditional black beret. Armoured regiments were also authorized to wear the cloth tank badge on the right sleeve. Regimental titles and the tank badge were usually the only adornment to the battledress.

Paratroops

In July1942 volunteers began to form the 1st Canadian Parachute Battalion; the 2nd battalion became the First Special Service Force. They had infantry uniform with maroon berets bearing the badge of the Canadian Parachute Corps (a formation that never got off the ground). Sleeves usually had the battalion title over the Pegasus patch over the airborne flash; a distinctive flash, 'Airborne Canada' on green, was developed late in the war. Officers had bright red backing to their shoulder insignia. Paratroops used British equipment and adopted British or American smocks and arms.

The First Special Service Force wore American uniforms with a Canada disc and a crossed-arrow disc on the lapels. The Shoulder Sleeve Insignia, or SSI, following US practice, showed the distinctive red arrowhead bearing 'USA' and 'Canada' in white lettering. This was placed at the top of the left sleeve, following US custom. Cap badges were generally the same as those worn by the Canadian Parachute Battalion.

Newfoundland

Volunteers from Newfoundland, a self-governing territory, were organized into the 57th (the 166th Field Regiment from November 1941) and 59th Heavy regiments of Britain's Royal Artillery. They wore a 'Newfoundland' shoulder title in red lettering (often removed in combat).

▼ GUNNER, 14TH FIELD REGIMENT, ROYAL CANADIAN ARTILLERY, 1944 *The newly issued Mark III helmet had camouflage netting, which was often used to carry items such as a first aid kit, or a packet of cigarettes.*

AUSTRALIAN AND NEW ZEALAND TROOPS

In 1939 the war seemed very distant from Australia and New Zealand. When Japan attacked, however, the conflict came much closer.

Australia

Although Australia had achieved the status of an autonomous state in 1926, in World War II Australian personnel would fight in Greece, North Africa, Italy, Asia and the Pacific. Uniforms initially resembled those worn in the previous war. Australian troops wore khaki service dress tunics with stand-and-fall collars (usually worn open) and five nickel buttons. These buttons initially bore the inscription 'Australian Military Forces' and a map of Australia, but later plain buttons were used. There were four generous pockets with scalloped flaps, and the breast pockets were pleated. Cuffs were pulled tight to make the sleeves seem baggy and a pleated back made for additional comfort. An internal pocket contained a field dressing.

In 1943 economies resulted in a simplified version being adopted. It was closer-fitting and often had plastic buttons; the lower pockets now had rectangular flaps. Officers had initially worn the open-necked tunic with khaki shirt and tie. Jungle attire consisted of bush shirts, jackets and denim shirts.

Trousers were long and baggy and usually gathered into canvas anklets with three buttons. Brown leather ankle boots were usually worn. Shorts were sometimes worn in the Mediterranean theatre, usually with puttees. Greatcoats, useful in the deserts of North Africa because of the low night temperature, were single-breasted khaki garments. It was worn free of insignia apart from the curved 'Australia' shoulder title.

Equipment was normally the 1937-pattern web equipment used by British troops. However, some 1908-pattern equipment was still in use, as was the 1903-leather bandolier. By 1942 these dated items had largely disappeared.

The insignia on hats and caps was still the rising sun above an Australian badge. It was pinned to the left-side of the slouch hat (to the brim). Insignia on the tunic consisted of the shoulder title 'Australia', which was curved, and the sunburst badge was worn on the collar points, although this was routinely abandoned.

◀ **Private, 2/5th Australian Infantry Battalion, 6th Division, 1941** *Australians were issued with the standard helmet or wore the slouch hat, which sometimes had the formation sign – seen here on the sleeve – pinned to the hat band.*

▶ **Private, 2/43rd Australian Infantry Battalion, 1942** *The greatcoat was usually worn free of insignia, so this unit's brown over blue disc is not visible. This unit's division distinguished itself at Tobruk and received T-shaped formation patches from then on as a mark of recognition for gallant conduct.*

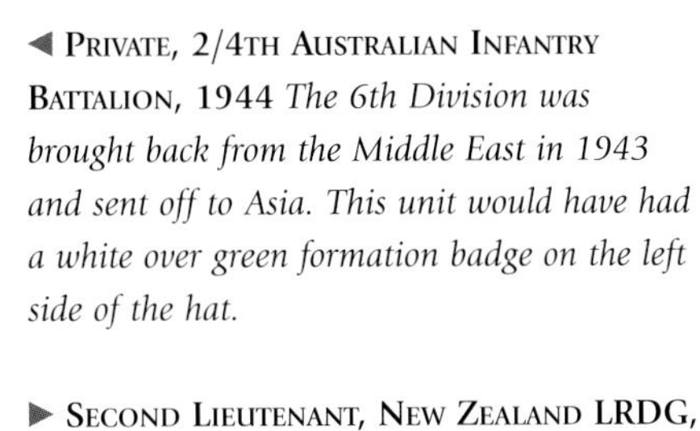

◀ **Private, 2/4th Australian Infantry Battalion, 1944** *The 6th Division was brought back from the Middle East in 1943 and sent off to Asia. This unit would have had a white over green formation badge on the left side of the hat.*

▶ **Second Lieutenant, New Zealand LRDG, 1943** *The Long Range Desert Group was a reconnaissance and raiding unit that drew much of its strength from New Zealanders and Rhodesians. Shoulder titles and scorpion badges were popular.*

Australian officers began the war with the peaked service cap, while soldiers wore the envelope-shaped side cap; attempts to introduce a canvas beret in 1944 were met with disapproval. The defining item of dress for the Australian soldier was the slouch hat in khaki, left side of the brim pinned to the crown bearing the Australian badge. There was a sand-coloured band, or puggaree and leather chinstrap. Australian troops also had access to the Mark I helmet from the previous conflict. This was worn with modified interiors and only until production of the Mark II satisfied demand; Australia manufactured 2 million such helmets, selling some to New Zealand and India.

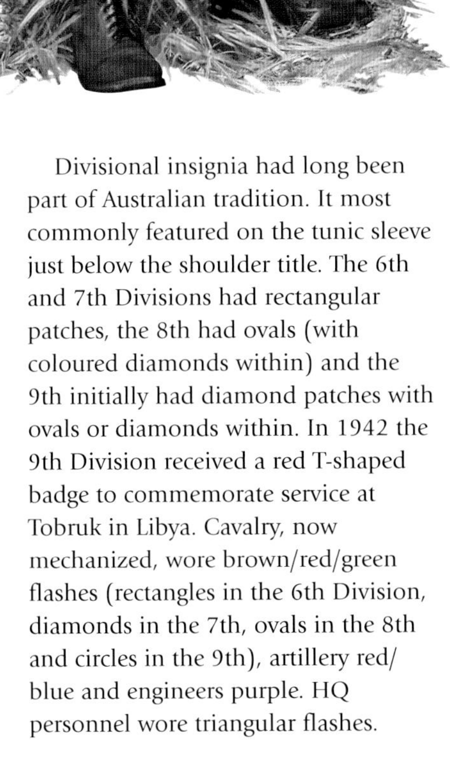

Divisional insignia had long been part of Australian tradition. It most commonly featured on the tunic sleeve just below the shoulder title. The 6th and 7th Divisions had rectangular patches, the 8th had ovals (with coloured diamonds within) and the 9th initially had diamond patches with ovals or diamonds within. In 1942 the 9th Division received a red T-shaped badge to commemorate service at Tobruk in Libya. Cavalry, now mechanized, wore brown/red/green flashes (rectangles in the 6th Division, diamonds in the 7th, ovals in the 8th and circles in the 9th), artillery red/blue and engineers purple. HQ personnel wore triangular flashes.

New Zealand

These armed forces wore service dress tunics or khaki drill shirts, lemon squeezer hats (with red puggaree band for infantry, although officers often preferred the peaked service dress cap) bearing the so-called Onward badge, a crowned wreath around 'NZ' with the motto 'Onward' below, also sometimes worn on the collar). Battledress was issued to troops (2nd Division) in Greece in 1941 (and later in Italy). Trousers with anklets were common in Europe, shorts more usual in Africa.

White lettering on black shoulder arcs bearing 'New Zealand' were common from 1941 (replacing metallic unit insignia, although this was sometimes retained), and battalion, brigade or divisional flashes were worn on the sleeve. These were complex with branch-of-service coloured geometric shapes appearing within a brigade patch. Cavalry had green and artillery had red/blue geometric shapes, which varied according to formation. The system was later simplified so that coloured felt denoted branch-of-service while shape denoted brigade.

In Asia New Zealand troops had slip-on shoulder titles in red lettering for the 2nd Division and black for the 3rd Division. These were worn on khaki drill shirts or bush jackets.

British helmets were worn. Armoured troops wore berets with red backing to their badges; cavalry did the same, but with green.

AFRICAN TROOPS

South Africa was the African continent's most significant supplier of manpower after 1939, but contingents from other countries in Africa also served far from home.

South Africa

The armed forces of South Africa were very small in 1939: its army, with 3,300 regulars, numbered fewer than 20,000 when reservists were included. These were drawn from those of European descent and were intended to operate in Africa; indeed, an infantry brigade was sent off to fight the Italians in East Africa in June 1940. This became a division in August 1940. Service in North Africa followed and South Africans were also used against the Vichy French in Madagascar.

South African units wore khaki drill dress. This mostly consisted of a sand-coloured tropical shirt, but officers also wore a more formal tunic with open collar, pointed cuffs and four pockets. It was worn with khaki shirt and khaki tie. The buttons bore the arms of South Africa and regimental badges were worn on the upper lapel, along with shoulder titles on the straps.

Numerous kinds of field jacket and bush jacket were used in Africa, from the old-style grey-green versions worn in the 1930s to the comfortable loose bush jackets adopted by many officers. Other ranks still wore the older-style canvas gaiter with four straps, which was popular because it gave the wearer some protection in the desert scrub; an economical two-strap version was also produced. By 1943, a mixture of British and American items were in use. South Africa did produce a copy of the battledress that was slightly browner than that in use in Britain. Those who volunteered for service wore an orange shoulder flash at the end of their shoulder straps and onto this a regimental device was sewn. Regiments were also recognizable by their distinctive cap badge.

South African divisions were distinguished by the traditional yellow and green flashes worn on helmets and sleeves. The 1st Division had a yellow over green lozenge, the 2nd had a circle and the 3rd (a reserve) had a square. The armoured division had a yellow triangle with green border; this division, formed in 1943, eventually served under American command in Italy. Rank was shown on the shoulder straps, either with blackened metal stars and crowns or following the British worsted-cloth tradition.

Most helmets were originally a variation of the Bombay bowler, solar topee or sun helmet. The Wolseley helmet had been phased out by 1939. A small number of South Africans in uniform in 1939 made use of the Mark I helmet, updated with new chinstrap and interior. These were supplemented by locally produced versions. South African factories then switched to manufacturing their own version of the Mark II and they produced sufficient numbers to equip their own personnel and supply the surplus to the Indian Army. The South African version was

◀ SERGEANT, NATAL MOUNTED RIFLES, 1943 *The tropical helmet came in a number of different styles, from the round Bombay bowler, to the more elegant topee. The South African example was manufactured in the 1930s and bears the regimental badge pinned to the front and has a sun curtain attached to the rear of the helmet.*

▲ *A propaganda poster, date unknown, celebrates the vital contribution to the war effort of troops from the British Empire.*

pierced with three holes on the brim to allow a cloth cover to be secured.

Armoured personnel (mostly from the South African Tank Corps, or the SATC-SATK) adopted the black beret. This was larger than the one worn by the British. The Special Service Battalion, manning armoured cars, added an orange/white/blue flash under their cap badge; Prince Alfred's Guard had a similar tradition with a red and blue flash.

The 1925 system of web equipment was adopted by South Africa. With its narrow braces and modified cartridge carriers, it was sometimes seen on troops in the early years of the conflict. They also made use of Braithwaite web equipment (issued in 1935), with its distinctive square-shaped two-part pack. Most South African officers still wore the Sam Browne belt.

Rhodesia

A number of Rhodesian units were formed and they came under South African command in 1942. They bore the title 'Rhodesia' on the orange shoulder flash. Their cap badge was usually the Rhodesian lion device.

West Africans

The most significant force drawn from this region was the Royal West African Frontier Force. This was composed of personnel from Nigeria, Sierra Leone, the Gold Coast and Gambia, but in one of those interesting footnotes of history it also contained around 400 Polish officers – sent from Britain to lead the corps.

Members of this force wore shoulder titles with the initials 'RWAFF', but also had distinctive regimental badges for individual units. A considerable proportion were sent off to Asia to fight the Japanese and there they adopted the slouch hat (or bush hat) and the jungle-green battledress (shirt, jungle) or bush jacket. As was customary, most insignia was kept off the sleeve, with the hat bearing a divisional sign – in this case the black spider on yellow rectangle of the 81st West African Division or the crossed spears on yellow shield of the 82nd West African Division.

King's African Rifles

The King's African Rifles were recruited in central and eastern Africa with regiments bearing the battalion number over 'KAR' on the shoulder and the hunting horn and crown cap badge. Again some troops found themselves in Asia and bore the black Rhino head on red badge of the 11th East African Division.

◀ **Private, Botha Regiment, 1941** *The orange tab on the shoulder strap was the mark of the South African volunteer who had signed up for service outside of his home country. The general policy seems to have been to place regimental shoulder titles in metal over these tabs, and this unit, raised in 1934, followed that practice.*

▶ **Private, 4th Battalion, Nigeria Regiment, Royal West African Frontier Force, 1944** *Two of the West African divisions (the 81st and the 82nd) were sent to fight in the Far East. The 81st Division included the 4th Battalion of the Nigerian Regiment and wore a black tarantula spider as a formation patch. The Force had a palm tree and scroll that was sometimes used as a cap badge, officers pinning it to their slouch hats.*

INDIAN TROOPS

India was potentially a huge pool of manpower for the war effort. It would go on to provide not only personnel but arms, uniforms and equipment for the war effort.

Although Britain had some reservations about arming Indians at a time when pressure was mounting to sever the ties between India and the British, necessity forced the imperial hand to draw on vast numbers of Indian military personnel. They were organized into the Indian Army and were largely officered by Europeans. Each Indian division had a complement of European troops (from the British Army in India), a practice dating back to the 19th century and an expression of British insecurity.

There were Indian officers. A military college had been founded in 1922, the year when the Army was completely reorganized. The college turned out commissioned officers (ICOs) but there were also a class of Viceroy Commissioned Officers (VCOs), and a few Indian officers were commissioned in Britain. Eight units were authorized to receive Indian officers – 7th and 16th Light Cavalry, battalions of the 1st and 14th Punjab, 5th Mahratta, 7th Rajput, 19th Hyderabad and the soon disbanded 1st Madras Pioneers. The programme was insufficient but war meant that Indianization was pursued with more vigour from 1939.

Burma was a slightly separate case, and in 1937 Burmese units were taken away from the Indian Army to become part of the Burma Army.

Indian uniform resembled that worn in the previous conflict. There was an assortment of khaki drill service tunics, tropical shirts and increasingly, from 1941, battledress tunics for those operating in the Mediterranean theatre. There, the khaki woollen pullover over khaki or grey flannel shirt would also become a regular sight. North Africa saw the use of khaki drill items in line with British practice. In Burma jungle-green items of dress would come to predominate. Trousers included the strange Bombay bloomers, long shorts that stretched below the knee. Many NCOs preferred baggy

◀ **Private, 8th Punjab Regiment, 1944** *Indian headgear came in a rich and varied number of forms when it came to full dress, mostly revolving around scarlet, blue and yellow. On campaign a khaki turban in everyday khaki, or the standard Mark II helmet, was the norm.*

▶ **Sergeant, 5th Mahratta Regiment, 1943** *This regiment followed the traditions of a light infantry regiment, even down to the bugle horn cap badge with ribbons and crown, which were reminiscent of that worn by the Durham Light Infantry (here the 'DLI' is replaced by a number 5 and the horn is slightly less decorative). This Havildar, the Indian Army infantry equivalent of a sergeant, would have had a red over green plume as an additional flourish on parade.*

◀ **Private, 7th Gurkha Rifles, 1942** *In 1942 the black cat shoulder insignia replaced a bolt of white lightning on a blue square for the 17th Indian Division. Regimental insignia, usually metal shoulder titles bearing '7.G.R.', were worn at the end of the shoulder strap, and many officers still had the regimental metal button bearing the number 7 between two kukri (a corruption of the Nepalese kukuri) knives.*

khaki trousers tucked into puttees. Ankle boots or sandals were worn.

Insignia consisted of regimental cap badges and metal shoulder titles (often replaced by slip-on khaki tabs with stencilled titles). The Indian Artillery, formed in 1935, had a gun cap badge but with a star above rather than a crown; Indian engineers had a star device. New badges were added as needed: the Indian Intelligence Corps, formed in 1942, had a star bearing an 'I' in a wreath.

Indians in Britain wore 'Indian Army' shoulder titles, with white lettering on red. Divisional flashes came into use, as with other British forces. Indian divisions had a wealth of coloured symbols, all worn on the upper sleeve or on the slouch hat when that was worn. Rank insignia followed British pattern, but VCOs were issued yellow-within-red strips for their shoulder straps in 1941; they also had different titles or address.

Equipment followed British pattern, although the older 1908-pattern equipment was more common than the 1937 pattern.

Specialists

Some 21 regiments of cavalry existed in 1939, uniformed in the traditional long khaki drill tunic (the kurta). In 1940 a process of mechanization began, most units receiving armoured cars. Battledress was preferred, as was the khaki turban rather than the standard black beret. Indian paratroops wore oversmocks or grey denim smocks as well as various form of paratroop helmet. The maroon beret was generally limited to NCOs and officers. The Pegasus badge – the same as that worn in Europe, but with the word 'India' placed below – was worn on the sleeve along with the 'Airborne' title and, if appropriate, wings.

Headgear

Although Indian soldiers received British helmets, many continued to wear their distinctive khaki turban. Slouch hats were popular in the jungles of Asia; the Garhwal Rifles, who were recruited in the Himalayas, wore such hats.

The turban varied according to religion, and also to regional preferences. Essentially, Muslim troops wore a cone-shaped skull cap (the kullah) and wrapped a khaki band (pagri) around it, the ends being fixed to the cap. Coloured pagri were used on formal occasions. Sikhs wore their traditional turban and troops from Madras wore a kind of pillbox khaki fez.

Gurkhas

The Gurkha rifle units wore slouch hats and insignia and distinctions generally followed the pattern adopted by British Rifle regiments. Metal shoulder titles were initially worn, then cloth slip-ons bearing a numeral and 'GR'; cap badges were worn on the slouch hat (the 10th traditionally had the badge or flash of tartan on the right side). The defining piece of equipment for these units was the curved kukri knife, worn in a leather scabbard.

Two parachute battalions formed from Gurkhas were also operational, wearing a crossed kukri and parachute device on a light blue square, with blades away from the chute for the 153rd Battalion, towards the chute for the 154th. The badge was worn on the sleeve or slouch hat; if worn on the sleeve, the 'Airborne' title was below. Some personnel wore the red beret.

▼ *British Indian troops examine a Nazi flag found in the Axis trenches of the Western Desert after the capture of Libyan Omar.*

THE UNITED STATES

The United States remained neutral in September 1939, and it wasn't until 8 December 1941, the day after Japan attacked Pearl Harbor, that American troops became embroiled in the war in the Pacific. It was another 28 months after that before they started to arrive in Europe – but material assistance to the Allies began well before. In the course of World War II the US performed a dual role in the fight against the Axis powers. On the one hand it fielded progressively more competent troops against German, Italian and Japanese forces in several different theatres and in varying conditions – from the cold Aleutian Islands to the deserts of North Africa. On the other, it provided a major industrial resource that met the Allied need for material and munitions: American vehicles, armaments, aircraft and ships were produced in vast quantities and were destined to be seen in every theatre of war, used by American, British, British Empire, Chinese and Soviet personnel alike.

▲ *Charging over rough Tunisian terrain, a US Army tank seeks out German armoured units in the wake of other American tanks whose tread marks have scarred the soil.*

◀ *A group of American soldiers look over a Japanese gun, which they had captured at Hollandia (in Dutch New Guinea), and afterwards used to shoot down enemy planes.*

AMERICA PREPARES FOR CONFLICT

In 1939 the United States was – more than any other time in its history – a sleeping giant. The decade of the 1930s had been blighted by the economic woes of the Great Depression, labour disputes (often resolved by using the army) and increasing social tension. Intervention in a distant conflict seemed like an unwelcome distraction and an unnecessary burden on a country reeling from two decades of apparent decline.

Isolation was the buzzword, something that appealed to many across the nation. 'Hitlerism' – the threat posed by German leader Adolf Hitler – was a distant problem, and many had little sympathy for imperial European powers that could be seen as getting what they deserved. Although the 'New Deal' economic policies instituted by the government of President Franklin D. Roosevelt were starting to have an improving effect, these and other aspects of domestic US politics distracted many from external affairs and obscured the clouds gathering on the horizon.

▼ *President Franklin Roosevelt delivers his 1941 State of the Union address to a joint session of Congress.*

▲ *Franklin D. Roosevelt and Churchill on the deck of* HMS Prince of Wales *at the Atlantic Charter Conference, which declared joint US and British war aims. 10 August 1941.*

Lessons of World War I

The United States had entered World War I largely unprepared and found that arming and equipping 3.5 million men was an enormous challenge even for a major economy. The situation was little better in 1939, although some important measures were taken in 1938 when the US Congress voted funds for rearmament. Those funds were deemed insufficient by the Army, which estimated that it needed $500 million to provide a modern, capable force for deployment. The problem was that in the lean years of the mid-1930s the US Army had used up its surplus stocks, and had not been able to stockpile weapons or equipment for any major increase in demand.

At that stage the authorities envisaged that mobilization would follow the trajectory similar to World War I, when up to 4 million individuals mobilized. Indeed the Protective Mobilization Plan of December 1938 was based on having 400,000 under arms, increasing by steps to the target of 4 million – a conception of mobilization with its origins in the General Staff's 1923 war plan. The logistical support of this initial protective force had, however, been improved, and an industrial mobilization plan attempted to ensure that sufficient equipment was delivered when and where it was needed.

The Rainbow Plan

The US government followed events in Europe closely. In November 1938 planners began to initiate the Rainbow Plan, which defined the numbers that would be needed but envisaged that it would be two years before substantial forces would be readied. Six months later the Americans had 190,000 regular soldiers under arms (50,000 overseas, mostly in the Philippines) with an additional 200,000 National Guard and 100,000 reservists.

Measures became more urgent when Germany overran Poland in a matter of weeks, shocking the British and French and surprising the Americans. A state of national emergency was declared on

8 September 1939. The Army Air Corps (subsequently reformed into the US Army Air Forces in 1941) received substantial funds to modernize and expand – enough to make 10,000 aircraft operational. The Navy, too, was given a freer hand.

The Army regulars and the National Guard was now composed of half a million men, increased in strength from August 1940 with new recruits required to serve for at least a year. It found itself able to start stockpiling weapons and munitions. Even so, the partial mobilization that followed meant that many men were being mobilized before the equipment they needed was available.

▲ *US Boeing B-17 bombers, flying in formation, demonstrate the country's increasing readiness for offensive warfare.*

Exporting to the Allies

On 16 May 1940, President Roosevelt signed the supplemental Military Appropriations Act, triggering the release of significant funds for aircraft production, munitions, uniforms and equipment. Industry responded and was further stimulated by demand from now-isolated Britain. When the Soviet Union was invaded in June 1941, it too asked for vast quantities of industrial assistance. This export of materials to key allies allowed the United States to avoid over-providing for its own still relatively restricted needs – for the number of Americans under arms in the autumn of 1941 was still relatively small.

▼ *A member of the first US expeditionary force to Europe, promised to Britain by Roosevelt, drinks tea at a Northern Irish port.*

Expansion

At that time the General Staff viewed Europe as the main theatre of operations. It envisaged that by the middle of 1943 sufficient forces would be available to launch offensives in Europe. These plans inevitably reflected American experience in World War I – they allowed for an expeditionary force operating alongside allies and with logistical support provided via transatlantic convoys and then stockpiled in the British Isles. The first goal of having 1.5 million men under arms was achieved by around the same time as these plans in late 1941. The Army had been expanded to 34 divisions, but having so many soldiers at home proved problematic. By late summer in 1941, there was a shortage of barracks – and increasing tension with civilians. The government responded by slowing mobilization and delaying the incorporation of National Guard units as long as possible.

This period was an extremely useful one because it allowed the training and induction of troops to continue and permitted the General Staff to extract useful lessons from the defeat of France in 1940 – as well as learning from what little accurate news was coming out of the Soviet Union in 1941. These lessons would play an important part in the development of US armoured capacity and tactics, as well as in the enlargement of the air force; mastery of the skies was seen as a crucial feature in German doctrine.

Still, progress was slow. In October 1941 only one infantry division was deemed to be properly equipped for overseas action, while 17 of the remaining divisions were only ready for the defence of the homeland. Of these 17 divisions, the majority were earmarked for use outside the United States, mostly in Europe. Methodical developments were, however, largely swept away by the Japanese attack on Pearl Harbor.

THE US ENTERS A GLOBAL WAR

The Japanese declared war on the USA on 7 December 1941 – adding, for good measure, a declaration of war against Britain and her empire the same day. The USA responded in kind the following day, supported by Canada and a host of Central American states. Then, in one of the most bizarre moves in recent history, Germany and Italy also declared war on the USA, on 11 December 1941. Suddenly the USA's unwanted war was global. The Americans would officially be at war with Germany, Italy and Japan from that December. Albania, Romania, Bulgaria and Hungary would also be at war with the United States – while Vichy France stood by, and Finland deliberately chose not to pick a quarrel.

Expansion was rapid. Pre-war targets were abolished and production and mobilization hurried forwards. The plan was to have 3.6 million troops ready in 1942, organized into 71 divisions. (Soon afterwards, the target was increased to 5 million.) Some 60,000 aircraft were to be produced, and 45,000 tanks. All this was needed to deal with the rather nightmarish scenario of a war on two fronts.

Japanese onslaught

The Japanese had not only attacked Pearl Harbor but they also launched assaults in the Philippines, Midway and Guam – where the attack came just four hours after news of the attack on Pearl Harbor filtered through. The Japanese onslaught was a surprise, even although tensions had been steadily increasing.

The Japanese had overrun large parts of China since 1937 and had built up forces in the Japanese-mandated Pacific islands. These islands – the Marianas, Carolines, Marshall Islands, Palau and Truk – had come into Japanese possession after the previous war and now served as useful naval bases. American garrisons on neighbouring islands grew increasingly suspicious of Japanese intentions, especially when reconnaissance planes began overflights in the spring of 1941. But the Americans had reduced their military establishments and saved money on the cost of building fortified emplacements.

When the attack came, it swept all before it. The Japanese stormed the Philippines: US staff being evacuated in February 1942, and the nadir of Allied fortunes in Asia came when the British surrendered Singapore in that month. Japan also took Guam and overran Borneo, even bombing Darwin in Australia, and occupied the Aleutian Islands, so taking control of a key point between the Soviet Union and Alaska. This led to fears that the Japanese would target the US mainland. In fact, Japanese aircraft only ever managed to bomb the US once (a light aircraft, launched from a Japanese submarine, dropped bombs on Oregon in September 1942). More damage was caused by Japanese fire

▼ *US Marine Corps soldiers gather around while officers including, far right, James Roosevelt plan an attack, September 1942.*

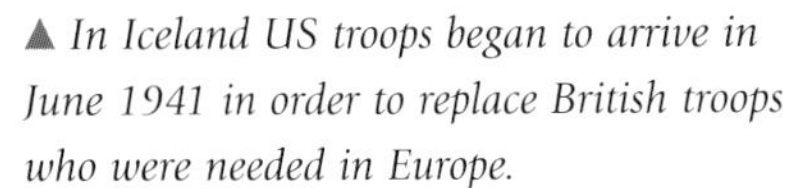

▲ *In Iceland US troops began to arrive in June 1941 in order to replace British troops who were needed in Europe.*

▲ *Colonel Cochran (right) of the US 1st Air Commando Group, and British Major General Wingate, brief their men in Burma.*

balloons, which were released in large numbers in 1944 and which carried explosives in the general direction of the United States and Canada: three days after release, gunpowder destroyed the balloon and the bomb load dropped. In all, around 300 of these devices seem to have been found or exploded in the United States and six people were killed.

US forces arrive in Europe

The American response inevitably took time to develop. Troops were also required in Europe. Iceland had been transferred to US rule in the summer of 1941 (following British occupation) and the garrison there built up over time. Troops of the 34th Infantry Division arrived in Britain in January 1942, but major operations did not begin until that November when the Americans were involved in Operation Torch, the landings in Morocco and Algiers (against the Vichy French, which led to the German occupation of the rest of France). Sharp fighting followed with German and Italian forces in Tunisia later that year and in 1943. From there, a major build up of men and equipment followed – and resulted in the invasion of Sicily and mainland Italy in the autumn of 1943.

The Americans were now stretched by Soviet demands for a second front in northern Europe – and British prime minister Winston Churchill's demands for more troops in the Mediterranean – and by the requirements of the Pacific theatre. Industrial output did, however, give the Americans an advantage over the Axis powers – who had overextended their armed forces, could not keep up with production and had lost many of their best units in the hard fighting of 1941 and 1942. Italy dropped out of the war in 1943, a significant development. Then the launch of the 1944 Normandy landings, and the establishment of Allied troops in southern France, began the rollback of German power.

Initially, the progress of the campaign was tempered because of the difficulty of keeping supplies coming in over increasing distances – as the Soviets were experiencing in the east; but, by late 1944, it was clear that the Germans would be defeated, and Soviet cooperation for the war against Japan had been enlisted by Roosevelt.

Forcing Japan's surrender

That final campaign against Japan was bloody and controversial. The Potsdam Declaration had called for unconditional surrender; the Japanese home islands had been bombed to destruction and Operation Starvation had been carried out to deprive Japanese civilians of food; the Soviets had overrun Manchuria in record time, following a declaration of war against Japan on 8 August, and by 18 August had already reached Korea and the Kuril Islands. On 6 August the first atomic bomb was dropped on Hiroshima, Japan, and the second followed on 9 August, dropped on Nagasaki. Japan surrendered a week later, bringing to an end America's war.

Truman's peace

It was President Truman who would decide the fate of a world emerging from war. Roosevelt, who had been duped by the Soviets, might have fashioned a different future. But Truman had declared in 1941 'If we see that Germany is winning we ought to help Russia, and if Russia is winning we ought to help Germany, and that way let them kill as many as possible.' He was highly mistrustful of the Soviet Union and was loathed by the Soviets. The new world order would not be entirely harmonious.

GENERALS AND STAFF

Generals had always allowed themselves liberty to dress as they pleased. Senior officers in the service of the United States were no exception.

US Army generals could be seen in a huge variety of dress. In part this stemmed from the fact that they served in various theatres, with varied climates, and naturally adopted warm clothing for Iceland and Britain, and followed the habit of wearing cotton shirts and trousers in the Philippines. However, in addition there were many generals who liked to create a distinctive identity for themselves – and the men they commanded – by wearing distinctive items.

◀ **Major General, 1941** *Generals in the northern theatres of the war still made use of the officers' long overcoat. A short overcoat with its own integral belt and notched lapels was also popular. Both types would appear with the black cuff braid that denoted a general officer rank.*

Stars of rank

The key distinguishing feature of officers of general rank was the system of stars. A brigadier general had one star; a major general, two stars; a lieutenant general, three stars; and a general, four stars. The rank of lieutenant general did not exist in 1925-39, then was reinstated and officers tied to a specific command, such as Hawaii, were also awarded this rank from 1940; similarly the rank of general was reinstated in 1940 – but it was rare, because only 18 officers were ranked as general or higher by the end of the war in Europe.

Towards the end of the war, five stars were introduced for the rank of General of the Army, which was created in December 1944. These stars were worn on the shoulder strap below an eagle badge. This rank was conferred on George C. Marshall, Douglas MacArthur, Dwight D. Eisenhower and Henry H. Arnold (of the air force). The five stars were worn in a pentagon shape, all other combinations were worn horizontally.

The stars insignia were worn on the shoulder straps of the service coat, with the US badge on the lapels, or on the shirt collar if this was being worn without a tunic. The various kinds of overcoat or cold-weather jackets would have had the stars mounted on the shoulder straps. All these insignia were generally in metal, although embroidered stars, sewn on to cloth patches, were sometimes used on the straps.

▲ *General Dwight D. Eisenhower led the Allied invasion on D-Day, and later became the 34th President of the United States.*

The insignia also appeared on headgear. For example, generals could make use of an envelope-style garrison cap, braided in gold, which had rank insignia on the left; various kinds of unbraided khaki caps were worn in the Pacific theatre, often with the star device. Campaign hats were usually plain, although they had gold braid, and service caps bore the coat of arms of the United States. However, helmets did usually receive the star device.

Prior to 1941 American generals also wore black cuff braid on the sleeves of their coats.

Many generals wore shoulder-sleeve insignia as appropriate. This included patches for army groups and army corps, but also geographic commands – south-east Asia, for example. Patches could also identify theatre headquarters –

◀ **BRIGADIER GENERAL, 1943** *Officers serving in the Philippines were advised to purchase two sets of khaki shirts with matching trousers, as well as formal attire. The service cap was not generally worn in that area, since the garrison cap or campaign hat (which offered better protection against the rain) was preferred.*

China, Burma, India (instituted in 1944) or Supreme Headquarters Allied Expeditionary Force (SHAEF – instituted in 1944 and replacing the headquarters European theatre of operations patch designed in 1943). Generals sometimes wore the divisional shoulder sleeve insignia.

General Staff

The General Staff Corps was created in 1903 to increase the efficiency of the Army. Members of this staff organization wore a distinctive star badge on the lapels of their service dress (a bronze version was sometimes worn on active service) and this three-quarter-sized version of the original was also worn on shirt collars or was moved to the breast pocket. This consisted of a five-pointed star bearing the gilt coat of arms of the United States (with enamelled shield on the eagle's front).

Aides-de-camp had their own special badge, consisting of an eagle above an enamelled United States shield. The design of this was fixed in 1936 and the appropriate number of stars was shown on the shield part of the insignia (two stars for an aide to a major general). Aides to the General of an Army simply had a blue shield with five stars rather than the United States shield.

Brassards

All this insignia was often insufficient to allow officers of the staff to perform their duties and staff officers took to wearing brassards as they had in 1917. This generally bore the letters 'GSC' although 'GSC' was sometimes replaced with a representation of the GSC badge. Other staff officers bore the numerals of their respective army, corps or division. Divisional staff had red brassards; corps staff, blue over white with red lettering; staff of armies, white over red with blue lettering. Headquarters staff would have blue over white over red with blue lettering.

Staff officers had pioneered the wearing of cuff braid, in black, on their coats. This was allowed until 1941 when the practice was dropped. Military Intelligence personnel had worn their own insignia of a sphinx and had yellow and purple intertwined braid on their caps, unless they were officers. However, these distinctions were largely discontinued in 1942 when intelligence officers were ordered to adopt the insignia of the unit to which they were attached or the infantry insignia. However, officers of the Counter Intelligence Corps, formed in 1942, had the right to wear a blue brassard with 'CIC' in yellow.

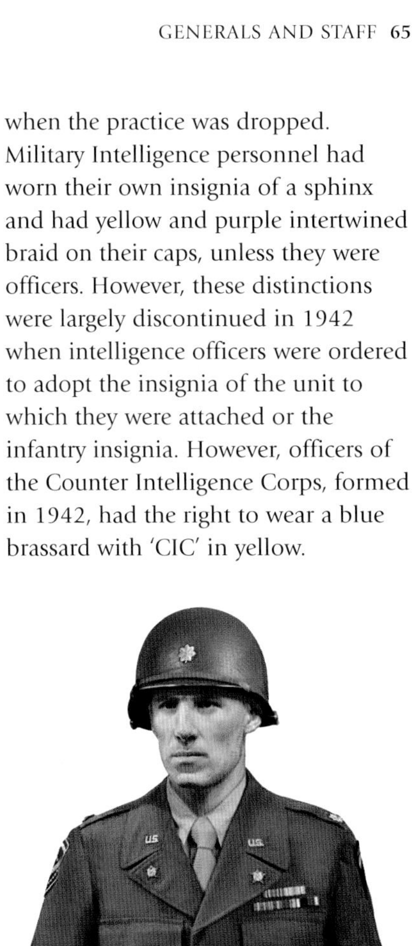

▶ **LIEUTENANT COLONEL, 1945** *This staff officer wears the SHAEF patch on his left sleeve, his right sleeve would have had the 'HQ ETO' patch. He also has two gold service stripes on the lower left sleeve showing length of service.*

INFANTRY

In 1941 the United States had to move quickly and improvise intelligently, to dress, arm and equip its rapidly expanding armed forces.

Troops who were already overseas – in the Philippines for example, or garrisoning Pacific islands – would draw on existing stocks. So, too, would the first brigades sent overseas to support the British. Some of these went via Iceland or Northern Ireland before arriving in mainland Britain.

American infantry uniforms were exposed to combat before a really practical form of dress had been developed. The result was that items were developed from experience gained in combat, and a number of designs of dress were adopted ad hoc or as a temporary measure. Standardization was not always possible and even though particular items of dress often proved themselves poorly designed they continued in use for lack of alternatives.

Service coats

American uniforms had changed since 1918. The unpopular and uncomfortable standing collar of the tunic adopted in 1912 had been abolished at the very end of 1926 and a new design with an open collar and lapels came into use. This notched lapel collar tunic (or service coat) was to be worn with a shirt and tie, and reflected trends in uniform then current in Europe.

The woollen 1926-pattern tunic was modified in 1939, allowing the back to be adjusted, and with belt loops to support the leather garrison belt; these loops were later removed. The tunic was fastened by means of four gilt buttons; it had four pockets with straight flaps and no pleats – all pockets were fastened with smaller buttons. A lighter cotton version was also issued. While smart, the uniform was not particularly well adapted to combat. In 1942 the design was adjusted, removing the rear pleats, and the garment was then deemed fit for use in garrison or on parade.

Parson's jacket

The garment that superseded it was the olive drab field jacket, sometimes known as the Parson's jacket after its

◀ **US4 Private, 133rd Infantry Regiment (34th Division), 1942** *However elegant the early war uniform might look, it was distinctly unpopular with the troops on active service. The wool of the tunic was impregnated with chemicals that made it smelly and, worse, rough to the touch.*

▶ **US5 Lieutenant, 10th Infantry Regiment (5th Division), 1942** *This junior officer wears the 1917-pattern helmet, which was unsuitable for World War II-era warfare because it offered no protection to the side or back of the head. It had been designed for use in trench warfare 25 years earlier.*

▲ *Lieutenant General Mark W. Clark and Secretary of the Navy James V. Forrestal with Nisei troops of the 100th Infantry Battalion, formed from Japanese living in Hawaii.*

designer, Major General James K. Parsons. First approved for use in 1941, this was a short jacket that extended to the hips. It was made from tough cotton with a fabric interior, had a fly front and was fastened with a zip – although the garment could be fastened close at the neck, and at the wrists, by means of buttons on a tab – behind five frontal buttons. The garment was often produced at low cost and in a hurry, and the zip often broke. It was popular with the troops, but senior officers were more impressed by British battledress.

The Parson's jacket was improved in 1943 with the 1943-pattern field jacket. This was tested in late 1943 and adopted shortly thereafter, becoming the mainstay of US troops in Europe. It was layered with an olive drab cotton exterior that gave off a slight sheen, and an optional padded interior that could be used in cold weather; alternatively, other jackets could be worn underneath, since the 1943-pattern jacket was roomy. The waist could be pulled tight with a drawstring, and the jacket was fly-fronted with six plastic buttons. The collar included a neck flap and had a detachable hood.

ETO jacket

Meanwhile – after Eisenhower's staff began to agitate for a new combat jacket in 1942 –work started on adapting the field jacket to bring it closer to the British design. The result, the European Theatre of Operations (ETO) jacket was made from British khaki wool, buttoned down the front, was pulled tight at the waist and had unadorned shoulders. Some 30,000 of these jackets were manufactured. A revised version had shoulder straps

▼ **Infantry Kit** *US infantry equipment was lightweight and relatively practical. Most bore the Army's ubiquitous badge of ownership, the black 'US' stamp.*

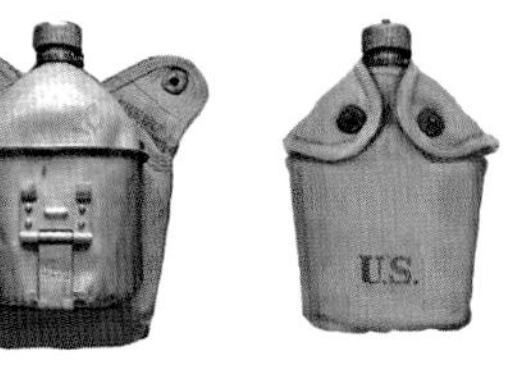

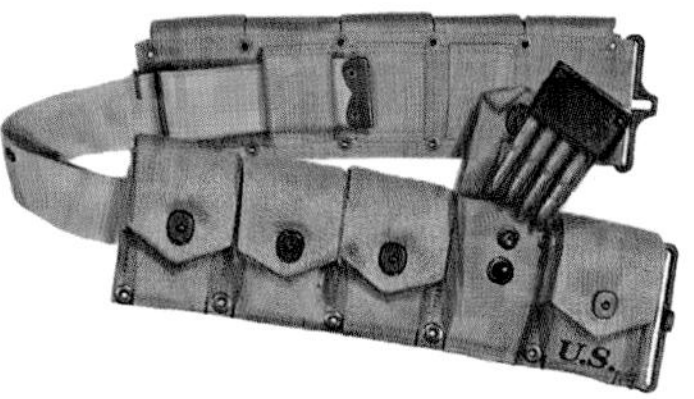

▼ **Sergeant, 168th Infantry Regiment, 1943** *He wears the new M1 helmet. This was a popular item, and a great improvement on the 1917-pattern tin hat; 22 million examples were to be manufactured, most by the McCord Radiator Company in Detroit, Michigan, US.*

and could be tightened further at the waist with an additional button. An Australian version of this garment was manufactured in green wool for use by American soldiers in the Pacific.

'Ike' jacket

While the ETO jacket was in use, the Quartermaster Corps was by 1943 working on its own version; at that time, it was of the opinion that the ETO item should no longer be made. The American field jacket issued in the autumn of 1944 was commonly known as the 'Ike jacket' after Eisenhower whose nickname that was.

▲ *A soldier serves chow to men of the 347th Infantry Regiment on their way to La Roche, Belgium. 13 January 1945.*

▼ **Private, 60th Infantry Regiment, 1944**
The M1 81mm (3.2in) mortar provided very effective supporting fire for infantry units and could fire between 18 and 30 rounds per minute. It was based on an original French design. The greatcoat is the melton wool overcoat. This proved restrictive in the front lines and was not highly regarded.

In the summer of 1944 examples began to appear in Europe. They were in wool, cut short at the waist, had a falling collar, interior pockets and two breast pockets with scalloped flaps. The jacket was baggier than battledress, and this was intentional so that additional layers could be worn underneath in cold weather. Officers wore tunics and jackets of the same type.

However, the garments were usually in superior cloth and lining, and were often privately tailored. Their service coats came in greenish olive drab but also in a chocolate-coloured cloth. Some 500 examples of the ETO jacket were specifically made for officers, again mostly tailored out of a darker, richer brownish or greenish wool.

Overalls and sweaters

Blue denim overalls had been standard issue as utility garments before 1941. In that year herringbone twill superseded denim for such items. These fatigue uniforms, with matching jacket and trousers, were hardwearing and popular. The one-piece overall, initially issued to armoured personnel, was also adopted by the infantry as a working uniform post-1944.

Wool sweaters were an important item of dress in the winter of 1944. Initially, these had not been regulation issue and soldiers had to borrow from the British or arrange for knitted items to be sent to them from home. A high-necked sweater was issued in 1944 with elasticated cuffs and waist.

Insignia

Infantry had used crossed rifles as insignia in the previous war. In 1922 these were slightly redesigned to show

◀ **Private, 423rd Infantry Regiment (106th Division), 1944** *This individual has the white mukluk first issued in 1942, with a canvas upper and sufficient insulation to keep the feet warm. These shoe pacs had canvas laces and a drawstring to keep them close to the leg.*

Officers wore the letters 'US' in metal pinned to their upper lapel, on both sides, while they had the crossed musket device below on the lower lapel. This device often bore the regimental number above it as part of the design. It was sometimes transferred to shirt collars when the service coat was not being worn. Such devices also made their way onto garrison caps. Regimental badges, usually in enamel, were also sometimes worn (such as the heraldic lion of the 28th Infantry Regiment) on lapels and caps, but the authorities disapproved of this distinctive insignia and they were rarely seen after 1942.

Divisional patches had become popular in 1918 as a means of instilling esprit de corps (good morale) in newly formed units. The first patches or shoulder sleeve insignia seem to have appeared some time in May 1918, but most were developed after the end of World War I. The inter-war period saw a marked rise in the use of these badges and by 1941 they were either machine-embroidered on a patch of olive drab backing (showing a thin border) or produced as a woven patch without backing. Some officers used bullion thread and patches made outside of the United States showed greater variation in styles and materials.

Personnel not assigned to any particular unit could wear an Army Ground Forces patch or an Army Services Forces patch. Failing that, they could wear an Army Group, Army (for example 5th Army in Italy) or Army Corps patch. A small number of Commands had their own patch – the China, Burma and India patch introduced in 1944, for example, or the Supreme HQ Allied Expeditionary Force patch of the same date. However, most troops bore a divisional patch on their left sleeve – an exception being the 158th Infantry Regiment, stuck in Panama, which wore a regimental crossed muskets. This device was shown on a collar disc: the disc came with different fastening mechanisms, the most common one by 1941 being with a retaining nut that allowed the disc to be removed and polished; clutch fasteners then became more common. This flat disc was worn on the left lapel whilst on the right a disc bearing 'US' was worn.

The crossed musket disc sometimes bore the company letter below, for example 'A' for Company A, 'HQ' for headquarters or 'S' for supply; 'MG' for machine gunners and 'HZ' for howitzer were also seen.

▶ **Private, 263rd Infantry Regiment (66th Division), 1944** *The poncho had initially been developed for use by the US Marines, but the Army began to test them in the summer of 1942. Eventually, coated cotton and nylon types were developed for infantry use. The capes could also be fastened together to make an improvised tent awning.*

◀ **Major, 115th Infantry Regiment (29th Division), 1944** *This European Theater of Operations (ETO) jacket was manufactured in Britain by an American firm. The garment had first been issued to elements of the Air Force and to troops of the 29th Division by way of experiment in 1943 and proved very popular.*

▶ **Private, 357th Infantry Regiment (90th Division), 1944** *The canvas leggings were fastened with hooks and laces. Putting them on and taking them off was troublesome (lacing from the bottom up was mandatory), and the hooks had a tendency to snag in undergrowth. They remained in service, however, for most of the war.*

patch, as did the Japanese-American 442nd (Nisei) Infantry. Troops in the Pacific were less likely to wear colourful insignia.

Service stripes were worn on the lower left sleeve and this initially authorized one stripe for each three-year enlistment term completed. Overseas service bars were introduced in the course of the conflict and were worn above the stripes. Each bar showed a six-month period of active duty overseas. Other distinctive emblems included the meritorious unit wreath worn, after 1944, on the right sleeve just above the cuff.

Marksmanship badges were awarded during the conflict but were not generally worn in the field.

Marks of rank

Officers wore distinctive rank insignia on their shoulder straps. In addition they had better quality uniforms, a service cap with eagle badge, a campaign hat with distinctive cords or garrison cap with distinctive braid.

Rank insignia for officers consisted of a gilt rectangle for second lieutenants, a silver rectangle for lieutenants and two joined rectangles in silver for captains. Majors had a gold leaf badge, lieutenant colonels had the same in silver. Colonels wore the eagle badge. Chief warrant officers had a brown oval with gilt centre; warrant officers had the same, but with brown ends. Warrant officers also wore a distinctive eagle badge rather than the officer's version.

NCOs wore chevrons on their sleeves. These were usually on black backing material and in khaki thread. However, there were a number of different styles. Silvered thread was also used, as was blue backing material. Brown gilded chevrons on olive drab backing were also seen. There were changes in 1942 when technical grades were added and when the First Sergeant rank achieved seniority and had a bar of lace removed from the base. Chevrons were not supposed to be worn with branch distinctions or marks of specialism but this was sometimes ignored by medical personnel especially. Combat leaders added a green cloth bar below their NCO chevrons.

Shirts

American troops had been issued with brown flannel shirts in World War I. However, the reforms of 1926 meant that a collared shirt of superior quality was now required. The 1934 coat-style shirt was the answer.

Two shirts were issued to each soldier. They had six buttons and two

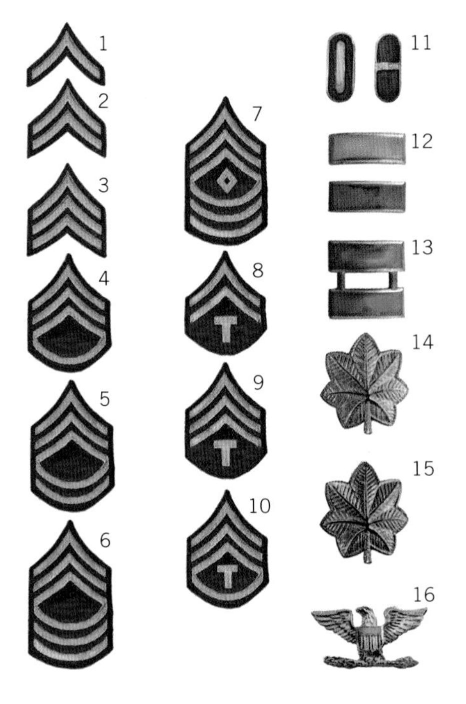

▲ **Rank Badges** *1 Private first class, 2 Corporal, 3 Sergeant, 4 Staff sergeant, 5 Technical sergeant, 6 Master sergeant, 7 First sergeant, 8 Technician 5th grade, 9 Technician 4th grade, 10 Technician 3rd grade, 11 (left) Chief Warrant officer (rank created August 1941), (right) Warrant officer, 12 (top) Second lieutenant, (bottom) Lieutenant, 13 Captain, 14 Major, 15 Lieutenant colonel, 16 Colonel.*

▶ **Private, 317th Infantry Regiment (80th Division), 1945** *The reversible parka was a very practical item. It could be worn with a standard liner or, in very cold conditions, a sheepskin liner and the hood, waist and cuffs could be drawn in tight. The parka was very popular in the mountainous conditions of central Italy in 1944.*

breast pockets. A revised version was issued in 1941, now with seven buttons and a collar that could be worn closed, with a tie, or looked sufficiently smart open.

In 1942 the so-called 'Special shirt' was issued; this had a band of cloth placed behind the buttons and a protective gusset fixed to the cuff to protect the skin from the possible effects of Mustard Gas. Flannel shirts were also reintroduced at that point.

The tie was usually khaki or black – until 1943, when an olive drab version was finally issued. Regulations allowed for the tie to be tucked into the shirt between the second and third buttons.

Trousers

In 1938 olive drab serge trousers were issued. They were straight, with two side pockets and two rear pockets. A fob pocket was also present at the front. As with the shirt, a Special version of trouser, with (Mustard) gas protection, was issued in 1942.

These styles of trouser were unsuited to combat situations and adjustable field trousers, which were baggier, were issued from 1942. Darker trousers were also manufactured to be worn with the 'Ike' jacket. In addition to these trousers, around 400,000 pairs of trousers were manufactured out of khaki wool in Britain. These also had two rear pockets and were cut straight.

A late-war pattern of trouser, known as the Victory trouser, began to make its appearance in late 1944.

Officers were also required to keep a smarter set of trousers for official duties. These were mostly the pale rose type known universally as 'pinks'. Many also continued to sport service breeches in dark olive drab or the light-coloured chino style.

Shoes and boots

The trousers were initially worn with dark brown leather service shoes. These 1939-pattern shoes were ankle-high with leather or rubber soles and a toe cap (withdrawn in 1943). Rivets were added to the sole from 1943 to provide more grip. These shoes were worn with canvas leggings or gaiters with a loop that fitted under the shoe; puttees were also quite common at the start of hostilities. The gaiters were not buttoned, but fastened with laces and a series of hooks and grommets.

Much more practical was the combat boot, first issued in 1943 but only becoming widespread in late 1944. This was the service shoe extended upwards with a leather gaiter fastened by buckles.

The paratroopers' boot was also popular and quantities were used by infantry units from 1942 onwards. Officers adopted the same footwear as their junior counterparts; the high cavalry boot of the inter-war period was now a thing of the past.

These items were never really satisfactory. The leggings were difficult to put on and uncomfortable when wet. The service shoes and leather gaiters shrank if exposed to damp for a period of time. As part of the attempt to solve the problem of infantry footwear, various kinds of overshoes were experimented with. These, known as shoe pacs, came in a number of forms from the white Alaskan mukluk to the laced rubber versions favoured in cold, wet climates. However, the item had to be permeable as moisture remaining within the item could freeze and cause frostbite. In late 1944 a jungle boot was finally developed, but came too late to benefit troops in the Pacific.

Overcoats

The American greatcoat, or overcoat, was a hard-wearing item little different from the one worn in World War I. The 1927 pattern was modified in 1939 and was now double-breasted, with two rows of brass buttons (replaced by green plastic buttons in 1942), open collar (or roll collar, as regulations had it), rear pleats and squared shoulders. The coat was long, heavy and uncomfortable when wet. Officers generally had their own coats tailored for them, preferring shorter cuts than those of the rank and file. In 1943, a regulation short overcoat was issued for officers, although trenchcoats and raincoats were also common.

Raincoats had been a standard issue item since 1938 when a long coat in an impermeable, rubberized fabric was introduced. It was of a simple design with five buttons, falling collar and slits in the side to allow access to equipment under the coat. A synthetic version of the same coat came into use later in the war.

The Marines had preferred ponchos to coats, but the Army was less impressed. After tests were carried out, coated fabric ponchos were issued – as well as the subsequently more common ponchos in synthetic nylon. The poncho had fasteners that could be used to fashion sleeves and a drawstring that closed the neck; the helmet had a tendency to funnel water down the back of the wearer's neck so this was a useful and popular addition.

Even more popular was the parka, which emerged in 1941, and the reversible parka, introduced in 1943. The Americans embraced the concept of layered protection wholeheartedly and the parka was baggy and worn over other items for optimal warmth. The 1943 pattern was reversible with a white side and an olive drab side (which often faded to light greenish brown). The garment was fly-fronted and fastened with buttons with zip behind. The hood buttoned around the collar and there were side pockets at the waist. Ski versions, with and without fur trim, made an appearance in 1941 and 1942 respectively.

Another useful item in cold weather was

◀ **Private, 41st Infantry Regiment, 1944** *Troops of the 2nd Division were issued camouflage clothing in 1944. It was useful in France that autumn, despite the number of friendly-fire incidents caused by Allied troops mistaking these unusually dressed soldiers for Germans.*

▶ **Lieutenant, 346th Infantry Regiment (87th Division) 1945** *This officer wears the popular high-necked sweater issued from 1944; 14 million examples were manufactured and this type of garment was to be a standard issue item for the next 50 years. He also has the knitted beanie hat or jeep cap.*

▲ **DIVISIONAL INSIGNIA** *US divisional insignia was a distinguishing feature of the US Army's uniform and was cherished as a distinctive badge by soldiers throughout the conflict.*

▼ **PRIVATE, 359TH INFANTRY REGIMENT, 1945** *This individual wears a newly issued garment in greenish olive drab. Over time, due to the effects of sunshine and washing, the material would fade to light green. This caused concerns because light green was completely unsuitable when it came to camouflage.*

the Mackinaw coat, or Jeep coat, first issued to drivers in 1938. It had a waterproofed outer layer and a thick wool liner that was also on the outside of the collar. The coat was double breasted and fitted close at the waist with a cloth belt. The 1942 pattern was an economy pattern with no wool collar and plastic buckle on the belt. A third, 1943-pattern coat was issued without a belt but the field jacket meant that this item was largely superseded before it could be supplied in large numbers.

Camouflage items were not especially common in the European Theater of Operations during the conflict. Some elements of the US Army in Normandy wore the herringbone twill camouflage jacket, with matching trousers, that had been first issued in 1943.

Helmets

American troops began the war reliant on the 1917-pattern helmet worn in World War I. This had been mass-produced in the United States during that conflict and had been kept in use throughout the inter-war period. It was by no means an ideal piece of equipment. It offered no protection to the sides of the head or the neck, having been intended to protect the top of the head of soldiers fighting in trench warfare.

Some improvements were made to the existing design and in 1936 the A1 pattern was issued, with a new interior and a new chinstrap. The older leather chinstrap had proved counter-productive because it did not release during a blast and the new fabric strap was more practical. The interior was of leather, giving a more padded, comfortable feel. This helmet, painted in a rough matt coating, was the most common form of head protection until 1942.

As war approached, attempts to design a new helmet intensified. The TS3 prototype, with its compressed liner and domed shape, proved the most successful and was adopted as the Helmet, Steel, M1 in June 1941. Initial samples were cast by a radiator company, but the helmet quickly went into mass production. It was a revolutionary design in that the liner, which could be adapted to fit most sizes of head by using a headband and neckband, was a distinct part of the helmet.

Helmets were manufactured from Hadfield manganese steel. Initial examples had an adverse affect on compasses and, from 1942, the helmet was demagnetized during the manufacturing process.

The helmet was heavy – 16 ounces (450 grams) heavier than the M1917 helmet – and experience showed that the chinstrap was insufficient; straps fixed at three points were soon developed. It also became clear that the impact of an explosion could cause the wearer's neck to be broken by the strap; this problem was overcome in 1944 with the development of a strap that self-released under impact. (Until that point, most soldiers simply did

▲ **Private, 19th Infantry Regiment, Pacific, 1944** *The herringbone twill jacket was usually worn with long sleeves and as tightly closed at the collar as was comfortably possible. This was to reduce the effect of insect bites, which blighted the lives of all soldiers in the Pacific campaigns.*

not fasten the strap.) The liner was also deemed too fragile, particularly in the humidity of the Pacific, and so this was later manufactured from plastic resin.

The M1 came into service in 1942, and was generally worn by American troops in North Africa and at Guadalcanal. It was generally painted a matt shade of olive drab, although ground cork could be added to the mixture to produce a rough, non-reflective coating. The matt paint had been shown to glisten when wet, which sometimes proved fatal in the permanent humidity encountered in the Pacific campaigns. Another way to overcome this was by the addition of a camouflage net that tucked under the helmet and could be further secured with an elastic helmet band. The net itself did not provide much by way of camouflage and did not break the profile of the helmet sufficiently.

Camouflage paint was also increasingly common, either green and brown patches, or white in winter conditions.

Markings on helmets were relatively common. Officers often added rank tabs, usually in white, and divisional patches were painted or stencilled onto the side or front of helmets. There were numerous variations on the standard divisional symbolism. It was not uncommon for battalions within regiments to paint additional identifying symbols on their helmets. For instance, the 7th Infantry Regiment used a fairly typical playing card device in white – with spades denoting the 1st Battalion, hearts showing the 2nd Battalion and clubs representing the 3rd Battalion.

Tropical helmets, such as the fibre sun hat, were common in hot climates in 1941. The fibre sun hat came with a leather chinstrap and numerous vent holes to cool the head. However, it offered insufficient protection.

Caps and hats

When the helmet was not in use the US Army made use of a great variety of caps and hats. These reflected traditions as well as the need for comfortable but smart off-duty headgear. The campaign hat, first introduced in 1911 and identified with the 'doughboy' of 1917, was still worn. It was round, with a domed crown – the so-called Montana crown, with indents on either side. It had vent

▲ *An American soldier wearing the ungainly standard issue jungle kit; a mosquito mask, rubber shoes, poncho and camouflage trousers.*

holes, a leather sweatband and chinstrap. The hat had cords around the base of the crown. For infantry, these cords were light blue, although officers had a gold and black cord and warrant officers silver and black. Some personnel wore branch insignia such as crossed rifles on the front of their caps. As the campaign hat was not waterproof, and not easy to carry, it was phased out.

Just as impractical, but smarter, was the peaked service cap. It came in dark olive drab and also a lighter shade. It usually had a brown leather peak and chinstrap, and a hat band in olive drab (and wet-weather covers came as an optional extra). It usually bore the officer's eagle device on the front or, for enlisted personnel, a disc bearing the coat of arms of the United States. The service cap was not to be worn in the Philippines, according to standing orders. Many officers adopted the so-called crusher caps, which had stiffening removed and gave the cap a flexible, but less than smart, appearance. Female personnel wore a round crowned peaked cap known as a hobby hat.

A more comfortable off-duty hat was the garrison cap. This was based on the French bonnet de police, was envelope-shaped and was easy to store and to carry. It again came in dark wool as well as light cotton to go with the summer uniform. Most garrison caps had piping in branch-of-service colours around the crown. Unit insignia was common before 1942, but from then on rank insignia was preferred over any branch-of-service or unit identifiers.

▼ **Sergeant, 105th Infantry Regiment (27th Division), Pacific, 1943** *Infantry had been distinguished by light blue colour distinctions from as early as 1851. This NCO has retained the colour piping along the garrison cap as a personal distinction. Caps without insignia and piping were also common in the Pacific theatre.*

Another popular cap was the knitted jeep cap with its short peak and band that could be lowered to keep the ears warm. This hat was first devised in 1941 and began to be seen in 1942. The intention had been for this peaked knitted hat to be worn under the M1 helmet. British commando hats were also popular with scouts.

Off duty, and while engaged in fatigue duties, soldiers made use of the modest fatigue hat with peak (and with domed or flat crown). It came in a number of variants, from the blue denim type seen in the 1930s to the olive drab versions common after 1943. A version with side flaps and wool liner was issued for cold weather. A round hat with vents and wide brim was also used in the Pacific campaigns.

Equipment

While the uniform worn by the GI was undergoing a process of radical change, American equipment remained relatively stable. This was thanks to the reforms in personal equipment undertaken in the late 1930s. Generally early-war canvas equipment was in khaki (light olive drab, or number nine), mid-war equipment began to be produced in the light green olive drab (number three) and later-war items began to appear in the green olive drab number seven.

A standard waist belt in webbing material was introduced in 1937. This had a metal point and an open buckle; closed buckles were also available. It did not support cartridge pouches; a cartridge belt, again in webbing, was produced for dismounted troops in 1923 and modified in 1938. It was designed to carry up to 80 rounds for the standard rifle. Additional ammunition could be carried in cotton bandoliers. Detachable suspenders helped spread the weight of the belt, although evenly spaced grommets along the base of the belt allowed other items to be suspended from it.

▲ **Private, 34th Infantry Regiment, Pacific, 1941** *The Pacific theatre was to prove a very demanding testing ground, not only for the men but also for their arms, uniform and equipment. Conditions were such that shoes, for example, had to be replaced every five months.*

Haversacks and packs

On their backs, soldiers usually carried 1928-pattern haversacks. These had a coat rolled over the top, and, usually, an entrenching tool strapped to the back. A meat-can pouch could be attached to the top for further

▲ *American soldiers from the 503rd parachute ski battalion rest in sleeping bags on the snow after hiking and skiing over rough mountain terrain during training.*

provisions. The bayonet, either the original design from 1905 or the M1 shorter version, was carried in a special fibreglass scabbard.

The 1928 pack was not perfect. In 1944 a new field pack was introduced, based on the pack used by Marines. It had an upper and lower section (known as the cargo pack). The top section was more like a rucksack and was manufactured from durable waterproof material. The 1945 modification, an improvement to strap fastening, came into use too late to be of service in the conflict.

Mountain troops could make use of a purpose-made rucksack that was first designed in 1942. It was a canvas bag with a drawstring at the top, roomy pockets and webbing straps. Early examples came on a steel frame and had a stomach band to provide stability and support. A 1942 modification allowed the frame to be discarded and included a chest band, which was more comfortable than the previous lower version.

Troops in the Pacific had initially struggled with standard-issue equipment. In 1943 the Quartermaster Corps unveiled the jungle pack. This was in olive drab or in camouflage material, had a drawstring and waterproof flap at the top and a compartment, closable with a zip, in which the canteen could be stored. The rest of the pack was rather like an oversized rucksack and was designed to carry rations, a hammock, medical equipment and clothes. Machetes, the Philippine Bolo knife or bayonets were strapped to the side. It has to be said that the sheer bulk of the pack, and the way the straps cut into the shoulders, made it universally unpopular.

The entrenching tool was usually the 1910 pattern, which had seen service in World War I. It came with a canvas cover, which buckled around the haft, and had a T-shaped handle (carried so that the handle was at the small of the back). Out of ten men, seven were to carry shovels and the remainder were to have pickaxes. A new folding entrenching tool was issued in 1943. This was an

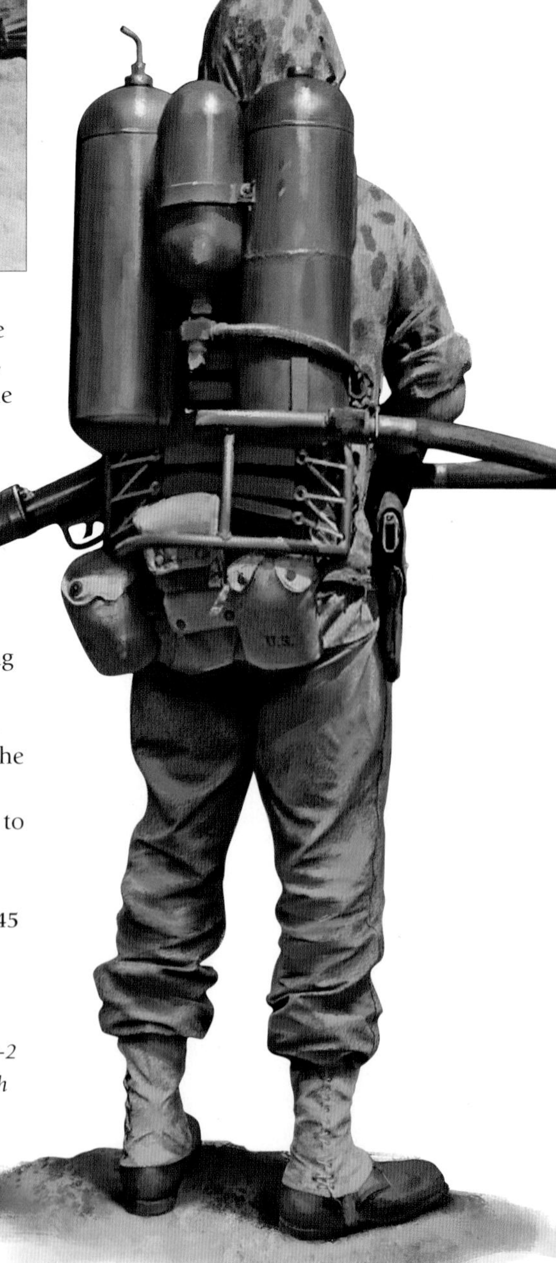

▶ **Private, 165th Infantry Regiment, 1945**
An important piece of equipment in the campaigns against the Japanese-fortified Pacific islands was the flame thrower. This private in the 27th Division carries the M2-2 flame thrower first issued in 1941. Although an improvement on earlier models, it still only had an effective range of around 30 metres (roughly 100 feet).

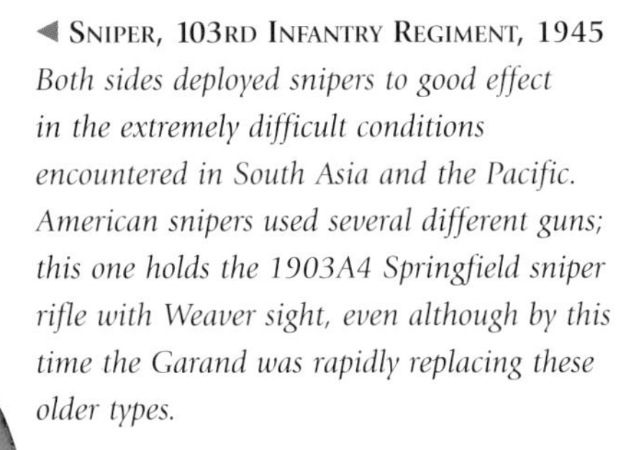

◀ **SNIPER, 103RD INFANTRY REGIMENT, 1945** *Both sides deployed snipers to good effect in the extremely difficult conditions encountered in South Asia and the Pacific. American snipers used several different guns; this one holds the 1903A4 Springfield sniper rifle with Weaver sight, even although by this time the Garand was rapidly replacing these older types.*

▶ **PRIVATE, 45TH INFANTRY REGIMENT (PHILIPPINE SCOUTS), PHILIPPINE DIVISION, 1941** *The Philippine Division was one of two unnumbered divisions to receive shoulder sleeve insignia; the other was the Americal. This had first been issued in the summer of 1942 and made use of the old Spanish imperial colours of yellow and red. The device was the head of the Philippine carabao.*

innovative, practical and extremely well-designed piece of kit. It was a shovel, hoe and pickaxe all in one. The handle was plain and attached to the blade with a metal hinge that could be adjusted to angle the blade differently. It also allowed the head to be folded over and stored in its canvas slip-on cover. This was usually light olive drab in colour, as opposed to the earlier khaki (olive drab number nine, but known as khaki) types.

Officers sometimes wore Sam Browne belts (which only became authorized for wear in the early 1920s and was usually worn with two shoulder belts in the field) but could also make use of the 1936-pattern pistol belt. This was worn with or without braces and was designed to house the ammunition pouch, the pistol (in holster, sometimes worn with a lanyard), a first aid pouch and a canteen. The 1928 pack was optional, and officers had greater freedom to modify their own equipment.

▼ *US troops in Panama in gas-masks pose for the camera. The gas mask was very rarely worn in combat.*

Gas masks

The United States had borrowed gas mask designs for the British and the French in 1917 and 1918. The first American design, the M1, was only issued after World War I. Despite its old-fashioned one-size-fits-all mask and large eyepieces the M1 continued into service into the 1940s. It was carried in a canvas bag, usually on the left hip (by the canteen). The modified M1A2 version, issued in 1935, was more common than the original 1919-pattern M1. In 1941 advances in rubber-moulding technology saw the introduction of the improved M2

▲ *US Medical corps load containers of blood plasma on to an army mule for transportation to a forward battalion aid station in Italy.*

mask. This came in different sizes, but it was heavy and difficult to handle. A lighter mask, the M3, was an improvement because it had a shorter tube and was produced so the eyepieces did not mist up. It was issued from 1942. The M4 mask, now in olive drab rather than grey, then came into use in 1943 and the M5, which did away with the long hose, was issued in 1944 (in time for D-Day – the Allied invasion of Normandy, France, on 6 June 1944).

A canteen (first issued in 1910) with felt cover was worn at the rear on the left and canvas bread bags or grenade bags could also be worn. Some of these were marked with the US stamp. A first aid pouch was also worn, usually suspended from the belt. Wire-cutters, torches, whistles, compasses and many other items were carried according to need.

A tan-coloured tent canvas (half of a two-man shelter) and five tent pegs were usually carried, with two men teaming up to create a tent. Infantrymen also carried a blanket.

Pacific theatre uniforms

Summer uniforms had been developed in the 1930s to offer some comfort to American troops garrisoning tropical stations. This usually consisted of khaki drill shirts and trousers in matching colour – the prescribed colour was sometimes known as Hong Kong khaki. In 1938 this concept was formalized and such uniforms were issued in numbers.

The herringbone twill (HBT) cotton suit, or one piece overall, were also extensively worn in the Pacific, becoming progressively more common after 1942. The suit consisted of a jacket-shirt and matching trousers.

▼ **Medic First Aid Kit** *A medic's bag would contain bandages, dressings, iodine, ointment for burns and wounds, scissors and pins.*

▶ **Medic, 386th Infantry Regiment, 1945** *Medics had the option of having the red cross on the arm as a brassard (with the medic's registration number on the reverse side), as well as painted onto the helmet.*

A darker shade of cotton was used from 1944. Tests were conducted to see which of HBT, poplin or Grenfell (Byrd) cloth offered the best comfort, durability and protection from insects. Byrd cloth won decisively but it was expensive and only seems to have been issued in to troops in Burma.

Marines popularized camouflage uniforms and the Army was not slow to see the advantages. A one-piece camouflage suit, or jungle suit, was issued in 1942. It was cut loose, to allow ventilation, but was long to protect from insect bites. However, it proved enormously unpopular because the lower part had to be removed completely to allow troops to perform their natural functions. The two-piece garment, issued in 1943, was an improvement but as Marines were mostly involved in beach landings the sandy-coloured and brown item was not especially useful for the Army. Snipers and scouts did, however, make use of some camouflage items.

The Pacific campaigns were an ordeal for the men and a severe test of their arms, clothing and equipment.

Mountain warfare

It should be noted that the US Army encountered extreme conditions in other theatres, too. Mountain troops were supplied with specialist gear to counter harsh, cold conditions.

This gear included the 1942-pattern mountain jacket (a specialist parka with hood and storm flaps), as well as a distinctive knitted shirt and matching trousers with roomy pockets. Rucksacks were also preferred to packs.

Ski or mountain boots were issued to troops of the 10th Mountain Division which, apart from a few specialist formations, was the main body of mountain troops. Ski boots had initially been trialled in May 1941, but subsequent modifications led to the design of the high-toed, rubber-soled ski boot that became standard issue.

◀ **Military Policeman, 3rd Infantry Division, 1944** *The 3rd Division had a blue square intercut with three white stripes to symbolise the three campaigns the division fought in during World War I. Divisional MPs were tasked with discipline, processing of prisoners and traffic control.*

▶ **Private, 85th Infantry Regiment (10th Mountain Division), 1945** *The standard-issued rucksack for mountain troops had been developed during field trials in 1941 and 1942. It had originally been worn with a steel frame, to keep the weight off the back, but, in the field, this frame was usually discarded.*

Medic and Military Police ID

Medical personnel had maroon and white piping on garrison caps and cords in those colours on campaign hats. The caduceus staff badge was worn as insignia (on coat lapels). Military Police were either divisional personnel tasked with discipline or were from the Military Police Corps (MPC), established in 1941. The MPC had two crossed pistols as branch insignia and had yellow and green cords on their campaign hats and piping in these colours on their garrison caps. Military Police (MPs) wore brassards and had 'MP' painted on their helmets.

CAVALRY

The United States Army was busy reforming its mounted units when World War II began.

Change of cavalry function

In World War I cavalry had been used for escort duties and had operated as couriers and messengers. The inter-war period saw intense debate as to what to do with mounted personnel; when World War II began the US Army still had two cavalry divisions – as well as ancillary units scattered around its territories and dependencies. Cavalry were being mechanized and would perform in the role of motorized infantry, but even so there were exceptions and the horse continued to play a useful role in certain situations – for example, in the difficult terrain of the Philippines. In 1943 the 1st Cavalry Division was converted to infantry, while the 2nd was later transferred into engineer or dock battalions.

Outside of the divisional hierarchy, the US cavalry performed reconnaissance and scouting functions. These were organized into cavalry groups from 1943; the 4th was, bizarrely, airborne cavalry as it was attached to the 82nd Airborne.

Dress

Cavalry began the war dressed like the infantry: service dress tunics with shirt and tie or field jackets, with Mackinaw coats or short overcoats in cold climates. Fatigue duties, drill and training were usually carried out in herringbone twill overalls – either the one-piece set or the separated jacket and trousers, the latter worn over the boots or leggings. This was worn with rank insignia, as, from 1941, was the olive drab shirt when worn without coat. Breeches were in olive drab wool or light khaki. They were either the rather uncomfortable elasticated 1926 pattern or older types, and all had cords below the knee that bound the garment tight to the calves and allowed the thighs to billow out. Breeches were generally worn with brown leather boots. A pattern of high boot that laced up the front was issued in 1931: these looked very smart, but lacing the boots all the way to

◀ **Trooper, 113th Cavalry Group, 1944** *This dismounted cavalryman carries ammunition in his cartridge belt, as well as in an additional bandolier. Previously the horse would have carried much of the cavalryman's load. His helmet sports the red horse of the 113th Group.*

▶ **Officer, 9th Cavalry Regiment (2nd Cavalry Division), 1941** *This officer wears a garrison cap. While the wide campaign hat had been popular with mounted personnel, it was unsuitable for use within vehicles, and so the smaller cap, here with its gold and black braid, was preferred.*

the top with the boot's system of holes and hooks took time and was unpopular. In 1940 a plain boot was introduced, and quickly adopted by many officers and men. These were worn with the 1911-pattern spurs. More common than the riding boot was the ankle boot, worn with buckled leggings (in leather, but sometimes in canvas). These had three buckles and were longer than those of the infantry.

The mounted cavalry generally retained the campaign hat rather than any side or field cap. The hat was worn with yellow cords for the rank and file (yellow having been introduced in 1855 as the branch-of-service colour) and officers had gold or silvered cord as per their infantry counterparts; the hat proved impractical for mechanized formations, who wore side caps.

Cavalry in the Philippines wore chino khaki shirts and breeches. The 26th Regiment served within the Philippines Department.

Cavalry generally adopted the dress and equipment of armoured troops from 1942 onwards – retaining, however, distinctive insignia.

Insignia

Cavalry insignia consisted of crossed swords. These were worn impressed on collar discs for the rank and file (sometimes with the troop letter placed beneath the swords) and as a distinctive gilt or brass badge by officers on their lower lapel. If the officer was wearing a shirt or overall, rather than service dress, the left collar took the crossed-swords badge and the right had the plain 'US' device. Sometimes the regimental numeral was placed above these swords. Regular cavalry units were numbered in single figures or tens, while National Guard units were numbered from 100. Reconnaissance squadrons continued this tradition of having the unit number included.

Divisional patches had been developed in the 1920s. The 1st Division wore a yellow shield with black diagonal and horse's head, the 2nd had a yellow shield with blue chevron and two stars above. Cavalry groups also developed their own heraldic symbolism, most famously the red horse of the 113th.

Equipment

Cavalry began the war equipped with the M1918 mounted cartridge belt (with nine pockets containing an eight-round clip for the rifle), as well as the M1918 pistol magazine pouch together with the M1916 pistol holster or the 1941 webbed version; pistols were generally carried on lanyards and were often the cavalryman's weapon of choice after swords were discarded in 1935.

Additional equipment and ammunition was generally carried on the saddle. The cavalryman's equipment was worn with first aid pouch and canteen. Cavalry did not carry entrenching tools, but many in the Pacific carried long knives or machetes.

The saddle in use in 1941 was the 1928-pattern McClellan (although officers used the smarter Phillips 1936 pattern). This had leather side skirts and, from 1940, plain wooden stirrups. Bridles were generally of the older 1909-pattern type. The rifle was kept in a leather scabbard to the front of the saddle while leather saddle bags – to which the mounted canteen could be strapped – were placed behind the rider.

▶ **SERGEANT, 26TH CAVALRY REGIMENT (PHILIPPINE SCOUTS), 1942** *This figure wears a Philippine Department seahorse patch (white seahorse on a dark blue background). This was worn by units, including this particular cavalry regiment, who were not attached to the Philippine Division.*

ARTILLERY

American artillery was in flux when war broke out, but a new doctrine and considerable investment in new material resulted in a modernized force by the middle of 1942.

Branches

America's Field Artillery was the larger of the two main artillery branches of the army. It had been enlarged from 1930 onwards and was, in 1939, still organized into regiments. In 1940 these were reorganized into battalions with associated support and an ammunition train.

The Coast Artillery Corps had been responsible for land and coastal fortifications, and all anti-aircraft, tractor-drawn heavy, railway and trench mortar artillery. In the 1920s there had been 18 harbour defence, two railway, six anti-aircraft and three tractor-drawn regiments. Trench mortars were taken from the CAC and heavy siege guns were assigned to the Field Artillery. In 1942 the anti-aircraft units were designated as battalions and broken up for deployment amongst the army; many became anti-tank units from 1944 onwards. Harbour and tractor-drawn units went the same way in 1944.

▶ **Lieutenant, 157th Field Artillery Battalion, 1945** *He wears the 1938-pattern Mackinaw coat originally intended for drivers. It was short and had a thick woollen collar and blanket-lined interior, making it ideal for combat situations in cold conditions. Later collars did without the heavy turnbacked lining. It was especially popular with officers.*

Dress

US artillery personnel were uniformed according to the differing styles in use among the infantry or cavalry. In 1939 much of the artillery had been horse-drawn. The 74th Field Artillery Battalion was one of the last to lose its horses, in the summer of 1942, the guns now being limbered to trucks or jeeps. This meant that field artillery either wore infantry trousers and leggings, or cavalry breeches and leather or canvas three-buckle leggings.

Hats were campaign hats with scarlet cords or garrison caps with scarlet braid.

Chemical mortar units had blue and yellow interwoven braid and tank destroyer units received their own colour (orange and black) only in 1943. The Ordnance Department had interwoven crimson and yellow.

Insignia

Regimental badges had been popular in the 1930s, but were being phased out when World War II began; even so, enamel badges can be seen on early war photographs on lapels and on shoulder straps. The branch-of-service insignia predominated, however. The artillery had long been distinguished by the use of the crossed cannon-barrels device, worn on collar discs or, by officers, on lapels or shirt collars. Battery letters were often placed below the crossed barrels, or battalion numbers placed above for officers.

The CAC had a different insignia. Superimposed over the barrels was a shell in an oval. Some of these devices can be seen worn by personnel in Europe, because CAC units provided air defence or were reorganized into anti-tank units and retained their traditional insignia.

Artillery generally adopted the divisional shoulder patch as it came into use. Only the chemical mortar battalions seem to have forged their own identity, with a mix of battalion patches worn on the upper sleeve. These battalions were deployed as standard mortar units to give support to the infantry.

Tank destroyers

The first battalions (the 93rd, 94th and 99th) were organized in late 1940. Initially seen to be part of the infantry, they retained infantry insignia, often adding an 'A' and a 'T' (standing for anti-tank) on either side of the muskets. Tank Destroyer Force was created in

◀ **PRIVATE, 599TH FIELD ARTILLERY BATTALION (92ND DIVISION), 1944** *General Eisenhower thought that more than 30 per cent African American personnel in a corps would be detrimental to its prestige. The US Army was a highly segregated organization, generally concentrating black personnel into specific units.*

▶ **SECOND LIEUTENANT, 120TH FIELD ARTILLERY BATTALION, 1943** *Artillery officers could wear their branch-of-service insignia on their shirt collars, although this made them prone to being picked out by snipers. Rank identification could come from rank insignia on the other collar or as here the helmet, which has a white rectangle to denote the owner's rank. The gun is the 75mm (2.95in) Howitzer.*

1942 and the units were elevated to a new branch of service and numbered in the 800s (National Guard battalions in the 600s). The 'AT' on the insignia now became 'TD' but, in March 1943, a new form of insignia was authorized. This was the M3 half-track – officially a "75-mm gun, motor carriage M3, in gilt metal" – and was worn as a lapel or collar badge by officers (on the left collar with the vehicle nose pointing right) and within a collar disc by other ranks. Very rarely, the battalion number was also added to the device.

The Force also established sleeve insignia based on the orange and black branch-of-service colours introduced in 1943. It mostly consisted of a black panther's head on an orange disc, with the panther chewing a tank; bizarrely, this initially resembled an American tank rather than a German design. Later versions had four, six or eight wheels on the tank tracks. Officers sometimes wore bullion-thread patches and the addition of battalion numbers to the patches grew increasingly common.

The 802nd Tank Destroyer Battalion was the only major unit to distance itself from the black cat, preferring to show a winged skull insignia. The skull was seen side on, in black with a red tongue, and it had a lightning bolt behind it in yellow. This insignia only seems to have been worn in 1943 before posting overseas.

Equipment

Artillery carried standard infantry equipment, although some adopted the carbine and the equipment preferred by armoured personnel; airborne gunners adopted that of the paratroops.

Machine gunners and bazooka-armed personnel also played an important role in artillery operations. Overall, in terms of artillery pieces, the US artillery had good, modern guns – the new 105mm howitzer and the 155mm howitzer – and was more mobile than the struggling Germans. The Americans were also assisted by field telephones (initially more reliable than radios) and had the crucial support of air observation spotters. Indeed, with Allied mastery of the air almost complete by 1943 surveillance, reconnaissance and air support was supplied in lavish quantities.

In short, the American infantry lacked the firepower of their German counterparts, and relied heavily on artillery and the USAAF to make up the difference.

ENGINEERS AND TECHNICAL TROOPS

The technical services – the Engineer and Signal Corps were increasingly important, and specialized branches of service.

Engineers

America's Corps of Engineers was a relatively old service, born in 1802 when engineer officers oversaw siege works and compelled the infantry to do the actual digging. In the 20th century engineers were more hands-on and were tasked with preparing defences, and preparing the way for troops going on the offensive (Engineer Combat regiments). In 1941 the service also became responsible for military construction duties (forming Engineer Construction battalions), including the establishment and maintenance of bridges; there were specialist heavy or light Ponton battalions (their name derived from 'pontoon'), as well as the Engineer Treadway Bridge Company.

Engineer officers were unique in that they had their own distinctive uniform button rather than the general service button in use by the rest of the Army. The engineers adopted the fortified tower by way of insignia; it was worn on the lower lapel or on the left collar of shirts by officers, and on collar discs by other ranks.

The branch-of-service colours were interwoven scarlet and white, worn as braid on a garrison cap by those other than officers and warrant officers or as cord on a campaign hat. Incidentally, the Quartermaster Corps, which had been responsible for military construction before December 1941, had buff as a service colour.

▶ **Private, 36th Combat Engineer Battalion, 1944** *He carries the SCR 625 mine detector, which was tested in late 1941 by the Corps of Engineers development unit and came into service in early 1942. It became the standard detector for finding metal-cased mines and was based on commercial models that made use of audio frequency to detect objects. The unit's dry-cell batteries were carried in a canvas bag.*

Other units attached to the engineers included armour engineer battalions, an airborne engineer battalion, an airborne engineer aviation battalion, engineer maintenance companies, plus engineer aviation battalions and engineer camouflage battalions. The most famous of the latter was the 604th Engineer Camouflage Battalion, which was based for a time in Britain and tasked with camouflage training and masking preparations for the planned invasion of continental Europe. Finally, General Service regiments carried out assorted construction tasks.

Regiments and battalions were increasingly incorporated into engineer combat groups from 1943.

Engineers generally adopted divisional shoulder patches, although some wore regimental versions – the 36th Engineer Combat Regiment had a white/red shield with a white seahorse. Engineers with the airborne forces would, therefore, have worn the appropriate divisional patch. Only amphibious engineers had the amphibious forces patch or wore the pocket patch of the amphibious training command – a red seahorse on a white disc, with a blue border. Just a few of these pocket patches were issued, but they were sometimes used as a special distinction.

Equipment

Uniforms generally followed the pattern in use with the infantry. Equipment was, inevitably, quite different. Engineers preferred the carbine to the rifle, assault engineers often utilising a pistol with 1936-pattern pistol belt; they often carried the handy M3 combat knife.

After 1944 many assault engineers took to wearing an assault jacket, the eight pockets of which enabled them to carry additional munitions and grenades.

◀ **Captain, 3rd Engineer Combat Battalion, 1941** *Engineer officers cultivated their esprit de corps, being part of a corps which dated its origins back to 1802. This officer would have had distinctive buttons bearing the motto Essayons ('We Shall Try'), a departure from the standard button in use by the rest of the Army.*

Another such item was the battle jerkin, which also allowed the wearer to carry extra munitions and specialist equipment.

Those assault engineers who took part in amphibious assaults – at Anzio or Normandy, for example – would have worn the 1926-pattern lifebelt. Equipment such as entrenching tools, picks, axes and wire cutters were also carried; they were usually the 1938 pattern. Specialized equipment would have included mine detectors, including the advanced SCR 625 with its detection coil and audio unit. The Army had its own mine laying (mine planter) service with crossed cannon barrels and a mine in a disc on the centre. Combat engineers participating in the D-Day landings in June 1944 carried a vast amount of additional equipment from assault ladders to explosive charges, flares, detonators and torches.

Chemical warfare had been a concern of the Army since 1917. In 1918 a branch of service dealing with chemical warfare was formed, with blue and yellow interwoven as branch colours. The insignia of the branch was a benzene ring over two retorts. This was worn on officers' lapels and on collar discs by other ranks. Chemical mortar battalions formed part of the Chemical Service but were deployed as standard mortar artillerymen during the conflict.

Signals

The Signal Corps had been around since 1860, and was expanded for World War II – a conflict that more than any other would rely on quick, accurate and effective communication. Its insignia consisted of two crossed signal flags with a burning torch between. The Signals Corps used interwoven orange and white as their branch-of-service colour.

Tasks mostly involved the establishment and maintenance of field telephone and radio communication. The EE-8 was the first effective field radio, coming into use in 1937, but the concept of mobile radio sets took off in the late 1930s. The 500 series made a huge difference to military communications, overcoming many of the problems associated with the heavy SCR 194. The most common was the SCR 511, which was extremely portable and came with a chest unit with mouthpiece, a radio receiver and transmitter, its own power supply and battery and a carrying case. It had a long pole that was rammed into the ground when the equipment was in use and nicknamed the pogo stick.

▶ **Sergeant, 56th Signal Battalion, 1944** *This Signals Corps NCO uses the SCR 511 radio telephone receiver and transmitter. This was originally conceived as a radio for mounted troops, and so was quickly branded 'the Horsey Talkie' following its distribution in 1942.*

ARMOURED TROOPS

The United States Army had experimented with tanks in 1917 and 1918, but years of neglect followed. It was only until the eve of the conflict in World War II that real progress was made in providing the armed forces with armoured capabilities.

An armoured corps was formed from two divisions in 1940 and light and medium tank regiments established with mechanized infantry, reconnaissance units (armoured cars) and mobile artillery support. Independent tank battalions were also assigned to support infantry divisions.

Insignia

The tankers had been relegated to a branch of the infantry before the war. Its first insignia had been that of a French tank, devised in 1917, but, in a sign of the times, this was abolished in 1921 and tankers were to wear the crossed muskets of the infantry with a 'T' in a disc superimposed. This proved unpopular, so the motif of a tank replaced the 'T'. This insignia lasted until 1942, when the armoured forces at last achieved some recognition as a free-standing branch of service. They became Armored Command in 1943.

They adopted a badge representing the Mark VIII tank in February 1942. It was worn on officers' lapels or shirt collars, or within collar discs for other ranks. This insignia lasted for the duration of the war. At the same time the tankers were given their own branch-of-service colours. These were intertwined green and white, worn as braid on garrison caps – but not by officers – or as cord on the campaign hat. The campaign hat was not practical for those serving in vehicles.

◀ **Mechanic, 66th Armored Regiment, 1943** *Overalls were worn under or over other garments. Early types had slits at the end of the leg that allowed the garment to be removed without taking off the boots. This slit was closed up with straps but later types were closed with studs, and also added an opening at the crotch for calls of nature.*

▶ **Private, 18th Tank Battalion, 1944** *Tankers' overalls were a practical garment that allowed the wearer to exit a vehicle without getting snagged, protected the body and clothes from grease, dirt and oil, and, just as importantly, kept him warm. The protective helmet could be worn with a wool-lined cotton liner in winter for additional warm.*

Armoured personnel wore divisional shoulder insignia. The shoulder insignia for armoured divisions was similar and based on the motif of a triangle divided into yellow (top), blue (left) and red (right). Superimposed over this was a red bolt of lightning and black tank tracks. The divisional number would appear in the yellow field at the top: there were the 1st to 14th divisions, plus the 16th and 20th. Independent tank battalions either omitted

▲ *A US military Sherman tank, followed by trucks of motorized infantry, move forwards from Anzio in Italy.*

their unit numeral or added the numeral in black thread. The Armored School used an 'S'.

Distinctive dress

Although armoured personnel could make use of any of the rich variety of dress available to the other branches of service, they also adopted some distinctive items for their own use. Tankers' clothing had to be close fitting and smooth, so that buttons or straps did not snag on the vehicle interior, and so that the tankers could clamber quickly out of the vehicle if need be. It also had to be warm, because the inside of a metal vehicle was terribly cold in winter.

The most popular product of the search to find a warm and practical top was the tanker jacket – or Jacket, Combat, Winter. Developed in 1941, this was short, warm, practical and simple to fasten and take off; it closed with a single zip behind a fly front. It came in olive drab or in khaki with mustard yellow lining and was made from water-proofed cotton. The lining was of blanket cloth and thickened at the collar, waist and cuffs. The only difference between the 1941 pattern and the 1942 pattern was that the former had horizontal pockets and the latter had vertical side pockets. The jacket proved very popular and was quickly borrowed by other branches of service, even though it had originally been intended only for tank crews.

To go with the jacket, a thick pair of trousers was also issued. These were effectively overalls – but were known as Trousers, Combat, Winter; they had cotton exterior and padded blanket lining. The overalls went up to the chest and had braces that went over the shoulder. A revised pattern, issued in 1942, had a zip at the groin to allow the tanker to relieve himself without taking everything off. The end of the leg was kept tight, with zips that allowed the overalls to fasten over the top of boots. Strangely, the overalls were worn under as well as over the tanker jacket.

Protection

The 1930s was the decade for experimenting with head protection for vehicle crewmen. The US ran a series of tests which, in 1938, resulted in a padded protective helmet, made of rubberized material, for use within tanks. This was actually only really issued from 1942 onwards; it replaced an earlier helmet – known as the Donut – that was more cumbersome.

The new tank helmet was light, well ventilated, had comfortable chinstraps and built-in earphones. It was painted olive drab, but the leather joins and leather padded front were usually in natural leather, as was the interior. A lined, cloth helmet was also issued for wear underneath the helmet in winter conditions. The tankers' helmet was supposedly of the right size to wear under an M1 helmet, although some tankers also used the USAAF flak helmet for additional protection.

▶ **Lieutenant, 32nd Armored Regiment, 1945** *The M38 tankers' helmet was adequate when it came to knocks and shocks, but it did not provide sufficient ballistic protection. Tank crews sometimes took to wearing the standard M1 helmet, but some also made use of the USAAF's M3 flak helmet and wore it over the M38.*

RANGERS AND SPECIAL FORCES

The United States had relied on the Marine Corps for raiding and for special operations in conflicts prior to World War II. However, the war that began in 1941 brought forth a new style of unit, composed of specially trained personnel.

Most of the major powers had neglected special forces in the inter-war years: the cost of training and equipping such forces was prohibitive. However, with the Axis occupying much of Europe, the need for raiding parties and special operations was keenly felt. The Americans established a number of specialist units to take the war to the enemy.

Merrill's Marauders

The 5307th Composite Regiment, codenamed Galahad, was a force of volunteers raised to fight in Burma, undertaking long-range raids against the Japanese. The unit was quickly rebaptized Merrill's Marauders after its commander, Brigadier General Frank Merrill. They wore the uniforms of their original unit and insignia was rare. They did, however, develop their own unofficial shield-shaped patch – with unit title above the shield, which was itself divided by a bolt of red lightening, quartered in green and blue and with a white sun upper left and white star lower right. There were numerous variations, some late-war machine-sewn examples and others locally produced in local cloth. Personnel were later absorbed by the 475th Infantry Regiment (part of the new Mars Task Force or 5332nd Brigade), which had a similar shoulder patch but with 'Mars' replacing 'Merrill's Marauders'.

▲ *Men of the 5307th Composite Unit patrol the Burmese jungle, under the command of Brigadier General Frank D. Merrill.*

Rangers

The first Ranger battalion was established in the summer of 1942 in Northern Ireland and sent for training in Scotland. It had been inspired by the British commando units and was led by William Orlando Darby. Once the name Ranger had been fixed, it was not long before distinctive insignia began to evolve. That insignia took the form of a scroll on the upper arm, reflecting British commando styles but suitably original. The scroll was not officially recognized. It had 1st on the first part of the scroll, then Ranger, then Bn on the right end (some locally made scrolls dropped the "th" after the numeral).

It was first used during the landings of Operation Torch in Africa in November 1942 and became popular with the first five battalions; a blue diamond piped yellow bearing the word 'Rangers' in yellow had been introduced and worn by the 2nd and 5th battalions in 1943, but was unpopular. The 6th Battalion, sent to the Pacific theatre and wearing the appropriate uniform, wore scrolls from late 1944 in imitation of their counterparts in the European theatre of Operations (ETO).

Ranger battalions were designated Ranger Infantry battalions in August

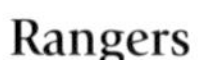

◀ **Private, 5307th Composite Unit (Provisional), Merill's Marauders, 1944**
Although the US Army did have its own machete troops operating in China, Burma and India tended to adopt local implements. Merrill's Marauders made good use of these in the jungles of Burma and this man's kukri, borrowed from the Gurkhas, would prove a useful addition to what is otherwise regular US Army equipment.

◀ **Private, 1st Special Service Force, 1944** *This was a special forces unit recruited from American and Canadian personnel. This individual carries the Johnson Light machine gun in southern France in the summer of 1944.*

1943. They were sometimes brigaded together into specialist forces such as the 6615th Ranger Force, established in North Africa in 1943. It consisted of the 509th Parachute Infantry Battalion, the 83rd Chemical Mortar Battalion and elements of the 1st, 3rd and 4th Ranger battalions. This latter was disbanded with personnel going into the 1st Special Service Force (and wearing both the Ranger flash and the FSSF arm insignia).

Rangers wore standard US infantry dress, but were adept at procuring the best items and the most practical equipment. For example, the 29th Provisional Ranger Battalion, formed from personnel from the 29th Division, and operating alongside British commandos, were amongst the first to receive the ETO jacket having first tested it in the mountains of the Scottish Highlands.

Special service

The 1st Special Service Force was founded in July 1942 and originally intended for service in Norway. It was composed of US and Canadian personnel recruited from a parachute battalion and was initially kitted out in winter dress, with the addition of a red arrowhead device bearing 'USA' across the point, with 'Canada' running down the head. Officers wore a crossed arrows device on their lapels or shirt collars. Other ranks wore the crossed arrows on a collar disc on their service coats. This device was also sometimes worn as a cap badge, particularly by the Canadians – who preferred regimental devices on their caps. A parachute oval was sometimes worn on the breast pocket. The unit seems to have worn a red, white and blue braid on the garrison cap and, in full dress, a similar fourragère or lanyard. The personnel had mixed Canadian and US items of dress until US styles began to prevail. Other marks of distinction included the use of the V42 fighting knife, designed especially for the unit, and the Johnson light machine gun.

The 474th Infantry Regiment was formed in January 1945 from the remnants of the 1st Special Service Force – then including the 1st, 3rd and 4th Ranger battalions – and the 99th Infantry Battalion, recruited from Norwegian personnel. This unit seems to have had a 474th patch on the left sleeve and the former unit's insignia on the right – arrow head, scroll or the Norwegian's red/blue Viking ship on a shield. The 474th's patch itself was something of a hybrid, with a blue ship on red arrowhead below a scroll.

▶ **Sergeant, 4th Ranger Battalion, 1944** *Rangers, rather like Britain's commandos, adopted dress that was as practical as possible. The only exception was their canvas leggings, which were difficult to fasten and tended to snag. The flannel shirt is here worn over a privately purchased wool shirt for some additional warmth.*

MARINES

The United States Marine Corps (USMC) had played a key role in American expeditions overseas and was rapidly expanded in the late 1930s on the presumption that it would again play a leading part in the conflict.

Navy troops

The USMC was part of the Navy and had grown from 20,000 men (20 per cent of the authorized strength of the Navy) in 1939 to 65,000 on the eve of war in 1941. They were heavily trained in conducting landing and amphibious operations in preparation for a rapid response in the Pacific or deployment to Europe or China; Marines had already been involved in the Shanghai evacuation of 1937. From that point on, the expansion of the USMC was quick and in a sense it became a specialist army within an army, with its own air force, paratroopers, armour and raiding units.

Marines would find themselves involved from Iceland in 1941 (under Army jurisdiction), then heavily in the Pacific and operating as small expeditionary forces and ships' detachments in every theatre of conflict. Different combat theatres called for different kinds of uniform – but so, too, did the kind of warfare in which the Marines specialized. As an organization, they were often in the lead in developing comfortable, practical items of dress and equipment and, under the auspices of the Navy, marines departed from standard US Army patterns.

The war, however, found the USMC unprepared for a modern conflict and many of the uniforms worn later would be improvized.

◀ **Marine, 6th Marine Regiment, 1941**
The Marine uniform worn in the first part of the early war revolved around forest green-coloured woollen items of clothing. This Marine wears the impractical service coat and has the small field-dressing pouch hanging from his belt. A larger pouch was worn in the Pacific theatre.

▶ **Marine, 4th Marine Regiment, 1941**
This individual wears the cotton (chino) khaki shirt worn in combat by Marines in the Pacific and the Philippines. Just visible is the white backing material that reinforced the button flap and made it more durable than the standard shirt.

Service coat

The service uniform consisted the impractical service coat, designed to be smart and hard-wearing but not really suitable for the battlefield. It was in green wool, and known as 'greens' by Marines. It had four pockets, the upper pockets with scalloped flaps and pleats. The tunic was worn with shirt, tie and matching trousers. This winter version was to be worn from

▲ MARINE, 5TH MARINE REGIMENT, 1942
This figure carries the rare, and rather unreliable, Reising M50 submachine gun, which had originally been intended for export to the Dutch East Indies but which was confiscated by the USMC when those possessions were overrun by the Japanese.

September to April when a khaki cotton version was to be adopted. This khaki version, usually worn without the tie, was used in combat in the early years of the Pacific conflict. It had two breast pockets with pointed, buttoned flaps and had the button flap lined with white cotton to make the item more hardwearing.

The trousers were worn with the tall Marine leggings (1910 pattern), made from strong canvas and with seven holes for laces up the side and a strap that slipped under the sole of the boot.

Combat uniform

The situation with combat uniform was not at all adequate. A temporary solution was the wearing of herringbone twill work uniforms, or fatigues – which for the Marines were in sage green. These were mostly two-piece uniforms with a sage-green jacket with three pockets, the one upper pocket, on the left, having a stencilled 'USMC' and insignia marking. In 1944 a modified version was issued. This now had two upper pockets, with vertical openings.

Trousers were also in sage green with two diagonal pockets to the fore, as well as a fob pocket often used for first aid materials, and two pockets to the rear. The number and styling of pockets was inadequate and the new version, issued in 1944, had two large cargo pockets down each thigh (fastened with a stud and flap), as well as a rear pocket designed to take the rain poncho.

Marines generally wore their boondockers, a hardwearing kind of leather boot, with all kinds of uniform. The Navy's black ankle boot was also used.

A camouflage suit was issued in 1943. This was a two-piece reversible uniform that came in colours that were not ideal for beach landings, making the use of the uniform unpopular with the Marines. There was a sand and brown side, and a green and brown reverse; the green/brown side had the pockets, sometimes stamped 'USMC'. It was issued to Marine Raiders in 1943 but was less common after 1944.

Although Marines did make use of a greatcoat (in forest green wool), a poncho was more practical in the Pacific theatre. This was initially in sage green, but a reversible camouflage version was also issued from 1943 onwards. The poncho came with buttons and it was supposed that it could be buttoned to another poncho to form a tent.

Headgear

The service cap, known as barracks cover, was usually worn with service dress. It came with interchangeable covers for use with either the winter or summer service uniform. It was usually worn at an angle by Marines keen to emphasize the individuality of their corps. Off duty, the ubiquitous pre-war campaign hat was favoured by

▼ *United States Marines pose on top of Mount Suribachi on the captured island of Iwo Jima with the American flag.*

the USMC. It was known as campaign cover and continued to be worn until 1943, when its use was largely relegated to training personnel. The garrison cap, with its simple envelope style, was adopted to be worn with the summer khaki uniform by the USMC, but received the derisive nickname of 'the pisscutter'. A utility cap, worn with the herringbone twill (HBT) fatigue uniform, was introduced in 1943. It had a short peak and bore the Marine insignia stencilled to the front. A HBT round hat with brim was also worn.

The Marines adopted the M1 helmet, although the 1917-pattern round helmet could be seen in the first months of the war. The helmet was often worn with a camouflage cover, especially as the war progressed. This was made of the same reversible patterned material as the camouflage poncho, with sand and brown patches on one side and green and brown on the reverse.

In the Pacific theatre the sun helmet (also known as a pith helmet or sun hat) was also common. It was made of fibre and usually bore the Marine insignia on the front. Although light and comfortable, it offered no real protection and was rapidly replaced.

Equipment

The USMC still made use of equipment carried during World War I (for example, the 1910-pattern haversack, with the 1917-pattern cartridge belt), although this was gradually discarded as it wore out. The 1928 system was an improvement but was not common in the Marines.

A new system of equipment was introduced in 1941 in light khaki with olive straps. This had a haversack, or field pack, with a blanket roll (a long or a short version) strapped to the top, often with tent canvas as a waterproof cover; there was also an entrenching tool strapped to the back in its own USMC cover, without the 'US' marking. A knapsack, for carrying spare clothes and boots, was also sometimes worn; when worn together – this was known as the transport pack. Officers had a green canvas field bag for their personal effects. The fastenings for most of these items were improved in 1943.

◀ MARINE, 1ST MARINE REGIMENT, 1945
The Marines acquired a stock of the highly accurate and effective Johnson 1941-pattern semi-automatic rifle, here carried by this officer wearing his frogskin camouflage uniform. US camouflage was going to be expanded to include camouflage for other theatres, but these largely remained plans when the war ended.

▲ *A relieved US Marine after the hard-won victory on Okinawa in 1945, the largest amphibious assault in the Pacific theatre.*

In addition, Marines wore a 1923-pattern cartridge belt (initially for ammunition for the Springfield rifle) and webbing belts in greenish canvas material – the bayonet was also in a cotton-coated scabbard, the 1942 version being of poorer quality than the original 1910 type. Additional ammunition was carried in canvas bags, usually stamped 'USMC', as was the gas mask carrier; gas masks were usually Navy types. The USMC had its own machete (USMC Machete, Intrenching) that came in its own canvas and leather sheath and also had a distinctive style of canvas cover for the water bottle closed by snap studs (lift-the-dot).

Insignia

The Marines had been distinguished by their globe, eagle and anchor device. These ornaments were worn by officers on caps, with the globe and eagle in white metal and the Americas and the anchor in yellow metal. It was worn on the campaign hat, and a simpler and smaller device was worn on the various kinds of soft side caps.

◀ CAPTAIN, 2ND MARINE PARACHUTE BATTALION, 1941 *This paramarine is wearing a T-4 parachute, carries the Thompson (or 'Tommy') gun and holds the ingenious collapsible Compax bicycle. He wears his rank insignia on the shoulder of his early pattern jump suit – quickly relegated to training exercises, as was the bicycle.*

▶ LIEUTENANT, 21ST MARINE REGIMENT, 1945 *It was rare for officers to wear rank insignia in the Pacific as this made them more vulnerable to Japanese snipers. Officers were therefore distinguished by their equipment and, on occasion, blackened insignia on the collar or cap.*

Marine officers shifted their rank insignia to the right side on these caps, and wore the Marine emblem on the left. Enlisted personnel wore the same device, but usually in bronze and most ornaments or devices were blackened in the field. The globe and anchor was to be placed on the left lapel of the early service coat, and also found its way on to shirt or HBT collars when the service coat was discarded. The anchor was placed to point forwards.

This Marine badge heraldry was also to be found on the units' buttons. These featured the eagle and anchor below 13 stars. These buttons were in bronze or later in plastic, simpler versions with just the name were worn on herringbone twill items.

Marine rank for officers generally followed the design adopted in the Army. Second lieutenants would have a bar in yellow metal, lieutenants would have one in silver and captains would have two in silver, and so on. Warrant officers, a rank established during the conflict, had a central red square added to the insignia of the second lieutenant. However, the Marines distanced themselves slightly from the Army when it came to NCO rank insignia. The chevrons were in olive green on red backing felt on the winter service uniform (worn September to April, or longer in colder climates, and known as Ables or greens) but such chevrons on light khaki cloth were the norm for Marines in action.

Shoulder sleeve insignia had only rarely been seen in World War I. Marines began World War II without such insignia. In 1942 the 1st Marine Brigade, organized as a provisional brigade sent to Iceland, wore a Polar Bear on black rectangle patch on both shoulders in British fashion. Then, in early 1943, the process began of adopting distinctive insignia for corps and divisions. The three corps quickly adopted sleeve shields (1st and 5th in 1943, 3rd in 1944). The 1st Marine Amphibious Corps had a whole range of insignia based on a blue shield with red diamond centre (Raiders adopting a skull device in the centre) and five silver stars. The six divisions adopted variations of cloth diamonds, shields or discs as sleeve insignia. The 2nd Division revised its insignia twice in 1943. A red parachute badge was worn on the lower left sleeve by Marines qualified as jumpers (the so-called Paramarines had been formed in 1941 and trained for airborne assault in support of amphibious operations). Service stripes, in olive drab on red backing, were positioned just above the cuff and worn tilted at an angle.

PARATROOPS

It took a while for the United States to establish the first units but, from that point onwards, growth was exponential.

Experiments

The early experiments in forming paratroop units led to the establishment of parachute-testing units, in 1940, parachute infantry battalions in late 1941 and then regiments (with supporting artillery and engineers). Then came the glider infantry regiments in mid-1942, raised and trained for glider-borne assault but not given the extra pay. The general rule when it came to uniforms and equipment was that the parachute infantry were issued with special dress and equipment and the glider infantry used infantry dress but borrowed items of equipment, and mimicked parachute infantry insignia.

It was essential that the paratroopers were issued with special dress as proper clothing made the difference between life and death. The search for suitable boots and helmets began in 1940. Experiments resulted in a wind-resistant one-piece suit, but it was too bright. The first approved suit was issued in 1941. This parachute jumper's coat was made of cotton, had a standing collar, was zipped up and had four pockets. It came with matching trousers that were elasticated at the ankle. Tests showed that the pockets were insufficient to carry the mass of equipment required by the average paratrooper. The pocket capacity was increased and a new suit was issued in 1942. This also had four pockets, closed with studs, and the upper pockets were angled inwards. It came with its own belt, but this was often discarded.

This practical suit was itself phased out from 1944, with many paratroopers then being dressed in field jackets suits (the 101st Division seems to have adopted this, the 82nd Division proved more conservative). Some paratroopers added knee patches and reinforced inners to their 1942-pattern trousers.

The 1917-pattern helmet, with its broad, round outline, was particularly unsuitable for airborne forces. As a stopgap measure the padded Ridell helmet was tried, or else aviation flying helmets were used. Paratroopers adopted the M1 helmet, but found that the chinstrap was problematic. The M2 helmet was issued in 1942 and was known as the D Bale helmet after its D-shaped chinstrap loops. A modified version of the M1 helmet, the M1C, designed for extra stability, was also issued to paratroopers. This had the liner fixed to the shell, A-yoke straps, which was a more comfortable arrangement, and an added chinpad. Even so the helmet still caused problems, the rear rim often digging into the neck upon landing.

◄ **US Paratrooper, 517th Parachute Infantry, 1st Airborne Task Force, 1944**
American paratroops tended to camouflage their helmets with paint, netting or camouflage material taken from parachutes or from tent canvas. The chinstrap was to be fastened when taking part in a jump, but many paratroopers then preferred to undo it once on the ground as it had a tendency to graze the face.

Boots

Jump boots were fundamental to increasing a paratrooper's chances of a successful landing. The American version was based on the experience gained by other armies. An experimental braced shoe had been used in training in 1940. By the summer of 1942 the standard rubber-soled jump boot came into use with up to 13 pairs of lace holes. It was popular and paratroopers generally tucked their trousers into the tall boot; this looked odd when the combat boot was worn.

Insignia

Paratroopers and glider troops were part of the infantry. They wore infantry badges, as appropriate, but also introduced their own specific insignia.

The paratroopers' metal jump wings were generally worn above the left breast pocket. These were sometimes set in a coloured oval or one in branch-of-service colour (red for artillery). Glider infantry had their own metal winged badge over their left breast pocket.

Many parachute and glider infantry regiments added their own regimental pocket patches, such as the black cat with parachute of the 503rd, but these were generally not worn in action. A dash of colour was added by the divisional patch (the Airborne Command's red shield with white glider and parachute was worn by non-assigned personnel, or a corps patch for the 18th Airborne Corps from 1944), or shoulder

▲ *A member of the famed 82nd Airborne Division arriving home in New York.*

sleeve insignia. These were primarily for the 11th Airborne (blue shield with white winged '11' in a red oval), the 13th (golden unicorn on blue shield), the 17th (golden eagle's claw on black oval), the 82nd (with its distinctive double 'A' in a disc) and the screaming eagle (on black shield) of the 101st. These patches were to be worn below an 'Airborne' tab. This was supposed to have been gold lettering on black cloth but older or noncomformist examples persisted – the 82nd preferred their white on blue, some artillery adopted white on red.

Garrison caps (with blue piping for other ranks) bore an oval badge, worn on the right by officers (with rank insignia on the left) and on the left by other ranks. There was a glider version, a parachute infantry version and, later, an airborne infantry version that combined the two. It was in white thread, or gold for officers, on a disc in branch colours.

Airborne divisions often wore call sign emblems on the right side of their helmet. These were usually variations on playing card symbols. The 101st had white circles, a diamond for the 501st PIB, a heart for the 502nd PIB, spades for the 506th and clubs for the glider infantry (327th and 401st). A white rectangle (or tick) denoted the battalion: 1st to the right of the symbol, 2nd below, 3rd to the left, HQ above. Paratroops deployed in France wore an American flag armband by way of recognition.

◀ **US Sergeant, 506th Parachute Infantry (2nd Battalion), 1945** *The gun carried here is the ingenious M1 carbine with folding stock. Easily carried in the confines of a transport plane, this was ideally suited for use by paratroopers. This sergeant wears the one-piece camouflage jungle suit, known as the frogskin suit. It had generous pockets but was heavy and uncomfortable to wear.*

▶ **Private, 325th Glider Infantry, 1944** *Glider infantry, known as glider riders, generally wore uniforms similar to those of the infantry, although they attempted to borrow certain items from their counterparts in the parachute infantry. The shoulder sleeve insignia shows he is one of the 82nd Airborne Division.*

AIR FORCE

The United States outproduced the Axis powers in aircraft manufacture and supported the Allied war effort with men and machines, effectively dominating the skies.

The US was quick to see the potential of a militarized air force. A small experimental unit had been formed in 1907, under the Army Signal Corps, and this unit became the Aviation Section in 1914, the Air Service in 1918 and the Air Corps in 1926. In the summer of 1941 the Air Corps became the Army Air Force; it only became independent of the Army in 1947. The interwar air force was tiny, but by 1942 had shot up to 9,000 machines and 400,000 personnel, and by 1945 had 2.5 million personnel and 64,000 machines.

▲ *The crew of an American flying fortress make their way to a debriefing session at an airbase in England following a bombing mission over Germany.*

◀ **Pilot, 373rd Fighter Group, 1944**
Pilots made use of different kinds of parachute. The one being worn here is the S1, first adopted in the 1920s and a seat-type, meaning that the chute sat at the rear of the pilot's waist. The life vest is the distinctive yellow Mae West.

Insignia

The winged propeller insignia was worn on a collar disc by enlisted personnel on their service coats. Officers wore the same device on their lapels, as well as on their shirt collars when the coat was not worn. The device also found itself on the various side caps worn during the conflict and sometimes under NCO chevrons. In 1920 the Air Corps had received the branch-of-service colours of bright blue and orange intertwined. This was worn as braid on the side caps of enlisted personnel or as cords on the campaign hat.

As with ground forces, the air force was quick to adopt colourful shoulder sleeve insignia. This was a generic Air Force patch (blue disc with orange wings carrying a red star in a white disc), insignia for geographic combat commands (Europe or the Far East, for example) and for specific air forces (1-15, plus the 20th, all based on a blue patch with orange device). Late in the war, support services were authorized to wear blue shoulder arcs bearing their designation in orange (Air Transport Command, for instance).

Many squadrons wore their own distinctive squadron patches on the sleeves of flying jackets or on breast pockets. As with the air forces of most other major powers, the USAAF adopted a series of wings to distinguish air crews. These white metal devices were worn over the breast pocket (a smaller version was worn on the shirt) and had variations for pilots (a shield), bomb aimers (a bomb), flight engineers (a propeller), gunners (a winged bomb) or observers (an oval).

In 1943 cuff insignia for specialists was introduced. This came in the form of inverted blue triangles with orange devices by specialism (a bomb for ordnance experts, a camera for photographers, a cog for engineers).

◄ **USAAF WAAC, Eighth Air Force, 1943**
The first members of the Women's Army Auxiliary Corps (known as the Women's Army Corps from late 1943) arrived in Europe in December 1942 and replaced British auxiliaries in support services. The WAAC had an insignia showing Athena's head in a Greek helmet, which came as a collar disk, lapel or collar badge for officers.

Flying gear

Uniforms worn on the ground followed the pattern established by the Army, with service coats being favoured by officers when off duty and overalls being worn for fatigue duties. When it came to flight gear, there was a large amount of variation – not surprisingly, given the rapid expansion of the service and the number of personnel involved, plus a rather flexible approach. Probably the most common, and certainly the most famous, item was the brown leather A2 flying jacket, which first made its appearance in 1931. It was comfortable, roomy and fastened with a simple zip. A more heavy-duty version of the leather jacket, with wool collar and heavy lining, was also issued (the B3, to be worn with matching trousers). In 1944 a cotton version, lined with artificial fur, began to replace the leather version, mostly as an economy. The jacket was usually worn with service trousers or breeches, or over overalls. Leather trousers were also popular.

Flying boots included the British fur-lined type, which fastened with straps, or the US-manufactured A6 type lined with wool. with a zip and strap.

In warmer climates a cotton khaki flying suit was worn, such as the one-piece A4 suit that was fastened with a zip and had its own integral belt. Flying suits became progressively more advanced as the conflict continued, but leather was always popular due to its ability to reduce burns.

Leather flying helmets were also the most common. The USAAF began the war with helmets that were poorly designed for use with breathing apparatus and communication equipment. The Type B6, with attachments to secure a mask, was an improvement. But the AN-H-16 with its integral receivers was really quite modern and also came in a khaki cotton version for use in hot weather.

The older flying helmets were worn with the B6 or B7 protective goggle but, again, the use of oxygen masks caused problems and the B8 goggles were designed to overcome this. These were also an improvement in the sense that the lenses were made of plastic.

Equipment included oxygen masks (early types just covered the nose, later masks were integral mouth-nose versions), life vests and jackets (the bright yellow B3 version being popular, as was the more cumbersome 'Mae West') and parachutes. These later came in variations worn on the lower chest, on the back and behind the individual (the S2). Pilots were allowed some latitude in equipment as well as dress, leading to some civilian items being used to supplement official issue.

► **Captain, 350th Fighter Group, 1944**
This fighter plane pilot wears the classic A2 leather flying jacket, a parachute, life vest and a first aid kit designed for use by US Airborne Forces. His shirt collar would display rank on one side and the USAAF insignia on the other.

GERMANY

Germany had astonished the world in the 1930s with its dramatic return to the world stage. Bitter and humiliated after defeat in World War I, and made more so by economic ruin, the Germans had become increasingly radicalized in the 1920s and the early 1930s. Adolf Hitler, leader of the National Socialist German Workers' (Nazi) Party and from 1933 Chancellor of Germany, seemed to offer a practical solution – even if his true vision for his country was shrugged at or misunderstood. He capitalized on economic growth to rebuild Germany's armed forces, and in the build-up to World War II won concession after concession from the bewildered French and British. Czechoslovakia was absorbed, Poland invaded; victory followed in the West. Then, in the greatest gamble of all, Hitler – buoyed by enthusiasm from a population who thought the war was already over – launched the invasion of the Soviet Union and set about exterminating those he decided were his racial and ideological enemies across Europe. His chief instrument for war was the Wehrmacht, which brought him victory in 1940 but could not hope to keep up with their leader's increasingly extreme demands.

▲ *Booted German NCOs and soldiers sit in the doorway of their transport wagon on the way to the front in 1940.*

◀ *Policemen salute Hitler as he passes through a cordon of SS in a German town in 1934.*

THE NAZIS AND THE ARMY

In May 1935 the Weimar Republic's Reichswehr was abolished and a new organization of armed forces (the Wehrmacht) came into being.

Germany passed the Law for the Reconstruction of the National Defence Forces, which brushed aside the concept that Germany was demilitarized and established the Wehrmacht under control of the Oberkommando der Wehrmacht (OKW), with Hitler at its head from 1938. The Wehrmacht encompassed forces serving on land (the Army, or Heer, was divided into the Field Army and the Replacement Army), at sea (the Navy, or Kriegsmarine) and in the air (the Air Force, or Luftwaffe). It also included the Waffen SS, a branch of the Schutzstaffel ('Protection Corps').

Hitler came to power in a democracy, but set about converting Germany into a totalitarian state. He did this by transferring power to bodies controlled by his National Socialist German Workers (Nazi) Party – first amongst these being the SS, an organization promoted to ensure the security of the Reich and commanded by Heinrich Himmler, from 1929 Reichsführer-SS.

▲ *Werner von Blomberg, Minister for War, Werner von Fritsch, Army Commander in Chief, Hermann Göring, Chief of the Air Force and Erich Raeder, Admiral of the Fleet, all salute before Hitler in 1937.*

▼ *Members of the Austrian Heimwehr wore the swastika as their army is inducted en masse into the German Wehrmacht in 1938.*

Racial purity

The Waffen SS was an armed force within the SS, initially established for policing duties. Its members – distinct both in uniform and manner of recruitment – had their own rank organization and were administered by SS departments. SS officers were supposed to uphold the Nazi ideology and act as Heinrich Himmler's racial aristocracy. (The Nazis claimed that Germans were members of a gifted and superior racial group, the Aryans, whose task was to safeguard the purity of their race and stamp out allegedly inferior races including Jews and Slavs.) However, non-Aryans joined the Waffen SS in numbers after 1943 and the ranks of the Waffen SS were stiffened by conscripts. They had not experienced the Army's officer corps training and were consequently looked down upon by Army officers, but they consciously adopted the elitism of shock troops and fought an ideological war frequently marred by atrocities.

The Waffen SS was not one of the branches of the SS that would be tasked with administering the death camps in which millions of Jews, Romany, homosexuals, communists and others were slain. These Waffen SS units (which steadily expanded during the war) were instead turned against external enemies of the regime and were assigned to the front line to fight alongside the Army and often under Army command.

The military and the Nazi Party

The Army was still the self-appointed bastion of military tradition, but inevitably it had also come under the regime's control and influence. Hitler's personal influence in Army affairs and promotions was considerable, and personnel had to swear a specific oath of loyalty to him. It was not unknown for senior officers to wear Party insignia on their uniforms, and cadets were on the receiving end of political indoctrination at officers' schools.

After World War II, it became common for Army officers to distance themselves from the regime and from the SS. The truth is complex. Some

Army officers were very strongly anti-Nazi – a group of plotters who tried to blow up Hitler in 1944 came from a minority highly critical of the regime; and, even from the early years, some dismissed the Nazi regime's rhetoric and obstructed any perceived political interference in the military. On the other hand, some officers were fervently pro-Nazi, having seen the regime restore Germany's prestige and furnish its armed forces with substantial resources. Many officers were allowed to be apolitical, so long as they did their duty.

That duty often made the German officer corps complicit with the regime. The German Army had demonstrated draconian tendencies in World War I, taking hostages, shooting suspected insurgents and starving occupied territories of resources. Now, with animosities intensified by racist and ideological bitterness, the Army went further, especially in the east.

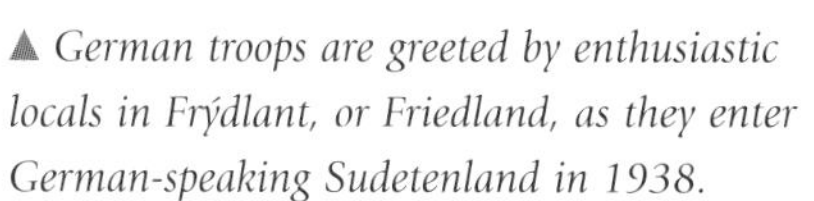

▲ *German troops are greeted by enthusiastic locals in Frýdlant, or Friedland, as they enter German-speaking Sudetenland in 1938.*

Reign of terror in the east

The occupied territories behind the Eastern Front were in the German Army's jurisdiction and that institution supported and perpetrated a veritable reign of terror amongst the peoples of the Soviet Union – repeated on a smaller scale in Greece, Italy, France, Yugoslavia and every other occupied territories. Partisans were shot in huge numbers, villages were randomly destroyed, foodstuffs confiscated and populations shipped back to the Reich to work as slave labour.

These were crimes performed by Army units (exempted from criminal charges by decrees drawn up before the campaign) using Army resources – as were the transportation of Jews to the death camps. Crimes against captured members of the Red Army were also common. A series of directives from Army, divisional or regimental officers enforced the shooting of commissars, Jewish prisoners, Asian-looking prisoners and women prisoners, then the mass starvation of Soviet prisoners of war; of these, 2.8 million died in just six months in the autumn and winter of 1941-42.

Such activities were a direct and sanctioned part of the regime's war aims. While in most areas there was collusion between the Army and the state apparatus, and acceptance in many cases of shared goals, in the east the war was conducted by an Army that seemed to want its own ideological conflict; it is significant that the east was, after all, controlled by the Oberkommando des Heeres (OKH), the Army's high command. This close partnership began to weaken as the chances of victory started to diminish towards the end of the war – especially after July 1944. The SS was expanded, and its influence extended, while the Army came under closer control and closer policing by an increasingly anxious German state.

▼ *A Nazi propaganda photograph shows a German official overseeing the distribution of food to Soviet forced labourers in 1943.*

FROM VICTORY TO DEFEAT

The Treaty of Versailles in 1919 had limited the size of Germany's Army, depriving it of heavy weapons, abolishing its air force and parcelling out its Navy to the victorious Allies. Germany preserved just a few surface ships, but submarines were prohibited.

The Third Reich (Nazi Germany 1933-45) set itself the goal of enlarging and modernizing German armed forces and, from there, being able to use them in an aggressive foreign policy that would necessitate conflict with Europe's leading military powers. German industry had the capacity and knowledge to turn out armaments in intimidating numbers, to the point where it could overtake British or French production. Germany had already shown a willingness, before 1933, to undermine the restrictions placed upon it by Versailles and Allied enforcement of the treaty had effectively ended by 1926.

▼ *Workers bring another Heinkel HE-111 twin-motored bomber to near completion in a serial-production German factory in 1940.*

All that was missing was the will. That will revealed itself in 1933. Under the Nazis, the military budget was tripled to 57 million marks. Aircraft production for the new Air Force (named the Luftwaffe in 1935) was intensified – although the number of pilots and crew still lagged behind. By March 1935 Hitler was boasting that his Air Force was equal to the Royal Air Force in Britain.

The strains imposed by this sudden national rearmament were immense and the internal contradictions they imposed played an important role in Germany's defeat.

Speed of expansion

The first major problem was one of manpower. Germany had a population of 80.6 million people in 1939 (38.9 million men) and, of these, 4.7 million were in Wehrmacht service in 1939. This meant that the armed forces had expanded massively over a short period of time, leading to shortages of NCOs and qualified officers. Casualties would only exacerbate this problem. There were some 15,000 officer casualties in the first nine months of the war against the Soviet Union, ten times the number lost in the western campaign of 1940. Replacements for other rank losses were also difficult to obtain and train under wartime conditions.

▲ *German tank design and their efficient production allowed them to dominate the battlefields in 1940.*

Added to problems caused by rapid expansion were the difficulties that arose when it came to equipping troops in any further expansion – the Wehrmacht had grown to 9.1 million personnel by 1942. There were also problems in supplying Allies and vassals: much of this was done using captured supplies, but these were of little use by 1942.

The re-equipping of the German armed forces was done at speed – and at great cost. In 1938 Germany was spending one-sixth (17 per cent) of her income on military expenditure; Britain's defence budget was 7 per cent in the same year. Raw materials were imported in vast amounts, but steel, oil and materials for the production of munitions were difficult to obtain cheaply. There was a great deal of waste; the German economy was not centrally controlled and rival factions

▲ *German troops position a 15cm Kanone, burying the tail end to absorb the heavy return after firing. This heavy gun was difficult to handle and unpopular.*

within the government controlled resources that might have been better utilized elsewhere. For a while the capture of foreign resources and the use of slave labour masked these deficiencies, and this also meant that German women were not employed in war-related work and that German workers did not see an increase in working hours. All this meant that Germany never fully transformed her economy into a war economy in the same way as, say, the Soviet Union did.

Outstripped by Soviets and Americans

By 1942 German military production was increasingly dwarfed in numerical terms by the Soviet Union and the United States. The US produced 197,000 aircraft between September 1940 and the end of the war; Germany struggled to produce 80,000 and did not always have the trained manpower even for these. The Germans also struggled in other areas. While the Soviets could count on 35,000 T34 tanks produced by 1945, Germany had a mere 5000 Panthers and 2000 Tigers (split across numerous fronts from 1944). Sheer weight of numbers and material counted against Germany in the long run and put enormous strain on a country that had stretched itself to achieve victory in 1940.

To an extent the Wehrmacht of 1939 was something of a facade. The concentration of overwhelming force at key selected points won victory after victory, but even so Germany was not especially well equipped with armour or aircraft in 1939. Only 14 out of 103 divisions were mechanized and the movement of supplies and troops was still dependent on horses and railways.

Some German weaponry was perhaps better than that fielded by the French and British in 1940, and qualitatively better than many Soviet weapons in 1941, but there was only some small advantage in just a handful of areas. (The German weapons, it must be said, were put to better use.) Germany never really had a technological advantage – and even although it produced some supremely effective small arms and armoured vehicles, it only did so at a time when the Allies were producing improved designs in greater numbers. Just as the initiative was lost by 1942, so too was any technological advantage.

Early successes undone

Germany was remarkably successful in the period 1939-41, overrunning western Europe without significant losses and conquering the Balkans and the Ukraine. This military achievement was based on a successful doctrine that was soon imitated by the Allies. However, Soviet resistance soon made it clear that sustaining the war would be enormously problematic for a Germany already struggling to maintain its war machine. For example, producing sufficient tanks to replace losses was already in difficult in 1941.

The German war machine was soon on the defensive, forced into guarding extensive coastlines or the vast expanses of Russian or Ukrainian plains. The scale of victory meant that Germany now became responsible for holding on to her possessions, and this meant that a new doctrine was needed – as well as the means to beat Allies who had rearmed and now had won control of the initiative. Germany's advantages were exhausted by 1941 and, from then on, defeat was only a matter of time.

▼ *The lot of the artilleryman was a difficult one; deafened in combat and forced to drag heavy equipment through mud between September and May.*

GENERALS AND STAFF

The uniforms worn by German generals resembled those worn by their counterparts in World War I. Perhaps this is not surprising in an officer class characterized by respect for tradition.

There were variations. While some generals followed regulations, which established a traditional style of dress, many more adapted their own dress to personal taste. German generals often retained the habit of wearing uniforms that reflected the uniforms of their original regiment or unit, and adding general-officer insignia. Panzer commanders flattered their troops by adopting panzer uniform with generals' distinctions; generals commanding mountain troops adopted the insignia and symbolism of mountain dress. The SS, which had its own rank structure, was a new formation but it too blended tradition with innovation.

◄ Major General (Africa), 1943 *The tall boots seen here were popular with officers in the early stages of the North Africa campaign but became less and less common. The shoe part of the boot was in natural leather while the upper part was in stiffened canvas in ochre or olive with leather reinforcement behind the ankle.*

Formal wear

German generals generally wore a formal tunic, known as a Waffenrock, often privately tailored, or adopted the standard tunic (Feldbluse) in use at the time. The most common variant in the early years of the war would have been the 1936 pattern, with its darker green-blue collar, five gilt buttons, four pleated pockets with scalloped flaps and straight cuffs. The collar would have a distinctive patch (a parallelogram) on either side consisting of bright red cloth with gilt oak leaf embroidery and two arabesques (known as Alt Larisch, and first worn by Prussian grenadiers in the 18th century). This traditional insignia continued in use throughout World War II although, in May 1944, generals of non-combat troops were allowed to wear patches in branch-of-service colours (also used as underlays to the shoulder straps).

These shoulder straps had entwined aluminium cord with gilt edging (all gilt for marshals) and a button by the collar, all with red underlays. They showed the specific rank as follows: Generalfeldmarschall, crossed marshals' batons in silver; Generaloberst (with rank of marshal), four pips, two centred, two at the shoulder; Generaloberst, three pips, one centred, two at the shoulder; General, two pips, one centred, one at the shoulder; Generalleutnant, one pip, centred; Generalmajor, no silver pip.

▲ *Erwin Rommel, pictured here in France in 1940, as a Major General, has opted for the less-formal side cap.*

Generals would be known as generals of infantry, cavalry, artillery, engineers, panzers, signals troops or mountain troops.

If a coat was not suitable for shoulder straps, a system consisting of black tabs with gilt bars and oak leaves was used. A Generalmajor would have one bar beneath an oak leaf, a general had three bars. Generalobersts added three silver pips; marshals added crossed batons.

An eagle emblem was worn on the tunic, in gold thread and on a base of dark blue-green material.

The rank of general field marshal was introduced in April 1936, and

▲ **INFANTRY GENERAL, 1941** *This general of mountain troops wears a 1928-pattern tunic in fine grey cloth. It was not uncommon for senior officers to have their tunics privately tailored and the tone of grey varied from light grey through to the field grey worn by most other members of the Army.*

lapsed between 1938 and July 1940 when nine new field marshals were appointed. A further nine generals were promoted to the rank in the course of the war. Field marshals had three arabesques on their collar patches, although there were variations: for example, Gerd von Rundstedt – commander of Army Group A in the German invasion of France in 1940 – sometimes wore a colonel's litzen on his collar (he was honorary colonel of the 18th Infantry Regiment), but with a marshal's shoulder straps.

Generals generally wore breeches in the same colour as their tunics. These billowed at the thigh and were kept tight around the calf with five black buttons. The garments had a double stripe in bright red down the outside seam. They were usually worn with riding boots. Greatcoats had bright red lining at the lapel, frequently buttoned over to show this distinctive colour.

Peaked caps followed the Army style, but with gold piping around the dark cap band and piping around the crown.

Insignia

The SS had its own rank system and those officers in the SS who were the equivalent of generals had their own insignia. The distinctive Army collar patches were not worn, instead black tabs were worn on the collar with both tabs having a distinctive three-leafed spray of oak in silver. In addition silver diamond pips were added below as follows: SS-Oberst-Gruppenführer, three pips; SS-Obergruppenführer, two pips; SS-Gruppenführer, one pip; SS-Brigadeführer, no pips.

These pips were also worn on the shoulder straps, which followed the Army style but were on a silver-grey underlay.

SS senior officers had black bands on their peaked caps with silver piping, and the Death's Head on the front of the cap band.

General Staff officers had a distinctive insignia on their collars. A more decorative collar litzen in aluminium (gold for officers at headquarters) with scarlet was worn on blue-green patches. As many officers on staff duty wore more formal dress, their tunics would have been piped in branch-of-service colours and their collar litzen would have been on patches in the same colour.

General Staff officers also had two crimson stripes down the outside of their breeches. Himmler's personal staff, the closest the SS had to a general staff, had dark grey as their branch-of-service colour but this was only shown on cap piping and on the underlay of the shoulder straps.

▶ **MAJOR GENERAL, 1942** *Binoculars were carried in a Bakelite or leather case but this was usually quite bulky and either left in the vehicle or on the saddle of the officer's horse. This general's cap has a gilded braid chinstrap that was usually kept on top of the peak and kept in place by a gilded button on either side.*

INFANTRY

German infantry uniforms were not radically modified when the Nazi regime came to power. They still, in outline, resembled those of the Weimar Republic. The regime limited itself to some modifications, but extensively overhauled the insignia in use by the new conscript army. Traditional elements of dress, however, persisted and continued to exist below the swastika.

German infantry regiments were expanded following the introduction of conscription in 1935. The vast majority were regular infantry regiments drawn from conscripts and the reserve (those aged up to 35), with the Landwehr (those aged 35 to 45) serving as a second reserve. The most fundamental change occurred in November 1942 when the infantry regiments were renamed as grenadier regiments; nine were designated as fusiliers.

▲ *Following victory in France, German troops parade through Freiburg in 1940. Note the way the men attach the helmet to the belt.*

◄ **Officer, 19th Infantry Regiment, 1940**
The Luger was the preferred weapon of German officers. It was worn in a leather holster (often blackened), which was buckled and suspended from the belt; 16 rounds of 9mm (0.4in) ammunition were generally carried in stiffened card containers.

Tunics

The standard Army tunic, or Feldbluse, was developed from the one worn by German troops in World War I. The Weimar Republic made few significant changes, but the new regime initially improvised some improvements and then, in 1936, manufactured large numbers of a modified-pattern garment for the much enlarged Army.

The 1933 pattern (issued in 1934) was modified in a series of improvements, so that by 1936 it had a much more practical lining (the 1933 pattern had only been lined at the shoulder); this improved the quality and durability of the garment. The tunic was supposed to be grey-green, but the manufactured garments actually came in a variety of shades, depending on where they were made, and had five blank buttons, two breast pockets (pleated and with scalloped flaps) and two lower pockets (larger than the breast pockets, but in the same style). The collar was of the stand and fall variety (closed with hooks) and was in dark green-blue cloth. Removable shoulder straps were buttoned onto the tunic by the collar and there were support straps for the belt at the waist.

The next few years saw some tinkering with this standard tunic. In 1940 the dark collar was discontinued for reasons of economy and, in 1941, a new pattern of tunic began to be issued with a sixth button down the front. In 1942 the pleats began to

◀ **Rifleman, 60th Infantry Regiment, 1940** *German infantry advancing into France usually wore helmets newly painted with anti-reflective slate grey paint. This replaced the satin green coating applied in factories and widely seen in Poland in 1939. This satin sheen made the helmet glisten when wet.*

▶ **Machine Gunner, 16th Machine Gun Battalion, 1940** *Machine gun battalions wore a distinctive Gothic 'M' on their shoulder straps above the battalion number. Being part of the infantry these battalions had white piping around the strap.*

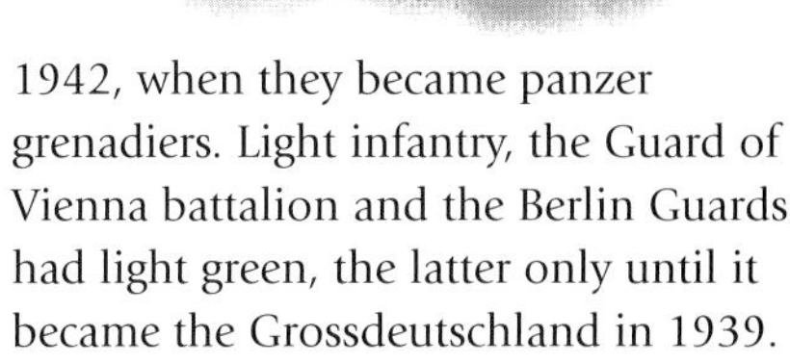

disappear from the pockets. Then, in 1943, the tunic was changed again. Now the scalloped pocket flaps disappeared and the cloth itself was a blend of 10 per cent wool and 90 per cent synthetic fibres lined with artificial silk, rendering the tunic uncomfortable and prone to irritate the skin. As dyes were also scarce, the colour of the tunics was no longer standardized.

A 1944-pattern tunic, based on British battledress, was issued in small numbers in 1944 and 1945. It had six buttons, but two of these were at the waist; it was tight-fitting and could be worn open at the collar. There were just two waist pockets. It is also worth noting that a large number of Austrian Army tunics, or captured and dyed Dutch tunics, found their way into German service.

Officers had similar tunics but they were manufactured in higher quality cloth, were often tailored (although they could be purchased from official suppliers) and had French cuffs. Lightweight summer versions existed and these came in a number of colours from sand to grey. A parade version with branch-of-service piping around the collar, down the front and around the cuffs was also sometimes worn. In addition, officers had the right to wear the more formal Waffenrock tunic, although this was rare by 1940; a white version also existed.

Shoulder straps

Tunics were to be worn with shoulder straps. These had pointed ends up until 1938, but they were then issued with rounded ends. Initially shoulder straps for other ranks were in dark blue-green like the tunic collar but, from the summer of 1940, they were field grey. The button at the top of the strap bore the company number.

Straps were piped in branch-of-service colours. This was white for infantry, fortress infantry, machinegun battalions, mortar battalions, frontier guards and bicycle units (who had switched from yellow to white in 1936). Motorized fusiliers attached to armoured units had grass-green straps (yellow for those attached to light divisions) between 1939 and late 1942, when they became panzer grenadiers. Light infantry, the Guard of Vienna battalion and the Berlin Guards had light green, the latter only until it became the Grossdeutschland in 1939.

In addition to any rank insignia, or any distinctive unit badges, the Germans began the war with a system of identifiers on their shoulder straps, although in January 1940 these numerals were scrapped in favour of slip-on bands with the same devices. The unit identifiers were either roman numerals (for districts or corps) or Arabic (for units). Above it was placed a Gothic or Latin letter to distinguish types of units. All these were in branch-of-service colours (or white metal for officers). They were sometimes covered by grey bands on campaign, but were commonly uncovered in 1939 and 1940 before being phased out.

Infantry regiments would just have the regimental numeral; fortress infantry added a Gothic 'F' above their unit number; machine gun battalions had a Gothic 'M'; mortar units wore a Gothic 'GW'. Motorized infantry added a Gothic 'S' when attached to armoured divisions or light divisions. There were also some unit-specific insignia, including the Grossdeutschland's 'GD' (after 1940). This insignia continued to be worn when the unit was enlarged to a division. In 1943 regiments within that division were supposed to wear cloth strips over their straps – grenadier regiments getting white and fusilier regiments getting red.

The Führer Grenadier Battalion wore an 'FG' between 1943 and August 1944, thereafter adopting the 'GD'. The Hoch und Deutschmeister Grenadier Regiment (formerly the134th) wore a cross insignia on their shoulder straps from 1944 to commemorate the Austrian origins of the regiment and the Felderrnhalle Regiment, which was an infantry unit before being reorganized as panzer grenadiers in 1943, wore the 'SA' symbol and three runes on their straps.

The opening of hostilities saw some changes as to how insignia was displayed and by December 1939 many units were suppressing unit insignia on the straps. Numerals or metal insignia were sometimes removed altogether. The strap was sometimes worn inside-out, or covered in a strip of cloth. In 1940 a band of grey cloth was issued to serve as a slip-on to allow the unit number to be easily removed. In reality, the situation varied from unit to unit, even though, as late as February 1944 regulations were calling for these bands to be worn in the field.

Tunic insignia

On the right breast, above the breast pocket, the tunic had an eagle badge. Essentially, these were the same as the eagles on the cap but larger. Some superior officers wore a metal version pinned to their tunics or gilt thread versions, but most badges were in aluminium or grey thread on a field grey or blue-grey cloth patch, grey predominating after June 1940. In 1944 this patch was sometimes triangular in form. There were many variations, but the most common were of the so-called BeVo-style weave and, by late in the war, most eagles were machine-sewn using poor quality synthetic fibres.

Another standard item of insignia were the collar litzen. These very Prussian military badges continued to be worn on tunic collars throughout the conflict and essentially consisted of two bars of lace with additional lace imposed to show branch colours. Dress versions for officers were in metallic lace and arm-of-service colour backing, but those worn in the field were of grey or aluminium thread and, by 1940, on grey-blue cloth patches. Those for other ranks were of inferior materials and, during the war, were often sewn directly to the collar.

The litzen for other ranks were modified during the course of the war. Older patterns with strips of branch

▲ **Senior Corporal, Machine Gunners, 62nd Infantry Regiment, 1943** *German infantry much preferred the black leather boot to the ankle boot. These boots were 35cm (almost 14 inches) tall, although over time they were made progressively shorter to save on leather. They had metal reinforcement to the heel and studs. The tall boot was something of a status symbol and the Austrians were mocked by the Germans in 1938 for their reliance on ankle boots.*

◄ *A troop of German infantry reserves, led by two officers on horseback, march to the front down a dirt road through Dobromil-Przemysl, Poland, c.1940.*

colours continued to be worn even though in 1938 a standardized style came into use with grey-green separating the grey bars and replacing the coloured strips. By 1940 the lace was grey, the pattern was simplified and the backing had disappeared.

Unit badges

Cuff bands are associated above all with the SS, but a number of units adopted them. Personnel who had fought in the Spanish Civil War were authorized the Spanien cuff band, although these were mostly technical advisors. The Grossdeutschland, an elite unit, should have worn cuff bands from June 1939, but black bands with gothic lettering were issued in October 1940.

The List Infantry Regiment (Hitler's old unit) were issued bands in 1943; the Felderrnhalle also had bands between September 1942 and June 1943. A band bearing the name of General Dietl was supposed to have been issued to some units in October 1944. It seems that officers of the 17th Infantry Regiment continued the tradition of wearing the Brunswick Death's Head, a badge which dated back to 1809. Cuff bands also existed for those personnel who had fought in Crete (mostly paratroopers), Metz (in 1944), the Kurland pocket and Africa.

Rank insignia

Senior German NCOs wore an embroidered aluminium-fibre edging around their collars and shoulder straps (the outer end of the sergeants' strap was unadorned). It was a style of ornamentation dating back to the 18th century. Tropical tunics had the same, but in a light brown thread. Junior NCOs then displayed rank insignia on their upper left sleeves of their tunics.

◀ **Rifleman, 504th Infantry Regiment, 1942** *Wartime modifications made the uniform plainer. The shoulder straps were now plain and devoid of ornamentation, and soldiers often wore their shirt collars out to cover the lace on the collar.*

▶ **Lieutenant, 116th Infantry Regiment, 1943** *The peaked cap shown here was the preferred headgear of German officers. This smart version has a blue-green band piped in white. The oak leaves are also on a blue-green backing cloth, although a more olive cloth was sometimes used. The leaves act as a wreath around the national cockade. It is worn without a chinstrap, and so there are no buttons on the side of the cap.*

▼ **Infantry Kit** *German infantry still carried a heavy burden, even though the pack was now lighter than before. From top left to bottom right: chocolate ration in a round tin; gas mask; canteen; cutlery set; gas mask cylinder; and belt buckle bearing its Gott Mit Uns motto.*

For corporals it was a single silver-grey inverted chevron on a patch of green-blue cloth; they added a pip if they had six years of service. Senior corporals had two such chevrons and the so-called stabsgefreiter, or career corporal, had two chevrons and a pip. Privates first class had a pip in a cloth disc on their sleeves. Senior NCOs, those traditionally entitled to wear sword knots, had their rank shown as pips on their shoulder straps, although sergeants had no pips – just the embroidered braid edging. Adjutants had one pip, aspirants had two and senior adjutants had three. Aspirants had cloth bands in branch-of-service colours to reflect their unique standing as officers in training. Officers wore a different style of shoulder strap dating back to 1864. Second lieutenants, lieutenants and captains wore aluminium or matt aluminium braid in a U-shape that was cut straight at the end of the shoulder. The braid was worn on backing cloth in branch-of-service colours and lieutenants had a gold pip, captains had two. For majors, lieutenant colonels and colonels the braid was interlaced. Lieutenant colonels had one pip, colonels had two.

For those items of dress that were worn without shoulder straps, cloth patches bearing rank insignia were developed and were issued in August 1942. These were designed to be worn on the sleeve of anoraks, snow and reversible anoraks, jackets and shirts as well as overalls for artillery and panzer troops. It consisted of horizontal bars on a black rectangle, officers adding oak leaves above their bars – so that a captain would have three bars with oak leaves above.

Officers and senior NCOs had the right to wear sword knots, and these were generally in aluminium braid but with a knot of coloured braid to denote regimental staff (dark green) or company within a battalion (white, red, yellow, blue and light green).

Reserve officers, and those of the Landwehr, were entitled to wear officers' straps, the only difference being that Landwehr officers had the military district number in roman numerals in white metal insignia.

Specialist badges

In July 1942 the Crimea Shield began to be issued to personnel who had participated in the conquest of the Crimea – this badge showed the eagle and swastika above the peninsula. In November 1942 the Nahkampfspange was authorized for personnel who had fought hand-to-hand with the enemy. It came in bronze, silver and gold and was to be worn above the left breast

◄ **Sergeant, 2nd Infantry Regiment, 1943** *Greatcoats that were designed for sentry duty were lined with sheepskin around the torso and were very warm. Too few were issued for the Russian winter. This sentry also wears the overboots made from felt and with a wooden sole.*

► **Sergeant, Grossdeutschland Regiment, 1942** *This NCO has a fur-lined peaked cap to protect him from the rigours of winter. It came with ear flaps and a thick lining. The fur was either white, as shown here, or black. It usually bore just the eagle emblem.*

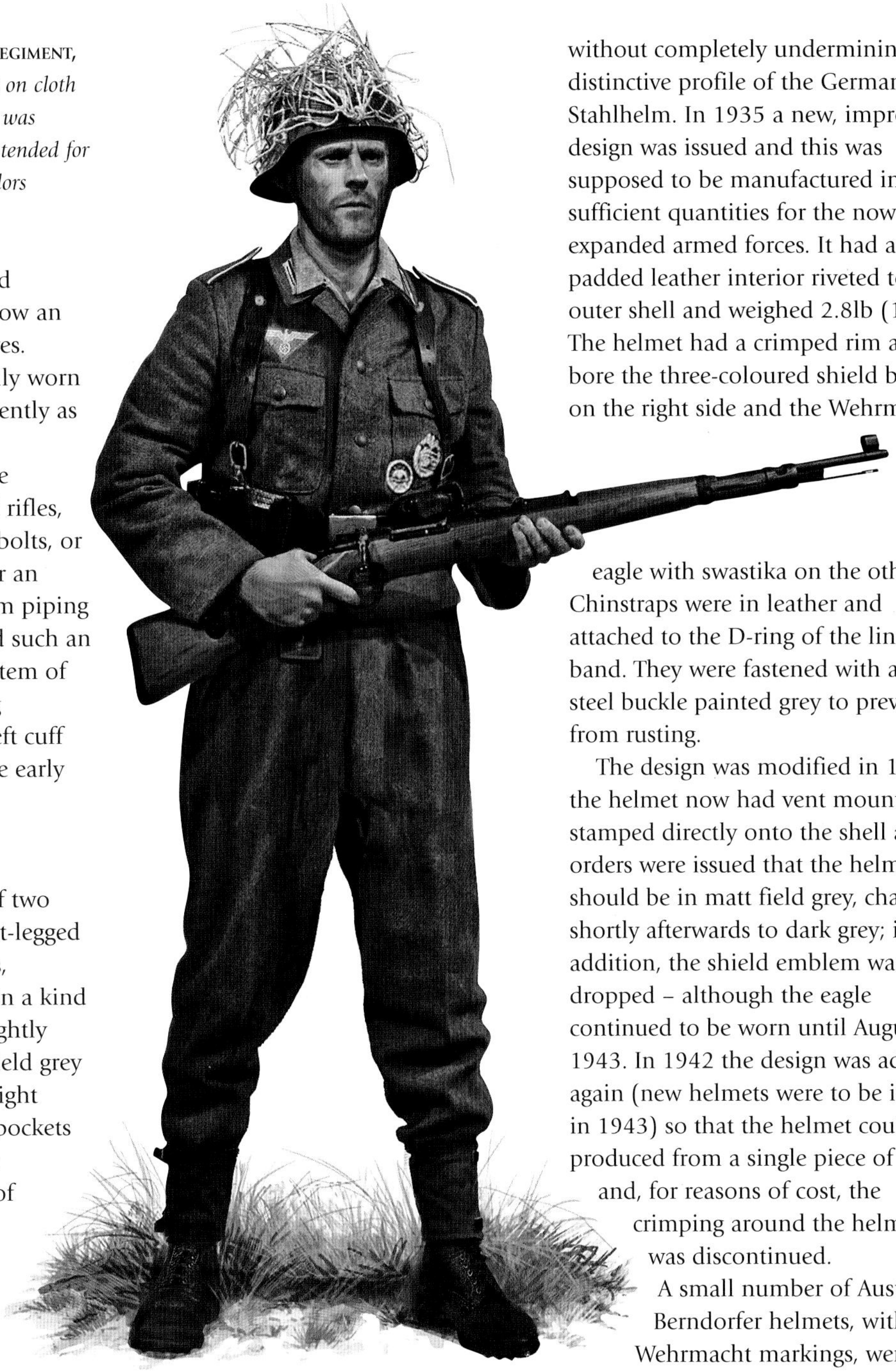

▶ **GRENADIER, 916TH GRENADIER REGIMENT, 1944** *The 1944-pattern tunic saved on cloth and resembled British battledress. It was issued in olive grey cloth and was intended for the Wehrmacht, as well as those sailors serving as marine infantry.*

pocket. It consisted of a crossed bayonet and hand grenade below an eagle and swastika on oak leaves.

Technical badges were usually worn on the right sleeve, most frequently as discs of field grey cloth with a specialist insignia in the service colour. Armourers had crossed rifles, radio operators had lightning bolts, or an 'M' with a lightning bolt for an electrical mechanic. Aluminium piping was added for NCOs who held such an official position. An earlier system of denoting marksmen by having aluminium bars sewn to the left cuff seems to have continued in the early years of the war.

Trousers

To begin with, trousers were of two main types. There were straight-legged trousers and, for many officers, breeches. These were initially in a kind of grey known as new grey, slightly different from field grey, but field grey was adopted in 1940. The straight trousers had two vertical side pockets and a small fob pocket on the front. Officers' breeches were of superior cloth and the inner leg was often lined. Piping down the outer seam was sometimes worn. In 1943 a kind of pantaloon was introduced, then in 1944 a baggy field trouser with under-foot ties was also issued.

Trousers were commonly worn with soft-leather marching boots or, increasingly, ankle boots and buckled leather gaiters (1933 pattern). Officers preferred the long riding boot, but by 1943 these were being discouraged and officers advised to wear trousers with gaiters (the older leather version or cloth gaiters issued in 1941) and ankle boots. These ankle boots were either of the 1937 pattern or the 1944 pattern, simplified with five lace holes down the front. Felt outer boots, for those on sentry duty, or for drivers, were issued in limited numbers.

Helmets and caps

The steel helmets produced between 1916 and 1918 were still in service by the early 1930s and were still being manufactured for the rump armed forces. (The Reichswehr was briefly interested in a plastic helmet being tested in 1932). Tests were undertaken at Thale in 1934 to improve the design and effectiveness of the old version without completely undermining the distinctive profile of the German Stahlhelm. In 1935 a new, improved design was issued and this was supposed to be manufactured in sufficient quantities for the now expanded armed forces. It had a padded leather interior riveted to the outer shell and weighed 2.8lb (1.3kg). The helmet had a crimped rim and bore the three-coloured shield badge on the right side and the Wehrmacht eagle with swastika on the other. Chinstraps were in leather and attached to the D-ring of the lining band. They were fastened with a single steel buckle painted grey to prevent it from rusting.

The design was modified in 1940: the helmet now had vent mounts stamped directly onto the shell and orders were issued that the helmet should be in matt field grey, changed shortly afterwards to dark grey; in addition, the shield emblem was to be dropped – although the eagle continued to be worn until August 1943. In 1942 the design was adjusted again (new helmets were to be issued in 1943) so that the helmet could be produced from a single piece of steel and, for reasons of cost, the crimping around the helmet rim was discontinued.

A small number of Austrian Berndorfer helmets, with Wehrmacht markings, were used by the Germans.

German troops wore several varieties of soft caps. A peakless side cap was issued in 1934 with the national cockade below an upturned chevron of service colour lace. It was originally tall, with the cockade at the top, but the cockade quickly dropped towards the base of the cap and, sometimes, the national eagle was worn above.

In 1942 a new version with buttoned-up flaps was issued, and in 1943 a peaked cap based on that of the mountain infantry was also produced. The peaked tropical service cap first

◀ MEDIC, 88TH INFANTRY REGIMENT, 1942 *Medical personnel were identified by the Alskulapstab and serpent device. This sometimes featured on the shoulder straps, but could also be worn in an oval on the right sleeve of the tunic. The collar litzen lace would also have bands of dark blue within the aluminium lace.*

▶ GRENADIER, 1053RD GRENADIER REGIMENT, 1944 *This grenadier has fashioned his tent canvas into a poncho. Essential equipment, including the entrenching tool, went into a protective sleeve made from compressed card edged with leather strapping.*

appeared in 1940 and was worn in the Balkans, Mediterranean and southern Russia – as well as in Africa. It had a light blue eagle on a brown cloth backing, a national cockade, chevron of lace, stiff pick and red lining.

Officers made use of similar caps, but also wore a soft cap with leather peak and grey crown. Their formal cap was the stiff-peaked Schirmmütze. This had a vulcanized black peak and cap band, and a dark green-blue band piped in service colours; these colours were also on piping around the crown. The cockade within oak leaves was worn on the front of the cap band.

Greatcoats and coats

In September 1935 a grey greatcoat with a blue-grey collar was introduced. It was double-breasted and with large side pockets. The darker collar was replaced by grey in 1940 and by a larger fold-up collar in 1942; a bulkier coat for sentry duty, the Wachmantel, with a cloth hood, was issued in small numbers. Greatcoats could be worn open at the collar by those personnel awarded the Iron Cross. Officers had the right to wear a long coat in leather, a raincoat, a cloak or a coat with a fur collar.

In addition to the long greatcoat, other outer wear items were developed. In the winter of 1942 a number of Army units made use of light grey working overalls to serve as camouflage in the snows of the Eastern Front; white cotton smocks were issued thereafter. Camouflage smocks, made out of camouflage tent fabric issued in 1931 were also popular, as were, later, camouflage items borrowed from the Italians and the SS.

A popular item was the reversible hooded parka. This was white on one side and olive or green on the reverse; a small number had camouflage patterns rather than oliver or green. It could be pulled close at the neck with drawstrings, as well as at the end of the coat. The mountain infantry version, with straps on the cuffs, under the groin and at the neck, was also popular. Sheepskin coats, as well as the Windjacke anorak, were also common. Removable shoulder straps could be worn on the Windjacke, the greatcoat and the leather coat worn by many motorcyclists.

Equipment

Army personnel were issued with a leather waist belt with a white metal buckles bearing the inscription 'Gott Mit Uns' ('God with us') around an eagle; officers could also wear a standard pronged buckle or, on more formal occasions, an oval buckle on an aluminium and black belt. A Y-shaped combat harness (only issued up to 1939) helped carry the load of supporting six blackened leather cartridge pouches – these dated from 1911; SMG ammunition was carried in a rectangular canvas pouch. Frogging for the bayonet and for the entrenching tool (with the shovel head being housed in a leather cover) was attached to the belt.

The 1934-pattern knapsack made from cow hide. It was rectangular and had blackened shoulder straps. Greatcoats and tent canvas were often strapped around the top. Aluminium mess tins and cooking pots were carried inside the knapsack. The replacement 1939-pattern knapsack had modified straps and buckles now that Y-shaped combat suspenders were no longer to be worn.

▲ *A Nazi propaganda photograph shows German troops taking possession of Tallinn, then known as Revel but now the capital of Estonia, in late August 1941.*

Canteens and flasks, mostly made from aluminium but later from coated iron painted khaki, and first issued in 1931, were worn under the knapsack or on the hip.

The distinctive metal gas mask canister (the 1934 pattern, the 1935 pattern with its improved fastening method or the longer 1938 pattern for the rubber mask) was also usually worn on the lower back. The most common version was the 1938 pattern. At the front an anti-mustard gas cape was often carried in a rectangular bag on the chest. Canvas bread bags were also carried, the most common being the 1931 pattern; the 1944 pattern included a rectangular pocket to house rifle-cleaning tools.

Lighter field equipment generally consisted of ammunition pouches, tent canvas, bread bag, flask, gas mask canister and a smaller olive-coloured canvas pack. The tent canvas, in camouflage material, was usually worn as a poncho or cape.

Officers often carried leather map cases, and were equipped with pistols (Luger or Walther) worn in a leather holster on the waist belt. A Sam Browne-style belt and shoulder belt was authorized in 1934, but the waist belt was often deemed to be sufficient. The belt could be used to support a dagger or bayonet; swords were no longer carried.

◀ **Infantry Sniper, 58th Grenadier Regiment, 1945** *This sniper carries a Gewehr 1943 semi-automatic rifle and wears a reversible parka which came with a wide hood. The coat itself was lined and padded, although the hood was not. The boots shown here are the 1942-pattern felt boots, which closed at the back with a strap and buckle at the top of the boot.*

AFRICA CORPS

German troops were sent to support the Italians in North Africa and, by doing so, threaten the supply lines running through the Suez Canal.

Desert combat

Plans were drawn up in late 1940, but it was only in early 1941 that German troops began to be sent from Italy to Africa. These were to be mostly motorized or armoured troops as the Italians had fared badly in the fast-moving fighting over huge distances offered by desert fighting.

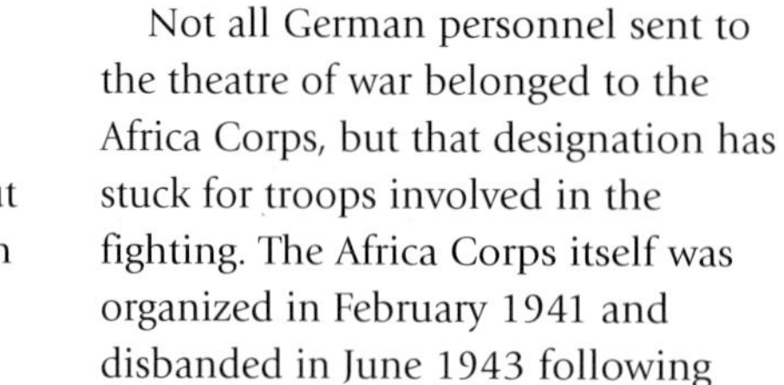

Not all German personnel sent to the theatre of war belonged to the Africa Corps, but that designation has stuck for troops involved in the fighting. The Africa Corps itself was organized in February 1941 and disbanded in June 1943 following defeat in Tunisia.

Initially, troops consisted of a small headquarters unit (guarded by a battalion of the 357th Infantry), the 90th Light Division and the 15th and the 21st Panzer Divisions (this latter formed from the 5th Light Division), plus various flak and supporting units. The Africa Brigade 999 (later a division of the same number) also served in Africa in 1943. It was significant in that it was a penal unit.

Tropical dress

The first troops to arrive in Africa wore the 1940-pattern tropical tunic. This was usually olive green in hue, but the conditions and the sun soon faded the material into a number of shades ranging from light brown to light green. The cut was similar to the field grey versions worn by troops in Europe. However, distinctions were usually on khaki material patches – so the patch for the tunic eagle device, the triangular patch for the rank chevrons on the arm and the shoulder straps were of khaki cloth. Litzen on the collar were of aluminium thread on a patch of khaki or light green cloth. A khaki shirt and khaki or black tie was worn with the tunic. Shoulder straps were piped in the branch-of-service colours. The Africa Corps consisted of very few standard infantry regiments, so most infantry straps were piped in the golden yellow of motorized infantry of light divisions, or the grass green of motorized infantry of armoured units. These straps were mostly plain and so devoid of unit numbers or camouflage slides.

◀ **INFANTRYMAN, 347TH INFANTRY REGIMENT, 1941** *This soldier is one of the first to be sent to support the Italians in North Africa. Subsequent arrivals would add the sleeve band bearing 'Africa Corps' and their eagle insignia on the tunic would be backed with a more appropriate olive material.*

▲ *Soldiers of the German Wehrmacht in Africa fit desert clothing and a sun helmet to a newly arrived conscript soldier in 1941.*

The Africa Corps armband was only adopted in July 1941 and was to appear on the tunic, greatcoat and the formal Waffenrock tunic. It was to be worn by members of units assigned to Africa, personnel in depots of such units and personnel sent to European hospitals. There were two designs, the common version in aluminium thread on a green cuff band with brown outer edge, or the later Afrika within two palm trees on khaki cloth.

Baggy pantaloons or trousers were popular in the heat of Africa and these were worn with the high brown boots, laced the full length up the front. Ankle boots and gaiters were commonly worn with the longer baggy trouser or Italian long trousers, or socks and boots with khaki shorts. Greatcoats, in brown or green woollen cloth, were also worn in order to cope with the cold desert nights.

◀ **Panzer trooper, 15th Panzer Regiment, 1942** *The side cap, in tropical colours, was also worn in Africa and came with a ventilation hole on either side of the cap. The pink lace over the national cockade has faded, but it shows that the wearer was part of a panzer division (as do the skull devices on the lower lapel).*

▶ **Sergeant, 3rd Aufklärungs Detachment, 1942** *Peaked tropical caps came in many variations. This individual's cap is piped in chestnut brown, which has faded to beige and goes without the inverted chevron of lace in branch of service colours, sometimes worn above the national cockade.*

Headgear

The first German troops sent to Africa generally wore the domed canvas (or felt) tropical helmet in khaki or light green. This had the normal eagle badge and national shield applied to the sides, was edged in leather and had a leather interior band. The lining was usually red, and the vent holes were placed at the top. Italian models were also used, and some Luftwaffe personnel even had blue versions.

The standard helmet, often painted sand brown, was unpopular because it was excessively hot to wear. A more practical item of headgear was the peaked cap. The tropical cap (known as the Afrikamütze) had been developed in 1940 and was manufactured in cotton twill from then on. The caps were lined in red, and two air vents allowed the head to cool. The cockade, on a cloth diamond or round patch, was on the front below a chevron or soutache or service-coloured lace (a convention dropped in 1942) and beneath the eagle emblem. Officers seem to have added silver piping to the top of the crown.

Armoured troops

There was a preponderance of German personnel in Africa belonging to armoured formations. In contrast to the situation in Europe, where panzer troops carefully crafted a distinctive look, armoured troops in Africa tended to follow the overall Africa Corps appearance, although some artillery personnel did wear the short jacket. In part this was because the black tunics and trousers of the panzer corps were impractical. Instead, panzer troops in Africa opted for the tropical tunic with shoulder straps piped in pink (or red for self-propelled artillery).

Panzer personnel did sometimes, however, attach the Death's Head emblem to their collars and a few troops wore the black side cap or peaked cap. Reconnaissance troops, of which there were a number of detachments, had golden yellow distinctions.

Sonderverband 288

This unit was raised from Germans who had experience of African conditions or of North African volunteers. Members wore a distinctive badge on the upper right arm – a palm tree in a wreath with a setting sun, all on a green disc. The unit became a panzer grenadier regiment in 1942.

THE SS

The initials SS stand for schutzstaffel, German for 'protective shield', and this elite corps was initially formed as a bodyguard for the Nazi leadership. As the war progressed their role expanded.

Waffen SS

In 1938 the Waffen SS was organized into four distinct regiments (Stanndarten), two motorized battalions, an engineer battalion and various supporting services. By the war's end there were more than three dozen divisions incorporating 800,000 personnel drawn from across Europe.

Tunic

The SS received its own tunic before the war began: which initially had a blue-green collar. It followed the Army pattern in other respects and in subsequent changes, mimicking changes in the Army pattern, with the loss of the coloured collar being the most notable alteration, the 1943-pattern tunic very much resembled the army pattern of the time. However, the breast eagle device was moved to the upper left arm and it had a distinctive design. Instead of litzen on the collar the SS wore two black tabs (piped in silver from the rank of Sturmscharführer upwards). On the wearer's right the black tab received the SS runes in aluminium thread, while the tab on the wearer's left received rank insignia.

Rank was shown on the collar and on the shoulder straps. The shoulder straps were black and were piped in branch-of-service colours. These generally followed the system of the Army – with white for infantry, red for artillery, black for engineers, lemon yellow for chemical troops, pink for panzer troops (although panzer grenadiers generally elected to keep the white of the infantry, spurning the grass green of the Army equivalent), yellow for cavalry and reconnaissance units, light blue for the train, dark

◄ **Private, 26th SS-Panzergrenadier Regiment, Hitlerjugend Division, 1944** *The camouflage smock came in a number of different variants. It was manufactured from light green cloth, and the pattern then applied. It was elasticated at the waist and at the cuffs and a cord, passing through 10 holes, closed the front. Most smocks came with slits in the front that allowed access to garments or equipment underneath.*

► **Corporal, 35th SS-Panzergrenadier Regiment, Reichsführer-SS Division, 1943** *Soldiers of the SS assigned to Italy, Greece and southern France often wore a robust shirt in khaki cotton. This came with ochre trousers, although camouflage trousers, as seen here, could also be worn.*

◀ **SS Adjutant, 2nd SS Panzer Regiment, 1944** *The Feldmütze Alter Art was comfortable and very popular. It had no stiffeners, giving the grey crown a soft look, and there was also the possibility of wearing it without the corded chinstrap seen here on top of the peak. The peak was vulcanised but was not especially rigid.*

▼ **Sergeant, 3rd Totenkopf Infantry Regiment, 1944** *This soldier carries the Sturmgewehr 44 which was light, easy to manufacture and accurate, but also capable of firing around 400 rounds per minute. Ammunition is here carried in rectangular canvas pouches that fastened with leather straps and buckles.*

▲ **SS Collar Badges** *1 Panzerschütze, 2 Panzeroberschütze, 3 Sturmmann, 4 Rottenführer, 5 Unterscharführer, 6 Scharführer, 7 Oberscharführer, 8 Hauptscharführer, 9 Sturmscharführer, 10 Untersturmführer, 11 Obersturmführer 12 Hauptsturmführer, 13 Sturmbannführer, 14 Obersturmbannführer, 15 Standartenführer, 16 Oberführer.*

blue for the medical services, orange for gendarmes and light green for mountain troops. A number of SS units bore ciphers or initials on their shoulder straps, such as the 'Leibstandarte' or 'Das Führer' cypher, or 'D' for Deutschland; very rarely, unit numerals were also worn on the strap but removed when on campaign.

Marks of rank

Rank was also shown on chevrons on black triangles (points down) below the eagle device on the sleeve. Green bars on black rectangular patches were worn by some officers on items of clothing that were not suitable for shoulder straps – superior officers had bars beneath an oak leaf device. On the lower sleeve of the tunic most units wore a cuff band signifying the SS division or, more rarely, the constituent regiment. This was usually black, inscribed in aluminium thread, with aluminium borders. Under the tunic a khaki shirt, with falling collar, was worn. This could be adapted to take shoulder straps. As the war continued these shirts, and the tunics, were made of poor quality fabric.

Unit types

Panzer troops usually wore the black short jacket, or Feldjacke. The pink piping around the collar patches was, however, discarded, and the Death's Head badge usually worn by Army panzer personnel was absent from the collar; SS collar patches featured instead, and officers had silver piping to the

▲ SS Second Lieutenant, SS Aufklärungs Abteilung, 1940 *Panzer and reconnaissance units largely began the war wearing a black beret, known as the basque beret. German troops had a relatively large version that proved too bulky to be worn inside the vehicle, and also proved to be difficult when headphones had to be worn. They were largely phased out in early 1941.*

collar. The shirt and tie worn under the tunic were usually black, as were the breeches or trousers, with only the crown of the cap on the officer's peaked cap and the ubiquitous side cap being in field grey. Self-propelled artillery crews usually had the short

► SS Female Auxiliary, 1943 *Women wore their own style of tunic and these usually had the SS runes within a black oval on the breast pocket. The sleeve badge indicates that this person worked in transmissions.*

jacket, too, but in field grey and with red distinctions.

In 1943 a distinctive camouflage jacket was issued to armoured crews. This was reversible, with camouflage material on one side and khaki cotton on the other. Mountain troops were accorded the right to wear the edelweiss arm and cap badge.

Headgear

Helmets were of the same type adopted by the Army – however, the SS had SS runes in black on a white shield on the wearer's right side of the helmet and a swastika party shield on the left. Helmets were more and more frequently covered with camouflaged helmet covers. This usually matched one of the patterns used in the manufacture of smocks and jackets, and the cover was pulled tight by means of a drawstring tightened under the rim of the helmet. The camouflaged helmet cover had first been tested in 1937, and 6800 examples had been delivered to SS personnel by 1939, in time to be worn by frontline troops embarking on the French campaign.

The SS wore a peaked cap from 1943 onwards: this had the distinctive Death's Head device on the front or two buttons that kept the ear flaps in place and above the SS eagle, usually on a patch of grey or black cloth. The standard side cap was also worn, this time with the Death's Head device below a chevron (point upwards) of braid in the branch-of-service colours. The eagle was then placed above the chevron point. The cap was either in grey, black or more unusually sand-coloured cotton.

Officers wore peaked caps with black bands and white piping (although branch-of-service colours were sometimes preferred) above the band and around the crown, which was in cloth the same colour as the tunic. On the front of the band was the Death's Head in white metal. The cap was worn stiff, but supports could be removed to give the cap a less rounded crown. Black berets were initially worn by panzer troops, but they were unpopular and quickly died out.

Although no SS units fought in Africa the tropical helmet was worn by SS troops in Italy and the Balkans.

Outerwear and equipment

Equipment generally followed that in use by the Army, although the SS had its own distinctive belt buckle showing an eagle clutching a wreath and a swastika with the SS motto: 'Meine

Ehre Heisst Treue' ('My Honour is called Loyalty'). Officers could opt to wear an oval belt buckle bearing the same device.

The most significant development in terms of outerwear was the camouflage smock, or Tarnjacke. This item, like the camouflaged helmet cover, was developed before World War II and became the first significant item of camouflage wear (discounting the use of the 1931-pattern tent cloth). The smock was reversible and came in a blend of cotton and rayon material, and proved to be well camouflaged and comfortable. It was closed at the chest by the means of cords, was elasticated at the cuff and drawn tight at the waist. There were a number of variations. Early camouflage patterns were in dark green, with darker and lighter green spots, then with black and brown added. The famous splinter pattern camouflage was issued in 1943, but was not unique to the SS. Subsequent patterns saw a palm leaf pattern, but the late-war variants were most usually a brown and black dot pattern (issued in 1944) on a light brown field.

A tunic of camouflage material, was devised in 1944 to replace the field grey version, but it was only issued in very limited numbers.

Divisional distinctions

The Leibstandarte SS Adolf Hitler wore the cuff band 'Adolf Hitler', the letters 'LAH' on the shoulder straps and SS runes on the collar patches. The Das Reich had 'Das Reich' cuff bands (from 1943); and SS runes on the collar patches. The Totenkopf had a skull insignia on the cuff band before 1943, when it was replaced with 'Totenkopf', and also had the Death's Head on their collar patch rather than the usual SS runes. The Hohenstaufen, Frundsberg and Hitlerjugend all had cuff bands and SS runes on the collar patch.

Himmler's bodyguard, the Reichführer SS, formed a panzer grenadier division in 1943. It had 'Reichführer-SS' on the cuff band, SS runes on the collar and, unusually, was uniformed in tropical uniforms. The Götz von Berlichingen panzer grenadiers were also formed in 1943, they had SS runes and a named cuff band, as did the Horst Wessel of 1944. The Florian Geyer Cavalry Division had runes on the collar patch and a named cuff band. Most of the personnel used the cavalry's distinctive yellow branch-of-service colour. The Dirlewanger Division, initially a brigade destined for those who had been transferred to punishment duty, had crossed gun barrels over a grenade on the collar patch.

▶ **SS Private, 1st Cavalry Regiment, Florian Geyer Cavalry Division, 1943** *The simple Feldmütze, or side cap, bore the SS skull and the national emblem of the eagle clutching a swastika. Both these devices were produced in aluminium or silvered thread – usually on black backing material, which was then sewn on to the cap. The cap itself was envelope-shaped, with a lower crown than the type produced in the mid-1930s.*

SS FOREIGN VOLUNTEERS

A large number of foreign volunteers from various countries joined the SS during the course of the war.

The Wiking Division

This panzer division took a number of western European volunteers. From September 1942 it had a 'Wiking' cuff title. Some regiments continued with a regimental title; the Germania regiment had a Gothic 'G' on the shoulder strap. The plan was to have a Viking ship device on the collar, but SS runes were commonly worn.

Balkan divisions

The Kama and Handschar SS divisions were mountain infantry raised in Croatia in 1944 and 1942 respectively. They had SS mountain troops' uniforms with a wheel device for the Kama and a scimitar-in-hand and swastika device for the Handschar. Both these Croatian units wore fezzes.

Albanians were grouped in the Skanderbeg division (mountain troops with double-headed eagle collar patch or crested helmet). Off duty, personnel wore traditional white caps rather than peaked caps.

Ethnic Germans formed the Prinz Eugen mountain division and had an Odal rune device on their collar and 'Prinz Eugen' band; a cuff title bearing 'Artur Phelps', to commemorate an SS general of that name, was worn by the 13th Regiment in the division from November 1944.

Other divisions

Latvians, Estonians and Ukrainians mostly formed Waffen Grenadier Divisions. Estonians seem to have had an armoured arm carrying a sword, Latvians three flaming stars – and the 2nd Latvian with a swastika. Ukrainians in the Galitzien Grenadier Division had a rampant lion patch, a device also worn by some personnel on a sleeve shield.

◀ **Private, 27th SS-Freiwilligen-Gebirgsjäger-Regiment, SS Handschar Division, 1944** *The Handschar Division was one of the stranger units of the SS, recruited as it was from Muslim personnel from Bosnia; some Arabs and Indians were later added.*

▶ **Private, 31st Waffen Grenadier Regiment, SS Galicia Division, 1944** *This division was recruited from Ukrainians and named after Galicia, once a province of ancient Poland. The lion rampant shown on the black collar tab was sometimes absent, in which case simple SS runes were worn.*

Dutch volunteers went into the Wiking Division. The Nederland Division, with a wolf-hook collar patch and 'Nederland' cuff bands (shortened from 'Legion Nederland'), also contained Dutch volunteers. The Langemark Division formed in 1944 (with a grenade device, or a three-armed swastika device worn also by the first unit of Dutch volunteers, the Westland). Belgians in the Wallonien Division had 'Wallonien' cuff bands and SS runes or the cross of Burgundy.

◀ SS Lieutenant, British Legion, 1944
A number of British and Dominion troops joined this corps and received a cuff title which bore the words 'British Free Corps' in Latin lettering.

▶ Private, 57th Waffen Grenadier Regiment, SS Charlemagne Division, 1945
This Frenchman is armed with a Panzerschreck in the ruins of Berlin. His uniform suggests that he previously served as part of the 8th (French) Freiwillingen-Sturmbrigade as they were issued with black collar patches and runes. Other Frenchmen, from the Légion des volontaires Français (LVF), for example, lacked these SS attributes.

French, Italians and Hungarians

The Charlemagne Division of Waffen Grenadiers was formed by French volunteers in 1945 with a cuff band and sword and wreath collar patch.

The Karstjäger Division served as mountain troops and had a crossbow collar patch device. Italians in grenadier divisions may have worn the fasces device on their collar. Hungarian volunteers were formed in Waffen Grenadier Divisions. with an 'H' device on the collar, or in the Maria Theresia cavalry division (cornflower device).

Danes, Norwegians and Finns

Scandinavians served in the Nordland division, with a sun collar patch, and the more famous Wiking Division. Troops in the Nordland seem to have worn Danish or Norwegian flags on shield arm patches. The Danish Free Corps had cuff titles bearing 'Freikorps Danmark', and albeit briefly, Danish flags instead of a collar patch device. It was later absorbed by the Nordland, as was a similar Norwegian legion. It had a Norwegian lion collar device and Norwegian shield badge on the sleeve above a cuff title. Finns serving in the Finnish Battalion, had a cuff title bearing 'Finnisches Frw. Bataillon der Waffen-SS' (Volunteer Finnish Battalion of the Waffen SS).

Soviet divisions

Russian troops formed two Waffen SS Grenadier divisions late on in the war. The first had RONA (POHA) shield patches (black Maltese cross on a white shield trimmed in red, beneath POHA) with a Maltese cross collar patch. It was absorbed by General Andrey Vlasov's army. The second just had an Orthodox cross on the collar patch. Cossack units, formerly recruited into the Army, were transformed into SS Cossack units in 1944. They did not change their uniform. The remnants of the eastern legions were reformed, some personnel making up a new SS Eastern Turkic detachment with a wolf's head insignia.

Other volunteer groups

A small Indian unit existed with a tiger head on the collar patch, as did a British free corps numbering around 30 men. This latter initially wore SS runes but a collar patch of three lions was adopted. It wore Union Jack sleeve shields and the cuff-title British Free Corps. Spaniards formed two SS companies, Bulgarians formed two regiments (with rampant crowned lion patches), as did Romanians (crossed swords with oak wreath device).

FOREIGN ARMY VOLUNTEERS

The German Army raised a number of units from foreign volunteers or prisoners of war.

Croatian

Volunteers from Croatia, organized by the client regime, were sent for service on the Eastern Front and were initially organized into the 369th (Croatian) Infantry Regiment. A Croatian shield with the traditional red and white chessboard pattern with the title 'Hrvatska' above was worn on the left sleeve and the shield was also on the left side of the helmet. The shield on the sleeve was later worn on the right sleeve.

► **Sergeant, 638th (French) Infantry Regiment, 1942** *The Légion des volontaires Français (LVF) was formed from anti-Bolshevik volunteers in France, mostly drawing on the various right-wing inter-war organizations (many of which had their own paramilitary formations).*

French

The Légion des volontaires Français (LVF), consisting of French anti-communist volunteers, formed a regiment in German service (the 638th Regiment) in late 1941. It wore a French tricolour shield on the right arm – also worn, but not systematically, on the helmet.

The Légion Wallonie – also known as the 373rd (Wallonien) Infantry Battalion – was formed from French-speakers in Belgium. It had a similar uniform to the 638th Regiment, but with the title 'Wallonie' and a Belgian flag shield. It was attached to a mountain division in 1942 and received 'Edelweiss' badges – the Belgian shield then being worn on the left sleeve.

Indian

In 1941 Indian prisoners and volunteers were recruited into the Free Indian Legion, also known as the 950th (Indian) Infantry Regiment. Uniform was German in style, although Sikhs won permission to wear grey or khaki turbans, but with a shield in Indian colours, a tiger and the title 'Freies Indien'.

◄ **Captain, 3rd Kuban Cossacks, 1943** *Slavs in German uniform had been expressly forbidden from wearing the German eagle insignia on the right breast. Instead they were issued with the grey and green emblem seen here.*

An Arab unit was formed in 1943, becoming the 845th German-Arab Battalion and serving in the Balkans. It wore tropical uniform with a shield bearing 'Freies Arabien' below an Arab flag and two white stars set in a red triangle and the same in Arabic above.

Soviet

The Germans initially raised units from ethnic groups such as Balts and Ukrainians who were deemed anti-

Soviet, but by the end of the war had a large number of former Soviet citizens in uniform. These varied from the ad hoc Hilfswilligen (Hiwis, often only identified by a white armband stating they were in Wehrmacht service) and Osttruppen, to the late-war units of the Russian Liberation Army (ROA).

Aside from the Balts and Ukrainians (who were gathered into auxiliary police units, with grey uniforms and black caps), six national legions were formed in 1942: Turkmenistan Muslim; Volga-Tartar; Georgian; Armenian; Azerbaijan; and North Caucasian. These all received national arm shields and coloured cockades. To these legions were added a number of Cossack units, the Terek, Don and Kuban units receiving their own designs of arm shields and cockades.

Cossack-style hats and breeches were worn with German tunics (often without litzen but with red collar patches, bearing crossed lances from 1943 and piped white for officers or green for troopers, and red shoulder-straps or piping). The Eastern battalions usually wore German tunics with green shoulder straps piped red, but without the German eagle or litzen. These units were usually used to form the ROA with a more formalized uniform. Personnel wore German uniform with an ROA shield (blue cross of St Andrew on a white disc on a red shield, beneath the Cyrillic POA). It also seems that they had a red and blue cockade and distinctive shoulder straps (with red piping) and collar patches (a white bar on a green patch). Only in 1944 did they start to wear German rank insignia and litzen.

A number of units formed the RONA (POHA) Army in 1943 – see the section on the SS.

Spanish

Spain had received assistance from Germany in the Civil War, and Spanish volunteers enthusiastically offered to join in Hitler's campaign against the Soviet Union in 1941. The 262nd, 263rd and 269th infantry regiments were formed by Spanish volunteers, these forming the 'Division Azul' ('Blue Division'). The name derived from the blue shirts worn by members of the Fascist militia, the Falange. Members of the Falange wore their cross-and-five-arrow badge on the national shield of their new German uniforms, with other members of the Blue Division having the unadorned Spanish shield badge (under the title ESPAÑA) and helmet badge. The unit largely returned to Spain in late 1943, although a reduced Blue Legion continued in German service.

In August 1944 the Army's volunteer legions were largely transferred to the Waffen SS.

◀ **Private, 263rd Infantry Regiment, Spanish Azul Division, 1942** *Spanish volunteers in the German Army wore a national sleeve badge on the right sleeve of their tunic and on their greatcoat. It came in two types, a simple tricolour badge (red over yellow over red) or the same but with a black iron cross pierced by five silver arrows.*

▶ **Sergeant, 845th German-Arab Battalion (Free Arab Legion), 1943** *The Arab Legion, recruited in North Africa and the Middle East, had a shield badge with Arabic motto. Arabic was also used on the shield badge of the Turkmenistan Legion, despite the fact that Arabic was not one of the languages used there.*

CAVALRY

German cavalry regiments had a long and distinguished history but were subjected to a complex reorganization when the Army mobilized in 1939.

Transition after World War I

The cavalry arm had not proved especially effective on the Western Front between 1914 and 1918, but played a more useful role in the war against Russia. Following the Versailles Treaty of 1919, the number of regiments was reduced – but not excessively so, because Germany was denied heavy weaponry. The regiments that survived were reorganized in 1935, but then largely converted to reconnaissance units in September 1939.

In 1935 five regiments were converted to panzer regiments, then the rest of the cavalry (renamed Kavallerie rather than Reiter regiments in 1936) saw some squadrons equipped with bicycles or armoured cars; only the first five squadrons were now mounted.

In September 1939, 13 cavalry regiments were converted into reconnaissance detachments, although the 21st and 22nd regiments were briefly raised in December 1939 as mounted units. Cavalry personnel undertook tactical reconnaissance, but in 1942 cavalry regiments began to be reformed on the Eastern Front, the most significant being the Regiment Nord, the Süd and the Mitte; some other ephemeral units, such as the 105th Regiment, were formed but their existence was short-lived.

Riders

Cavalry were uniformed with a standard Army helmet, side caps and tunics. The distinguishing colour of the cavalry arm was yellow, and so shoulder straps for other ranks were piped in this colour. Even after many of the units were converted to reconnaissance detachments, mounted personnel retained the yellow colour as a sign of distinction

◀ **Lieutenant, Nord Cavalry Regiment, 1943** *The German Army saddle had been introduced in 1925, to be taken from stock when the previous saddle was worn out. It came in five sizes, was manufactured from wood and linen (with some metal plates), covered in leather and with leather skirts, all padded on the underside. Equipment, including a gas mask for the horse, was then arranged around the saddle.*

▲ **Sergeant, 21st Cavalry Regiment, 1940** *German cavalry had been accustomed to carrying their equipment in saddlebags but as cavalry were performing a more demanding role, often on foot, tests were made to convert one of the saddlebags into a backpack. This was first tried in early 1940 and was then worn on the Y-straps. These straps were quite practical, although the back strap came in one size only.*

and tradition and even some motorized units, which should have had brown piping, retained yellow; this particularly seems to have been the case with cavalry personnel making up the 24th Panzer Division, who should have had pink piping but clung on to yellow.

On the cloth side cap the strip of lace above the national cockade was yellow. Officers had yellow underlay on their shoulder straps, with piping around the band and crown of their peaked caps. One unusual addition to the shoulder strap was the upturned horseshoe worn by officer-instructors of riding schools. These individuals tended to have piping in the carmine pink of the veterinary service rather than the yellow of the cavalry. Vets wore serpent insignia on their shoulder straps along with the veterinary company number in Arabic numerals.

Breeches were standard issue for mounted personnel. Officers often wore garments of a superior cut, with chamois leather lining along the inner thigh to reduce wear and tear from constantly being in the saddle. Riding boots were worn with buckle-on spurs.

Distinctions

While cavalry regiments had worn their unit number in Arabic numerals on their straps, reconnaissance units added a Gothic 'A' above their new detachment numeral. Cyclists added an 'R' (after 1936, previously they had used infantry service colours), instruction detachments had an 'L' (but no numeral) and remount or central training schools wore their district numeral in roman numerals. Yellow was also the distinguishing colour of motorized infantry in light divisions. When the Regiment Nord was formed it decided to continue the tradition of wearing the Prussian Death's Head on their peaked caps and on their shoulder straps – a symbol that had begun life as the insignia of Prussia's Leib Hussars. The insignia was in silver for other ranks and gold for officers. The regiment became the Feldmarschall von Mackensen Regiment in 1944, but the tradition continued – and a black cuff band bearing the von Mackensen name in aluminium thread, and between borders of such thread, was also then worn at the cuff.

Farriers wore a round cloth disc with an upturned horseshoe, master farriers added a pip below the horseshoe. Other specialist badges generally followed the examples worn by the infantry, but usually in yellow rather than white.

Equipment was similar to that worn by the infantry, but a lot of equipment was carried on the saddle. The cavalry had its own Y-belt (adapted in 1940 to carry one of the saddlebags on the rider's back), with three straps of blackened leather connected by an iron ring. On the waist belt hung the ammunition pouches, a bayonet suspended using frogging, a canteen and gas mask canister.

▶ **Private, 105th Cavalry Regiment, 1942**
The cylindrical gas mask container was a distinguishing feature of the German military, and contained the 1938-pattern gas mask. The cylinder came in two sizes, 27.5cm or 25cm (10.8in or 9.8in); and was produced in large numbers from 1930.

Arms

German mounted personnel tried hard to retain the sabre. It was still commonly seen being carried by mounted troops in 1940, but largely died out from then onwards; the lance, synonymous with German cavalry in World War I, had been abolished in 1927. The most common German sabre was still the 1897 pattern, although many officers carried their own personal side arms.

The most common type of saddle was the 1925 pattern in natural leather. It came in five different sizes. Leather saddle packs were placed on either side or worn on the rider's Y-belt; the rider placed a rolled grey blanket and camouflage tent canvas behind him, to his left usually carried a bucket-type carbine holster – although the carbine was sometimes worn slung over the shoulder.

ARTILLERY AND ENGINEERS

German artillery and engineers enjoyed a formidable reputation. Artillery became progressively motorized, and technical troops became more and more specialized.

Artillery

Aside from artillery attached to infantry units, including mortars and flak (which used infantry service colours distinguished by a 'GW' or an 'FL' respectively), German artillery included field regiments, horse artillery, motorized units, mountain artillery, flak, fortress, railway and self-propelled artillery.

Artillery, unless it was mounted or motorized, followed the principles of infantry uniform (with mountain infantry being uniformed like mountain infantry), but had, with few exceptions, red as a service colour. Field artillery had the unit number on shoulder straps, horse artillery (one regiment) added a Gothic 'R' above their numeral. Flak detachments had a winged howitzer insignia with the detachment number while observers added a 'B'. Landwehr artillery seem to have worn their district number in Roman numerals. Railway artillery added an 'E', although armoured trains had pink as a service colour. Artillery units forming part of the Grossdeutschland division had 'GD' added to their shoulder straps.

Units tasked with laying down smoke cover (Nebeltruppen) had burgundy as a service colour. Train units, often charged with carrying munitions, had light blue as a distinguishing colour.

Self-propelled artillery were slightly different in that, from 1940, they began to wear the panzer-style jacket – but in grey. The short jacket was worn with a khaki shirt and sometimes a black tie, and had seven metal buttons down the wearer's right-hand side. The upper collar was limp and bore litzen with red lace.

Shoulder straps were to have red piping or backing cloth for officers; unlike panzer troops, these artillery units were not supposed to wear the Death's Head on their collar patches. However, it seems that they did wear such insignia as, in 1943,

◀ **Lieutenant, 242nd Sturmgeschütz Brigade, 1943** *Self-propelled artillery were caught between thinking of themselves as tankers and being part of the artillery. The result was a hybrid uniform. This officer has the black peaked cap common to the panzer units. This had two buttons (sometimes also painted black) that let down a flap to cover the ears, and was piped around the crown in silver or aluminium thread.*

▶ **Lieutenant, 1st Horse Artillery, 1940** *German horse artillery had been formed into a group of mounted artillery, but this was transformed into a regiment of horse artillery at the end of 1939. The Gothic 'R' on his shoulder strap, which would be in gilt metal for officers, stands for Reiter.*

they were ordered to be removed. Motorized anti-tank units seem to also have worn the Death's Head. These overalls meant that adjutants wore their rank insignia on the sleeve in the form of aluminium-coloured rings. Specialist metal badges were worn on the tunic, for example the flak or coastal artillery badges.

Engineers and pioneers

German engineers were mostly organized into Pionier battalions. A Pionier was a specialist assigned a range of engineering combat activities, and these troops were often employed to open the way for an assault or to cover a retreat; casualties were heavy.

The general uniform was as for the infantry, but with black distinctions. They had battalion numbers (in black bordered in white thread) on a dark green-blue shoulder strap or on a grey-coloured strap. Engineers assigned to fortresses had a Latin 'F' with their battalion number, while railway engineers had an 'E' over their detachment number. Personnel in the Grossdeutschland Division again added the entwined 'GD' insignia to their shoulder straps. Technical troops, a category that only became operational in 1942, had a Gothic 'T' and instructional personnel had an 'L'. Tank engineers intertwined black and white on their shoulder straps. Bridging units did not wear a distinguishing insignia, but engineers based on river craft did have an anchor device on their shoulder straps. Labour battalions had initially worn light brown as a service colour, as had reservist engineers, but these changed to black in October 1943 in reward for good conduct. Personnel charged with overseeing prisoner labour squads had a pick and shovel device on their straps.

▶ **Pioneer, 11th Pioneer Regiment, 1942** *German flame throwers had proved their worth in World War I. A less bulky model was produced in 1935 and an improved model of that (the Flammenwerfer 41) was brought out in 1941 and began to be used in 1942. It was lighter and contained a mix of tar and petrol.*

While the uniforms of the pioneers followed the style of the infantry, equipment differed. In March 1941 a special backpack was introduced. Canvas side pouches were to be worn instead of ammunition pouches – these pouches were drawn tight with draw strings and were supposed to carry grenades. They also had a lined compartment for the gas mask and side pockets for ammunition. The backpack contained a mess tin but also compartments for smoke grenades and explosive charges. This equipment was to be issued to selected individuals.

Additional equipment included the entrenching tool, suspended from the waist belt, an axe (with a leather cover over its head), a saw in a black leather sheath, and a pioneer's toolkit in black leather. Wire cutters, in long or short versions, had their own black leather covers and were suspended from the belt. Officers tended to restrict themselves to the carrying of pistols and whistles as badges of authority, as well as selected specialist equipment.

◀ **Lieutenant, 291st Artillery Regiment, 1940** *A German artillery officer would have made good use of his field telephone to communicate with headquarters, or to liaise with other batteries or neighbouring units. This type, the ubiquitous Feldfernsprecher 33, came in a Bakelite case.*

Communications

Personnel wore lemon yellow as a service colour from April 1936, when the colour was changed from light brown. Personnel tasked with experimental testing wore a Gothic 'A', those involved in interpreting intercepted transmissions had a Latin 'D'. Oddly, war correspondents also had lemon yellow branch-of-service colour, but this was only until 1943 when the colour was changed to grey, coincidentally also the colour of the propaganda units.

PANZER TROOPS

Thanks to early victories over Poland and in western Europe in World War II, panzer units won a tremendous reputation. A distinctive uniform accompanied their enhanced status.

Blitzkrieg

Under the Versailles Treaty of 1919 Germany was banned from having tanks, but by 1934 the treaty was largely irrelevant and the Army set about raising and equipping armoured units – initially called combat vehicle troops, but renamed armoured troops in 1938. The troops were to be dressed in black and to receive the Death's Head emblem as a mark of distinction, because Prussian hussars had worn black with silver lace and had a skull on their caps, so tradition was maintained. The skull was also worn by stormtroopers and the Freikorps, so appealed to the Nazi elite.

The distinctive double-breasted short jacket, issued in black, was supposed to have been worn by tank crews while in the vehicle. It was worn with a grey shirt (later field grey) and black tie, and the top of the jacket was usually left undone to show these items. Cuffs were buttoned to allow the crews to wear gloves comfortably. The collar was initially piped in pink (golden yellow for reconnaissance troops and an unusual white-and-black for engineers), and service colour was also shown on the piping around the black shoulder straps and the officers' strap underlays. The collar was largely unpiped, and free from NCO braid, by 1942: NCOs wore lace around the cuff instead. Collar tabs showed the silver Death's Head and these tabs were also piped in service colours – again discontinued from 1942 as coloured lace became scarce. Collar litzen were restricted to a few staff officers. The tunic had the usual eagle device in aluminium thread on a black patch of cloth. Self-propelled artillery had red distinctions (and grey tunics) if they were independent formations, or pink if they were within panzer units.

Trousers, also in black, were buttoned at the ankle (to give a baggy look) and had a strap that fitted under the foot and stopped the garment from riding up. Greatcoats

◀ **Sergeant, 6th Panzer Regiment, 1940**
Headphone receivers with the ingenious throat microphone (Kehlkopfmikrofon) were an important piece of equipment for the tankers who rolled into France in 1940. The headphones were sometimes worn over one ear, with one ear uncovered so that the tanker's own crew could be heard.

▶ **Sergeant, 33rd Panzer Regiment, 1942**
This panzer NCO has been awarded the Iron Cross but also wears the panzer combat badge. This was issued to tank crews who were veterans of three battles fought on three separate days. The cuff bands denote rank, as do the pips on the shoulder straps and the metallic piping around the strap edges (not worn around the collar).

◄ **Private, 11th Panzergrenadier Regiment, 1944** *The tank destroyer sleeve badge was issued to those individuals who had single-handedly knocked out an enemy tank. This panzergrenadier wears canvas gaiters and ankle boots; by 1944 these were much more common than the early-war leather boots.*

► **Lieutenant, 7th Panzergrenadier Regiment, 1945** *This officer is barely distinguishable from his men and wears a camouflage smock to cover his field grey tunic. He does, however, carry the rare MP-43 assault rifle, which usually found its way to elite units or officers.*

were as for the rest of the Army, but these were not popular or especially practical for panzer troops and so parkas or anoraks were preferred. In 1941 a practical overall was issued. It had a large pocket and was usually made from thick grey material, allowing it to be worn as winter wear over the black tunic. Rank was shown on rectangular patches; green bars and oak leave combinations denoted rank.

Headgear

Panzer units were issued with black berets padded with artificial sponge to prevent head injuries, lined with oil cloth and bearing the national cockade in oak leaves on the front, below an eagle device. It was elasticated around the edge to keep the item in place, and there were six air vents to allow the circulation of air. The beret was largely abolished in January 1941, after which only drivers of armoured cars generally wore it. In March 1940 a black side cap had been authorized for panzer troops, and the wearing of the grey side cap had been banned; khaki items were worn in the south, and then in Africa. A soutache of pink lace was worn above the cockade and officers added aluminium or silver piping around the top of the caps. In 1943 a peaked cap was introduced usually embellished with insignia as per the side cap.

Equipment was kept to a minimum. Most crewmembers had a pistol to hand, but seldom wore a holster, which could snag in the confines of a tank. The Germans were the first to issue throat microphones in 1935 and replacing them, in 1938, with a variant that was used for the next seven years. This, the Kmfa, was modified, but never entirely replaced; an economy version was brought out in 1944.

Special insignia

The Grossdeutschland Division had an entwined 'GD' on their shoulder straps and a cuff band on the sleeve, the Felderrnhalle units wore a distinctive insignia of an 'SA' badge and runes on their shoulder straps after June 1944, as well as a cuff band. The 90th Panzer Grenadier Division wore a badge representing Sardinia and a sword. The 24th Panzer Division used yellow piping, distinguishing themselves as former cavalrymen. The 19th Panzer Division wore a wolf's hook device on its caps, while the 116th had a hare.

Panzer grenadiers

Motorized infantry were renamed as panzer grenadiers in the summer of 1942. They were given distinctions in grass green (darker green than the mountain infantry), although a few clung to yellow or pink with their distinctive Gothic 'S' (for Schützen).

MOUNTAIN TROOPS

Germany had raised specialist units for operations in mountainous regions in World War I, and the Wehrmacht continued the tradition.

Formation

Germany's mountain troops were principally formed of regiments of mountain infantry (the Gebirgs Jäger). By the end of 1940 there were 13 active regiments, with an unusual numbering: the 13th, 85th, 91st, 98th, 99th, 100th, 136th-139th, 141st, 142nd and 144th. More were added in 1941, and some high mountain battalions were also added in 1942; two Ski Jäger regiments were also formed, as well as some ad hoc battalions partially created from cycle battalions.

The mountain infantry should not be confused with the Jäger battalions that were formed as light infantry in 1942, but which performed the standard infantry role; the Jäger battalions also has light green piping but had a green oak leaf badge on their sleeves and in metal on their caps. The most famous unit among these was the Brandenburg Division.

Tunics

Mountain infantry wore infantry tunics (in all their variations), but with shoulder straps piped in light green. The regimental number initially appeared on these straps, but – as with the infantry – bands were placed over this designation or the numeral was removed. The tunic was sometimes modified so that the collar could be buttoned to ensure that the collar remain upturned.

◀ **Private, 12th Mountain Infantry, 1944**
It was common for German soldiers to have award badges pinned to their tunics. This mountain infantryman has the infantry assault badge (also known as the infantry combat badge). It was first awarded in December 1939, in silver, but a bronze class began to be awarded, too, from 1940 onwards and this was intended for motorized units. It consisted of an oak leaf wreath and a rifle under an eagle and swastika.

In addition, mountain troops were authorized to wear an edelweiss arm patch on their right sleeves 16 cm above the elbow. First issued in May 1939, the edelweiss patch had white petals, yellow stamen and green leaves below. It was surrounded by a chain device in aluminium thread. The insignia was issued on a disc of green blue, or field grey, but rarely sewn directly on the sleeve cloth. Mountain personnel assigned to other units sometimes continued to wear this insignia, and this was officially authorized in 1944.

Caps

Mountain troops did wear steel helmets on occasion, but far more common was the peaked cap. The mountain troops' peaked cap (bergmütze) had two buttons which, when undone, let down ear flaps. Above the two buttons were the national cockade (sometimes worn on a disc of green blue cloth) and the standard eagle. On the left side of the cap was a metal edelweiss badge, with the stem pointing towards the front – regulations were strict, it was decreed that the badge should be 20mm above the base of the cap band; the centre of the flower was often painted yellow, or in gilt for officers. In the summer months a grey or green shirt was worn, and this usually also bore the edelweiss emblem.

Greatcoats were dispensed with. Most mountain troopers preferred the reversible anorak (Windbluse), an ingenious item was of impermeable cloth (a blend of cotton and rayon, but subsequently mostly rayon); one side was white and the other light brown, olive or grey. The Windbluse had three chest pockets and came with a hood.

The cotton Windjacke was also worn. This was double-breasted, and was usually in light-brown cloth. It had four exterior buttons, two vertical ones above the hip and two horizontal ones

◀ **Private, 13th Mountain Infantry (Gebirgsjäger), 1940** *German mountain infantry tended to wear field grey breeches with leather straps to bind them tight to the calf. Some then opted for alpine socks, but green or field grey puttees were also common and these would have a buckle to stop them unravelling. These were worn above the natural leather boot (with ankle padding, gripons and seven lace holes).*

at the waist. The coat was usually worn with detachable shoulder straps, indicating the wearer's rank. The 1940 pattern was also worn by SS mountain troops.

Winter wear

The reversible Windbluse was often worn with reversible trousers (Windhose). When these were not worn, mountain troops had pantaloon-type trousers (berghose) that were tied below the knee, had two side pockets and a frontal pocket for a fob watch. They were baggier than the Wehrmacht standard-issue trousers. They were often worn with grey green puttees, which came in a number of different sizes, or with long alpine socks.

Ankle boots, specially adapted for mountain terrain, were also worn. These were made of brown leather with a band of field grey material lining the top to cushion the ankle. Crampons could be attached to the wooden soles (which, in any case, had metallic grips).

Shoulder straps were light green, but supporting troops belonging to mountain divisions usually retained their branch-of-service colouring: artillery would have red, engineers would have black and reconnaissance troops would have yellow.

Mountain troops did not carry knapsacks, but opted instead for an olive-coloured rucksack with black leather straps. First issued in 1931, this contained the usual mess tin and personal items, with tent canvas inside or worn as a poncho. Otherwise, standard infantry equipment was carried (with the addition of ice picks, ropes and snow goggles).

Ski troops

The Ski Jäger, of which there were two numbered regiments as well as various detachments, wore badges based on that of the Jäger – that is, green oak leaves in a blue-green disc piped in aluminium thread on the sleeve, and a metal oak leaf device on the side of the cap; they had two skis across the sleeve badge and a single ski across the cap badge.

▶ **Captain, Skijäger-Regiment, 1943** *The German Army had many gloves, from the white ones worn on parade, through the grey ones worn by officers (with one or two buttons at the wrist) to the field grey textile gloves issued to other ranks. White camouflage gloves were also issued. This officer wears a privately purchased skiing glove of a type popular in the 1930s.*

PARATROOPS

Deprived of an air force by the Treaty of Versailles, Germany had to wait until the mid-1930s before embarking on a crash course of experimentation with paratroops (Fallschrimjäger). The results were successful and the Germans were amongst the most innovative exponents of the tactical use of airborne forces.

In 1937 an experimental company of paratroops was formed by the Army. Until 1938 these paratroopers wore white piping on their shoulder straps with a Gothic 'L', and then 'FJ' in Gothic letters until January 1939 when they were transferred to the Luftwaffe. Expansion followed rapidly and there were finally 41 numbered regiments (numbered up to 63, but there were gaps) plus ad hoc units and battalions of paratroop machine gunners, mortar personnel and anti-tank detachments initially identified by Gothic lettering on the shoulder straps. The strangest units of all were the projected regiments of paratroop panzers formed in 1944 – but these, perhaps wisely (given the potential difficulty of airdropping heavy equipment), were abolished before seeing action.

▲ *German paratroops land and collect their chutes to prevent the wind from catching them and dragging them across the ground.*

Specialists

Paratroops then adopted the Luftwaffe tunic in blue with collar tabs in golden yellow, a colour also shown on the shoulder strap piping. These tabs showed the different ranks by means of insignia representing a bird in flight. NCOs had different numbers of such insignia, officers added oak leaves below and officers from major upwards had wreaths around the bird symbol. Rank was also shown on the shoulder strap as well as, for NCOs, aluminium chevrons on dark blue triangular patches (point down) on the sleeve.

Tropical tunics were worn by paratroopers deployed to southern Italy, the Balkans and southern Russia but many chose to wear just the tropical shirt with or without collar tabs, but often with shoulder straps attached. Most paratroopers wore the distinctive light green cotton smock over this tunic. The first pattern was thought to have too many zips, so a simplified pattern was issued as the war began. It stretched down to the thigh, had generous waist pockets, vertical pockets at the top and was worn without straps – so officers showed their rank on dark blue sleeve tabs or did without recognisable rank insignia. The initial designs were step-in types, which were not especially popular or practical, and subsequent designs closed around the thighs with a series of studs. The Luftwaffe eagle was shown on the breast of the smock. Camouflaged versions, initially based on patterns used for tent canvas, began to appear later. Even by 1941 the splinter-pattern smock was still relatively rare. From 1943 on paratroops in Italy made good use of stocks of Italian camouflage smocks and material.

Greatcoats were not worn, but a variety of anoraks and parkas, including the useful reversible green/white hooded anorak, were very popular. Trousers were designed uniquely for paratroopers. Usually

◄ **Paratrooper, 2nd Fallschirmjäger (Paratroop) Regiment, 1940** *The Germans were advanced when it came to specialist equipment for airborne infantry. In addition to the practical smock, which reduced snagging and served as an overcoat worn over the field tunic, the paratroopers also had jump boots. These were in blackened leather and were laced up the sides (with 12 pairs of lace holes).*

worn with knee pads, they were of a generous cut, with a side pocket for the essential knife – paratroopers often needed a wooden-handled penknife to cut themselves free from their parachutes.

Helmets

The Luftwaffe introduced a specific helmet for paratroops in 1936. The 1936-pattern helmet was much lighter than that worn by the Army and had additional padding to the interior. The helmet was modified and, in 1938, an improved helmet appeared. This had a very secure grey leather chin strap and additional padding initially made out of chamois leather but, subsequently, synthetic materials. It was painted field grey, had the Luftwaffe eagle on one side and the national shield on the other; this was discontinued after 1940. Air vents were positioned just above these insignia. The field grey colour was not popular and helmets were subsequently painted green (or khaki or white, depending on circumstances). Camouflage nets and helmet covers were also added to break the helmet's rounded profile Paratroops wore distinctive blackened jump boots that laced up the side and had generous rubber soles.

Equipment

By 1941 most paratroopers were armed with MP40s since the carbine was not deemed sufficient; when jumping, they carried ammunition in appropriate pouches strapped to the leg – after landing these could be worn at the waist. Officers often preferred pistols. The FG42 automatic rifle was developed for paratroopers. Personal equipment was often kept to a minimum, paratroops keeping a flask and bread bag with them but little else.

◀ **Corporal, 5th Fallschirmjäger (Paratroop) Regiment, 1944** *The paratroopers' helmet was usually painted in matt field grey and with a Luftwaffe eagle emblem on the side. The chinstrap was of a special type that gave stability, but could also be released quickly. The strap itself was usually grey or black, but was often lined with chamois leather for extra comfort.*

▶ **Sergeant Major, 3rd Fallschirmjäger (Paratroop) Regiment, 1943.** *This individual carries the newly developed FG42 automatic rifle (Fallschirmjägergewehr 1942). The paratroops, being part of the Luftwaffe, made use of separate procurement channels from those used by the Army and this enabled them to order and obtain some unusual items of equipment and weaponry. This particular gun was first used in German paratroopers' daring rescue of Benito Mussolini from captivity in the Apennine mountains in September 1943.*

Containers, known as Waffenhalter, were dropped with the troops and these were later designed with small wheels so they could be pulled along.

German parachutes were, by all accounts, unsatisfactory. The common types were the RZ16 and RZ20, but these were poorly designed and difficult to control during the jump – which led to numerous landing injuries. The harness was securely attached to the chute with clips, but this also led to problems when landing: paratroopers either found themselves at the mercy of the wind or stuck, perhaps under fire, while trying to release themselves from the chute.

LUFTWAFFE FIELD DIVISIONS

The Luftwaffe began to form divisions for service in the field in the summer of 1942. There would eventually be more than 19 such divisions fighting on all fronts.

Regiments

A Luftwaffe field division was formed by Luftwaffe personnel, but such divisions were transferred to Army authority and so were then designated as field divisions (L). They were based on Luftwaffe Jäger regiments and fusilier battalions (and field regiments), with associated supporting personnel – artillery, anti-tank and engineer detachments.

Experimental storm regiments had been formed as early as 1940, but it was only in 1942 that the concept of Luftwaffe infantry really took hold. The Meindl Division (formed from field regiments in 1942) was in addition to the numbered divisions. Another such was the Hermann Göring Brigade – which began life as a regiment, was enlarged to a brigade in the autumn of 1942 with grenadier regiments and Jäger regiments and became a division in 1943; it was outside Army jurisdiction. It became a panzer division, then, in 1944, was rebranded as a paratroop-panzer corps.

The survivors from Luftwaffe field divisions were supposedly to be organized into an SS division (Reichsmarschall) late in the war, but the conflict ended before activation.

▼ *Luftwaffe pilots receive their orders from General Milch at an airfield in Berlin.*

Insignia

Shoulder straps in the field division were in blue cloth with the appropriate piping. This was red for flak and anti-tank artillery, pink for engineers, dark yellow for signals troops, dark blue for medical staff and green for the infantry. Infantry were mostly organized into Jäger regiments, but it seems that initially infantry carried on wearing the yellow patches of Luftwaffe ground troops, replacing these with green in late 1943. It seems that fusiliers serving in field divisions had the white distinctions of the infantry rather than the light green of the Jägers – something that became more common from July 1944. The 20th Division was a little unusual in that its officers adopted yellow as its predominant branch-of-service colour.

Gendarmes were given orange distinctions. Troops belonging to Hermann Göring units followed a slightly different system, with white collar patches piped white for grenadiers, pink for panzer units (green tabs piped in pink were used by anti-tank units), red for artillery and black for engineers. The panzer regiments of this formation usually wore the Death's Head device on their patches and most personnel wore the distinctive cuff band. Senior NCOs added aluminium braid around the edges of their straps and around their collars. Rank was also shown on the sleeve as chevrons on a triangular patch of blue cloth (facing point down). This had a black edge. Senior NCOs and officers had wings rather than this chevron device. Rank was also shown on the collar tab. This was unusual in that it was in green for the Luftwaffe divisional elements and piped in the branch-of-service colour (so an engineer

▶ **Fusilier, 43rd Luftwaffe Jäger Regiment, 1944** *There was a wide variety of camouflage material in use in the late-war Wehrmacht. This jacket comes complete with camouflage shoulder straps and is fastened by five buttons. At this stage these buttons were of synthetic material or plastic, although some officers retained painted buttons.*

◀ **Senior Corporal, 64th Flak Regiment, 1944** *Luftwaffe Flak troops had red as a branch-of-service colour and such units played an important part in attempting to stem the effects of Allied air superiority. This corporal wears the silver Flak badge instituted in July 1941 and designed by the notable German designer of war badges, Wilhelm Ernst Peekhaus. It was generally awarded for acts of bravery or for reaching 16 points (four points were awarded for hitting an aircraft, two if other guns were also firing at that aircraft when it was hit).*

would have green tabs piped black), but with the addition of silvered bird insignia (affectionately known as gulls). A private would have one, a lieutenant would have one over a strand of oak leaves, a major had one within a wreath of oak leaves. Senior NCOs added aluminium piping along the bottom and side edge, officers had such piping all the way around their patch.

Tunics were predominantly blue, until replaced by the Army's grey items. This Fliegerbluse tunic bore a Luftwaffe flying eagle clutching a swastika device on the tunic breast, but did not have pockets. Although greatcoats were issued with collar tabs or collar insignia sewn directly to the collar, a more popular item in combat was the camouflage smock, usually in splinter pattern. This was a simple garment, and cheaper to make than the paratroopers' smock, with five buttons and two buttoned waist pockets. Shoulder straps (sometimes in camouflage cloth) could be attached or tabs worn on the sleeve. The Luftwaffe eagle was usually stitched to the smock on the wearer's right. Trousers or pantaloons were also initially blue for these units, before being replaced by the Army's field grey as Luftwaffe stocks were depleted.

In the Mediterranean and southern regions (fighting mostly in Italy and the Balkans), tropical tunics were worn, with sand-coloured trousers or shorts and sand-coloured caps or side caps. Helmets were often painted mustard yellow.

The Luftwaffe field divisions wore a variety of headgear. The helmet, with Luftwaffe eagle device on the wearer's left side, was worn (with or without camouflaged helmet covers or with helmet netting for camouflage) as was the side cap (again with Luftwaffe eagle). Luftwaffe field divisions did not make use of the paratroop helmet, although it seems that in Italy some members of the Hermann Göring units did. In 1942 the Luftwaffe imitated the Bergmütze of the mountain troops by introducing a soft peaked cap in blue – this had a single button to the front to keep the ear flaps in place.

Luftwaffe divisions used a great variety of Army items, from anoraks to puttees, and, over time, the distinctive elements of Luftwaffe dress gave way to standard Army items. Some Luftwaffe units in Norway also made use of SS parkas and mountain gear.

▶ **Grenadier, 1st Hermann Göring Panzer Grenadier Regiment, 1943** *This unit fought in Italy, and a blend of dark-coloured items for use in northern Europe, and khaki items used in the south, was common. The cuff band or title was in silver or aluminium capital letters (Latin lettering) with white piping above and below. It was to be sewn 16cm (6.3in) above the end of the right sleeve. These were to be placed above cuff braid if any was worn; some senior NCOs still had cuff rings on their tunic cuff.*

THE LUFTWAFFE

The Luftwaffe won victory after victory in 1939 and 1940, but from then on it was downhill – as Germany's pilots and ground crews battled to stem the tide of Allied air superiority.

Luftwaffe personnel generally wore blue rather than the Army's field grey. Tunics mostly consisted of the popular Fligerbluse with shoulder straps, or for officers, the more formal tunic, all with the Luftwaffe eagle on the chest and with collar tabs on the stand and fall collar (or upper lapel of the formal tunic, which was then piped in aluminium braid). The shoulder straps were in a cloth that matched the colour of the tunic and were piped in branch-of-service colours. For the Luftwaffe these were white for generals, carmine red for staff officers, yellow for flying officers, bright red for artillery (predominantly flak), golden brown for signals troops, dark blue for medical staff, pink for engineers and light green for air-traffic control and direction. Flak units initially had their regimental number (or district number in Roman numerals) on their straps, but these were later covered up, removed or turned over for camouflage purposes.

Rank generally reflected the system in use within the Army, with NCOs adding aluminium braid around the edge of their shoulder straps and collars, and officers having aluminium-braded shoulder straps on underlays in branch-of-service colours. Rank was shown on the sleeve, either as aluminium chevrons on blue triangular patches (points down) just above the elbow or for senior NCOs and officers as a series of bars and wings in gold, positioned in the same place. Rank was also shown on the collar tabs, which were in branch-of-service colours and showed birds in flight (above an oak leaf insignia for officers and within an oak wreath for officers above the rank of major). Luftwaffe generals had gold devices on white collar patches.

◀ PILOT, 52ND FIGHTER SQUADRON, 1940
Pilots could make use of a number of different kinds of eye protection. There were goggles that were held in place with a green elasticated strap. These had interchangeable lenses (dark or clear) and were often produced by the P.M. Winter workshop. There were also Bakelite flying glasses (Splitterschutzebrille) that came with a peg to secure them to the nose or with an elasticated band.

▲ *Pilots of the German Luftwaffe board their type He 113 fighters in July 1942.*

Officers generally wore the standard peaked cap (with blue crown and Luftwaffe eagle and a cockade within winged oak leaves); other ranks favoured the side cap or from 1943 the peaked cap – not always in blue. Standard steel helmets (with the Luftwaffe eagle in white) were used by ground crew. Members of the civil defence services (Luftschutzwarndienst-LSW) used captured helmets or the so-called Gladiator helmet issued in small numbers from 1938.

Tropical dress

Luftwaffe personnel were posted to Africa, the Mediterranean and southern Russia and, in these warm climes, opted for topical dress. This was different from the khaki dress worn by the Army because it was of a very light sand-brown colour while the Army had a light sand-olive. Tropical caps, with peaks, were produced in cotton twill with a linen lining but, surprisingly, no air vents. The Luftwaffe eagle, on a patch of khaki cloth, was stitched to the top of the cap, with the cockade (also on a flash of khaki cloth) placed in the front centre of the band. Officers sometimes added aluminium piping around the crown or wore the more formal black-peaked cap with black cap band, cockade and winged oak

◀ PILOT, 106TH KAMPFGRUPPE, 1940
Bomber and reconnaissance pilots tended to favour the blue cotton flying suit because it came with artificial fur lining and kept the pilots warm at high altitude. It had an opening from the right shoulder to the left waist and this was closed with a zip. There were also zips at the groin, over the pockets and at the cuffs.

▶ PILOT, 27TH FIGHTER SQUADRON, 1942
Luftwaffe personnel in Italy, the Mediterranean and North Africa were issued with the domed tropical helmet. A blue version briefly made an appearance, although sand-coloured khaki was more common. The six-button tunic was also in sand-coloured khaki and Luftwaffe personnel in North Africa were entitled to wear the Africa Corps cuff title.

leaves. The crown was either blue or white. The most common tropical tunic was the six-buttoned, open-collared version with four pockets.

Flying equipment

Flying suits came in a number of different types. The most common were the dark blue suits that zipped from the left thigh to the right shoulder. These were fur-lined and had a fur collar, although summer versions existed in thinner cotton and without the fur. Further zipped openings were placed under the groin and down the side and inside of the lower leg. The cuffs also had slits that could be tightened with zips. There were also zipped pockets on the thigh as well as side pockets. The trouser legs were tucked into tall blackened flying boots (also with zips down the side) but, by the middle of the war, separate flying jacket and flying trousers were also manufactured. Fighter pilots often preferred leather jackets worn over the flying suit trousers.

Airmen wore brown leather flying helmets with goggles in flight, together with large leather gauntlets. Flying helmets usually came with integrated headsets that were covered in brown leather because they were sensitive items. Parachutes, life jackets (either inflatable or a bulkier version worn from 1943 filled with kapok fibres for extra buoyancy), oxygen masks (with two or three straps) and wrist compasses (or compasses attached to the belt) completed the picture. Most pilots were armed with pistols kept in the side pockets of their flying trousers.

Distinctions

Cuff titles were introduced in 1935. Commemorative cuff titles of blue cloth, with aluminium Gothic lettering, were issued to particular squadrons. These mostly commemorated aces of the last war, such as Max Immelmann or Manfred von Richthofen, although some Nazi officials and Luftwaffe senior officers were also accorded the same honour. In Africa pilots sometimes added an Afrika cuff band, others had the Legion Condor distinction or that commemorating operations over Crete (the Kreta band). A number of pilot, observer and glider pilot badges, and other awards, were worn on the tunic or, selectively, on the flying jacket.

THE SOVIET UNION

The Soviet Union had emerged from a bitter civil war, the repression and famine of the 1930s and a massive process of industrialization to assert itself as a great power. Although Germany's Nazi leader Adolf Hitler was convinced this was a facade, and that by kicking in the door he would make the whole system collapse, he was proved wrong by 1942. The brutality of the German assault, and the horror unleashed on the Soviet peoples, brought a significant and quick response. A wave of patriotism, and a sense that the Germans were waging a war of extermination, meant that those serving in the Red Army achieved the status of heroes. Often they were. Conditions on the Eastern Front (or, from the Soviet point of view, the Western Front) were horrific. The scale of the fighting was immense and without question it was the most significant campaign in the history of modern warfare. Victory there was central to the defeat of the Third Reich and the liberty of Europe.

▲ *Three Soviet infantrymen, sporting medals in the field, as was customary, pose for the camera with their Shpagin-designed submachineguns.*

◀ *Two USSR soldiers ride alongside a column of destroyed German vehicles in the Ukrainian city of Odessa, in April 1944.*

THE RED ARMY

The conflict on the Eastern Front was the pivotal campaign of the war, and saw 80 per cent of the fighting. Even during the brutal campaign following the Western Allied landings in Normandy in 1944 there were still twice as many German troops on the Russian Front as there were in the west.

The scale of the fighting, and the destructive nature of the conflict meant that the price for victory or defeat was incredibly high. The Soviets destroyed 600 enemy divisions and inflicted 4 million casualties on the Axis. The Soviets lost 8 million soldiers dead and 16 million civilians. Material damage was also significant: 6 million houses were destroyed and 100,000 farms. The country was impoverished by the conflict and lost the cream of its youth.

Misleading historical accounts

Perhaps because the sheer scale of the war on the Eastern Front is daunting, the conflict and the Red Army's role in it are poorly understood in the West. But there is an ideological dimension to the problem too. Soviet armed forces are too frequently seen through the prism of the Cold War that followed on from 1945. For nearly 40 years after the war the only detailed accounts of the Soviet military came through the portrayal and images of the USSR at war created by the defeated Wehrmacht generals.

▲ *Joseph Stalin, dictator of Soviet Russia, casts his ballot in the Lenin election district of Moscow during the first election to be held under the new constitution, December 1937.*

▼ *Soviet cavalry parade through Moscow on 7 November 1941 to mark the anniversary of the Bolshevik Revolution.*

That portrayal consists of waves of unthinking infantrymen throwing themselves against German machine guns, herded forwards by detachments of the Narodnyy Komissariat Vnutrennikh Del or 'People's Commissariat for Internal Affairs' (the NKVD), the Soviet law enforcement agency, shooting those who turned back. Of outdated and ineffective aircraft and tanks – apart from the lucky T34, Of a merciless political repression that would mean the Gulag (forced labour camp) or execution for any wrongdoers; and of the bitter winter, the saviour of the Soviet Union.

These accounts continue to dominate, but obscure a more complex picture. The Red Army faced a steep learning-curve, but emerged as a formidable fighting force. If it had relied simply on fear and harsh

weather it would not have achieved victory against as formidable an opponent as the German Wehrmacht.

Winning required well-motivated and well-equipped soldiers. The Red Army, just as with any successful fighting force, was not motivated by fear. True, discipline was strict. But the concept of NKVD troops mowing down the faint-hearted behind the front line is a myth; fleeing personnel were rarely shot because the army was in great need of manpower; for example, between August and October 1942, during the German push into Stalingrad, 140,755 soldiers were detained for being absent from the front; of these, 1,189 were executed while 131,094 were returned to their units. Nor was it the case that failure would mean being sent to the Gulag. Western historians often repeat that Soviet prisoners released from German activity were treated as traitors and imprisoned as punishment for not fighting to the death. This clearly isn't so as, after the war, by 1 March 1946, of the 4.1 million Soviet citizens repatriated from the West, 2.4 million of them had returned to civilian life, 0.8 million had rejoined the Army, 0.6 million had joined Army reconstruction units and 0.2 million were sent on to NKVD filtration camps for further questioning or detention.

Motivation to fight the Germans came from elsewhere. Most soldiers were aware of what had happened in the territories occupied by the Germans, how prisoners of war were murdered or starved to death and civilians treated as slaves. Many knew this was a war of survival – and this, combined with a surge in patriotism and a growing thirst for revenge, were often motivation enough.

As for the myth of 'General Winter' (the key role played by winter conditions), while the Soviets did have experience of fighting in cold weather, they were by no means exempt from its problems – as the Winter War against Finland so ably demonstrated. Indeed, the mud and then the cold seriously hampered Soviet capabilities just as much as they did their enemies.

▲ *Soviet troops and a KV1 on Moskovsky Prospekt during the siege of Leningrad, which lasted from September 1941 to January 1944.*

Shortages

Initially the Soviet soldier was not especially well prepared for the new kind of warfare about to be unleashed by the Germans. As with other armies of the period, there were important shortages, perhaps not unsurprising given the sheer scale of the Red Army. There was a lack of motorized transport, poorly armoured tanks and flimsy fighter planes. For the infantry, shortages of automatic weapons and anti-tank guns were particularly problematic. These limitations were insignificant when fighting the Japanese in 1939, but were critical when facing the well-armed Germans. In addition the dearth of good equipment, when combined with failures at the strategic level, meant that effective kit was poorly utilized, especially in the early years of the war.

Stalin and the German attack

One area in which the Wehrmacht generals did make a valid point in their accounts of the Soviets' war was with regard to the interference by their leader Joseph Stalin in military affairs. Between 1934 and 1938 Stalin conducted a series of purges of leading Soviet figures whom he accused of being internal enemies. The effect of this was to reduce the number of officers by 4 per cent; but, the most dramatic loss was at the head of the armed forces – where the entire high command was effectively removed and disposed of. The effect on morale was significant, as was the costly reorganization that followed the promotion of younger personnel.

Stalin's meddling was just as fatal on the eve of the German invasion when he insisted that reports of German preparations be ignored. NKVD border forces had gone on high alert on 18 June 1941, but were told not to shoot at aircraft overflying Soviet territory. Troops were not told to concentrate – and they remained dispersed and unprepared, despite clear indications that the Germans were massing.

When the onslaught came, it was terrible. The Germans were at the gates of Moscow and Leningrad before they had a significant setback and it was only with immense difficulty that they were turned back – and then, amazingly, rolled all the way back to Berlin. Only a motivated, effective, determined Army could have achieved such a reverse of fortune.

HARD LESSONS

The Great Patriotic War (the Soviet defeat of Nazi Germany in 1941–45) is a story of going from epic defeat to total victory. The first few months after the German invasion (as well as a number of campaigns in 1942) saw Soviet forces beaten by the Germans time after time. The Air Force was largely destroyed on the ground, the Navy was kept desperately at anchor, and Army division after Army division was dispersed, destroyed or captured.

The Soviets had been warned. Germany had rearmed, played a decisive role in the Spanish Civil War (1936–39) and had swept to victory in the west in 1939–40. In the east the Japanese had received a bloody nose at Soviet hands in 1939, but had overrun much of China by 1940. But the truth was that the Soviets were still absorbing these lessons when the Germans struck.

▼ *The German Wehrmacht and a cameraman from the Nazi Propaganda unit, cross the border of the Soviet Union on 22 June 1941.*

Unprepared for battle

The Soviet staff estimate in 1940 was that it would take five years fully to modernize the armed forces. In fact, between 1928 and 1938 plans were being drafted, redrafted, revised and changed so that the whole concept of an operational war plan became mired in confusion. In 1940 it was discovered that the most recent plan dated from March 1938 and took no account of the numerous developments between then and July 1940. Subsequent discussion envisaged a German strike into the Ukraine – which the Germans had occupied in 1918 and which would provide them with an abundance of raw materials. It did not properly foresee a German surprise assault at great speed and all along the line. These theories meant that the Red Army was badly deployed and, when the blow came, was not concentrated in these poorly selected positions.

The idea that the Soviets were sufficiently prepared to launch a pre-emptive strike against German forces has now largely been dismissed as fanciful. The Soviets' own plans for mobilization were not properly developed or implemented by May 1941 and the staff expected mobilization to be complete in some areas only by 20 July 1941. The result was that the Red Army was not really capable of defending itself. Individual units would fight well, and in desperation, but the Red Army would not act as a co-ordinated force and only rarely gained local superiority. It is customary to blame Stalin or communism for these shortcomings, but the situation was not so dissimilar from that prevalent in a number of western countries in 1940.

Reforms and improvements

The Spanish Civil War and war with Finland had revealed shortcomings in Soviet tactics, equipment and strategic assumptions. This led to an overhaul of armoured forces in particular, reforms that were still being put into effect in 1941. Reforms in an army of

▲ *Soviet tanks advance into battle carrying infantry. This is a classic image of the Red Army at war.*

5 million soldiers were inevitably complex and confusing, especially given the urgency of the situation. Particular deficiencies were highlighted, but only partially addressed by 1941. Soviet armour was numerous and some particular models – for example, the diesel KV-series and the T34s – were remarkable. However, most of the 12,782 tanks in the western districts in 1941 were placed in newly established armoured divisions that were still working out how to operate together as well as to combine their strength with infantry, artillery and air support. These were areas in which the Germans excelled. The Soviets learned the hard way, and at great cost, but, ultimately, they overtook the Germans when it came to combined-arms operations and Operation Bagration, the immense offensive that drove the Germans out of the Soviet Union, would demonstrate a conclusive superiority.

Deficiencies in armour were augmented by problems when it came to combating tanks. The Soviet 45mm (1.8in) anti-tank gun could penetrate a thickness of 38mm (1.5in) armour from 500 metres (1,600 feet) and 50mm (2in) armour from 100 metres (330 feet). Most German tanks had 50mm thick armour that rendered Soviet infantry vulnerable. Soviet artillery was well trained, but lacked mobility. Both these issues were tackled. Steps were quickly taken to augment infantry artillery and increase the firepower of infantry divisions. Artillery and infantry were made more mobile, and given armour and air support. Inadequate communication equipment in 1941 eventually gave way (with support from the US Lend Lease programme) to more modern systems and related improvements in command and control.

New Army, improved weapons

The old Army was literally and metaphorically destroyed in 1941. In its stead came a newer and more cautious military that soon wrested the strategic initiative from the Germans and built on small victories to achieve the stunning success at Stalingrad in 1942–43. In order to make this possible, Soviet industry was harnessed to the war effort. Much has been made of the feat of moving factories eastwards to avoid the Germans, but just as important were modifications made to the design of weapons so that they could be manufactured outside of arsenals and armouries, and produced quickly, cheaply and in great numbers. The number of semi-automatic Tokarev rifles surpassed 1 million in 1941, while 16 times more of the Ppsh submachine gun were produced in 1942 than had been made in 1941. By the middle of 1942 350,000 units were being produced per month.

Finally, a significant change came at the top. Officers learned their trade the hard way. Some 25 per cent of officers in 1941 had war experience, but the rest were poorly trained. This was also the case with the high command, which had also been gutted by the purges. This weakness was exacerbated by the fact that Stalin had interfered excessively in all aspects of military affairs until he felt it was no longer appropriate to link his name with defeat. His insistence that Soviet armies go on the offensive, time and time again, against a superior, fast-moving enemy, led to massive losses. When he relinquished responsibility, and allowed his increasingly experienced generals control of their own troops, the situation improved significantly. A number of intelligent, aggressive and talented Soviet generals emerged, Georgy Zhukov being the first amongst equals.

▼ *Georgy Zhukov, Marshal of the Soviet Union, poses in all his finery following the defeat of Germany in 1945.*

GENERALS

The rank of marshal of the Soviet Union had been introduced in 1935. There were five such individuals in 1940. The rank of general did not exist before 1940; instead, those in command of brigades, divisions and armies were known as kombrig, komdiv and kommandarm (first class and second class), plus marshals. In 1940 the system changed to major-generals (plus specialisms in the aviation, armoured, artillery, engineering, technical and staff services, with more being added in 1942), lieutenant generals (with specialisms as above), colonel-generals, army generals and marshals of the Soviet Union. In 1943 marshals (with specialisms) and senior marshals were added as ranks below marshals of the Soviet Union.

Generals had a degree of flexibility when it came to dress. Many adopted distinctive styles and items of dress used by more junior officers and, when at the front, ditched regulations in favour of more subdued, or more elaborate, dress.

Kittel tunic

In 1940 generals and marshals generally wore the kittel or open-necked French tunic. The kittel tunic had a stand and fall collar and was closed by five buttons. It had two breast pockets and was piped (generally in raspberry, although the cavalry maintained the traditional blue, and marshals and army generals always had raspberry piping) at the straight cuffs (pointed for aviation) and around the collar (additional gold piping was present for senior generals, set within the red piping). The kittel or French tunic was generally in khaki but a white version existed for summer use; generals commanding armoured troops favoured steel grey, while aviation generals adopted dark blue, at least before 1941. The collar tabs were in the shape of a lozenge and these were in branch-of-service colours (black for artillery, raspberry for infantry, blue for cavalry), apart from marshals and army generals who had red patches, with gold piping along the top edge.

Actual rank was shown by combinations of gold stars; red enamel diamonds had been used to designate the rank of commanders before 1940. A major-general had

◀ **Marshal, 1940** *Senior officers of the Soviet Union were uniformed in a simple but practical way. The only decoration consisted of rank insignia, awards and brass buttons, which from 1940 bore the seal of the USSR.*

▶ **Lieutenant General, 1941** *Winter uniform consisted of the astrakhan hat and the double-breasted greatcoat with brass buttons. In 1940 the cuffs on the greatcoat went from being pointed to being straight.*

▲ *General Emil Fred Reinhardt's 69th Division meets officers of General Vladimir Rusakov's 58th Guards Division on the Elbe.*

two stars, a lieutenant general three, colonel-generals four, army generals five and a marshal a gold star and wreath. Branch-of-service insignia were also sometimes worn, depending on the taste of the individual officer. Rank was also shown on the lower sleeve in the form of chevrons in gold and a gold star (which was larger for marshals and army generals, and smaller for the rest) piped in red or light blue for aviation generals. Up to the rank of colonel-general, the chevrons were in gold with a lower strip of the appropriate branch-of-service colour; army generals had gold chevrons with a red chevron above and thin red chevron below, while marshals had two gold chevrons on a red background with a gold star and wreath in between.

Coats and caps

Greatcoats, which were grey and double-breasted, bore the same rank devices but also had piping around the collar, cuffs and down the right front of the coat. Breeches were generally dark blue, with the appropriate piping down the outer seams and between gold generals' stripes. Long trousers with shoes could also be worn.

Generals and marshals wore the appropriate peaked cap but they had gold leaf embroidery on the peak and a yellow lace decorative strap. Simple white or khaki versions were preferred when in the field. In addition, they had the right to wear the tall fur papakha cap with red crown and yellow lace. It bore a round gold cockade with a central red star. This was also worn on the peaked cap.

1943 reforms

In 1943 shoulder boards were introduced and the collar patches described above were phased out. Shoulder boards for general officers were in gold thread (silver for some non-combatant roles such as medical or provost services) or khaki, and were piped in red (blue for aviation, raspberry for technical and supply services). Some generals wore branch-of-service insignia on their boards, but generally only rank stars were shown. Major-generals had one silver central star; lieutenant generals had two, aligned along the centre of the board; colonel-generals had three; army generals, four; marshals, a silver star within a gold wreath; senior marshals, a large gold star; and marshals of the Soviet Union had a gold star and, by the collar end of the board, a disk showing a hammer and sickle on a blue globe within a gold wreath (supported by 11 red bars representing the 11 constituent republics of the Soviet Union), all beneath a red star (the seal of the Soviet Union).

Tunics were generally piped as before, with red for senior generals or with branch-of-service colours for the more junior generals or specialist generals. Greatcoats received shoulder boards, too – as well as a rectangular tab that was in the colour scheme previously mentioned.

Equipment for generals was usually restricted to a leather belt with a star-design buckle and the integrated system of belts and equipment (map case, holster) issued in 1932. Sabres and daggers were also worn as a mark of authority.

▶ **Lieutenant General, 1944** *Shoulder boards, which had fallen out of favour since 1917, reappeared in 1943. This lieutenant general would have had two silver stars on a board of golden interwoven bullion thread. A brass button, by the collar, bore the Soviet seal.*

NKVD

The NKVD (Narodniy Kommissariat Vnutrennih Del or People's Commissariat for Internal Affairs) has received a great deal of attention in recent years, but confusion over its role and how it was organized persists. In the Soviet Union of the late 1930s and the war years it was the entity charged with security. To enable it to function effectively, it had its own troops, administered separately from those of the Red Army.

Evolution

The NKVD had evolved from the Cheka, the Bolshevik security service. In 1934, the formation of the NKVD was seen as a step towards simplifying the complex Bolshevik system. The NKVD was tasked with internal security, guarding state installations and dealing with internal dissent. In practice this meant that the NKVD was responsible for the border or frontier troops, guarding factories and prison camps and, when the 1941 war began, escorting supplies to the front (railway security and convoy troops). The NKVD's strength in eventually grew to more than half a million men and women by 1942 and included rifle regiments (some motorized), armoured battalions, convoy troops and artillery units as well as trained personnel dropped behind German lines to support the partisans (the so-called OMSBON brigade). It also had its own small air force, which, in 1941, consisted of a single regiment and several independent squadrons.

Later counterintelligence once again became part of the NKVD's role, although this largely became the task of the NKGB in 1943 (a task shared with the so-called Smersh or counter-espionage directorates).

NKVD uniforms generally followed the style of the uniform worn by the equivalent branch in the Red Army, so that NKVD rifle or interior

◄ **PRIVATE, 132ND BORDER GUARD REGIMENT, 1941** *Frontier guards were tasked with securing borders and patrolling lines of communication. The rectangular pocket lamp attached to his tunic is the Elektrit type common in the 1930s.*

▲ *The NKVD were notorious for political executions, such as here at Katyn, but also brutally killed border guards and rifle units.*

troops would follow the infantry style, and NKVD tank battalions would follow that of armoured troops. However, the NKVD had its own distinguishing insignia.

NKVD rifles

The NKVD uniform had evolved since the Revolution. A new uniform defined in 1935 and issued in 1936 drew on some of these traditions. The most common uniform was the khaki gymnastiorka tunic shirt or French tunic, with open-necked collar with shirt and tie. Dark-grey tunics were rare, although they were worn by NKVD personnel in armoured units. By 1940 the collar tabs for NKVD troops were dark red with a central raspberry stripe (gold for officers) and piping (gold for officers). There was also raspberry piping around the collar for officers (officers would have raspberry piping on their blue breeches) and at the cuff. Interior and rifle troops had the crossed rifles and target infantry badge on their collars (not always worn). Rank insignia generally followed the Red Army pattern but there were stars on the sleeve rather than chevrons and from 1940, a gold triangle in the corner of NCOs' collar patches.

◀ **Sergeant, 14th NKVD Rifle Regiment, 1941** *Some 13 rifle divisions were formed from personnel of the law enforcement agency Narodnyy Komissariat Vnutrennikh Del (NKVD) during World War II. When not wearing the 1935-pattern peaked cap in NKVD colours, shown here, they wore standard Soviet helmets.*

▶ **Major, 290th NKVD Rifle Regiment, 1943** *In 1943 NKVD officers began to wear the smart kittel tunic with light blue piping at the collar, around the shoulder boards and on the straight cuffs. Unusually, the leather waist belt was worn under the tunic; it supports the Tokarev pistol holster.*

Greatcoats were of regulation pattern and the shape of the collar tabs followed that worn by the Red Army. They were in dark red with raspberry piping along the top of a shield-shaped patch. The cap worn by NKVD forces had a black peak, red band and a blue crown. The crown and band was piped in raspberry and bore the red star badge.

NKVD personnel also wore a distinctive insignia on their upper left sleeve, although this was often dropped when on campaign. It consisted of a hammer and sickle, with a sword above, in a silver wreath on a red background.

There were some modifications to this basic uniform in 1937 (political officers were now to have raspberry piping instead of gold). The oval badge was to be worn on both sleeves and ranks were changed to bring them more in to line with the Red Army equivalents. The biggest change was in 1943, however, with the return of shoulder boards (pagonii) and the absence of collar patches on the now slightly raised collar of the gymnastiorka. For officers, this or the tunic had blue piping at the cuff (usually absent on the summer tunic) and blue piping was also worn on khaki breeches.

The NKVD had a unique shoulder board shape and this was not as long as the Army's equivalent. The boards used on campaign were khaki, with blue piping for officers and NCOs and blue stripes (or brown for NCOs), in a style that followed the Army's system of red piping for other ranks (red boards piped blue for service dress). Sometimes NKVD rifle units painted their regimental numeral onto the boards, adding the letter K after their numeral; railway security troops added the Cyrillic letter 'Ж' and industrial security added a Cyrillic 'P'.

Border guards

There were border units attached to the Army, Navy and Air Force. They all wore distinctions that were added to the standard uniforms worn by the equivalent non-NKVD service. Border regiment personnel wore Army uniforms, but with green collar patches piped red or gold for officers. Their caps had a black band piped red and a green crown piped red. The 1943 uniform had green piping on the shoulder boards (and on officers' cuffs and breeches). The naval border force wore naval uniforms with sailors' caps with the inscription МОРПОГРАН–ОХРАНА Н.К.В.Д (coastguard of the NKVD). The NKVD's border air force wore Air Force uniforms, but with green patches piped red and green rank stars piped red on the sleeve.

INFANTRY

The backbone of the Red Army consisted of rifle regiments. These were dressed and equipped as uniformly as possible. A regiment was composed of three battalions and while the majority of the personnel consisted of infantrymen there were also various specialists within the unit's organization. Each battalion had anti-tank, mortar and heavy machine gun personnel, increased after the Winter War against Finland of 1939-40, and a platoon of signals troops. Regiments also included medical personnel and additional supporting artillery, signals, engineers and reconnaissance troops such as scouts. A rifle division would require additional logistical support (including a field bank), reconnaissance, technical troops (chemical companies from 1941), armour and artillery.

Specialists

Whilst most rifle regiments were of a standard or regular type, there were also some specialist mountain units, motorized and mechanized regiments (with personnel often armed with automatic weapons) and machine gun battalions. From 1941 onwards, there were also rifle units that received Guard status. In support of the Soviet war effort, and in addition to these different kinds of rifle regiments, there were also armed militias, penal units and, of course, partisans.

Red Army infantry had improvised uniforms until 1919, when a more systematic approach was taken. The civil wars were still raging, and it was not possible to supply uniforms throughout the Red Army, but the 1919 uniform with its arrow-headed chest straps and pointed caps were recognizably different – the irony being that a uniform in this style had been rejected by a commission tasked with designing a new uniform in 1914. These were abolished by 1924 when a new uniform, for soldiers of the recently established Soviet Union Army, was issued.

The next major development was the creation of the 1935-pattern uniform and it was this standardized dress that was most commonly seen when the Soviets went to war against Poland in

◀ **Private, 609th Rifle Regiment, 1940** *This infantrymen has the 1937-pattern cartridge pouches common to Soviet infantry. These came in natural leather, blackened leather or waterproofed canvas with leather straps. An additional pouch, wider and usually made from cloth, was sometimes also worn.*

▶ **Private, 37th Rifle Regiment, Winter, 1940** *Greatcoats came in a variety of cloths and colours from the grey preferred by regulations to the brown khaki used by suppliers in the south of the Soviet Union. The greatcoat was a comfortable garment, lined at the shoulders and at the chest, and adjustable thanks to a cloth belt to the rear.*

Ranks in 1940

Krasnoarmyeets (Red Army man)	Private	plain
Efreitor*	Corporal (introduced in 1940)	gilt triangle
Mladshiy Serzhant*	Junior Sergeant	gilt triangle, red triangle
Serzhant*	Sergeant	gilt triangle, two red triangles
Starshiy Serzhant*	Senior Sergeant	gilt triangle, three red triangles
Starshina	Sergeant Major	gilt triangle, four red triangles
Mladshiy Leytenant	Second Lieutenant	red square
Leytenant	Lieutenant	two red squares
Starshiy Leytenant	Senior Lieutenant	three red squares
Kapitan	Captain	red rectangle
Maiyor	Major	two red rectangles
Podpolkovnik*	Lieutenant Colonel	three red rectangles
Polkovnik	Colonel	four red rectangles

* introduced in 1940

1939 and Finland (in the Winter War of 1939-40) and were on the receiving end of the German invasion in 1941.

Tunics

The distinctively Russian tunic-shirt, or gymnastiorka, had its origins in the 19th century as a garment used by Russian soldiers while on fatigue duty. It had evolved into the main uniform for other ranks in World War I and in 1935 was established as the key uniform for all ranks. There was a summer version in cotton and a winter version in wool. Unlike its Czarist predecessor, this uniform collar had had a stand-and-fall collar since been changed in 1929. This bore the collar patch in branch-of-service colours (with piping) and rank insignia. There were now three buttons down the front of the tunic and tunics were sometimes fly-fronted. There were two breast pockets with scalloped flaps secured by two further buttons. The cuffs were straight and were tightened by two further buttons. Sleeves were reinforced for other ranks with additional material. A collarless shirt was worn under the tunic and a false collar (in white, to ensure the soldier kept his neck clean) cushioned the neck.

The officers' version was similar to this but was not reinforced at the elbow. It had piping around the collar and at the cuffs. The pockets were supposed to have had rectangular flaps, but scalloped versions were also seen. Many officers opted for the popular French tunic. This was named after the British general and had an open collar, lapels, six large buttons and four pockets (the top two pleated, the waist pockets hidden). It was piped in service colours at the cuffs and worn with a white shirt and dark (usually black) tie.

Collar insignia

The rectangular collar patch was red (magenta) for infantry; from 1940, a central red stripe was added. It was piped in black for other ranks and in gold for officers. Rank insignia was worn in the form of red enamel badges in the form of rectangles, squares and triangles and a gilt triangle in the top corner for certain ranks. The various combinations are given here:

Political officers – of whom the most junior, zamesitely politruks and mladshiy politruks, were the most significant at regimental level – had a red star and hammer-and-sickle insignia on the lower sleeve – also shown on the greatcoat sleeve.

Behind the series of rank indicators on the collar was a branch-of-service badge. For infantry it consisted of crossed rifles on a target insignia. It was not universally worn. These badges were issued to some units in 1940 and by 1942 seem largely to have been restricted to NCOs and officers.

▶ **Officer, 77th Rifle Regiment, 1940**
When not wearing the off-duty side cap soldiers would have worn the 1936-pattern steel helmet. This was in use in the first years of the war, but from 1941 it was common to see Soviet units using a mix of the older pattern as well as the newly issued 1939 pattern. This was because reserves coming up to the front were often supplied with the newer model.

▲ **Private, 321st Rifle Regiment, Summer 1941** *The majority of Soviet infantrymen were armed with the standard Mosin rifle. Although this was an old design it had been modified and improved in 1930. Most Mosin rifles were made at the Tula arsenal before the German advance shifted production eastwards.*

The insignia was attached to the collar by prongs pushed through the collar material and splayed out behind. Photographs also show that some Red Army personnel sewed the barrels and butts of the rifles on the insignia to their collar to prevent them falling off.

In addition to the rank insignia on the collar, Red Army officers and NCOs also sported chevrons on the lower sleeves of their tunics. Chevrons were officially abolished in August 1941, but seem to have survived in many cases. Initially, they were combinations of red chevrons, of different thicknesses, worn points down. A second lieutenant would have three thin chevrons, a captain one thicker chevron. The system was altered in July 1940 so that red and gold chevrons were intermingled. A captain would have a gold chevron, then red then gold, a lieutenant colonel the same but with a thicker lower gold chevron.

Trousers and boots

Trousers also came in summer cotton and winter wool types. They were baggy at the thigh and bound below the knee so that they could be worn tucked under puttees or into boots. The trousers could be tightened by a cloth strip pulled through a small buckle. NCOs had the option of wearing blue pantaloons and officers also could wear blue, with red piping, or khaki (also piped).

Boots were either ankle boots (worn with khaki puttees), mostly of the blackened 1938 pattern with hobnails, or a more traditional leather boot issued to front line troops in 1939. These were worn with foot wraps, which – unlike socks – created a snug fit and were deemed more comfortable when boot sizes were limited. The 1938-pattern tall boot had a studded sole. Leather leggings were sometimes used with ankle boots. For troops operating in extreme conditions a boot made out of compressed felt was issued.

Greatcoats

The standard greatcoat was made of thick woollen cloth. Officers preferred grey, but the coat was generally brown or khaki for other ranks. The brown greatcoat closed to the side with hooks (and had a fly front) and had straight cuffs and a pointed stand-and-fall collar. Lozenges in the branch-of-service colour were placed there. These were magenta for the infantry, with black piping being restricted to the top end. The coat was long, falling to 35cm (14in) from the ground.

Politruk, 638th Rifle Regiment, 1941 *This political officer was tasked with troop morale, education and political morals. He wears the distinguishing mark of the political officer, a red star on the sleeve. This was officially abolished in the summer of 1941, because the Germans were executing political officers, but the star continued to be worn until 1943.*

Rank insignia was displayed on the lozenge. The officers' version was double-breasted and later versions had a rectangle displaying service colours in appropriate piping, with one top button. Officers also had the right to wear a waterproof gabardine riding coat.

In February 1941 it was decreed that the other ranks' greatcoat should be worn by officers as well, and that rank distinctions should be removed from the greatcoat sleeves and collar patches. This regulation was, at best, partially adopted. It had been a tradition for Russian soldiers to roll their greatcoats and to wear them across the torso. This was continued in the Red Army, many infantrymen rolling the coat and binding it where the two ends met (and then sometimes tucking the ends into the mess tin). The same could be done with the tent canvas.

A number of other coats would make their appearance during the war as well, all intended to protect troops from the extremes of the climate. A double-breasted sheepskin coat (the polushobok) was popular, with or without a wool collar and cuffs. It had raglan sleeves to enable gloves or mittens to be worn with ease. In 1941 the most popular coat, the padded telogreika was issued; it had matching trousers, but these proved less of a success. It was closed with four buttons and was reinforced at the elbow. It was usually worn free of any insignia. A double-breasted duffel coat in khaki (with four pockets) was also issued in limited numbers from 1937.

Gloves, balaclavas, fur pelisses and scarves were used in great numbers, especially in the bitter conditions found at the northern front around Leningrad. The Red Army was careful when it came to the weather, and regulations stipulated what was to be worn at what particular temperature.

Dress for different temperatures

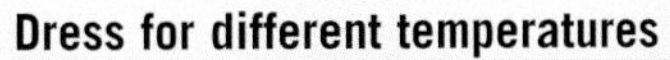

More than +25°	No 1 light cap, cotton tunic and breeches
From +20° to +25°	No 2 light cap and cotton tunic and breeches
From +15° to +20°	No 3 cap, wool tunic and breeches
From +10° to +15°	No 4 cap, wool tunic and breeches
From 0° to +10°	No 5 the same, with greatcoat
From 0° to -6°	No 6 as above but with gloves
From -6° to -10°	No 7 as above but with fur hat
From -10° or lower	No 8 the same but with ear flaps worn

◄ **NCO, 12th Rifle Regiment, Summer 1941** *This soldier wears the Ssh. 1936 helmet designed by Alexander Schvartz. It was unpopular with the troops, being unstable, ungainly and offering poor protection.*

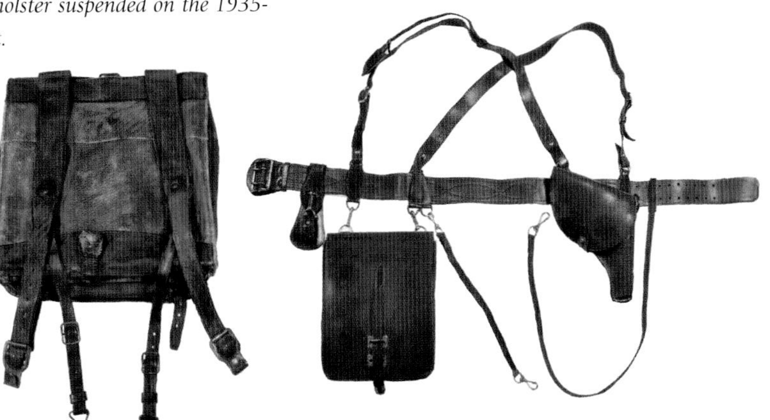

▼ **Soviet Infantry Kit** *The 1936-pattern backpack below was produced in enormous quantities, but most were lost in the first year of the war. The 1939-pattern campaign bag, right, which resembled a rucksack, was easier to produce and more common from 1941 onwards. Officers generally wore a map case and pistol holster suspended on the 1935-pattern belt.*

Helmets

The Soviet Union initially made use of Sohlberg helmets (from 1916) or French Adrian helmets with insignia filed off and a red star painted on the front (frequently bordered in gold for officers). There were too few helmets and so plans were drawn up for headgear of Soviet manufacture. As a temporary measure the 1928 helmet was produced, based largely on the Adrian, whilst tests continued on various prototypes.

In 1936 a new model went into production, known as the Ssh. 1936 (with Ssh standing for Stalshlyem, or steel helmet). It had a pronounced visor (rather like the original German steel helmet issued in 1916), a high dome and a flared rim designed to protect the side of the head and neck. It was manufactured in a hurry, and quantities went to Spain to equip the Republicans, but it was unpopular with Soviet troops because it was unstable and uncomfortable when running. Nevertheless, this was the helmet most commonly seen during the invasion of Poland, the Winter War of 1939–40 and the 1939 campaign against the Japanese.

A modification was made to the flared rim, the air vents and the lining (making it more cushioned) in 1939. The helmet was usually painted in satin or matt paint, usually green, and sometimes had the red star on the front, with or without the hammer and cycle. The vast majority had canvas chinstraps. It continued in service throughout the war (some troops in the Far East wore it in 1945 when the Red Army attacked Manchuria), but a new model, the Ssh. 1940, was produced in massive numbers and largely replaced it.

▲ *The massed power of the Soviet infantry, in their 1936-pattern helmets, parade through Moscow in December 1939.*

◄ **Private, 253rd Rifle Regiment, 1943**
This way of carrying the tent canvas or folded greatcoat wrapped around the soldier's torso, was very common. The ends were tucked into the round 1926 pattern mess tin. The tin did, however, also have its own green canvas cover that was pulled tight by means of a drawstring.

Older models, such as the Adrian, were worn by militias and air-defence organizations, for example during the Leningrad siege.

This new Ssh. 1940 helmet was robust (made from a single piece of steel), simple to produce and despite still being a little unstable was relatively comfortable; it had leather interior or padding made from specially treated cloth. It weighed the same as the previous model and came in three sizes. The design is said to have been partially based on the Italian helmet designed in 1933.

The chinstrap was usually canvas (sand-coloured or light green), with a metal buckle (painted light green), with post-war helmets being given a Y-shaped strap (to help stabilize the helmet). The strap was 30cm (12in) long and attached to a lug that was itself attached by a cotton strap to a rivet in the side of the helmet.

Most helmets were manufactured at Lysva, but some were also produced at Leningrad during the siege.

▲ **Private, 365th Rifle Regiment, 1941** *Decent winter camouflage uniforms were rushed into service following the Winter War of 1939–40 against Finland. Costumes such as this could be worn with warm felt boots (valenki) or the standard leather boot, as here, which had relatively good grip.*

The helmets were in the main painted light green, although naval troops received grey helmets. Camouflage paint was sometimes applied (in styles that reflected Soviet camouflage clothing) as very few helmet covers were supplied.

Caps

The Red Army had a bewildering amount of headgear. When the helmet was not being worn, field caps were probably the next most common item. These had a duck-billed peak in black or khaki, a coloured band with red star badge, a chinstrap and a khaki crown; the 1935 pattern was flatter than the 1924 version. The band was magenta for infantry, and the crown had magenta piping. The cap was the same for all ranks, and could be worn in a khaki-only version in the field.

A side cap, the famous pilotka, was also very common and it came in many shades of khaki. This was usually worn with a red star badge (usually made of enamel, sometimes of cloth), which for officers was on a disk of cloth in branch-of-service colours (prohibited in 1941). Officers preferred to have piping on the cap. In the hot south of the USSR and in central Asia, the panama was a popular hat. It was a round brimmed cotton hat issued from 1938 with obligatory red star.

Another cap, this time something of a leftover from the 1920s was the pointed boudionovka. This was in khaki or grey fabric, dome-shaped and with a small cloth spike. The cap had flaps that could be buttoned to the side or buttoned under the mouth to create a kind of balaclava. The infantry had a red cloth star with inset enamel star on the front. During the Winter War of 1939–40, this cap was found to be unsuitable for the northern winter, but it was still a popular item (especially when worn under the helmet).

The replacement winter hat was the chapka-oushanka, with two flaps tied over the top of the hat and could be secured under the chin. It came rounded or in a squarer shape and could be worn under the helmet. It was issued in large numbers from 1940 onwards. The original fur or woollen winter hat was the chapka-finka, issued in smaller numbers from 1931. It was made from merino lambswool or fur and a cloth crown and padded interior. There was a single fold-down flap that covered the neck and the ears and this then had fur or wool on the inside. A red star badge was worn on the front. Officers wore a taller cap, the papakha, which was usually in grey wool or fur with a red or grey crown.

▼ **NCO, 42nd Rifle Regiment, 1942** *The padded jacket worn here was immensely popular with the troops. It was fastened with five metal buttons, although these were often replaced by plastic ones later in the war, and also had a wooden button that was used to tighten the cuff.*

Equipment

Established Soviet frontline infantry were generally well equipped from 1941, but hastily raised units rushed to the front in 1941 and 1942 experienced shortages. Most infantrymen had a leather belt (canvas became more common later) supporting natural leather cartridge pouches. These were of earlier patterns or in the new 1937 pattern, which was a double pouch worn on each hip. Submachine gunners either had a round pouch in cloth for the drum or a pouch that could take three box magazines. An entrenching tool with hood and a bayonet scabbard were suspended on the back of the belt.

Infantry wore the compact 1936-pattern knapsack that had tent canvas (doubling as a poncho) strapped around the top and sides in a horseshoe shape. The mess tin, which was enamel or aluminium and had its own integral cover, was strapped to the centre of the pack. A more practical rucksack was introduced in 1939. This was of durable canvas with leather straps (canvas from 1941) and two roomy pockets on the back. Another popular item was the assault pack of 1930, a khaki duffle bag with drawstrings that also served as straps and went over both shoulders. Flasks were usually of the 1938 aluminium type and came with a canvas cover that allowed them to be attached to the belt, usually at the small of the back. Gas masks came in many forms, the most common being the BNT5 of 1930 or the Sch M1 of 1938 with vulcanized facemask. It was worn in a khaki canvas bag.

Grenades were carried in canvas bags or tucked into the belt. The most common types were the 1930 stick grenade, the heavy 1940 anti-tank grenade or the improved F1 fragmentation grenade. Common weapons included the Mosin-Nagant 1930-pattern rifle (carbines became common later, especially for tank riders), the Tokarev semi-automatic SVT-40 and the PPsh-41 submachine gun (the PPs-43 after 1943).

Officers wore an integrated system of belts and equipment first issued in 1932. It consisted of a waist belt with distinctive star buckle or two-pronged buckle, leather suspends that went up over the shoulders (sometimes forming a 'Y' at the back or else continuing as two straps) and helped support the pistol holster (worn on the right front) and document or map case. The pistol – usually the older Mosin-Nagant or the new Tokarev 1933-pattern gun – was attached to the waist belt by a leather lanyard. A whistle, with its own cord, could also be attached to the belt

▼ **Private, 72nd Replacement Regiment, 1943** *The Soviet helmet was generally issued in a matt green colour, but in fact colours varied from khaki or olive to bright apple green. It was often painted in winter and Soviet troops also added red stars or, more rarely, slogans.*

▲ **Captain, 151st Rifle Regiment, 1943** *Officers generally favoured the 1932-pattern equipment that consisted of belts, braces, map case and pistol in holster. The belt had two prongs, although the 1935-pattern belt, with its metallic Soviet star, was popular.*

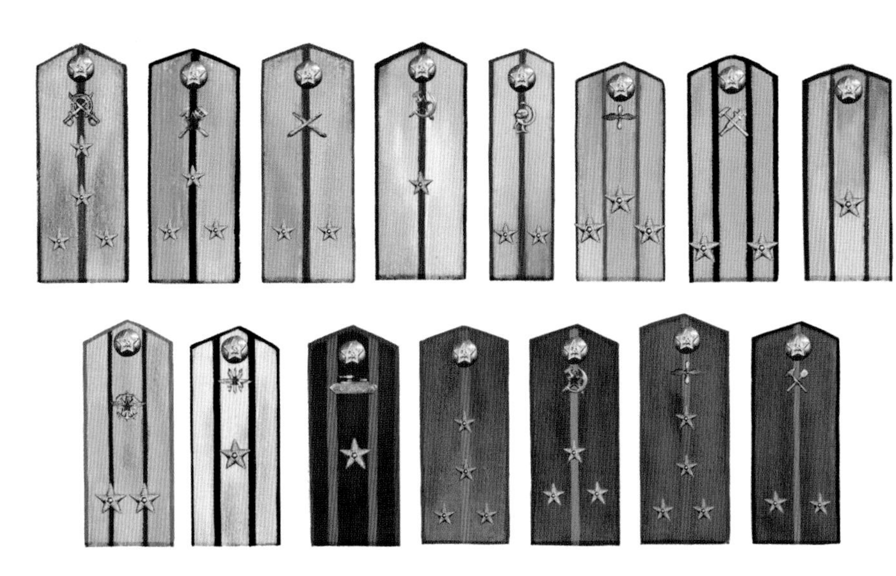

▲ SHOULDERBOARDS *From top left to right: captain (cavalry); lieutenant (topographical staff); lieutenant (artillery); 2nd lieutenant (quartermaster staff); lieutenant (medics); colonel (aviation); lieutenant colonel (technical); major (infantry).Bottom row: lieutenant colonel (railway troops); major (engineers); major (armoured); captain (infantry); lieutenant (quartermaster staff); captain (aviation); lieutenant (sappers).*

and kept in a leather cover. A canteen and canvas bag were often added to this system and an additional belt for sword or dagger could also be added.

Insignia

Although there were a great number of badges awarded for marksmanship or issued as rewards for completing training courses (usually aluminium with red enamel), and medals were often worn at the front, specialist cloth insignia (denoting units or specialism) were rare.

Just as in other armies, distinctive wound badges were, however, introduced during the war. In July 1942 an order was issued stipulating that a red cloth strip would signify that the wearer had been badly wounded and a yellow strip that the wearer had been lightly wounded. They were to be worn above the wearer's right breast pocket. They were then stacked up in chronological order from that point onwards. The average number of stripes is not known, but in the Red Army 1,226 officers, 1,553 NCOs and 1,200 privates were wounded seven or more times and 2,496 officers, 3,395 NCOs and 3,234 privates were wounded six times in the war. Some 1,480,324 individuals were wounded once and qualified for one strip.

▶ PRIVATE, 4TH RIFLE REGIMENT, 1944
This infantryman, wearing the Russian greatcoat, carries the 1944 pattern Mosin carbine – an indication that the quality of Soviet small arms was improving, but a reminder that not all infantry were armed with semi-automatics or SMGs.

Wartime changes

In August 1941, in response to heavy casualties and to reduce problems faced when uniforming large numbers of replacements, orders went out that the coloured collar patches be replaced by khaki versions – and that the red enamel rank insignia be painted green, too. Many units ignored this order. If this subdued colour system was adopted, units either obtained some of the new patches issued in small numbers, improvised in the field or, as a very practical step, the coloured collar patch was removed in its entirety. Almost immediately afterwards, further orders instructed that all metallic buttons be replaced or painted over in khaki. The cap badge was also painted with green paint.

1943 regulations

The most noteworthy change came in 1943, when a new uniform was introduced (authorized in January, introduced by 15 March). Much of the older equipment continued to be worn (supplemented by items supplied through the US Lend Lease programme, such as British or American boots and belts), but the uniform underwent a revolution.

Out went the collar patches and rank insignia, for the new uniform now favoured a more traditional look and seemed modelled on the uniforms of 1914. In January 1943 regulations were issued that established a new style of tunic.

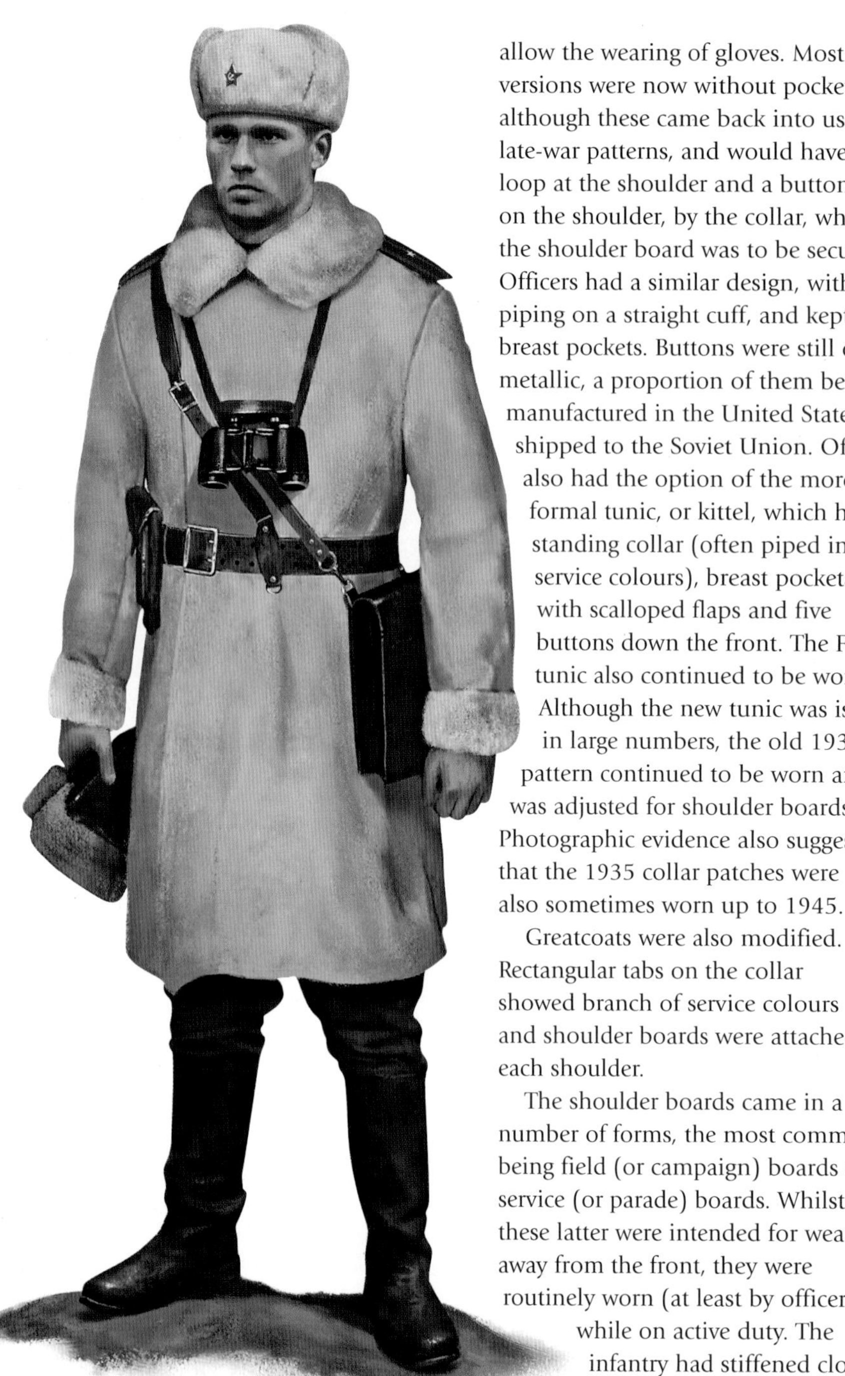

▲ **Major, 242nd Rifle Regiment, 1945** *The coat seen here, the poluchubok, was made of sheepskin and had fleece at the collar and at the cuffs. It was very warm and was adapted so that it could take the appropriate shoulder boards.*

It was to have shoulder boards and a standing collar closed by two buttons to the front of the collar and three down the front. It came in summer or winter versions, the winter one being in wool with buttons at the cuff to allow the wearing of gloves. Most versions were now without pockets, although these came back into use in late-war patterns, and would have a loop at the shoulder and a buttonhole on the shoulder, by the collar, where the shoulder board was to be secured. Officers had a similar design, with piping on a straight cuff, and kept the breast pockets. Buttons were still often metallic, a proportion of them being manufactured in the United States and shipped to the Soviet Union. Officers also had the option of the more formal tunic, or kittel, which had a standing collar (often piped in service colours), breast pockets with scalloped flaps and five buttons down the front. The French tunic also continued to be worn. Although the new tunic was issued in large numbers, the old 1935 pattern continued to be worn and was adjusted for shoulder boards. Photographic evidence also suggests that the 1935 collar patches were also sometimes worn up to 1945.

Greatcoats were also modified. Rectangular tabs on the collar showed branch of service colours and shoulder boards were attached to each shoulder.

The shoulder boards came in a number of forms, the most common being field (or campaign) boards and service (or parade) boards. Whilst these latter were intended for wear away from the front, they were routinely worn (at least by officers) while on active duty. The infantry had stiffened cloth boards in khaki on campaign, piped magenta. Parade boards were magenta piped black. NCOs added red stripes across the board according to rank (three for a sergeant).

Officers had khaki boards piped magenta, with one or two magenta stripes running along the board and with stars positioned according to rank. The parade board was of gold fibre piped magenta with magenta stripes and dark gold stars. The boards were held in place by a button that was intended to be concave but was usually flat.

Guards units

Order number 303 of 18 September 1941 converted four rifle divisions (the 100th, 127th, 153rd and 161st) into

▼ **Private, 244th Rifle Regiment, 1945** *The simple side cap was the most common type of headgear in use when the helmet was not being worn. It came in many shades of khaki, from olive to sand-coloured, and was usually worn with a reduced version of the red star. This star was sometimes camouflaged with green paint.*

Guard divisions. These were issued with a special standard and a badge was created and issued in 1942 to be worn on the tunic. These were generally worn in combat, as a mark of distinction. Interestingly, the plans to issue the Guard units with distinctive uniforms were scrapped, but these designs were later used for the new 1943 pattern uniforms. The quality of uniforms issued to units with Guard status was the same as that issued to standard units. However, it is true that the Guards were preferred when it came to equipment such as improved versions of small arms or motor vehicles. There were 119 infantry divisions with Guard status by 1945, plus three motorized rifle divisions. Guard corps also contained units that were not of Guard status and who, therefore, did not wear the Guard badge. Officers and NCOs added the designation Guard before their rank, for example Guard lieutenant.

▶ **Scout, 188th Guards Rifle Regiment, 1945** *The camouflage smock had been developed in 1941, but was not widely used until the end of World War II. It came in ochre with green artificial leaves, but also in green with brown leaves. It had a hood and a mesh to mask the face could also be worn.*

Snipers and scouts

The Red Army encouraged individuals to become snipers. There was no special uniform for these individuals, although they wore a number of badges – the 'excellence at sniping' badge was introduced in 1942. They did make use, however, of camouflage, as did Red Army scouts. These latter were handpicked individuals formed into platoons who were sent on ahead to reconnoitre locations and to capture prisoners for information and intelligence.

Camouflage items varied according to season. White smocks, hoods and trousers were issued in winter. Heavy casualties in the Winter War of 1939–40 led to the rapid adoption in 1940 of white items for winter wear. The white smock was as long as the greatcoat, had a generous hood (to accommodate the helmet) and had drawstrings at the neck and at the cuffs. It was closed down the front with nine white buttons and was usually worn over the padded jacket or a sleeveless fur or wool top and felt boots.

Experiments with camouflage led to the adoption, in 1938, of the so-called amoeba pattern for army fabric (a post-war term). In winter/spring it was to be of green cloth with patches of black and in summer/autumn it was to be of green cloth with brown patches. It came as a cagoule with hood and a facemask, and baggy trousers. A helmet cover in the same style was issued in very limited numbers. In 1941 another style of camouflage was issued, this time with a pattern designed to represent foliage. It was also green, and the pattern came in various forms of brown, although there were a number of local or seasonal variations.

◀ **Sniper, Rifle Regiment, 1945** *This sniper uses the Mosin rifle, but with the addition of a 3.5 power PU telescopic sight. These came with a mount and usually had a serial number that linked it to the rifle. The sight was carried in its own carrying case.*

Another kind of camouflage suit also made an appearance in 1943. This was a two-piece green suit with strips and knots of hessian attached to break the wearer's profile. It had a hood and facemask, and was popular with scouts.

Snipers would probably have carried their scopes in a protective cover on the waist belt. The 1930 sniper rifle was issued in large numbers, but the SVT40 was regarded as superior.

Mountain detachments

The Red Army had specialist mountain detachments. These followed the regulations for infantry described above, but also made use of special items of dress and equipment. The most significant was a dark-grey double-breasted jacket and matching trousers in waterproofed cloth. These were worn with alpine socks (in grey or white) and ankle boots. Rectangular collar patches showed rank distinctions (there was no piping around the collar for officers) and red chevrons were initially worn above the cuff for officers and NCOs.

This uniform was worn with fur hats or helmets and a number of variations of coats were also worn, often in dark grey and with fur collars or hoods. Civilian goggles and climbing equipment were in use.

Ski troops were formed on an ad hoc basis after 1940, many scout units taking to skis in winter. There were no specialist regiments. Ski troops adopted the white camouflage smocks and gloves, and wore them with white over trousers, ski boots and alpine socks.

▶ **Private, 902nd Rifle Regiment, 1944** *The PTRD anti-tank rifle held by this private was designed by Fedor Degtyarov and could fire armour-piecing rounds capable of penetrating 40mm (1.6in) of armour from 100 metres (around 325 feet). It became less effective as the war continued largely because German armour was developed to offer better protection.*

◀ **Guard, 141st Guard Rifle Regiment, 1944** *This NCO, a member of an elite, decorated unit, wears a winter version of the tunic in good-quality cloth. For officers and many NCOs the pocket flaps were visible, but the tunic was tailored in such a way as to render the pockets themselves invisible.*

Medics

The Red Army's medical personnel had green as a distinguishing colour. Between 1935 and 1943 this was shown on collar tabs (piped red) and on the cap band (the crown of the cap being piped red). Officers had gold piping around the tab, and red piping at the collar and cuffs. A gold badge representing a chalice with entwined snake was worn on the collar; this was silver for vets. The coloured collar patches were supposed to have been suppressed in 1941, but they persisted.

◀ **Private, 1st Special Mountain Detachment, 1942** *This mountaineer wears civilian ski goggles and a wool jumper. He would have carried civilian mountain equipment, but he is heavily armed with standard Soviet infantry weapons.*

In 1943 shoulder boards were introduced – these were narrower for non-combat personnel. These were khaki piped red for campaign dress. NCOs added brick-red stripes and officers had the same, but as thin stripes running from end to end. Parade boards were silver piped red for officers and green piped red for other ranks. Medics carried a canvas shoulder bag (with red cross) that contained bandages, dressings and first aid medicines. A white brassard with red cross was only rarely worn.

Militia

Soviet militias were mostly recruited in 1941 for the improvised defence of Leningrad (13 divisions) and Moscow (17 divisions). They were poorly equipped, wearing civilian items of dress, outdated helmets and equipment. A number added armbands or improvised insignia. They were quickly absorbed into front-line units. Those captured by the Germans were usually classified as partisans and shot or sent to serve as slave labour.

Penal units

Much has been written about the penal units of the Red Army. In 1941, as an emergency measure, a number of units were formed from Gulag inmates who were granted the right to win their freedom. They initially continued to wear their black penal overalls and have been called the 'black divisions'– but these could also have been confused with units of workers' militia in factory overalls. The situation in the disciplinary companies is clearer. These received those convicted of military offences and were to serve a period of time in these units before being released back to normal formations. From 1943 officers wore infantry shoulder boards but of a much thinner design. Rank and file wore standard Red Army uniform, but devoid of any insignia or awards.

Female soldiers

Women soldiers were initially confined to non-combat roles – such as medics, runners or drivers – but, as the war dragged on, more and more Russian women found themselves armed and at the front. Women generally wore a tunic (buttoned the reverse way to the male equivalent), with a skirt in khaki or the regulation blue. These were worn with black stockings, black socks and boots. They had the option of wearing a distinctive beret from 1941 onwards and this was in very dark blue or a number of shades of khaki. A single-piece dress was issued in 1941 (modified to take narrow shoulder straps in 1943) with belt and pockets in the skirt.

▼ **Medic, 467th Rifle Regiment, 1944** *Female personnel wore tunics of a similar style to that of their male counterparts, although they buttoned on the other side. When the helmet was not worn, a dark blue beret was preferred, although it was not especially practical in winter.*

FOREIGN TROOPS

The Soviet Union raised a number of units from peoples who had been exiled by German occupation of their homelands, and a smaller number from prisoners of war.

The Poles were, in a sense, both exiles and prisoners. The Czechs were formed from a handful of political refugees and military personnel who found themselves in Soviet territory. Some Romanian units were recruited from prisoners of war relatively late in the conflict and found themselves dressed and equipped as Soviet troops. The most bizarre unit was the Normandy-Niemen squadron, recruited from French pilots who had made their way through Iran and into the Soviet Union in order to fight the Germans. There were also a number of Spaniards who had come to the Soviet Union following defeat in the Spanish Civil War.

Poles

The history of Polish troops in Soviet service is complex. Polish prisoners of war were released from Soviet captivity in 1941 and began to form units under the command of General Anders. These troops were sent on to Iran in 1942. Other Poles were formed into the Tadeusz Kosciuszko infantry division in 1943 and this grew to corps size, merged with the communist resistance in Poland and formed the LWP (Ludowe Wojsko Polskie) in 1944. A distinctive cap badge was created in 1943 (a Polish eagle without crown and shield), which was worn on Polish peaked caps (manufactured to Polish designs in the Soviet Union) or stencilled (or even painted white) on the Soviet helmet.

Pre-war rank distinctions seem to have been retained on the tunic's shoulder straps (most Poles wore the 1943-pattern Soviet tunic) and these were combinations of stars and bars. Some tunics with stand-and-fall collars were also issued, in khaki, and these had breast pockets and shoulder straps. Service dress versions of these tunics may have had pennons in new branch-of-service colours affixed, but this was rare – infantry would have had blue over yellow. Equipment was of Soviet design, as were boots and greatcoats. Specialist troops, such as tank troops and engineers, made use of specialist Soviet items and, for example, wore the padded tankers' helmet.

◄ **Captain, 2nd Infantry Regiment, Tadeusz Kosciuszko Infantry Division, 1944** *The Polish-style tunic was manufactured in the Soviet Union, as was the cap. Infantrymen were authorized to wear pennons in blue and yellow on their collars, but these were rare in the front line.*

▲ *Many of the Polish soldiers that were captured in 1939 would end up fighting as part of the Red Army from 1943.*

The Poles fought in the liberation of Poland and ended up taking part in the fighting for Berlin's Reichstag.

Czechs

A small group of Czechs had been captured when the Soviets overran eastern Poland in 1939. An independent battalion was formed from these men in February 1942.

The personnel were initially dressed in Soviet tunics and trousers and were without insignia. In the summer of 1942 they received British battledress (intended for General Anders's Polish Army) and supplemented these with Red Army greatcoats, equipment and caps. (There were some British helmets.) Weapons were standard Red Army issue. The unit had grown to be brigade size (infantry and tank battalions) by 1943 and corps size (with supporting air force and paratroops) by mid-1944. Over time the British appearance of the troops disappeared altogether, with Soviet uniforms becoming the norm. They wore a distinctive cap badge, consisting of the Czechoslovak rampant lion in a shield. It was in white metal. It seems that later crossed swords were added behind this device.

Romanians

Two divisions of Romanians were eventually raised for Soviet service. The most significant was the Tudor Vladimirescu Division, which became active in 1944. A secondary division, the Horia, Closca si Crisan Division was formed, but had not completed its organization by the time Romania swapped sides. The Tudor Vladimirescu Division was uniformed and equipped by the Soviets and received a distinctive white metal cap badge (bearing the letters 'TV' on a flag within a laurel wreath) and wore a similar badge on the tunic. The second division was to have the same but bearing 'HCC'.

French

General de Gaulle had initially envisaged a French infantry division in Soviet service, but practical problems convinced him that a fighter group was a better step. The Soviets agreed in March 1942 and the pilots began flying Yak fighter planes in early 1943 (apparently preferring the local design to Hurricanes). The pilots wore a mix of Soviet and French items, and ground crew also made use of some British battledress.

The pilots were initially given French blue peaked caps, showing the eagle badge and rank. They wore blue open-necked tunics with white shirts and black ties; rank was shown at the cuff or as strips on a dark rectangle on the front of the flying jacket. The flying jacket was either privately purchased or issued by the Soviets: a leather and fur Canadienne jacket was popular. It showed rank and the unit insignia (two lions) as a metallic badge on the breast. Boots, parachutes and flying helmets were of Soviet manufacture.

Spanish

Non-Soviet citizens were not permitted in the Red Army before 1941. That changed with the German invasion, and Spanish refugees from the Spanish Civil War enlisted. The fourth company of the NKVD's special brigade was composed of Spaniards. They wore Soviet uniforms and items of civilian clothing if they were parachuted behind the lines to operate alongside partisans.

◀ **Private, 1st Czech Independent Battalion, 1943** *This Czechoslovak soldier is dressed for a winter in the Ukraine, complete with felt boots. He is armed with the new PPsh-43 submachine gun. This was simple to produce, effective, and therefore turned out in huge quantities.*

▶ **Pilot Normandie-Niemen Squadron, 1943** *Although the Free French had toyed with the idea of creating an infantry regiment, the availability of pilots, who had been stranded in the Middle East, meant that a fighter squadron was created instead. It blended Russian equipment with French items of uniform, with most pilots retaining the blue cap of the French Air Force with a cross of Lorraine prominent.*

CAVALRY

The Red Army cavalry was relatively at full strength in 1941. Cavalrymen had proved their worth in the Russian Civil War of 1917-22 and would continue to do so on the difficult terrain of the Eastern Front.

Mounted infantry

Cavalry now served as mounted infantry: one man guarded eleven horses at the rear, while the rest of the troop went into action on foot. They proved useful for reconnaissance, were adept at covering the huge distances on this massive front and were highly mobile in winter and in the muddy seasons (providing rapid response or raiding). They were deployed either within cavalry divisions or on detachment to rifle and armoured divisions.

Early uniforms

The cavalry uniform had evolved along similar lines to that of the infantry. In 1935 a new uniform was defined and issued from 1936: it consisted of the khaki gymnastiorka with blue collar tabs piped black. Officers had gold piping around the tabs and blue piping around the collar and cuffs. The same rank symbols as used in the infantry were worn on the collar. A gold branch-of-service badge was worn towards the back of the collar, held in place by metal prongs that were folded behind the collar cloth. This badge depicted crossed sabres over an upturned horseshoe; and was first authorized in 1922, this seems to have fallen out of favour and was not listed as an official emblem in the 1935 reforms but appeared again in 1943. However, it does seem to have been worn throughout that period.

◀ **Captain, 65th Cavalry Regiment, 1941** *This cavalryman wears standard officers' equipment and is armed with a Mosin carbine. Officers had the option of carrying a sword (with a leather sword knot used to prevent the sword falling to the ground) and a Nagant revolver. This rather heavy gun was carried throughout the war.*

▶ **Sergeant 2nd Guards Cavalry Regiment, 1944** *This Guards cavalryman sports the Guards badge on the right of his standard tunic. He wears the long black boot common to infantry and cavalry – the boot had a heel that made it suitable for stirrups. A metal spur was attached with leather straps.*

Cavalry wore breeches throughout the war. These were baggy around the thigh and were usually dark blue. Officers could also wear khaki versions with blue piping down the outer seams. Breeches had two pockets and could be tightened below the knee. These were worn with high leather boots that were supplied together with strap-on spurs. Blackened ankle boots and gaiters were also sometimes worn because the cavalry boot was not comfortable for dismounted service.

Headgear consisted of the peaked cap with blue band and blue piping along the top of the khaki crown. The leather chinstrap was usually worn down and the peak was either black or khaki. The pointed boudionovka cap was also common before 1942 and this was worn with a cloth star in blue at the front, bearing within it a red star with hammer and sickle device. Helmets, fur caps and side caps (often in blue) were also worn.

The 1943 uniform

Just like the infantry, the Soviet cavalry received new uniforms in 1943. The rank and file received the tunic with standing collar, officers wore a similar tunic (piped at the cuff) but could also wear the kittel tunic with blue piping around the collar. Shoulder boards were worn and these were khaki piped blue for other ranks (NCOs had red stripes across the board according to rank), while officers had khaki boards with red stripes running along the board on their campaign dress versions.

For service dress – supposedly worn away from the front but also commonly seen on the battlefield – the boards for other ranks were blue piped in black (with yellow stripes for NCOs), while officers had gold bullion boards that were piped in blue and had blue stripes along the boards, and a combination of stars to show rank. The cavalry insignia was also sometimes displayed on the board, up near the button by the collar. A variation was the reconnaissance insignia given to scouts before 1941. It had crossed sabres and a theodolite and binoculars.

Unit numerals were rare. There were 17 cavalry divisions with Guard status by 1945 and personnel within those divisions wore the Guards badge.

Greatcoats

The cavalry (and horse artillery) wore greatcoats that were longer than those used by foot soldiers. These stretched down 18–22cm (7–9in) from the ground. They were either in brown woollen cloth or grey (which was favoured by officers), and had cotton lining to the waist and to the sleeves – these were reinforced at the elbow. The collar was closed at the neck by means of a hook and eye and there were five buttons down the front. The back of the coat was split to the waist and the coat could be tightened using a cloth belt and two buttons.

Greatcoats bore blue lozenges (piped black or gold) before 1943 and, from then on, shoulder boards were worn and the collar received a blue rectangular tab. A quilted jacket was also common. This had a standing collar that had the standard collar patches in blue. The padded telogreika was also worn, although the matching trousers were not popular with mounted personnel.

Equipment

Cavalry carried swords into action. These were normally the 1927-pattern shashka sabre (without hilt guard) or the older model dragoon sword with guard, which was worn with a belt that went up over the shoulder. The sabre and the bayonet were in scabbards that were bound together. Cartridge pouches for carbine ammunition were worn on the leather belt and greatcoats were often worn wrapped around the torso.

Officers carried pistols and map cases on their 1932-pattern leather belt with suspenders. Cavalry were initially armed with carbines, but submachine guns became much more common after 1943. The Degtyarev anti-tank rifle, which was a heavy piece of equipment, was carried on brackets on the saddle of a packhorse. The gun could be fired from the horse. The saddlebags contained 120 rounds of ammunition.

▶ **Trooper, 134th Cavalry Regiment, 1941** *This cavalryman carries his slightly curved sword, along with cartridge pouches for his carbine. Additional ammunition could be carried in canvas bandoliers or kept on the saddle, where the bulk of personal items were carried in saddle bags behind the rider.*

COSSACKS

Although those Cossacks who fought in German uniform have received a great deal of attention, Cossacks in Soviet service far outnumbered the collaborators.

Cossacks had always played an important role in Russian armies as scouts and light cavalry. The Bolsheviks eventually won them over to fighting for the Reds and Cossacks were largely integrated into the Red Army by the 1930s. They lost their autonomy, and were numbered as part of the regular cavalry, but they still maintained distinctive and traditional elements for their uniforms. By 1941 Cossacks were mostly drawn from the Don, Terek or Kuban regions, where warriors had strong traditions of horsemanship and of serving as mounted troops. They would largely remain as such during the conflict.

Don Cossacks would form two divisions in the Red Army, Kuban Cossacks formed three and Terek Cossacks had one. Cossacks drawn from the peoples of the Caucasus and central Asia were briefly raised, but were not deemed to be politically reliable and were disbanded or absorbed into the regular cavalry.

Early uniforms

The essential uniform was that of the Red Army cavalry, whether the 1935 pattern with blue collar patches (worn with rank insignia and the crossed sabres and horseshoe cavalry badge) or the 1943 pattern with khaki shoulder boards and blue piping. In 1936 a tunic similar to the 1935-pattern khaki version was introduced, which was again khaki but had blue piping around a standing collar and down the front lapel of the tunic.

Headgear usually consisted of a peaked cap, usually that of the cavalry (blue cap band, khaki crown with blue piping), although the Don Cossacks wore a cap with a red cap band and blue crown with red piping. Breeches, which were usually dark blue in the early stages of the war, and boots with spurs were worn. Cossacks sometimes borrowed additional items such as the quilted telogreika jacket and trousers or waterproof capes, just as their counterparts in the regular cavalry did.

Cossack cap, tunic and Circassian

The traditional elements of uniform consisted first and foremost of a black lambskin cap. The cap worn by the Terek and Kuban Cossacks was slightly shorter than the version worn by Don Cossacks. This was in black and 2cm (0.8in) wider at the base than it was at the top. It bore the standard star with hammer and sickle badge. The crown of the cap was scarlet for the Kuban Cossacks (with decorative cruciform lace in black for privates and NCOs, and gold for officers) and blue for the Terek Cossacks. Don Cossacks had brick-red crowns to their taller caps.

The Cossacks also had the option of wearing traditional tunics (originally in silk) rather than their khaki service tunics. These had been brought back into service in 1936, almost as an addendum to the 1935 regulations. These tunics, known as a beshmet, were scarlet with blue piping around the collar (blue and gold for officers).

► **Cossack, 39th Guards Cavalry Regiment, Don Cossacks, 1944** *The padded jacket was a popular item amongst the Cossacks because it meant that the cumbersome and drab greatcoat could be dispensed with. A longer tunic for mounted personnel, which was also padded, had been issued in 1931, but it was rare.*

◀ **Cossack, 40th Guards Cavalry Regiment, Kuban Cossack Regiment, 1943** *Soviet soldiers had a white detachable collar under their tunic. This was to prevent painful rubbing of the neck, but it also allowed NCOs to check that the troops were staying clean – it formed part of the inspection.*

▶ **Major, 24th Cavalry Regiment, Kuban Cossacks, 1942** *The khaki tunic seen here under the traditional riding coat was generally discarded when the individual was in full dress. Instead, the traditional silk or satin shirt, in red for Kuban Cossacks and with standing collar, was preferred.*

The collars bore the standard collar patches then in use and they could be fastened at the neck by means of hooks. They had baggy sleeves and were worn tight around the waist and flared below. The same tunic in light blue was worn by the Terek Cossacks.

Over this tunic a black traditional coat, or Circassian, could also be worn. This had the traditional pockets for decorative metal cartridges (usually nine) and was in grey for the Terek Cossacks and dark blue or black for the Kuban Cossacks. The coat had unusually large and wide cuffs, often turned back to reveal the facing colour of red or blue. It usually had rank insignia on the sleeves. If this garment was not worn, a black felt cloak was preferred. This could be tied at the neck by means of leather straps. Finally, a coloured hood could also be worn. This was edged in black, but was grey for the Don Cossacks, scarlet for the Kuban Cossacks and blue for the Terek Cossacks.

Many of these items were officially suppressed in 1941, but they continued to be worn right through the conflict.

Cossacks were equipped with standard cavalry equipment. This generally consisted of the 1927-pattern shashka sabre (without hilt guard), carbine, bayonet, leather suspenders and sword belt (worn over the shoulder). The sabre and the bayonet were in scabbards that were then connected closely to each other. Officers added pistols and map cases. Cossacks adapted this basic equipment as necessary, adding decorative belts and frogging and using traditional whips and bridles; they sometimes rode bareback or had the standard blue horse cloth with red star. Cossacks rode the traditional small and medium-sized ponies and this made them especially mobile in winter and during the muddy season.

The vast majority of Cossack units were awarded Guard status and so had the right to wear the Guards badge on their tunics.

▼ *Pavel Kamnev of the Kuban Cossacks was awarded the Order of Lenin in 1942 for service in the Caucasus.*

ARTILLERY

-The Red Army had emphasized the development of new technology and munitions in the 1930s, and the artillery branch had made great steps towards modernization – with an emphasis on mobile automatic weaponry. Although there were shortages (only 1,382 serviceable anti-aircraft guns instead of the required 4,900), and a great deal of material was lost in 1941, Soviet artillery emerged as an effective and dominant force on the Eastern Front. Artillery served in position, on foot, mounted and as mechanized troops – this became increasingly common from 1942 onwards.

New developments, such as the increased use of self-propelled artillery and the deployment of rocket launchers, came to play an important role by the end of the war. In addition, revisions to the way mortar, anti-tank and anti-aircraft artillery were used meant that these branches were now much more effectively deployed among other arms of service.

Early uniforms

The artillery uniform was generally like that of the infantry, although some mounted field units had uniforms with similarities to those of the cavalry. The 1935-pattern khaki gymnastiorka had black collar tabs with red piping and a red central stripe. Officers had gold piping around the tabs and red piping around the collar and cuffs. The same rank symbols as used by the infantry were worn on the collar. A gold branch-of-service badge was worn towards the back of the collar and this showed crossed cannon barrels; privates were supposed to wear stencilled designs but these were popular and many adopted the metal badge. These came in a number of variations. Each barrel (based on a 17th-century cannon barrel) was to be 28mm (1.1in) long.

Greatcoats had the black lozenge piped red or gold with the artillery insignia and rank insignia. These coats were of infantry length for most artillery, but of cavalry length for mounted field batteries. The insignia was subdued in 1941.

In September 1942 those

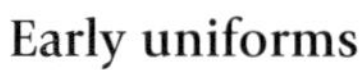

◀ **Officer 642nd Artillery Regiment, 1944** *The helmet seen here was often abandoned in winter, giving way to a more comfortable fur hat. The 1940-pattern helmet had six rivets to the crown, and these supported an improved lining, whereas the 1939 pattern had three rivets.*

▶ **Gunner, 248th Light Artillery Regiment, 1941** *This artilleryman carries standard equipment for Soviet foot soldiers. He has a leather belt to carry the leather cartridge pouches, a canvas bread bag and an aluminium cup. The canvas gas mask carrier is swung behind the bread bag.*

officers who had gained technical qualifications were granted the right to call themselves captain of artillery and technical services, major of artillery and technical services, lieutenant colonel of artillery and technical services and colonel of artillery and technical services. Insignia remained the same.

Peaked service caps had black bands, khaki crowns and red piping around the crown. Boudinovkas and pilotka side caps had red stars on a black background.

In 1943 shoulder boards were introduced and collar tabs abolished. Other ranks had khaki shoulder boards in field dress and these were piped red (with red rank bands for NCOs) and had the artillery logo stencilled (or more commonly the metal insignia). Officers had the same and with red stripes and silver stars, plus the metal insignia. Service dress meant black shoulder boards piped red (with yellow rank bands for NCOs) and, for officers, gold boards piped red and with red stripes and silver stars. Unit numerals were sometimes worn on the shoulder boards, the number being followed by a Cyrillic 'Б' if a brigade was designated. In the spring of 1943 the self-propelled artillery were assigned to the armoured branch of the Army, and received the appropriate shoulder boards.

Anti-tank units

Different branches of the artillery were not generally distinguished from each other. The only exception was for anti-tank units. In June 1942 instructions establishing the design of a special insignia for anti-tank personnel were issued. It was intended that a black rhombus should be worn on the upper sleeve of the left arm and that it should be piped red. In the centre of the 9cm (3.5in)-wide badge would be the artillery crossed-cannon badge in gold for officers and yellow for other ranks. The other ranks' yellow version does not seem to have been issued but 24,000 patches with gold thread were handed out from July 1942. Some patches with stencilled insignia in yellow paint were then issued to make up the numbers required. The badge was to be worn on tunics and greatcoats, although it seems that anti-tank gunners in armoured and mechanized formations did not wear the badge. There were six artillery divisions with Guard status by 1945, seven mortar divisions and six anti-aircraft divisions. Artillery personnel in these formations wore the standard Guards badge on their tunics.

Equipment

Artillery equipment aped that in use by the infantry and cavalry. Carbines were preferred to rifles. Specialist equipment was required in large numbers to assist with obtaining accuracy of fire. Binoculars had 6x (times 6) or 8x magnification, periscopes up to 10x; the large or the artillery stereoscopic tube was the most advanced. Other devices included the aiming circle (or BMT), mounted on a tripod or pole with a spike that could be pushed into the ground, and range finders, mounted on tripods. A periscope could be added so that calculations could be done under cover. Some officers carried a simplified aiming device, which was pocket-sized and looked like a compass but was used to direct mortar fire.

▲ **Sergeant, 989th Howitzer Regiment, 1944** *This veteran of the artillery wears wound stripes on the right of his tunic, as stipulated by regulations. Red stripes were awarded for wounds that required treatment, yellow stripes were for serious wounds. Multiple stripes were sometimes sewn on to backing material.*

◄ **The M10 (15mm)** *This Soviet howitzer was produced between 1939 and 1941.*

ENGINEERS

Technical troops provided an essential service during the Great Patriotic War (the Soviet defeat of Nazi Germany in 1941–5). The Red Army developed a number of highly specialised units between 1935 and 1945 to assist in offensive and defensive operations.

Specialists and engineers

Engineers and pioneers played an important role in designing and building obstacles and defences, or in paving the way for an infantry or armoured assault. Signals and communications units helped in establishing or maintaining communications.

◀ **Private, 95th Signal Battalion, 1941**
Signals personnel wore the signal branch-of-service insignia on black patches piped blue. Signals troops belonging to other branches of service kept the insignia but changed the distinguishing colours as appropriate.

Pontonniers built and dismantled bridges. Railway troops maintained and organized movement by rail and chemical warfare troops prepared to counter the enemy use of poison gas.

Soviet engineers generally copied the uniform of the artillery, but they were distinguished by black tabs and blue piping. The 1935-pattern tunic would have black collar tabs, blue piping (gold for officers) and rank insignia. A badge of crossed spade and pick was set at the back of the collar. Officers had gold-piped patches and black piping around the collar. The same combination of gold-piped patches and black piping was extended to greatcoats and to their lozenge-shaped badges.

Peaked caps had black bands and black piping; side caps had red stars with, for officers, a black disk of underlay and black piping. The old boudionovka pointed cap had largely been phased out by 1940, but was still seen (usually being used as a balaclava under the helmet). The engineer's boudionovka had a red star with black disk underlay.

Engineers assigned to armoured or aviation units generally followed the uniform design of that particular branch of service, but with the engineering insignia.

Changes in 1943

The 1943 regulations saw a switch to shoulder boards. These were khaki piped black (or black piped black for service dress) and khaki piped black (with red stripes and silver stars) for officers; service dress meant gold shoulder boards piped black with black stripes. A shoulder board did not usually carry a unit numeral, but this was not impossible; numerals followed by a Cyrillic 'Д' denoted airborne battalions.

Sappers had the engineering insignia, but as they were essentially infantrymen they kept the infantry uniform. Pioneers, who were charged with entrenching and fortifying positions, had crossed axes as their branch insignia. Electromechanical engineers, tasked with maintaining power supplies and securing cables, wore engineer uniforms (a special insulated overall had been developed in 1930 to protect them from electrocution), but with a crossed axe and spade device with thunderbolts.

Equipment

Engineering equipment included the standard long-handled spade, pick and wire-cutters. Assault engineers were developed from 1942 and they were given specialist equipment to assist in preparing enemy defences for attack. They made use of flame-throwers such as the LPO50, with its three tanks of fuel and its rifle-inspired lance, or mine detectors such as the VIM203 detector – although dogs were also trained to detect mines.

They sometimes supplemented their equipment with body armour. This had been developed in 1941 and a special cuirass – linked using buckles and straps to a lower abdominal protector – was issued in 1942 as the SN42 (SN standing for stalinoy nagradnik or 'steel vest'). It was lined, had additional padding around the neck and was strapped on with a canvas belt. It was mostly painted matt green, but these sets of equipment were also painted with camouflage

◀ **Private, 29th Engineer Regiment, Winter Dress, 1941** *Soviet radio equipment was reasonable but insufficient to the needs of the rapidly expanding armed forces. This was a problem shared by other powers. The Soviets overcame the problem by producing more, especially portable radios, and obtaining telephone cable and sets from the United States of America.*

paint in various styles. The vest was principally designed to protect against shrapnel in urban fighting, but it could also stop a pistol round. It weighed 3.5kg (7.7lb), so was not especially popular and a double-thickness cuirass was relegated to use by snipers firing from the prone position.

Technical troops

Signal and communications troops wore the same design of uniform as the engineers, but were distinguished by blue piping around their collar patches and around the officer's collars. They also had blue piping on their peaked service caps. Their badge was a winged thunderbolt with a red star. In 1943 they adopted the engineers' uniform altogether, only keeping their traditional badge as a distinction.

Signals troops made use of field telephones such as the UNA-F28 version from 1928 or the upgraded 1942 UNA-F42 version. Radio backpacks (the A7) and two-man radios (issued in 1938 and in 1942, and given the designation RB-M) were also carried into the field, as were radios, field telephones and transmitters supplied through the US Lend Lease programme. The main shortage was of telephone cable; the Allies would eventually supply 16 million km (almost 10 million miles) of cable, which had a short life in the Russian winter.

Technical troops (those outside of the specific categories given here, such as fuel mechanics) had a hammer and calliper badge in 1935.

Bridging units had their own badge of crossed axes over an anchor. Railway troops, surprisingly, had a similar badge of a crossed hammer and anchor, then from 1936 crossed hammers over an anchor over a winged star. They were also distinguished by red brassards bearing their insignia and, from 1943, by a black diamond badge piped green showing a yellow badge of winged wheels. Chemical troops had a gas mask badge with crossed gas canisters, but otherwise were dressed as engineers; their gas mark badge was replaced by the badge of technical troops in 1943. Insignia on the shoulder boards of topographic troops was only authorized in 1943: it was a red star on the engineers' badge.

Technical troops generally carried carbines in the field because these were more manageable than the longer rifle.

▶ **Private, 8th Guards Sapper Battalion, 1943** *The SN42 body armour was issued in limited numbers to assault engineers. It was most famously used in the street fighting at Stalingrad and, to a lesser extent, at Leningrad. It offered some protection from ricochets and mines, but it also helped protect the wearer from flamethrowers.*

ARMOURED TROOPS

Soviet armour developed significantly in the 1930s. Light tanks, heavy tanks and armoured cars formed the core of tank regiments and independent battalions, while armoured cars (and later motorcycles) played an important role in reconnaissance units. As the war developed, self-propelled artillery grew in importance, but personnel carriers were rare; infantry often rode into battle on tanks.

Tankers

In June 1941 there were 150 tank regiments; 25 more were added in July 1941. Armoured troops also included armoured car units and reconnaissance units equipped with motorbikes – rare in 1939, but increasingly common from then on.

From 1935 onwards, armoured troops had the right to wear a steel-grey uniform based on the artillery pattern. This meant a tunic with a stand-and-fall colour or an officer's French tunic, with open collar and white shirt with black tie. The breeches were also supposed to have been in steel grey, but few were manufactured in this colour and even the steel-grey tunics were rare by 1941, when they were abolished. There was also an overall in grey, green or dark blue. First issued in 1935, this was a single piece, fastened with a zip and tightened with an integral belt. It was worn over the uniform.

Grey or khaki tunics were worn, the collar insignia was the same. It consisted of a black collar patch piped red (or gold), the usual rank insignia and a bronze tank badge – slightly modified in 1940; these were usually issued in pairs. Officers had red piping around their collars and on their breeches. Caps had black cap bands, a grey or khaki crown and red piping around the crown. Side caps were usually khaki, although a few officers seem to have acquired steel-grey versions. The collar patches, rank insignia and greatcoat tabs were subdued in 1941, and rank chevrons on the sleeves abolished.

Motor units attached to tank formations dropped the tank insignia for a pair of winged wheels worn on the collar. Signals units used their distinctive winged thunderbolts on the black collar tabs.

◀ **Tanker, 47th Tank Regiment, 1941**
Tankers had the choice of wearing khaki or steel grey tunics or overalls fastened with a zip down the front. The leather jacket was popular, whether it was specific to armoured crews or one borrowed from the air force.

▶ **Second Lieutenant, Reconnaissance Battalion, 210th Tank Regiment, 1941** *This officer wears the wheeled steering wheel with wings device used for personnel serving vehicles. He now serves as part of the crew of an armoured car and has retained his original insignia.*

◀ TANK COMMANDER, 36TH TANK REGIMENT, 1942 *The padded helmet was developed in the mid-1930s and for its time was an innovative and ground-breaking piece of equipment. It came in painted fabric but a leather version also existed.*

▶ TANKER, 75TH SEPARATE TANK BATTALION, 1943 *The padded jacket was well suited for all manner of troops. Tankers took to it not only because it was warm, but also because it had some fire-resistant properties.*

Changes in 1943

In 1943 the basic uniform changed with the introduction of the 1943-pattern tunic and shoulder boards. These normally retained the tank badge by the button close to the collar (further down for other ranks). The shoulder boards were khaki piped red (with red stripes and yellow stars for officers) in the field, with service dress consisting of black boards piped red for other ranks (with gold bands across for NCOs) and gold boards piped red and with red stripes for officers. Although unit numerals on the shoulder board were rare, they could appear. This numeral was followed with the Cyrillic 'Б' if a brigade rather than a regiment was denoted or the Cyrillic 'ГБ' if a Guards tank brigade; 12 armoured corps had Guard status by 1945, and nine mechanized corps. Motorcyclist units added an 'M'.

Leather items

The most distinctive part of the armoured troops' uniforms was the tankers' helmet. This had first been produced in leather in 1934. That pattern had three combs of leather running over from the padded front brim to the back of the wearer's neck. There were also earflaps, which buckled under the chin, and these had smaller flaps over the ears themselves; these smaller flaps could be kept in place with studs. The helmet was modified in 1936. More padding was added (horsehair or artificial wool) to the top and sides, and a strap and buckle over the top of the helmet allowed it to be kept rigid. The neck flap could turn up and the flaps over each ear also received a buckled flap. The leather helmet was now covered with an artificial coating to increase durability. Fur-lined versions also existed.

The other significant item of uniforms for the armoured troops was the leather coat – leather was more fireproof than many of the materials available at the time. The first type of black leather coat was issued in 1929. It was double-breasted and had five buttons and closed at the collar with a hook and eye. The 1934 pattern had four buttons, breast pockets and two vertical pockets at the sides and two waist pockets. It had Raglan sleeves that could be tightened over gloves. The 1937-pattern coat was similar, but without the Raglan sleeves. All these coats came with matching leather breeches that could be bound below the knee and worn with boots or puttees. Armoured personnel could wear the standard infantry greatcoat (with appropriate branch-of-service colours). Until 1943 this had the black (piped red or gold) lozenge, but from 1943 a green rectangular tab piped in red denoted armoured troops.

MARINE INFANTRY

The Soviet surface fleet rarely strayed from its bases. Personnel were often called to act as infantry during moments of crisis, but also mounted some amphibious operations.

There were two kinds of marine infantry. The first, the naval infantry brigades, were composed of sailors armed and equipped as infantry, who protected naval bases, ports and waterways. There were 42 brigades of naval infantry and these formations initially retained their naval uniforms, although as they became more permanently stationed on land they gradually adopted Army uniforms – but with some distinctive features. Then there were the naval rifle brigades. Although these were originally composed of naval personnel, they were absorbed into the Army and were commanded by Army officers and uniformed as per Army units while perhaps retaining the Navy belt and cap.

Black devils

Soviet sailors were uniformed in a V-necked tunic, or bushlat, which usually had the traditional striped shirt showing beneath. This was dark blue, giving rise to the marine infantry nickname of 'black devils', and the formal version had a lighter blue turnback collar folded over the shoulder with three white stripes around the edge – very similar to the uniforms of other navies. Breeches were also dark blue and were usually tucked into leather boots.

Greatcoats were dark blue and fastened with metallic buttons bearing an anchor device; a blue double-breasted pea coat was also issued. Naval personnel wore a leather belt with a distinctive belt plaque showing a star (with hammer and sickle) and anchor device. Insignia was shown on the sleeve (as red or yellow stars and gold bars on the lower sleeve, although political officers had a red star piped yellow and NKVD units had a yellow star piped green). A specialist badge was worn in red on the upper left sleeve. An infantry badge was introduced for naval infantry in 1941; this had a yellow anchor and rope on a blue disk also piped in red.

◄ **MARINE, 143RD MARINE INFANTRY BRIGADE, 1942** *Soviet marine infantry were usually uniformed in naval styles of dress. This individual has an Army helmet – the Navy was authorized to wear helmets painted dark blue.*

► **CAPTAIN, 7TH MARINE INFANTRY BRIGADE, 1942** *Marine officers generally wore the tall leather boot, which was both robust and comfortable. The top of the boot was left supple and soft, which meant that after a few months of wear the boot looked creased.*

▲ *The Russian Baltic fleet was trapped around Leningrad but its personnel served during the siege of the city.*

Fleets

Naval infantry wore peaked caps with black bands and white crowns. Ratings also had naval round caps that were dark blue and had two ribbons behind (with anchor devices). The cap usually bore the name of the fleet in gold as shown in the table below.

A more general title of military fleet ('Военно-морской флот') was worn by some naval detachments. Very rarely a ship's name was used on the cap – only usually the name of a major vessel. Some of the bands were in orange and black, denoting that the unit had been decorated with the Order of the Red Flag.

Standard Army helmets were worn (usually in grey or dark green) and Army equipment was issued. The naval infantry had the habit of wearing belts of ammunition crisscrossed over their shoulders and of carrying naval daggers; they were armed with standard Red Army firearms.

As the war progressed Army uniforms began to replace naval dress. Khaki tunics and padded jackets were worn over the striped shirt, and khaki breeches replaced the dark blue naval versions. The distinctive naval infantry badge continued to be worn on the sleeve, as did the naval belt. Sailors caps also continued to be worn.

Shoulder boards

In 1943 shoulder boards were introduced and, for naval infantry, these were worn on predominantly khaki tunics; rank continued to be shown on the lower sleeve as a yellow star over a combination of gold bars. Service dress boards were dark blue and gold for officers (piped dark blue and with dark blue stripes). The only exceptions were for engineering and non-combat personnel, who wore silver boards. The button by the collar bore an anchor device. The shoulder board could bear the initials of the relevant fleet, that is 'С Ф', 'Б Ф', 'ЧФ' or 'ТФ', usually in yellow. Rank insignia meant a single yellow stripe across the board for a senior sailor, two for a petty officer, three for a sergeant, a thick bar for a senior sergeant and a thick bar running along the board for a sergeant major. Officers had their rank denoted by combinations of stars and stripes – yellow on the dark blue field board, dark blue on the service dress board. Officers and specialists serving in a particular branch of service had naval uniforms, but kept the shoulder board colouring and design of their particular branch of service – so naval aviation officers effectively had Air Force boards on naval uniforms.

Insignia also included the Guards badge. There were a number (perhaps as many as four) naval versions of the Guards insignia, the most common being a clasp of blue and orange ribbon (vertical stripes). The naval version was only used for a limited period of time and the Navy switched to the standard Guards badge in 1943 to harmonize the awards system.

▼ **MARINE, 5TH MARINE INFANTRY BRIGADE, 1942** *This marine infantryman is ready for assault and is equipped like his infantry counterparts – the cap and shirt indicate his naval origins as does the belt buckle. He carries an RGD33 grenade from his belt.*

Fleet name		Cap title
Northern fleet	(operating around Murmansk/the Arctic)	'Северный флот'
Baltic fleet	(operating around Leningrad)	'Балтийский флот'
Black Sea fleet	(operating around Odessa)	'Черноморский флот'
Pacific fleet	(operating around Vladivlostock)	'Тихоокеанский флот'

PARATROOPS

The Soviets were among the first to see the potential of specialist paratroops and glider-borne infantry.

In 1930 an experimental group of military parachutists was established in Moscow. Following on from those initial trials, training schools were established for the evaluation and training of troops in this form of warfare. By 1936 battalions had been formed and in 1938 there were six operational brigades.

▲ *A Soviet pilot puts on his PD6 parachute, the kind most often worn by aviation personnel and paratroops.*

◀ **Paratrooper, 4th Battalion, 8th Airborne Brigade, 1942** *Paratroopers wore helmets as well as the famous pilotka side cap. However, as a mark of prestige as much as anything, many retained their peak caps with band-of-service colour (light blue) on the cap band.*

They were involved in operational jumps despite being largely used as infantry. In 1945 Soviet paratroopers, who had by then been granted Guard status, captured the last Emperor of China, who was then ruling the Japanese puppet state of Manchukuo.

Airborne battalions were originally to consist of paratroopers and glider-borne infantry, but a lack of suitable aircraft meant that very few Red Army personnel were ever sent into action using gliders. Paratroops consisted of male and female personnel and were uniformed accordingly.

Tunics

Uniforms followed those of the infantry, but with Air Force insignia; the Air Force had been entitled to wear dark blue tunics and trousers between 1935 and October 1941, and such items were still seen later on in the war. The 1935-pattern tunic was mostly in khaki and it received light blue collar patches (piped black or gold), rank insignia and the winged propeller badge towards the back of the collar. Officers had light blue piping on their tunic collars and cuffs and down the outer seams of their blue breeches. They had the option to wear the French open-necked tunic and this was worn with white shirt with detachable collar, and black tie.

Peaked service caps had light blue bands, dark blue crowns and light blue piping around the crown. They also had a special badge that had a wreathed red star below golden wings. Side caps were initially dark blue piped in light blue, but khaki caps became more common from 1941 and these sometimes had light blue piping.

The 1943 changes saw the introduction of shoulder boards. These were khaki piped light blue for other ranks' field dress and khaki piped light blue with red stripes, propeller insignia and stars for officers. Service dress called for light blue boards piped black and gold boards piped light blue and with light blue stripes respectively. Officers had silver stars and silvered propeller badges, other ranks had stencilled badges, metal badges or did

▲ **Paratrooper, 1st Battalion, 214th Airborne Brigade 1942** *The rucksack, issued in 1939, contained the mess tin (in cover), toiletries, a change of linen and rations. It was more popular than the heavier 1936-pattern haversack.*

without. Other branches assigned to paratroop units kept their branch insignia, but added the Cyrillic 'Д' after their unit numeral if this was shown.

Insignia followed the pattern worn by the infantry, but a number of different paratrooper badges were worn, usually above the wearer's left breast pocket. An open parachute on a blue lozenge below a red star was the first such badge and was issued from 1933 onwards. Instructors added a silver aeroplane motif and moved the star to under the canopy. Some 16 airborne divisions had been awarded Guard status by 1945 and these units were entitled to wear the Guards badge on their tunics.

Equipment

To this basic dress were added standard infantry equipment, camouflage smocks and standard infantry helmets, although these were rarely worn in combat as the paratroopers' distinctive peaked cap was seen as a mark of special distinction. New designs of camouflage equipment were issued to Guard scouts, snipers and paratroopers, so paratroops were generally well provided for. They also received extra pay and bonuses according to the number of jumps they made. The Soviets did not design a specific helmet or jump suit for paratroopers until much later, but leather flying helmets were sometimes worn while airborne. The only distinctive item of dress was a fur-collared waterproof parka, designed to keep the wearer warm at high altitude, and khaki or dark blue overalls that resembled those worn by tankers and armoured personnel.

A small naval paratroop unit saw action around the Black Sea in 1943. It was uniformed as above, but with naval belt buckles, the traditional striped shirt and sailors' caps.

Parachutes

The chutes used by enlisted men were generally square cotton with an area of approximately 60 square metres (70 square yards). The parachute was semiautomatic in operation, and was also equipped with a handle release for use in emergencies. Other ranks did not use reserve chutes. Officers generally made use of a round chute, also made of cotton, with approximately the same area as that used by other ranks. It also had both a manual and a semiautomatic operation. Officers were, however, equipped with a silk reserve chute. The standard training parachute was the PD6 , sometimes also used by officers on operations. For most jumps, however, the square PD41 chute was used, which opened more quickly and was used for low-altitude jumps.

▼ **Paratrooper, 1st Parachute Battalion, Manchuria, 1945** *The panama hat had proved popular from 1938 in central Asia and with troops stationed along the Chinese border. This hat has been borrowed from the infantry.*

AIR FORCE

The Soviet Air Force consisted of an Army Air Force (VVS, or AKA from 1942) and a Naval Air Force (an air arm operating as part of the military fleet or VMF). The Army Air Force had developed from embryonic units that flew during the Russian Civil War of 1917-22 into a large air service equipped with modern planes by the mid-1930s. As was the case in other European countries, these planes were very dated by 1941. Following a steep learning curve, the Soviets achieved dominance of the air over the Eastern Front by mid-1943.

Organization

Founded in 1918, in early 1939 the VVS had 360,000 personnel, organized primarily into fighter aviation regiments, bomber (plus long-range and night bomber) regiments, reconnaissance and spotter regiments, transport regiments, ground crew (and logistic, medical and mechanical services) and guards, together with airborne infantry. Later ground-attack regiments became more common.

Dress

The Air Force enjoyed the right to wear dark blue tunics (other ranks gymnastiorka, officers gymnastiorka and officers open-collar French tunics) and breeches or pantaloons. The tunics had light blue collar patches (piped black or gold), rank insignia (initially also worn as red chevrons on the sleeve) and the winged propeller badge at the back of the collar; from 1942 technical staff had a similar device in gold but with a red enamel star in the centre of the propeller, replacing the technical branch-of-service badge worn to that date. Officers had the collars and cuffs of their tunics piped in light blue and light blue piping down the outer seams of their blue breeches. They had the option to wear the French open-necked tunic and this was worn with white shirt (with detachable collar) and black tie. Dark blue greatcoats were also issued and these had light blue lozenges with black or gold piping along the top, branch-of-service insignia and rank insignia. These dark blue items

◀ **Lieutenant, 142nd Transport Regiment, 1941** *Pilots had some latitude when it came to dress – for example, the 1935-pattern tunic was issued in blue, steel grey or, as here, khaki. The blue and steel grey versions were rarer as the war went on; the blue version was supposedly withdrawn in the autumn of 1941, but it proved resilient.*

▶ **Pilot, 22nd Fighter Regiment, 1942** *This pilot wears the leather combination flying suit adapted from 1940. A heavily padded and buoyant winter version was especially popular among pilots flying with the Northern Fleet.*

▲ *The Soviet I-16 fighter plane saw service in Spain and over Poland. Most were destroyed in 1941.*

were supposedly abolished in October 1941, to be replaced by khaki items. Even so, blue items persisted at least until 1943.

The peaked service cap had a light blue band, dark blue crown and light blue piping around the crown. The cap had a special badge with a wreathed red star below golden wings. Side caps were initially dark blue piped in light blue, and many pilots clung on to these items for the sake of tradition. Female pilots usually wore the beret.

The 1943 changes saw the introduction of shoulder boards. The boards were khaki piped light blue for other ranks' field dress and khaki piped light blue with red stripes, propeller insignia and stars for officers. Service dress called for light blue boards piped black and gold boards piped light blue and with light blue stripes for officers. Officers had silver stars and gilt propeller badges; other ranks had stencilled badges or metal badges – or did without. The button by the collar was with a hammer and sickle emblem (an anchor for naval aviation). A shoulder board could carry the regimental numeral. The number followed by a Cyrillic 'Ш' letter denoted a ground-attack aviation unit.

In addition to these standard items of dress and insignia, there were a number of variations of pilots' badges. These were embroidered patches worn on the upper left sleeve. The pilots' badge was in gilt thread and had a winged propeller with red star at the centre and crossed swords. In 1942 the technical staff received their own arm badge with crossed hammers and naval pilots had an anchor rather than swords or hammers. Fourteen air corps had been granted Guard status by 1945 and members of Guards units wore the standard Guards badge.

Flying gear

Soviet pilots generally wore brown flying helmets and wore their uniforms under flying gear. The helmet came in many different versions but the 1940 pattern was the most common. There was a leather summer version or a winter version in fur-lined leather. The 1940 pattern had black moulded rubber ear cups that could have been adapted to receive radio receivers. There was a chinstrap (with buckle) and later models had a laryngophone (throat microphone) built in.

The flying jacket used by Soviet pilots was mostly the 1935-pattern long leather coat (in black or dark brown), usually fur-lined in the winter. It was often worn with leather trousers (also fur lined) and felt or fur-lined boots. A one-piece flying jacket was also developed. This came in light brown with a fur collar and lining, had a button to tighten the cuff and was fastened with a zip (a version with five buttons and a fly front was also issued). It had a pocket on each thigh (closed with a button) and most pilots carried a leather map case over their shoulder. Pilots carried pistols.

A shortage of specialist equipment meant helmets, buoyancy and flying jackets supplied through the US Lend Lease programme. Some Lend Lease aircraft were also operational: the Soviets received 1,000 Spitfires, 3,000 Hurricanes (modified to receive additional armament) and 2,500 P-40s. The bulk of aircraft were, however, of Soviet design and build.

▲ **Lieutenant, 46th Guards Night Bomber Regiment, 1943** *This female pilot has the pilots' badge on the upper left arm. It consisted of crossed swords behind a red star, all on winged propeller. This badge had been introduced as early as 1924.*

OTHER ALLIED POWERS

The process by which a coalition came into being to fight the Axis powers was neither smooth nor systematic. At one point in 1940, Britain (with her empire and people who had fled continental Europe to take refuge in Britain) stood alone, until following Axis aggression Greece joined and temporarily increased the alliance. However, 1941 was a turning point: the Axis attack on the Soviet Union and the German and Italian declaration of war against the United States fashioned a large and powerful alliance. As important as the big powers were, a host of smaller nations supported the aim of defeating the Axis, whether it was because they themselves had been victims of Axis aggression, because they saw supporting the Allied war effort a matter of moral solidarity or because they saw an opportunity.

▲ *Danish personnel, in their distinctive helmets, undertake anti-aircraft training in the final days of peace before the German invasion.*

◀ *A Belgian infantry regiment, armed with Lebel rifles, parades before its colonel in the summer of 1939.*

ALLIES, GREAT AND SMALL

The countries that faced the Axis in the war, and the eventual coalition that emerged to win victory in 1945, were a diverse collection of nations and peoples. There were victims of Axis aggression and there were those who rallied to the side of victory and threw in their lot to defeat German domination of Europe and Japanese supremacy in Asia. There were political opponents of Fascism and there were those who perhaps sympathized with right-wing politics but, out of patriotism, opted to fight against the far right. Inevitably, also, there were the reluctant warriors, those who were forced into uniform to wage a war they knew or cared little about.

Alongside the Allied nations were volunteers from countries that officially remained neutral. Irish men and women volunteered for service in the British armed forces. Portuguese personnel volunteered for Allied forces and her sailors participated in supplying the Allies. Individuals from Axis countries also fought for the Allies. There were Germans and Italians in the French Foreign Legion, and the Soviets raised Romanian units from prisoners and had German and Italian collaborators.

▼ *China had to wait for Allied equipment, but by 1945 large numbers of Chinese troops were using US or Soviet material.*

War in China

The first to feel the horrors of war were the Chinese. China had emerged from a period of turbulence and chaos, when warlords governed her lands, only to find herself the victim of an aggressive Japan. The Sino-Japanese War of 1937-45 was a horrible calamity that led to millions of deaths, but 1945 did not bring peace. The two significant victors in the war against Japan, the Communists and the Nationalists, embarked on a bitter war for control of China that would see the Communists emerge as winners and the Nationalists confined to the island of Formosa (Taiwan).

▲ *Polish infantry dressed in smart parade uniforms are photographed in Warsaw in the dark days of 1939.*

German aggression in Europe

The Czechs were the next to suffer – their country was occupied before any declaration of war. Czech personnel escaped to the Soviet Union, to France and then on to Britain. Czech lands were occupied; the Slovaks split away and joined the Axis. Poland was the next victim, doubly so. Poland had pursued a misguided policy in the 1930s that led to the country being isolated and surrounded by hostile powers. Inevitably, it was coveted by Germany (the country had absorbed territories that had belonged to Germany) and the Soviet Union was hostile (Poland had waged war on the Bolsheviks and controlled much of eastern Ukraine). Yet it had also picked fights with Lithuania, the Czechoslovaks and Hungary. An accord with Romania – and last-minute agreements with France and Britain, who opted to support Poland rather than ally with the Soviets (the Soviets had proposed a pact in April 1939, but were spurned, leading to them seeking agreement on Poland with Germany) – did not lead to material assistance in 1939 and Poland found itself divided between its traditional enemies. Poles

went into exile, as they did before, and fought in large numbers in British uniforms and, after 1941, as part of the Red Army. Many Italians fought alongside the Allies from 1943.

The Germans overran Denmark with ease, and fought to occupy Norway – achieving this despite French and British intervention. Next came Belgium, Luxembourg and the Netherlands. Soldiers, sailors and airmen from all these countries would continue to fight in Allied uniform. The biggest surprise was France, with its powerful Army and enhanced reputation. The Republic fell in a matter of weeks, surprising the Germans and much of the world. Most of the country was occupied, with the Germans establishing naval bases all along the Atlantic coast and supporting a collaborative regime (Vichy) in the south of the country. But Free French made their way abroad to continue the fight, and the Resistance in France continued the struggle (often against terrible odds).

The Germans then turned on Yugoslavia, overrunning a country that had avoided German diplomatic attempts to woo it to join the Axis alliance. That country was dissolved and split between the Italians, a new Croat state and a Serb rump under German control. But a significant resistance movement developed, fuelled by atrocities and excess. From Yugoslavia the Axis invaded Greece, which had been engrossed in war with Italy. Greece too developed a significant resistance movement that would largely be suppressed after 1945 in a bitter civil war.

▼ *A French instructor trains a female volunteer in England in a camp of the Free French Forces in 1942.*

Countries switch sides

Axis defeat seemed inevitable by 1943. Many of the countries that had supported the Germans switched sides when liberation approached. In the west the Germans had already dissolved the Vichy state and liberation in 1944 led to hundreds of thousands flocking to the French colours and going on to participate in the invasion of the Reich. In the east the Romania and Bulgaria successfully switched sides and fought alongside the Soviets in 1944 and 1945, and the Finns followed a similar path. The Hungarians attempted to come to terms but the Germans intervened, dragging the country down into apocalyptic fighting in 1945.

▲ *These Free French soldiers, also known as the Fighting French, parade at a base, probably at Camberley, in England in 1942.*

Other allies

In addition to these major states, there were other valuable contributors to the Allied cause. Brazil sent an expeditionary force (which is beyond the scope of this book) following its declaration of war against Germany and Italy in August 1942. Many Central American states had done this on a unilateral basis following US entry into the war, and Mexico did the same in May 1942. Turkey – having followed a policy of neutrality, but also supplied goods to Germany through Bulgaria – entered the war on the Allied side in February 1945.

BELGIUM

Belgium's Army was small and had been neglected since World War I. It relied on a core of line infantry supported by some elite units and a relatively large number of cavalry.

Infantry

Belgian infantry consisted of line infantry regiments, carabiniers, chasseurs, grenadiers and mountain troops (the Ardennes Jagers). The infantry wore a brown or dark khaki Adrian helmet weighing 1kg (2.2lb). First introduced in 1915, it was modified slightly in 1931, sporting a Belgian lion motif and differing slightly from French helmets by having a flatter front and rear peak and black lining. A side cap, or bonnet de police, was worn off duty. The officers had peaked caps with a crown badge below the Belgian cockade. The regimental numeral featured on side caps and shoulder straps (below a crown).

Belgian line infantry tunics were introduced in 1935. They had six buttons (bearing the Belgian lion), four pockets, shoulder straps (with a button by the collar) and pointed collars. They were in a browner shade of khaki, and for line infantry had a red collar patch on the pointed collars piped in blue; blue piping was also used on side caps and the officers' caps. Officers wore jackets with open collars and pointed cuffs, a khaki or green shirt and a tie. NCOs were distinguished by stripes on the lower arm and usually had tunics that were of a finer cut.

Rank was shown as a series of stars within the collar patches. The grenadier regiments, of which there were two, were distinguished by a burning grenade on the collar patch (also worn on the greatcoat collar), together with a motif that replaced the crown on the officer's caps and was also worn on the shoulder straps; fortress units had a tower device. The chasseurs were uniformed as per the line infantry, but with green collar patches faced yellow; cyclist companies were identified by a bicycle wheel on the collar and side cap. The carabiniers were uniformed in a similar fashion, but without the yellow piping; instead, they had a hunting horn device on their caps, shoulder straps and collars. The Ardennes Jagers, with seven regiments, were differentiated by having red piping to their green collar patches, but they also had a special boar's head device on collars and on

◀ Private, 7th Infantry Regiment, 1940
The Belgian Adrian helmet was modified in 1931, the only real change being to the decorative lion. This was given a more ferocious appearance by opening the mouth and displaying the teeth. Helmets were usually painted a matt greenish khaki.

▶ Captain, 1st Chasseurs Ardennais, 1940
These chasseurs were elite troops formed to operate in the Ardennes. They had a distinctive wild boar device that was worn on the units' dark green beret (sometimes above the battalion number).

▲ SECOND LIEUTENANT, 12TH ARTILLERY REGIMENT, 1940 *Artillery officers had peaked caps when not wearing the Adrian helmet. These caps had red piping above the crown and crossed cannon barrels by way of insignia. This was all below the black-within-yellow-within-red Belgian cockade.*

their distinctive green berets. Machine gun battalions wore the battalion number in Roman numerals on their shoulder straps and had an eight-pointed star on their collars. Most troops wore the double-breasted khaki greatcoat (with five buttons) or carried it rolled over the knapsack.

Cavalry

Belgian cavalry consisted of guides, lancers, mounted Jagers and chasseurs. In general, the uniform was similar to that worn by the infantry, although riding boots and breeches were worn and the greatcoat was shorter.

Shoulder straps still had the unit number beneath a crown, but facing colours and distinctive devices designated the branch of service. The two regiments of guides had amaranth collar patches, piped in green, and this colour was also worn on the officers' cap bands. A device consisting of crossed swords beneath a crown was worn on the front of the cap, and this device was often worn on the side cap and greatcoat collars too. The four regiments of lancers had white facings, piped blue, and wore a crossed lance device on caps, side caps and greatcoats. They had the regimental numeral on the side cap and the shoulder straps – in this case, there was no crown.

The two regiments of mounted Jagers had yellow collar patches faced blue and their device consisted of a hunting horn and sabre. Again, no crown appeared on the shoulder strap. The two regiments of mounted chasseurs had dark blue collar patches piped in red, but this time with a grenade badge (repeated on the shoulder straps and caps). Regimental devices on the straps were replaced by the letter 'R' for remount depots.

Technicians

Troops assigned to armoured cars had white facings piped in scarlet. They also had the letter 'C' as an insignia on side caps and caps, while personnel assigned to the tank regiment had scarlet facings piped blue with a helmet and crossed canon barrel device. Both types of unit wore berets, and had French-style leather helmets for use within the tank.

Belgian artillery were uniformed as per the infantry, but were distinguished by dark blue facings piped red and crossed canon barrels on their caps and greatcoats – apart from fortress artillery, who had the initial letter of the fortress ('N' for Namur, for example) on their caps. The army's engineer battalions had the traditional black piped red facings and used a Roman helmet as a motif on collars, greatcoats and caps. The shoulder strap bore the battalion number in Arabic numerals and the helmet, although officers just had the Roman helmet. Train personnel had light blue distinctions faced in dark blue and either the battalion's number on the shoulder strap, in Arabic numerals, or the corps' number, in Roman numerals, if personnel were assigned to a specific corps. A wheel device was used on side caps and greatcoat collars.

▶ TROOPER, TRANSPORT BATTALION, 1940 *The 1935-pattern tunic had collar tabs shaped in a lozenge. This style replaced the more rectangular type worn on the older style tunic with standing collars. Train units had light blue piped at the top with dark blue.*

CHINA

China suffered greatly in the war, but 1945 did not bring peace. Those elements that had fought the Japanese went on to wage a bloody civil war until 1949.

Power struggles

China had become a republic in 1912, when the last emperor abdicated and the rule of the Qing dynasty came to an end. The dominating force in the new republic was the nationalist party, the Kuomintang (KMT) – which, from 1927, ruled from the capital, Nanjing. The party instituted a series of reforms, establishing a modern army (known as the National Revolutionary Army from 1925 onwards) and defeating the feuding warlords who had plagued the country for decades.

Led by an energetic commander-in-chief, Chiang Kai-shek, China's armies embarked on a radical modernization programme that involved the Soviet Union and Germany in training and re-equipping the Army and a small Air Force. As the KMT slid politically to the right, the Chinese rejected Soviet aid and, from 1933 onwards, favoured assistance from German Nazi leader Adolf Hitler. The programme was not entirely successful in creating a unified, well equipped and uniformed force. Local autonomy and lack of resources meant that many of the plans remained undeveloped and that Chinese forces would take to the field in whatever uniform was available. A further complication was that the communists, who had initially collaborated with the KMT, developed their own armed forces, usually known as the Chinese Red Army, although this was largely restricted to Yenan province.

Japan, the growing military power in the region, had conquered Manchuria and its military now looked to destroy China. The Japanese seriously underestimated Chinese forces and the fact that outside intervention would unify once-warring factions. The war began in July 1937 and Japan seized Beijing and the ports, soon controlled the Yangtze valley and destroyed Nanjing.

◀ **Private, Big Sword Company, 1936** *Units equipped with traditional Chinese warrior swords were fielded against the Japanese, often acting as assault troops with Mauser pistols, swords and grenades. The practice died away in the first year of the war as the swords were too heavy.*

▲ **Private, 303rd Regiment, 1937** *The majority of Chinese troops were uniformed in a relatively haphazard way, depending on season, climate and availability. Most did at least wear the cap badge seen here, the white star on a blue disk.*

To combat this onslaught, China initially relied on its 143 existing divisions. The army was predominantly infantry-based, with some cavalry and artillery. There were just three battalions of armoured cars in 1937, and these were quickly destroyed.

▲ *General Chiang Kai-shek inspects a company of officer cadets at Wuhan, in 1940.*

Chiang Kai-shek lost the best of his units in the fighting of 1937, but preserved a reliable core to continue the fight while the KMT and Mao tse-tung's communists made use of partisans and guerrillas to harry the Japanese. Stalemate ensued in 1939, with the KMT operating out of their new capital, Chongqing. Overall, KMT forces were badly led, badly supplied and poorly equipped, at least initially, but they tied up hundreds of thousands of Japanese troops and made a significant contribution to ultimate victory.

Revolutionary Army

The uniforms of the National Revolutionary Army were developed in the mid-1920s. They initially drew on existing blue-grey uniforms with their simple tunics and peaked caps, but also on stocks of khaki tunics with standing collars used extensively by forces based in Szechuan. Puttees were worn high on the leg and footwear consisted of sandals or ankle boots, with officers preferring cavalry boots. Civilian items were also used. Regional variations also played a part, with troops in the north making use of fur hats and greatcoats, while those in the south accessed horizon blue cloth for their uniforms from French Indochina.

This confusion in dress was matched by a lack of helmets and equipment. The NRA made some progress by 1936, defining a new uniform, and did at least establish a system of rank insignia and unit distinctions, the first step along the road towards homogeneity. German supplies were used to uniform and equip a number of divisions (dealt with below), and imports of small arms made a significant difference to improving the Army's effectiveness. Officers were, inevitably, better off than their men, many of them providing their own uniform. The style of their uniforms was based on those devised for the cadets of the Whampoa Military Academy.

▶ **Private, 524th Regiment, 1937** *There were Chinese units that were very well equipped having, ironically, benefitted from German supplies. This unit, which fought at Shanghai, was part of the German-equipped 88th Division and was uniformed complete with the 1935-style German helmet.*

Variations

The idea was to have a summer uniform in light cotton khaki, and a winter uniform based on grey (and often with a padded tunic for extra warmth) or, in some regions, a brown khaki. The infantry were to be supplied with a peaked cap bearing the white KMT star on a dark blue background, or fur caps. Officers were to wear a peaked cap with a high crown, rather like those fashionable in Europe. They might also wear a better-tailored version of the peaked cap.

A locally manufactured helmet known as the 'plum blossom variant' was also intended for issued. This was based on the Japanese 1922 design, but slightly modified to be lower in the crown, and more like the Brodie helmet worn by British

and American troops in World War I. It had a distinctive visor and was thicker along the base, where the steel was rolled over to form the rim. It was topped with a five-leafed blossom design that covered four air holes. The lining was riveted to the shell at four points and the chinstrap, which was normally of canvas, was buckled to lugs on either side of the helmet. It seems to have received the KMT star on the front by way of insignia.

This helmet was not produced in sufficient numbers and the Japanese invasion put an end to production. The French had supplied a large number of the original Adrian helmets to China, especially when the new model introduced in 1926 made the older style redundant. The British too had sold Brodie helmets to the Chinese. Both of these variants had the KMT star. The tunics were to have four pockets, a standing collar and no shoulder straps. They were buttoned with wooden buttons, or sometimes silver or gold for officers. The collars bore patches in branch-of-service colours as well as rank insignia. The infantry had red patches, the cavalry had yellow, the artillery blue and engineers white. The small numbers of medical personnel were supposed to receive green, while transport and mechanized troops were to have black; the 200th Division had been equipped with Soviet-supplied tanks and were acting as armoured troops. Generals had gold collar patches with a single triangle set in the centre to denote a major general, two to denote a lieutenant general and three for a corps commander. Officers also used these gilt triangles as well as a gold bar running the length of the collar tab, and gold piping all around it. Second lieutenants had a single triangle, lieutenants had two and captains had three. Majors had two gold bars and a single triangle, lieutenant colonels had two triangles and two bars and colonels had three triangles and two bars. NCOs used collar patches that were unpiped and had a single triangle for a private, two for a senior private and three for a lance corporal. A corporal added a black bar behind the triangle, a sergeant had two triangles with the blue bar and sergeant majors had three triangles and the blue bar. These devices were often repeated on field caps or forage caps.

The Air Force followed the same principal. Chinese divisions often wore a divisional or unit patch above their tunic pocket or on the upper left arm. This was sometimes piped in service colours but there was no standard approach.

◀ **Captain, 3rd Artillery Regiment, 1937** *China was a melting pot when it came to weapons, uniforms and equipment. European powers sold surplus stock and new models, while the Soviets and Germans provided training.*

Gunner, 3rd Artillery Regiment, 1937 *These Chinese artillerymen are using a German-produced 20mm (0.8in) Flak 30 gun exported to China in the 1930s.*

▶ **Private, Communist Forces, 1944** *The Communists were largely only distinguished by the red stars on their caps, making use of whatever uniforms and equipment they could lay their hands on.*

There were a number of different greatcoats in use, but padded jackets or civilian items were also worn as needed. Greatcoats and blankets were often worn rolled around the body, as knapsacks were rare. Weapons were an odd mix of Chinese-manufactured rifles and pistols, imported (Mausers and Browning pistols) or captured items. Canvas ammunition pouches and bandoliers were common for rank and file infantry. Officers wore a ceremonial dagger or sword, cavalry carried lances and swords and some infantry personnel were also equipped with swords.

German divisions

The 3rd, 6th, 9th, 14th, 36th, 87th and 88th Chinese divisions were trained and equipped by German advisers. They wore a light khaki summer uniform and a darker woollen uniform that was usually brownish-green, although grey had been intended. These troops also wore the German 1935 model helmet, mostly painted grey, with KMT symbol; a few of the earlier 1916 model helmets were also delivered. China had purchased 220,000 of these helmets from Adolf Hitler's Germany and they were delivered in 1936. These troops also wore leather equipment (including cartridge pouches for ammunition, mostly for use with Mauser rifles) and gas masks. Officers had Sam Browne belts and, usually, Browning pistols.

Chinese in Burma

Some 20 Chinese divisions were brought into India and took up positions in Burma in 1942, later forming Force X and Force Y. These were equipped with British and American equipment and uniforms. Force X would receive American M1 helmets and the 1943-pattern jacket, whilst the 6th Army received British helmets and web equipment.

▲ **Female Partisan, Communist Forces, 1940** *The C96 Mauser, with its odd wooden stock that doubled as a holster, was extremely popular in China. Numbers fell into Communist hands in the 1930s after being issued to Chinese police and military during the warlord era (1916-28).*

Collaboration

Some Chinese collaborated with the Japanese occupiers and client regimes – known as the Provisional Government and the Reformed Government – were established. These had troops wearing Japanese equipment, Chinese uniforms and a distinctive five-petal flower badge (with the petals in white, blue, orange, red and black).

Communist forces

The Communist troops who joined the Japanese provided their own equipment and were uniformed in khaki or grey, but with the distinctive red star as insignia and a red armband for commanders. The New Fourth Army in the south and the Eighth Route Army joined forces with the KMT for some time. These troops seem to have adopted KMT insignia rather than wearing red stars, and this included a distinctive patch worn on the upper left arm. They used mostly captured weaponry and whatever equipment they could lay their hands on.

DENMARK

Throughout the 1930s Denmark steered a pacifist course through the turbulent waters of European politics, even though the country was especially vulnerable to German aggression.

When the Germans invaded, the Danish regular army attempted to meet the threat, but the government capitulated after six hours of fighting.

The Danish Army was composed of Royal Guards (the Royal Life Guard Regiment being infantry, the Guard Hussar regiment being the cavalry), six infantry regiments (numbered 1–5 and 7, with 6 being converted into a mechanized unit), a cavalry regiment (the Jutland Dragoons), three artillery regiments and assorted technical troops.

In terms of uniform and personal equipment, Denmark was in a state of flux in 1940. A new khaki uniform had been ordered in 1923, and this was to be worn with brown leather equipment and a new, distinctive helmet. In fact, existing supplies (the 1915 style of grey uniform) were still being worn in 1940 as it was policy to wear out stock before replacing it. The Life Guards differed slightly by wearing a grey-green tunic in the same cut as the khaki version. The khaki tunic had a stand and fall collar and was fastened with six bronze buttons – which for infantry showed crossed rifles below a crown, and for the Life Guards had a royal cipher below a crown. The tunic had four pockets, with the breast pockets being pleated. Officers wore a tailored jacket with an open collar and lapels. The shoulder straps on these tunics and jackets were khaki, buttoned by the collar and unadorned for other ranks, but rank distinctions were shown on them for NCOs (sergeants and sergeant majors) and officers. Other NCOs (corporals and senior privates) had rank chevrons on the lower cuff. The rank distinctions consisted of a silver bar for a sergeant, positioned in the middle of the strap, and two bars for sergeant-majors. Officers had gilt rosettes, three large rosettes for a colonel, three smaller ones for a captain, two for a 1st lieutenant and one rosette for a 2nd lieutenant.

In winter a black double-breasted greatcoat was worn. This had been issued in 1910 and had buttons in the branch-of-service style.

Khaki trousers were worn, rolled up above either brown or black ankle boots. Officers wore leather boots and had Sam Browne belts and pistols. Leather equipment was supposed to be brown. There was a belt, supporting a single cartridge belt containing 40 rounds. The belt also supported the bayonet frog. Many troops were still wearing black leather equipment. A leather backpack was being phased out, and troops were switching to a canvas backpack often supplemented by a bread bag and a mess tin. Gas masks were also carried. The backpack was more suitable than the knapsack with rolled blanket, as the blanket interfered with the helmet and restricted a soldier's head movement.

▶ **Trooper, Jutland (Jyske) Dragoon Regiment, 1940** *There were two cavalry regiments, the Guards, who retained a grey uniform, and the Jutland Dragoons, in brownish khaki. By 1940 these were mounted on bicycles or the Nimbus motorbike.*

The 1923 helmet

Denmark began thorough tests on various kinds of helmet in 1915, but towards the end of 1923 adopted a unique design – and this began to be produced in 1924. It was domed, with highly sloping edges that gave a good level of protection to the neck and the sides of the head. The helmet carried a coat of arms, had a leather chinstrap and a lug through which a strap could be slotted to allow the helmet to be secured to the belt or backpack. The helmets were supplied by Glud & Marstrands and manufactured from Swedish steel but they proved unpopular with the troops. They were deemed unstable and the air vents were too wide, making the helmet's inside drafty. Modifications took place in 1929, with a buckled strap then being fitted.

Officers generally preferred to wear a peaked cap. This had a khaki crown, a white cap band, a coat of arms badge, which was larger for generals and staff officers, a Danish cockade (white within red within white) and a black peak. Off duty, a khaki forage cap or side cap was worn. For other ranks this bore the Danish cockade, while NCOs had a brown textured band running around the crown.

▼ **Lieutenant, 3rd Foot Artillery Regiment, 1940** *Officers wore a peaked cap that had a khaki crown, white band and brown lacquered peak and leather chinstrap. The cap band bore the Danish royal coat of arms and the crown had the Danish cockade (red with gold outer ring).*

Other arms

The Danish cavalry generally followed the pattern above. The Guard Hussars wore khaki tunics, breeches and leather boots. Their buttons were the same as for the Life Guards. The Jutland Dragoons were uniformed in the same way, but with buttons bearing crossed sabres and a horseshoe below a crown. Artillery were uniformed as per the infantry, but with buttons bearing crossed cannon below a crown, and for engineers this was a spade and a cannon barrel. Pilots wore officers' uniforms but with wings above their right breast pocket.

The end

Germany dissolved the Danish Army in 1943. Some Danes had emigrated and fought for the Allies in Allied uniform while others volunteered for service with the Germans, either in the Waffen SS or as part of the short-lived Schalburg-Korps. This unit generally wore Danish forage caps with the Danish cockade, the khaki uniform with SS badges (rank badge on the left collar tab and a wheeled swastika on the right collar tab), a Danish shield bearing hearts and lions on the sleeve and the Schalburg cuff title.

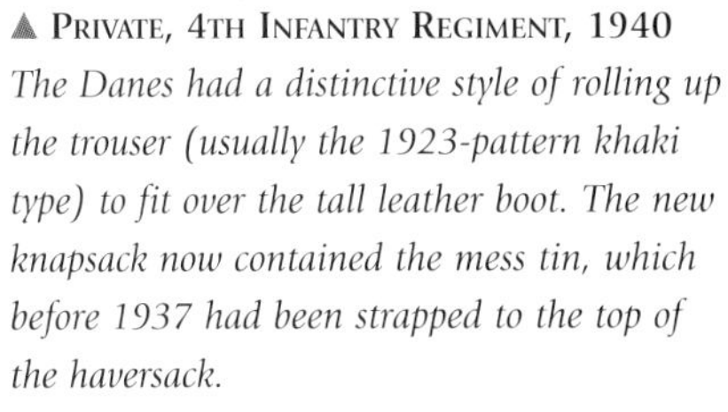

▲ **Private, 4th Infantry Regiment, 1940** *The Danes had a distinctive style of rolling up the trouser (usually the 1923-pattern khaki type) to fit over the tall leather boot. The new knapsack now contained the mess tin, which before 1937 had been strapped to the top of the haversack.*

FRANCE

France was the pre-eminent power in Europe between World War I and World War II. The country had emerged victorious from the slaughter of World War I. She won back lost territory in Europe and expanded her empire in Africa and the Middle East. Above all, she had a large and respected Army. In the 1920s the French Army was equipped with tanks, modern aeroplanes and machine guns. A crisis of confidence in the 1930s led to the building of the costly Maginot Line – a string of defensive fortifications, named after French minister of war André Maginot, along much of the country's eastern frontier – but even so France knew that she could rely on an enormous number of troops. These were French troops (recruited from within the French borders), North Africans (including French settlers) and foreign troops, as well as colonial forces. French troops, North Africans and members of the Foreign Legion were under the control of the Ministry of National Defence and War, while colonial units were administered by the Ministry of the Colonies.

Organization

French infantry had won World War I and had a tremendous reputation. Infantry included line, light infantry, mountain infantry and fortress units, as well as a number of foreign units, notably the Foreign Legion (five infantry regiments with another being raised in Syria in 1939) and, by 1940, a number of Polish exiles.

Cavalry were in the process of reforming into motorized units. French tank units mostly consisted of bataillons de chars de combat – combat tank battalions, the 45th of which was provided by the gendarmes (police) in May 1940. A smaller number of bataillons de chars légers (light tank battalions) were also established.

French artillery – which included mountain, anti-aircraft and fortress units as well as field artillery – was well equipped and numerous. Technical troops included the bridging train (seven battalions),

◀ **General of Brigade, 1940** *Generals followed the fashion of other officers in the French Army but went without collar patches and used a system of stars to denote rank. Headgear for campaign dress was the distinctively French-style kepi, in khaki, but sometimes showing the decorative chinstrap and with a lacquered peak.*

▶ **Private, 255th Infantry Regiment, 1939** *The French infantryman still depended on his greatcoat, or capote, to keep him comfortable. This was buttoned back because the wool was heavy when wet and this impeded movement.*

▲ **Private, 95th Infantry Regiment, 1940**
The French had developed a two-piece pack system. An upper pack contained essential items, a lower pack less pressing supplies. The blanket was rolled on top and an entrenching tool, or an axe or wire cutters, strapped under the blanket.

13 regiments of engineers (pioneers were part of the infantry), seven regiments of sappers/miners and two regiments of railway troops. All these units were broken up and redistributed among the other divisions in September 1939.

Colonial units included infantry, cavalry and technical troops and were recruited in the colonies with native personnel and French officers. French citizens, including those resident in the colonies, served in specific colonial units or in penal units sent to the colonies, and Frenchmen resident in the colonies made up most of the famous Zouaves (light infantry units particularly associated with North Africa).

The French Air Force was large. Its aircraft production was greater than that of the Germans. The Air Force was organized into 67 fighter squadrons, 66 bomber squadrons and 30 reconnaissance squadrons (plus reserves).

Generals

There was a degree of freedom for generals when it came to uniform. By 1940 most wore a tunic with breeches. The 1929 officers' tunic, with seven gilt buttons, straight cuffs and pointed collars (along with four pockets, the upper pockets having scalloped flaps), was favoured. This did not have shoulder straps: instead, a raised, embroidered bar of cloth was attached at the end of the shoulder. Breeches were mostly in light khaki or faun, with reinforced inners.

Many generals opted to wear the standard greatcoat, adorned at the cuff with stars of rank, but raincoats were also common – as was the Raglan riding coat in green. This was a shorter and lighter version of the greatcoat favoured by many French officers. Brown riding boots, or ankle boots with puttees, completed the uniform.

They wore a dark blue kepi with red crown and gold Austrian knot decorated with gold oak leaves or a simplified khaki kepi with oak leaf embroidery restricted to the base of the crown but silvered stars; a general of brigade had two stars. These stars could also feature on the Adrian helmet, where they were to be positioned around the insignia that marked the wearer's branch-of-service – for instance, a grenade for an infantry general. The stars were also worn on the tunic sleeves, just above the cuff.

Equipment generally consisted of a Sam Browne belt with binoculars, a map case (small or large), a pistol in holster and a cane (which replaced the sabre). Gas masks were often carried in the first few months of the war.

Infantry

The profile of the French infantryman had changed little since 1918. Horizon blue had gone, confined to some

▼ **Helmet Badges 1937–41** *1 Infantry (a grenade), 2 Artillery (bomb and barrels), 3 Engineers (armour), 4 Light Infantry (a horn), 5 Medics (the staff and snake), 6 North African troops (a crescent), 7 Colonial troops (an anchor), 8 Tankers (a helmet), 9 Armoured car (Medusa head).*

◀ **PRIVATE, 5TH INFANTRY REGIMENT, 1945** *The French Army in 1944 to 1945 simply had to improvise. It made use of Adrian helmets, often with the cross of Lorraine, as well as American M1 helmets, and was often equipped with British or US equipment (such as the cartridge belt seen here).*

▶ **CAPTAIN, 99TH INFANTRY REGIMENT, 1940** *Other ranks of infantry had their greatcoats while officers had the more elegant coat, or manteau, which was authorized for wear in the field. It came with or without shoulder straps and was made from much finer material than the greatcoat.*

hastily formed reservist formations and the odd greatcoat, and mustard-brown khaki was almost universal by 1939.

The 1935-pattern tunic, with six buttons, was commonly worn with a khaki shirt and tie. The walking out version of this tunic was also seen in the 1940 campaign, and this came with piped shoulder straps and piping on the cuff (scarlet for infantry), a style also adopted for the walking out greatcoat. The 1938-pattern tunic – also seen during 1940 – had five buttons, but was distinguished by buttoned flaps. Concealing a unit's identity from enemy eyes was important, however, and coloured collar patches were highly visible; the solution, ordered in April 1939, was a buttoned flap that could conceal the collar patch. This was to be either an integral part of the new clothing or sewn on to older patterns of dress – an order that required officers with privately tailored items to disguise their patches as best as possible. Many infantrymen did without the tunic altogether, preferring a pullover or just the cotton khaki shirt.

From 1938 officers could wear an open-collared tunic, with shirt (white, with detachable collar) and black tie. They often retained their gilt buttons with grenade insignia.

The collar of the tunic bore distinctive collar patches. For infantry, these consisted of the regimental numeral in dark blue (gold for officers and senior NCOs) with two chevrons of lace (in blue) above the number (known as soutache lace). Regional regiments, composed of reservists formed on mobilization, had white soutache lace. Machine gun battalions had yellow lace and battalion numbers. Pioneers (infantry units tasked with labour such as digging trenches) had numerals, but no soutache lace. Officers had similar devices, but their tunic collars were more pointed and the insignia was therefore in a diamond shape; if they wore the open-necked tunic, the patch was worn as a small lozenge above the lapel. Many regiments had enamel badges worn on the breast or on the coloured lanyard; the lanyards were by now often restricted to ceremonial dress but they came in colours reflecting military awards given to the regiment – that is, red for units issued the Legion of Honour.

The distinguishing feature of the French infantryman was still his greatcoat. The double-breasted pattern that was adopted in 1920 served up until 1940 and was made of good-quality wool with straight cuffs and no shoulder straps. Insignia was worn on the collar. Officers wore a number of different items, from the 1932-pattern single-breasted overcoat to the fur-coloured canvas jacket (the Canadienne) or a leather jacket in black or khaki. Rank was shown on the cuff or on a tab on the chest. It came in the form of stripes (gold for infantry), with captains having three stripes, majors four, and so on. NCOs usually had diagonal strips above the cuff rather than the chevrons worn on formal occasions.

▼ **Chasseur, 7th Battalion of Chasseurs Alpins, 1940** *The beret was the distinctive mark of French mountain troops. It was known, affectionately, as the tarte and had been designed to be big enough for the wearer to place his feet in it during the night.*

Infantry helmets

French infantry still relied on the Adrian helmet to protect their heads. The model in use in 1940 was the 1926-pattern helmet painted in matt khaki. It was issued to a limited extent in 1926, to some selected units in 1935 and almost universally in 1939. The dome was made from a single piece of manganese steel; a crown was added that helped to conceal eight ventilation holes bored into the top of the dome. Many helmets bore the 1915 style insignia, but in 1937 a new oval badge began to be used on helmets. The original 1915 insignia for infantry was the bursting grenade bearing the letters 'RF' (for République Française) and in 1937 this same device was placed inside an oval disk.

When the helmet was not being worn, a side cap, or bonnet de police, was used. This was identical to that worn in World War I, although in khaki, and it was largely unadorned for the rank and file. Officers had rank insignia on their caps but also sometimes stitched collar tabs or numerals to the cap.

Officers wore the peaked kepi or helmet. The most common type of kepi was the 1919 pattern in very dark blue with red crown and Austrian knot. Infantry officers had the regimental numeral in gold on the front. The peak was of stiff, lacquered card and the (decorative) chinstrap was of thread with gold fibres.

Infantry wore trouser breeches of a type first issued in 1922. Of the same colour as the tunic, they extended to just below the knee with a cuff of white cotton that fitted tightly to the top of the calf. They were relatively baggy but the so-called golf trousers, adopted in 1938 and issued in early 1940, were much more roomy. They also finished below the knee and had drawstrings at the end of the leg to bind the garment closely to the calf. Infantry wore puttees in khaki and had ankle boots in natural leather, mostly of the 1917 pattern. Officers still preferred cream-coloured breeches and cavalry boots, although breeches with matching cloth puttees were also

▲ **Lieutenant, 2nd Bataillon of Chasseurs a Pied, 1940** *These chasseurs had originally been light infantry, trained for skirmishing, although the name was largely symbolic. Nevertheless the chasseurs retained the use of the hunting horn as a device on their helmets – as seen here in the new oval.*

popular – as were a new kind of elasticated wool puttee in khaki or white, helpfully marked 'left' or 'right'.

New equipment was only partially issued by 1940 and many infantrymen went into action with equipment that resembled that in use in 1916. The new equipment had two cartridge pouches (these were made more rigid in 1937) on the standard-issue leather belt and two comfortable and wide suspenders over the shoulder (meeting at the top of the back and forming a single suspender down to the back of the waist belt). The 1935-pattern canvas and rigid backpack was worn, with an additional compartment suspended underneath, as well as a canteen and gasmask (an ANP 31 in a canvas bag).

▲ *General Charles de Gaulle inspects part of General Philippe Leclerc's 2nd Armoured Division, near the Arc de Triomphe in Paris, 26 August 1944.*

◄ **FRA7 Private, 91st Battalion Alpin de Forteresse, 1940** *Fortress troops were deployed to protect France's frontiers. Mountain troops found themselves defending the Alpine frontier, as well as serving in the Maginot Line. Most Alpine fortress troops retained the traditional beret, but lacked the hunting horn of the chasseurs.*

Light infantry

The regular infantry were supported by two kinds of light infantry. Originally these had been skirmishers, but by the 1930s they were regarded as elite infantry. There were the Chasseurs à pied and the elite mountain troops, the Chasseurs Alpins.

Chasseurs à pied had helmets with a hunting horn device (with the letters 'RF') until 1937, after which the design was placed in an oval disk. They wore blue side caps, piped in yellow and with yellow hunting horns. Officers had blue kepis with blue crowns piped in silver and silver numerals.

Chasseurs wore a dark blue shirt and tie and dark blue tunic. The collar insignia consisted of a yellow battalion number over a hunting horn, all below two strips of yellow soutache lace; oddly, the distinguishing colour was green for the insignia on the greatcoat. The horn and numeral were silver for officers and senior NCOs. The greatcoat was the standard khaki version, although khaki or dark blue capes were also worn.

Equipment followed the pattern of the line infantry, but rucksacks rather than knapsacks were often preferred. Officers had silver rank distinctions. Officers and men had dark blue trousers or breeches and dark blue or khaki puttees.

Chasseurs Alpins wore a large beret known colloquially as the tart, with a horn badge or grenade badge; if they wore a helmet, this carried the grenade badge. In other respects they followed the Chasseurs à pied. However, as mountain specialists they developed a range of specialist items, from white camouflage suits and sheepskin jackets to canvas windjacks and parkas. One such item was the 1940-pattern khaki anorak, which was issued to troops taking part in the Norwegian campaign of that year; many fought with whitened leather equipment. Ski

▲ **Trooper, 1st Motorized Dragoons, 1940** *The dragoons were also divided and this unit was one of five regiments designed to be transported into battle and issued with the 1935-pattern helmet for motorized troops. Three others – the 13th, 18th and 29th – were assigned to tanks.*

troops, formed into squads from specialists of the Chasseurs Alpins, were outfitted in these items, but also used canvas gaiters or high wool socks and waterproofed mountain boots. They had a dark blue or yellow star on the sleeve as distinguishing insignia. Some 10 battalions of Chasseurs des Pyrénées were raised in 1939 for service in the Pyrenees. They were uniformed as the Chasseurs Alpins, but with blue insignia on the collar (battalion number, lace and horn).

Groupes Francs, often formed from light infantry personnel, were used as assault troops in 1939 and 1940. They were formed ad hoc, and largely went into action with improvized insignia – a red skull on a blue disk or the skiers' star badge, for example.

Fortress troops

The fortress infantry inevitably played an important role in a military strategy that included the defensive Maginot Line. There were fortress infantry regiments and Alpine fortress battalions. The fortress infantry had brown berets. Their greatcoats and tunics received a khaki sleeve title (with blue or gilt lettering) designating the region of France they were to protect (for example, 'Vosges' or 'Meuse'). Units in the Maginot Line had a distinctive beret badge in silver (worn on the left by officers, on the right by NCOs and privates) and a waist sash. The Alpine fortress battalions were uniformed like Chasseurs Alpins (but with three strips of soutache lace) with blue berets and a blue- or gold-lettered title showing either 'Alpes Maritimes' (74th, 75th and 76th battalions), 'Durance' (72nd Battalion), 'Maurienne' (71st) 'Tarentaise' (70th) or 'Ubaye' (73rd). Additional battalions were assigned to these places in 1940, as well as to Queyras (92nd Battalion).

Cavalry

French cavalry was in the process of being motorized. In 1939 there were 32 French cavalry regiments. Six were cuirassiers (six more were partially raised) and, of these, the 5th, 9th and 11th were mounted while the 4th, 6th and 8th were motorized. Of the 16 dragoon regiments (seven more were partially raised), the 6th, 8th, 19th and 31st were mounted; the 9th, 10th, 20th and 30th were partially mechanized; the 13th, 18th and 29th were given tanks; and the 1st, 2nd, 3rd, 4th and 5th were motorized.

Cuirassiers and dragoons generally wore the 1935 six-button tunic in khaki with breeches (or golf trousers), boots or gaiters (mostly the 1921 pattern) with ankle boots; the walking

▼ **Trooper, 4th Hussars, 1940** *The four regiments of hussars were split between mounted (the 1st and 4th) and motorized (2nd and 3rd) for reconnaissance. This uniform is for mounted personnel, complete with leather gaiters.*

◀ **Captain, 12th Artillery Regiment, 1940** *Many officers still had the right to ride while their men marched, and so had the choice of wearing leather gaiters, as here, or the elegant Chantilly riding boot. Breeches also indicated officer status.*

out version of the tunic had light blue piping on straps and cuffs. Cavalry were supposed to stain their gaiters and boots black, but natural leather was also worn in 1940. They wore the Adrian helmet with grenade badge (sometimes in an oval), and officers wore a dark blue kepi (with regimental numeral) or helmet. The cuirassiers were uniformed in tunics with dark blue collar tabs and regimental numerals and lace in red; an extra strip of lace was worn by the mechanized cuirassiers, in violet. The traditional button colour for French cavalry had been silver, so NCOs and officers had regimental numerals embroidered in silver thread. The dragoons had the same, but with white numerals (sometimes red if the walking out tunic was being used) and lace. A star was supposed to be added to the collar patch of motorized dragoons so that they had two strips of white lace, a strip of violet a numeral and a star, but this only really appeared on reservists' uniforms.

Light cavalry were divided between chasseurs and hussars. There were six chasseur regiments, two of which were motorized (the 7th and 11th) while the 1st, 8th, 12th and 18th were mounted. The four hussar regiments were divided between mounted (the 1st and 4th) and motorized (2nd and 3rd). The light cavalry were uniformed in a similar fashion to the dragoons, but with light green regimental numerals and lace on the collar patches of the chasseurs and sky blue for the hussars. Officers wore light blue kepis, helmets or side caps, often decorated with Hungarian knots for hussar officers. The cavalry generally received the MAs36 rifle, so no bayonet was carried; they carried ammunition either in pouches or in a natural leather bandolier. Belts and equipment of the 1916 pattern were most common. Personal equipment was kept to a minimum.

The five armoured car regiments (and three groups) were generally equipped like light cavalry, but with violet numerals and lace on their blue collar patches. They had a distinctive Medusa's head insignia on their 1935-pattern helmet for mechanized troops or Adrian helmets.

Reconnaissance units, generally drawn from the cavalry regiments and armoured car groups, had a complicated history. Essentially, the GRDI (infantry division reconnaissance groups) and the GRCA (army corps reconnaissance groups) were formed during or after

▶ **Captain, 13th Battalion of Combat Tanks, 1940** *Tankers across Europe favoured the beret. The French version was in black or very dark blue, and was lined in satin for officers. The beret bore the badge of the armoured troops, a medieval helmet over crossed cannon barrels.*

▶ **Scout, 24th Group de Reconnaissance de Corps de l'Armee, 1940** *The carbine was the 1892 pattern, modified in 1916. It was generally slung over the shoulder when mounted, although this sometimes injured the rider; if a pack was being worn, it was attached to the pack's straps.*

mobilization. The GRDI were uniformed like the chasseurs (but with three chevrons of lace on the collar patch), the GRCA like dragoons (but again with three chevrons of lace). The reconnaissance units were mostly issued with the 1892 carbine as these units were newly formed and issued with equipment from the stores.

Motorcyclists belonging to these units wore the 1935 helmet for mechanized troops, a waterproofed cotton tunic (paletot) and 1935-pattern overcoat with Raglan sleeves (although these were officially withdrawn when it was clear that they were insufficiently waterproof) or the improved 1938-pattern canvas coat. They wore collar patches on their sleeves with buttonable flap for concealment.

Artillery

The French artillery's distinctive insignia was the red collar patch with dark blue regimental numerals and two strips of lace. Motorized artillery groups had three strips, while those assigned to cavalry or mechanized cavalry units had two strips with a star insignia. Officers had the numeral and star in gold thread. The 110th, 111th, 310th and 320th were colonial artillery units, but numbered and uniformed like metropolitan units.

Artillery helmets had a bursting grenade (with 'RF') superimposed on crossed cannon barrels; these were placed in an oval in 1937. Fortress artillery tended to wear khaki berets and also sleeve titles with regional names in blue on a red background. Anti-aircraft artillery consisted of the 401st to 409th artillery regiments and although they wore regimental badges they were not distinguished by any specific branch insignia.

Engineers, specialists and armour

French engineers followed similar principles, but they had black collar patches with red numerals and lace; some engineering units raised from forestry employees had a hunting horn in red added to their patches. Those attached to specific fortified points had black sleeve titles with red lettering. Engineer helmets had a cuirass and crested helmet (with 'RF') placed in an oval in 1937. Signals troops did away with numerals on their collars and instead had red bolts of lightning; signal specialists in the infantry or chasseurs had the same device as a red or yellow sleeve badge. Train (transport) units had light green collar patches with red numerals (no soutache lace).

Armoured troops' branch colour was green and this could be seen on the cuffs and shoulder straps on the tunic; the battalion number on the collar was in grey or rarely green, with grey lace. A grenade insignia was sometimes present, and certainly used by the 45th Battalion, raised from the gendarmes. Officers and NCOs had numerals in silver. The 1935-pattern black leather coat was the most highly favoured item of dress. Officers wore their rank insignia in the form of stripes on a blue or black tab on the front of the coat. Headgear consisted of a black beret that was mercilessly boiled to reduce its size and had the tankers' helmet and crossed gun barrel device on the front. The 1935-pattern helmet for mechanized troops had the same stamped insignia but with 'RF' in addition. Overalls or breeches were worn.

Tank regiments had their own enamel or metal insignia, but the divisional badge could also be worn – as could the badge of motorized units (a flaming star over tank tracks) introduced in 1935.

Medical personnel had a gold caduceus in laurel wreath device on a crimson (doctors), purple (dentists) or green (pharmacists) patch. This device also appeared on the Adrian helmet.

North African troops

Zouaves and Algerian, Tunisian and Moroccan Tirailleurs formed the bulk of the North African infantry. They generally followed the style set out for the French infantry above, but with some characteristic features. Zouaves had red collar numerals and soutache lace on their tunics and greatcoats, while the Tirailleurs had light blue; the Moroccans added a light blue star below the numeral.

◀ **Corporal, 9th Zouaves, 1940** *The Zouaves continued to wear their distinctive headdress, or chechia, in 1940, although a more subdued khaki version was also worn on campaign. When on campaign, the chechia was worn without insignia (crescent and regimental numeral).*

▶ **Private, 4th Regiment of Tirailleurs Senegalais, 1940** *The Senagalese would have anchor devices on their Adrian helmets, showing the connection between the Ministry of Marine and colonial troops. A red chechia was worn off duty.*

They all wore Adrian helmets with a crescent below the letters 'RF' (placed in an oval from 1937 onwards), but sometimes the unit number replaced the 'RF'. Instead of side caps, they wore red or khaki chechias (a floppy, non-rigid cloth fez), sometimes with a crescent, sometimes unadorned. Officers, most of whom were from mainland France, usually preferred to wear the peaked kepi. This usually had the regimental numeral on the front above the characteristic device of the troops the officer was commanding (crescent or star). Goumiers, or Moroccan auxiliaries, adapted French uniforms to their own tastes or wore a native uniform in light cotton (a gandoura). Over these items, they often wore colourful hooded capes made from wool (djellabas). They were grouped into Tabors (battalions), and consequently known as GTMs. Their headgear was of all kinds, from US, British or Adrian helmets to black berets or native caps with cloth wrapped around them like a turban (khiouts or rezzas).

North African cavalry consisted of the Spahis – Algerian, Tunisian and Moroccan light cavalry. They were uniformed like French cavalry, but with yellow numerals and lace on the blue collar patch; the Moroccans, again, added a star, but only from 1941 onwards. Khaki turbans or the red chechia often replaced the helmet. Some Spahi helmets bore a star rather than the crescent device.

The Chasseurs d'Afrique wore light khaki cotton tunics (1921 pattern) or wool tunics (1920 pattern) with blue collar patches and yellow regimental numerals and lace. Officers often retained the smarter tunic with standing collar and pennon-style collar tabs. The chasseurs wore the cavalry coat, breeches and boots or leather gaiters with ankle boots. Headgear consisted of the chechia in red or the tropical helmet in light khaki. Adrian helmets were also common from 1940 onwards, and officers often wore the sky blue kepi. Saharan companies had yellow stars and crescents with soutache lace on blue collar patches.

Colonial troops

The colonial troops consisted of the colonial infantry regiments (again with French personnel) and various indigenous units from Africa (such as the Senegalese Tirailleurs), the Middle

▲ LEGIONARY, 2ND REGIMENT OF THE FOREIGN LEGION, 1940 *The Foreign Legion had green regimental numerals and two stripes of soutache lace, although cavalry had the same with a grenade badge on a dark blue patch. The white kepi cover leaves the peak and a red circle of the crown uncovered.*

► FOREIGN LEGION COLLAR INSIGNIA
1 The 11th Infantry of the Foreign Legion, 2 Legionary based at a depot, 3 Officer of the Foreign Legion, 4 Officer at depot, 5 The 2nd Regiment, 6 Cavalry.

East (the Levant troops) and south-east Asia. Colonial units were generally distinguished by an anchor device on their Adrian or tropical sun helmets, kepis and on their collars.

They wore light khaki shirts, tunics (sometimes in the double-breasted paletot style or the 1935-pattern tropical tunic) and shorts or trousers and a light khaki version of the standard infantry greatcoat. The colonial infantry regiments had red numerals and soutache lace on their collars, but with a red anchor below the regimental numeral. NCOs had red braid distinctions, officers gold. The Senegalese Tirailleurs and troops from Madagascar had yellow as a distinguishing colour for their numerals, anchor device, soutache lace and NCO chevrons. They also had yellow piping around the collar of their paletot tunic. They wore the chechia, most officers (Europeans on the whole) preferring the sun helmet with anchor badge. Artillery followed the principles above, but with the addition of an anchor.

The Levant troops consisted of Lebanese chasseurs, Syrian infantry and cavalry, squadrons of Levant line cavalry and various native cavalry detachments (mostly consisting of Druze, Kurdish, Alaouite or Circassian cavalry). The Lebanese chasseurs had violet collar patches with yellow soutache lace, battalion numerals and a cedar tree. Syrian infantry had the same, but replaced the cedar with a crescent. The squadrons of line cavalry in the Levant had light blue patches with two strips of soutache lace in violet and the squadron number on a crescent. They wore standard colonial khaki dress, but added elements of local dress (such as the chechia) as well as red waist sashes. The native cavalry wore traditional costume, but did adopt French collar patches. That of the Druzes was light blue for the 1st squadron, red for the 2nd, green for the 3rd, dark blue for the 4th and black for the 5th (with the squadron number below a star).

▲ *A group of Tirailleurs, French colonial infantry, from Senegal, captured in northern France in 1940.*

Foreign Legion

The African Light Infantry was not part of the Foreign Legion, but a penal unit that served in the colonies. It had violet battalion numerals and soutache lace and a hunting horn device, which was sometimes absent on the collar but was also worn on the 1931-pattern tropical helmet.

The Foreign Legion fought in many theatres and so adopted the uniform appropriate to each theatre: in the desert, sand-coloured shirts, 1935-pattern tunics in light khaki and shorts with sun helmets (1931 pattern) or white kepis; in Europe, khaki greatcoats and Adrian helmets, with grenade badges. Their distinguishing collar patches were green regimental numerals with soutache lace for infantry and light green with a grenade below on a blue patch for Legion cavalry.

▲ *A group of delighted French pursuit pilots display the cross from a German aircraft that they have shot down.*

Polish troops

Some 30,000 Polish troops joined the French army in late 1939 and were involved in the Norway campaign or were stationed in France or the Levant (the Carpathian brigade). Polish exiles made use of French uniforms and equipment. These were generally devoid of insignia apart from the white Polish eagle badge attached or painted on the Adrian helmet, brown beret (in the style of fortress infantry) or side cap. Some units attempted to continue Polish traditions for collar insignia, but most infantry had plain collars or a French blue collar patch with two strips of yellow lace. A Czech division was being trained at Agde, in southern France, but were not ready for combat when the Germans invaded in 1940. Two regiments, uniformed in French style, were attached to the 23rd and 239th (light) divisions respectively.

◀ **Paratrooper, 1st Regiment of Chasseurs Parachutistes, 1944** *Two battalions of this regiment were formed in 1943, but they never parachuted into action. They were equipped with American jump boots, helmets and tunics but had a distinctive parachute patch and French helmet insignia.*

French Air Force

The Air Force had a helmet badge with winged star and the letters 'RF'. Two kinds of helmet were available from 1937, either the standard army Adrian helmet or a helmet based on the armoured troops' peakless version; both were dark blue with a black leather strap. The same winged star was shown in yellow on the collar patch (with green soutache lace), but Air Force personnel wore a great variety of uniforms and much of it was non-regulation. Pilot officers preferred a wide-crowned peaked cap with eagle badge and bands of gold thread denoting rank.

Rank was also shown as gold bands around the cuff of the dark blue tunic; the cuff and hat bands followed the same principle (with a captain having three bands, a lieutenant two and a second lieutenant one) or as gold tabs on black patches on the overcoat or flying jacket. NCOs had two strips of gold piping around the cap band and chevrons above the cuff (two gold for senior sergeants and sergeants, orange for senior corporals and below).

Breeches and boots were worn, with a great number of flying jackets in various different styles.

Defeat in 1940

The 1940 campaign was a disaster and French forces either surrendered or went into exile. Those that surrendered went on to remain in the reduced Vichy armed forces, went home or joined the Resistance.

The Resistance is beyond the scope of this work, but the exiles, known as the Free French or Fighting French, became more and more important in the course of the war. They fought in Africa and Italy, played an important role in liberating their homeland and ended the war advancing into Germany and Austria.

Rebirth of French armed forces

The uniform history of French forces between 1943 and 1945 is chaotic. Troops fighting outside of France generally attached their old insignia to new uniforms supplied by the British and Americans. This was particularly true of the French forces forming up and training in North Africa, who were subsequently used in Italy and in the invasion of the south of France, with many ending up in Alsace in 1945. For example, collar insignia would be applied to the sleeves of British battledress and regimental and divisional badges would be worn. Adrian helmets were still common, but British and American helmets were also adopted, with the French flag painted on the side and anchors, horns, grenades or the cross of Lorraine painted or attached on the front as appropriate.

The liberation of France confused the picture still further, with tricolour armbands and cross of Lorraine badges seen in large numbers as ex-Resistance personnel were merged with the Allied-equipped regular units in an ad hoc fashion. Newly raised units, from the first paratroopers to infantry battalions, all showed a similar mixed uniform style – with new items starting to emerge by 1945. One innovation was the reintroduction of coloured side caps in late 1944. Infantry were to have blue caps with red piping (yellow or green for light infantry), artillery had black piped red and cavalry units (mostly made up of colonial troops) adopted red.

◀ CAPTAIN, 1ST REGIMENT CHASSEURS D'AFRIQUE, 1940 *Officers in this unit had the choice of wearing either the high domed tropical helmet or the light blue kepi with a red crown and black peak. The kepi usually had the regimental number; the sun hat was free of insignia.*

▶ SECOND LIEUTENANT, 4TH REGIMENT OF TIRAILLEURS MAROCAINS, 1945 *American uniforms and equipment predominated among those units which were formed and equipped in North Africa. This particular regiment added their original collar tabs to their sleeves, and adopted a republican device for the helmet, in an effort to maintain an appearance that was distinctively French.*

GREECE

A devastating war with Turkey, which ended in 1922, bankrupted Greece, and the armed forces then faced a long period of neglect.

The Hellenic Land Army consisted of 56 regiments of infantry confusingly numbered up to 72. Reservists in 1940 and 1941 brought the total to 92 regiments. Numbered among these were the Evzones, who also had their own number – so, for example, the 42nd Regiment was also the 5th Evzones. They were light infantry who qualified as elite troops. There were three cavalry regiments, the second of which was mechanized and disbanded in March 1941 so its personnel could be used as part of other armoured units. In addition, there were three motorized regiments in the process of forming when the Italians attacked.

Infantry

The khaki (or olive) tunic worn by Greek infantry was based on the 1912 pattern. The tunic was closed by five dark brown or black buttons, had a stand and fall collar and four pockets closed by buttoned, rectangular flaps. There were shoulder straps, with a button by the collar and no cuffs. There was a single pleat to the rear, although some British-supplied tunics had two, and the tunic was lined in cotton.

It seems that most other ranks did not wear collar tabs (which were red for the infantry), preferring an unadorned tunic, although tabs were usually present on the khaki greatcoat. Trousers matched the tunic colour, and puttees were used by all ranks.

NCOs wore yellow chevrons on the sleeve; sometimes of an older style and piped in branch-of-service colours and worn near the cuff, more often they were above the elbow and all-yellow.

Officers had a finer tunic with lapels, and this was worn with a shirt and tie (usually khaki). The tunic had metal buttons and collar tabs in branch-of-service colours. This was red for infantry, but the tab also bore a white metal grenade. The shoulder straps bore rank distinctions. This was one silver star for a second lieutenant, two for a lieutenant and three for a captain. Majors had one star and a crown, lieutenant colonels two stars and a crown and colonels had three stars and a crown. The most junior of generals had a star, a crown and crossed sabres.

◀ **Private, 18th Infantry Regiment 1941** *For troops in the south, and fighting in Crete, British equipment made up for a shortfall in Greek supplies. The British helmet, seen here, was issued to Greek troops in 1941, and to those who went into exile from then on.*

▶ **Corporal, 6th Infantry Regiment, 1940** *Greece had been equipped with large quantities of Adrian helmets in the 1920s, but in 1934 a new helmet was authorized. It was issued in time for the war with Italy and was, ironically, of Italian design.*

▲ **Private, 1st Evzone Regiment, 1940** *These elite infantrymen generally wore puttees and baggy khaki trousers with ankle boots on campaign.*

The Evzones usually wore standard infantry uniforms and equipment, but conserved at least some of the distinctions that set them apart from the line infantry. This would mean one or more of either a pleated skirt (khaki rather than white), pompoms on boots or the famous fez.

Headgear

Greece had received numerous Adrian helmets in 1918, many of which bore the symbol of a cross on a shield beneath the crown. Sometimes the crown was missing because it had been scratched off during the country's republican years between 1924 and 1935. More common was an Italian helmet that first made its appearance in 1934 and was adopted by the Greeks in 1939. The Italians produced the steel helmet (seemingly from quite inferior steel), then the Greeks fitted out the insides and painted the helmet (khaki or green in some units).

A relatively large number of British Mark II helmets were supplied from 1940 onwards to make up for the shortfall in Greek helmets. Some officers wore the helmet, but many preferred a peaked cap that resembled the cap worn by British officers. It was khaki with a leather chinstrap and a cockade beneath a crown. For generals the peak was lacquered and adorned with gold braid. For most ranks a khaki field cap was used.

Equipment

Officers preferred the Sam Browne belt. Other ranks used equipment that had changed little since the conflict with Turkey in the 1920s. A brown leather belt supported three double cartridge pouches in brown leather and a bayonet frog. Bread bags and canvas knapsacks were also worn, as were entrenching tools. British or German Dräger or Auer gasmasks were sometimes carried.

Other troops

Greece's cavalry regiments were uniformed in khaki tunics with green collar tabs, breeches and riding boots. They wore helmets and side caps. Officers had green collar tabs and peaked caps. A handful wore Italian-made leather coats when acting as part of mechanized detachments or as reconnaissance troops. Mechanized forces were largely underdeveloped as Greece only had two Vickers tanks and 11 Renault tanks. Artillery were largely uniformed as the infantry, but with black distinctions (train units had light blue, signals personnel had dark blue and engineers had purple). Medical staff had violet collar tabs.

The Greek Air Force was divided into an Army Force and a Navy Force. While Navy aviators largely used naval uniforms and insignia, Army Air Force pilots and observers were uniformed in dark blue. The cut of the cloth followed that of infantry officers, with a tailored tunic, light blue shirt and black tie. Pilots wore silver wings above the left breast pocket, and rank was shown as white piped dark blue braid on the cuff.

▶ **Second Lieutenant, 1st Artillery Regiment, 1941** *Greek officers emulated their British counterparts when it came to dress. The cap bore the Greek crown over the light blue and white Greek cockade. Shirts were usually white or khaki, ties olive or khaki.*

NETHERLANDS

The Dutch had 24 infantry regiments before mobilization (expanded to 48 by reservists) plus a regiment of grenadiers and Jagers with Guard status and border infantry battalions.

Dutch uniforms had not seen substantial changes since the reforms undertaken in 1912, although some modifications were made in 1938. In 1940 the uniform consisted of a blue-grey tunic and trousers – or breeches for officers and mounted or mechanized personnel. The tunic had a standing collar that was lined for comfort and could be closed by means of a hook. The tunic was closed with seven brass buttons and had two pleated breast pockets closed with a scalloped flap. It had rolled shoulder straps. The officers' tunic did not differ greatly from that worn by other ranks, but had two additional pockets (unpleated) lower down and piping in branch-of-service colour to the cuff (blue for line infantry, orange for grenadiers and green for Jagers).

For line infantry the collar was piped in dark blue (with a yellow band below for musicians) and rank insignia were worn to the front of the collar. Senior privates had a white metal button to the front of the collar, NCOs had a yellow metal disk set towards the collar centre and yellow chevrons piped in blue on the sleeve. Officers wore silver stars on the collar to denote rank – one star for a 2nd lieutenant, three for a captain and one star plus a yellow metal bar for a major. Cyclists wore a bicycle wheel insignia on the collar in yellow, grenadiers had an exploding grenade and Jagers had a hunting horn.

Dutch infantry wore side caps when off duty, and these were piped in blue (orange for grenadiers, green for Jagers) and had the regimental numeral on the left-hand side (or a grenade badge for grenadiers or hunting horn for Jagers). Officers wore a stiff kepi with an orange cockade and, below, a cap band bearing a unit designation (usually the regimental numeral) and piped in branch of service colours. A helmet that resembled a rounder version of the Adrian had been introduced in 1916, but this was replaced in 1934 by a new version that had first been tested in 1928. This helmet was domed, sloped to cover the nape of the neck, and was usually finished in apple green. The helmet had a disk bearing the lion of Nassau emblem on the front, a slit (so it could be attached to a belt) on the rim and a black chinstrap riveted to each side.

▼ **Private, 9th Infantry Regiment, 1940**
Dutch infantry wore a distinctive helmet with lion badge, but off duty preferred a simple side cap made out of the same cloth as the tunic – with the regimental numeral or rank insignia in orange.

▲ **Private, 42nd Infantry Regiment**
The greatcoat was double-breasted and was first issued in this style in 1912. Greatcoats usually had their collars piped in branch-of-service colours (blue for infantry).

A grey double-breasted greatcoat (with distinctive insignia of rank stars on the collar) was worn in cold weather. Infantry wore trousers and puttees, officers preferring breeches and boots. Officers wore Sam Browne belts and carried pistols.

Cavalry

The Dutch had four regiments of hussars and a regiment of cavalry. Acting as mounted infantry, they were partially equipped with bicycles, but cavalrymen were also sent to form armoured car squadrons for reconnaissance and motorcyclist despatch riders. The uniform was similar to that worn by the infantry, but had white metal buttons and insignia and no piping to the collar. Mechanized cavalry/armoured car personnel had a badge showing an armoured car. The hussar regiments wore a black busby before 1940, but this was usually replaced on active service with the standard helmet. Personnel assigned to serve with motorized formations or as despatch riders tended to prefer leather coats.

Technical troops

Dutch artillery wore infantry uniform, but had their collars and caps piped in red. Officers wore red piping on their cuffs, and a crossed cannon device on their collars (crossed artillery shells for heavy artillery). Horse artillery were as for the cavalry, but with crossed cannon barrels on their collars; anti-aircraft gunners had a strange insignia of crossed cannon barrels superimposed on a propeller. The bridging units had red piping with anchors on their collars, while engineers had light blue piping and a crested helmet or if in a signals detachment bolts of lightning. Medical staff had crimson piping. Most Air Force personnel retained the uniform of their original unit, but added a propeller badge to the collar and if a pilot or observer wore gilt wings on the breast pocket. Ground staff wore uniforms that resembled those of the infantry, but with light blue piping.

Dutch colonies

The Dutch had small detachments in the Caribbean and in Suriname, but more substantial forces in the East Indies. This force was the Koninklijk Nederlandsch-Indisch Leger (KNIL) and it numbered 75,000 men in 1941 (the Dutch declared war on Japan in December 1941). These troops, which included infantry, cavalry (operating armoured cars) and artillery, as well as a small air force (the Militaire Luchtvardienst of the KNIL), wore uniforms that had come into force in 1938. The uniform was a greenish khaki colour, and was made of fine cotton. The infantry wore a hunting horn badge on their collar, cavalry had crossed swords and the artillery crossed cannon barrels. Although helmets were worn, a round slouch hat was much more popular. It had one brim pinned up with the orange cockade.

◀ **Captain, 37th Infantry Regiment, 1940** *Officers could chose between a tall kepi, as seen here, or a helmet with leather lion's badge – the lion was the lion of Nassau of the Dutch royal family.*

▶ **Trooper, 1st Hussars, 1940** *Dutch cavalry were unsurprisingly largely mounted on bicycles in 1940. However, a few were tasked with driving armoured cars or motorcycles and these personnel were issued with leather coats and crash helmets. The helmets were not popular and most troopers wore the standard helmet or side cap.*

NORWAY

When the Germans invaded in April 1940, Norway had a small Army with supporting air arm and an important Navy together with its own Air Force.

The Norwegian Army had only partially mobilized when the Germans attacked and, despite Anglo-French support (bolstered by Polish exiles), most resistance was over by June 1940. The king went into exile and Norway was ruled by a collaborationist regime made infamous by Vidkun Quisling, who seized power with Nazi backing and governed as Minister-President in 1942–5.

The Army of 1940 consisted of a Guard regiment, 16 infantry regiments, two rifle battalions, three dragoon regiments and three artillery regiments with mountain and anti-aircraft batteries, together with an engineer regiment. There were also some ski companies. Mechanization was largely irrelevant to Norway, due to the terrain, but the dragoon regiments were in the process of being converted into mechanized and cyclist units.

The standard Norwegian uniform consisted of a grey-green tunic. This had initially been introduced in 1912 and was sturdy, loose (so warm clothing could be worn underneath) and well made. It was closed with silver buttons bearing the Norwegian lion, hidden by a fly front. The four pockets also had pointed flaps with hidden buttons and no pleats. These pockets were wide and roomy, and could be used to carry ammunition. The stand and fall collar was closed with hooks and piped in red for the infantry, and this piping was also shown on the straight cuff – cuffs had been simplified in the 1930s. There were no shoulder straps. Officers sometimes wore a similar tunic, but with shoulder straps, pointed cuffs and pleated pockets. This seems to have been rare. Trousers of the same grey-green colour were worn, most usually with puttees or long socks. Officers had red piping, but this was not universal. The trousers were again loose fitting so that additional garments could be worn underneath for warmth. Grey, double-breasted greatcoats with shoulder straps (which showed officers' rank insignia) were worn in winter.

Rank

Rank was only shown on the collar, with general officers having a beige decorative collar tab and star decorations (and they were also distinguished

◀ **Private, 12th Infantry Regiment, 1940**
Norway's own helmet was in short supply despite being an elegant and rather practical design. The mountain rucksack was practical and hard-wearing and based on civilian designs of the period.

▶ **Private, 15th Infantry Regiment, 1940**
Norway maintained stocks of tunics, helmets and equipment, but these proved insufficient when the army was expanded to meet the German invasion. This infantryman has been fortunate in that he has been issued with Norwegian materials.

◀ **PRIVATE, ALTA BATTALION, SKI COMPANY, 1940** *Ski troops wore the standard greenish blue tunic and cap with white snow smocks, trousers and gloves. The Norwegian cap had two ear flaps that buttoned to the side, a flexible peak and a soft crown. It bore the Norwegian cockade.*

▶ **LIEUTENANT, 3RD MOUNTAIN ARTILLERY BATTALION, 1940** *As well as much needed heavy weaponry, Britain supplied the Mark II helmet; this was usually worn without insignia, although a few officers added the Norwegian coat of arms.*

by gold buttons bearing a crossed batons device) and field officers having silver stars on their collars. NCOs had horizontal red stripes on the cuff (one for a corporal, two for a sergeant) and on the field cap. The field cap was of grey-green cloth, with a soft peak and ear flaps that could be buttoned to the side of the cap. It had a Norwegian red within white within blue within white cockade and sometimes had red piping along the crown – although this was rare. In addition some troops made use of the 1931 helmet. This was based on the Swedish design and modified in 1935 by the addition of the Norwegian lion within a shield crest (this helped the troops recognize the front of the helmet quickly). It was painted dark green, lined, with a leather chinstrap. It was not especially common and deficiencies in 1940 were made up by the British Mark II helmet.

Equipment

Norwegian equipment was simple and kept to a minimum. A brown leather belt with simple buckle supported one or two brown cartridge pouches for the standard Krag Jørgensen rifle; a few carbines were issued to technical troops and the 1925 or 1930 model sniper rifle was issued to NCOs and selected personnel in the rifle and ski units. Some troops made use of the Madsen light machine gun and carried larger and sturdier ammunition pouches that were closed with a buckle. The steel bayonet scabbard was also attached to the belt by means of frogging. Officers used pistols, but some also had bayonets.

Norway's cavalry uniforms were virtually identical to the infantry. They were differentiated by hunting horns on their silver buttons, and cavalry boots. Some of the cavalry serving as motorcyclists or in reconnaissance units had leather overalls, but these were very rare.

Artillery troops were dressed as for the infantry but had a rosette on gold buttons, with engineers having a crested helmet device on silver. Personnel belonging to transport or supply units had a device representing a rubber tyre on their gold buttons. Pilots wore silver wings flanking a Norwegian shield above their right breast pocket and had silver buttons showing propeller blades below a crown. It seems that Air Force personnel opted for green piping rather than red.

During the war

Many Norwegians preferred exile and service in Allied uniform, while others joined collaborator units such as the Rikshird. They wore a dark blue tunic and trousers with a brown shirt and black tie. A blue field cap was also worn. Arm badges (a red circle with a yellow cross and two swords) and cuff titles were also worn. Vidkun Quisling's bodyguard, the Foregarden, were uniformed in infantry uniforms with a 'VQ' cipher on the collar and the cross and swords badge on the sleeve.

POLAND

Poland mobilized on 29 August, cancelled the mobilization and then mobilized again on 30 August 1939. At that time there were 84 infantry regiments in 1939, each comprising three battalions. In addition, there were six mountain infantry regiments, and frontier guard battalions.

▼ PRIVATE, 31ST INFANTRY REGIMENT, 1939
The leather cartridge pouches were robust and well made. They were attached to the waist belt and supported with leather braces. There were three on each side. The system resembled the German pattern from 1909.

The artillery consisted of field, anti-aircraft and fortress units, but was in a state of transition. Field artillery was in the process of mechanization, but was still largely horse-drawn.

Polish cavalry were divided into four types. The bulk consisted of 27 regiments of traditional lancers (pułki ułanów), 10 regiments of mounted rifles (pułki strzelców konnych) and three light horse regiment (pułki szwole erów, derived from the French chevau-leger). Then there were the motorized elements, formed in 1939, and the cycle companies. Personnel from the 24th Lancers were amongst the first to have their horses replaced by motor vehicles. The cavalry differed only in uniform, all were supposed to operate as mounted infantry. Technical troops included engineers, signals and chemical troops.

The Air Force was small, organized into 15 squadrons of fighters, nine squadrons of bombers and 19 observation and liaison squadrons.

The 1936 version of the uniform was the most common one when the Poles went to war in 1939, although elements of the 1919 pattern were still visible and some reserve units were uniformed in this style. There were two versions of the 1936 pattern – a wool winter uniform in grey-brown-green and a lighter cotton uniform worn between May and September. Many units were wearing their summer uniforms when the Germans invaded. The summer versions were sand-coloured; older examples of these uniforms faded to an even paler khaki.

Infantry

Uniforms for infantry consisted of a tunic with seven buttons bearing the Polish eagle. The tunic had four pockets, with flaps, and shoulder straps. These bore the unit numeral and rank insignia, although the unit number (or monogram) was often removed on campaign and slip-on regimental distinctions were sometimes used instead. The tunic's collar was stand and fall and closed by means of a hook and eye. The 1936 uniform had called for a dark blue collar patch with silver zigzag lace and

▲ CAPTAIN, 5TH INFANTRY REGIMENT, 1939
This Polish officer wears a matt-painted helmet that has been camouflaged with pieces of cork to reduce the glare that even matt helmets could create when wet.

a strip of yellow piping to the rear edge. This patch was not usually worn on the campaign uniform, although photographic evidence suggests that some personnel had such distinctions in September 1939.

Infantry either wore the 1931-pattern helmet or a number of different styles of cap (see below). Equipment consisted of a leather belt – the 1936 pattern had one single-prong buckle, the 1927 pattern had two. The belt carried two triple cartridge belts, for a total of 90 rounds per man. This was normally for the Mauser rifle, a variant of the German model from World War I. While carbines were issued to machine gun companies within infantry battalions, they also went to cavalry, artillery, engineers and train troops. Infantry carried an entrenching tool and bayonet (of which there were five variants issued in almost as many years) suspended from the belt.

Infantrymen also carried a canvas haversack for personal effects and a knapsack. The most common type, issued in 1932, was made from thick waterproofed canvas. It had shoulder straps and was connected to the cartridge pouches to the front. The greatcoat and blanket (and sometimes tent canvas or tarpaulin) were rolled on top of the knapsack and the aluminium mess tin and cup were attached to the outside. Poland produced its own gas mask, the 1932 model with its green accordion respirator pump, tube and facial protection. It was carried in a canvas bag and worn below the knapsack.

Trousers (issued in 1937) were straight-legged, replacing older versions that had been gathered at the knee. Officers continued to wear breeches like this, usually privately tailored. Infantry wore ankle boots in leather (blackened and waterproofed) usually worn without puttees.

The 1924 greatcoat had branch-of-service coloured stripes sewn horizontally across each collar. The shoulder straps were plain (unlike the 1919 version, which had metal numerals), but slip-ons could be used to designate units as with the tunics.

◀ **Private, 7th Infantry Regiment, 1939** *The Polish haversack, or Tornister, had been issued in 1932 and was made of robust material with cotton straps. The mess tin was usually strapped to the back and additional bags containing personal items were suspended below. These had belts that were worn over the shoulder to cross the chest.*

▶ **Private, 2nd Mountain Rifles (Podhala ski Rifles), 1939** *These mountain troopers wore capes rather than greatcoats. This individual wears long puttees, which were more common in these units than the short gaiters worn by the standard infantryman.*

Headgear

Poland inherited a number of helmets and in 1919 her army was wearing French Adrian types, the German steel helmet and the Austrian Berndorfer, as well as odds and ends from various other sources. The most common helmet was undoubtedly the French Adrian helmet, supplied to the Poles after World War I. This included helmets with the Polish eagle device, but also unadorned items. In 1939 Poland's cavalry wore the Adrian helmet rather than their own design.

German and Austrian steel helmets were in storage throughout the inter-war period and in 1939 motorized troops could be seen

▲ **Lieutenant, 9th Lancer Regiment, 1939**
Although lancers were armed with carbines (with bayonets) rather than lances, they also carried swords. Officers generally preferred swords (the 1922-pattern curved sabre) and pistols (1935-pattern standard issue).

▲ **Lancer, 2nd Lancer Regiment, 1939**
Polish lancers were still wearing the Adrian helmet which had come into use in 1919. (Poland had purchased stocks of the French helmet following independence.) The helmet bore the distinctive crowned eagle, although the new nation was a republic.

wearing these items. This was partly because of shortages, but partly because the new Polish design was deemed to be too heavy for such mobile troops. However, the helmets were refurbished by being fitted with new liners and with the distinctive Polish chinstrap.

Poland issued a new helmet in 1931. For its time it was an advanced item of equipment, offering good protection and comfort for the wearer. It had been developed by a commission based in Warsaw whose members took inspiration from Swedish helmets and helmet interiors, and were impressed by the quality of Swedish steel. A prototype was released for testing in 1930 and then modified; the helmet, now made from a steel alloy, entered production in 1931 and began to be issued the following year. More than 300,000 were produced, and this was insufficient for the needs of the Army. The helmet was domed, with an elevated rim to the front and a very short peak. The rim to the side and rear was uniform, giving a straight edge. It was relatively robust, and the padded lining and modern chinstrap provided stability. This chinstrap had a chin pad for added comfort and a distinctive fastening system. Most helmets were painted matt khaki-green, but some helmets were issued with a textured finish created by adding fragments of cork to the paint – the Salamander effect. This made for a rough finish, which broke the profile of the helmet. The border guards had a Polish eagle attached or pinned on their helmets, but most other units had unadorned items.

When a helmet was not worn, the most common form of headgear was a peaked cap called the rogatywka polowa. This came in a number of forms, the stiffened 1935 pattern being as common as the 1937 pattern, but older softer versions from 1919 and 1927 also coexisted with the newer models. The 1937 peaked cap had an embroidered eagle badge, or was plain with a buckle and cloth peak. It had fold-up flaps that could be let down for ear protection in winter. The crown was noticeably less square and softer in later versions. A simpler fatigue cap, without peak or brim and known as the furazerka, was also worn. A 1937-pattern service dress cap consisted of a black lacquered peak, black chinstrap and a band in service colours. Above the band was an eagle and a squared khaki crown (point to the fore).

Officers wore silver piping on their service dress caps, silver stars according to rank, and metal eagle badges on their field caps. Their tunics were cut in the same style as those of the rank and file but they added stars and, if colonels, lieutenant colonels or majors, two silver bars to their shoulder straps. The lace on their collars was more ornate. Greatcoats had the service colour strips on the collar and appropriate combinations of stars on the shoulder straps. NCOs had rank insignia on their shoulder straps, either a combination of silver bars, piped red

▼ Corporal, 1st Light Horse Regiment, 1939 *The light horse regiments wore a peaked cap with a high crown, but otherwise were equipped as per the lancers – here with the 98a carbine slung over the shoulder.*

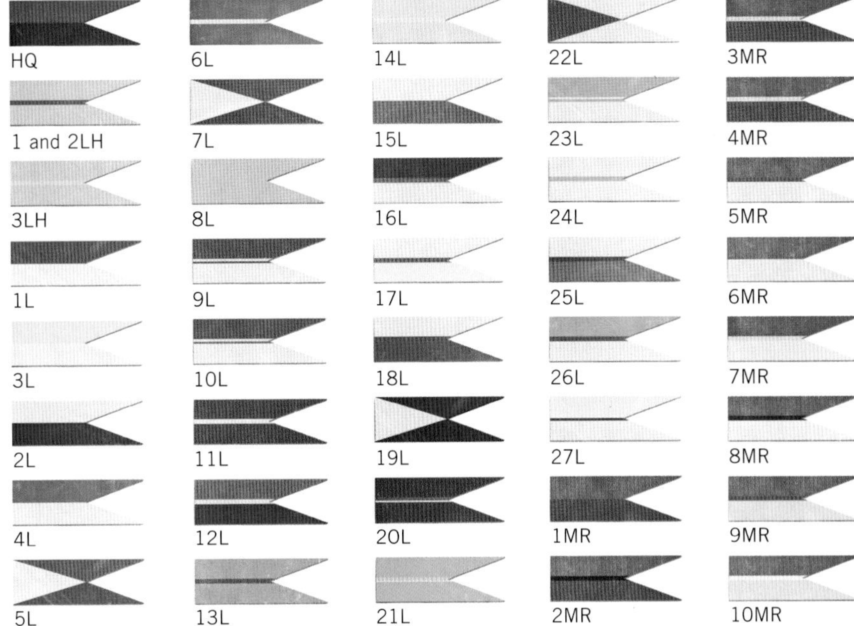

▲ Polish cavalry collar insignia in 1939 *(LH = Light Horse; L = Lancers; MR = Mounted Rifles).*

or for sergeant majors and sergeants a combination of chevrons and silver braid around the edge of the strap. NCOs wore a band of this silver-edged red lace on their service dress cap bands (a chevron for sergeants and above). Musicians wore swallows' nests on their shoulders in service colour with white piping.

Border guards

These troops followed the infantry pattern of uniform, but had round caps rather than square-topped field caps. They had blue as a service colour, with green piping on the crown of their caps.

The only other distinctive type of infantry was the mountain troops, or Podhale Chasseurs, named after a mountainous region in southern Poland. These troops wore a round felt hat, with domed crown and eagle's feather; a hat with a flatter crown, known as the huculski, was worn by the 11th Carpathian Division. There was a silver band around the base of the crown, an eagle badge and rank stars as appropriate. A distinctive symbol of a broken cross (often mistaken for a swastika) and pine branches, was worn on the tunic collar either above the zigzag lace on the service uniform or at the collar points on plain collars. These troops did not wear greatcoats but opted for a khaki cape with service lace on the cape collar as well as the units' emblem. The cape was usually worn over the left shoulder.

Artillery

In the Polish artillery troops followed the standard uniform in terms of tunic and trousers or breeches. Field artillery service colours were dark green with a strip of red piping or, for the heavy artillery, scarlet. The anti-aircraft batteries had green piped in yellow. Horse artillery had green as a service colour, piped in black. Engineers had black collar patches or strips of lace on their greatcoat collars with a scarlet strip of lace to the back of the collar tab or above the black lace on the greatcoat. Signals troops had the same, but with light blue lace rather than scarlet. Pioneers had scarlet as a service colour, medical troops had dark purple (piped blue) and train units had light blue (piped red). Most technical troops still had Adrian helmets rather than the newer-pattern Polish style.

Polish military police – known as Zandarmeria, the Polish transliteration of French gendarmerie – had bright orange as their distinguishing colour, with cap bands and collar patches on tunics in this colour. Piping was yellow, so the greatcoat had a strip of yellow over orange braid on the collar. Personnel wore a crested helmet badge on their left breast pocket.

Cavalry

Poland's military was still attached to the concept of mounted cavalry. This was partly a matter of tradition, but also due to the fact that the cavalry had proved its worth in the war against Bolshevik Russia of 1919-21. Nevertheless Poland did have mechanized units, too, and had gone to some lengths to develop this branch of service. Tank battalions, armoured battalions, reconnaissance companies (with tankettes and armoured cars) and motorized brigades (motorized infantry and artillery, with tanks) were formed or forming by 1939.

Be that as it may, the Polish armed forces took great pride in their cavalry. The branch was uniformed and equipped to a high standard, rigorously trained and well led. Unit pride was such that different squadrons had horses of different colours: trumpeters were still mounted on grey horses and horse artillery were to have black or dark brown horses.

Cavalry wore the standard tunic and had reinforced breeches. There was no single service colour for the cavalry, but instead different regiments had different distinguishing colours for their hat bands (service dress) and wore swallow-tail lance pennon insignia on their collars; this was rare on campaign, when cavalry collars were plain and devoid of insignia and zigzag lace. Detached and headquarters reconnaissance squadrons had scarlet over blue. Lancers and mounted rifles wore the square-topped caps, while the light horse were uniformed with round-topped versions like the border guards. Cavalry regiments either had the regimental numeral or a distinguishing monogram. For example, the 1st Light Horse wore 'JP' rather than '1' because their honorific title was 'Josef Pilsudski' after the Polish statesman and leader of the Second Polish Republic. They wore the device on removable slides on their campaign dress shoulder straps; these devices were worn attached, in a more permanent fashion, on the service dress uniform.

The cavalry were equipped with a Y-suspender belt, waist belt, six cartridge pouches, entrenching tool and bayonet. They carried grenades in a canvas bag and had a canvas bread bag for food and personal items. They wore 1931-pattern leather boots that were looser on the leg and of rough natural leather, blackened or impregnated to be waterproof. Men were armed with carbines and one of any number of patterns of sabre. Lances were not generally carried in the field, but guidons were. Officers carried pistols – the ViS 9mm ($^{3}/_{8}$in) pistol from 1935 onwards, usually secured around the neck with a leather lanyard – and had tall black leather boots. Saddles were of the 1936 pattern or older versions.

▲ *Polish soldiers during the Warsaw Uprising of 1944 wear a mix of captured German material and old Polish uniforms.*

◄ Insurgent, Warsaw Uprising, 1944 *The Home Army had very little by way of supplies from the Allies and had to make do with older Polish items, plus whatever they could capture from the Germans. Polish national colours, worn as brassards or around helmets, distinguished friend from foe.*

Technicians

Mechanized troops were largely uniformed in the style of their respective branch (infantry, cavalry and artillery, and so on), but there were some distinguishing features. The branch-of-service colour was orange – so cap bands and collar patches were

▲ **Partisan, Eastern Poland, 1945** *Polish parties and were liberally supplied with uniforms and equipment by the Soviets in 1944 and 1945. This individual carries the PPsh-41, with its drum of ammunition.*

in this colour; piping was in black. The service dress would have required a pennon of black over orange on the collar and campaign dress still would have had a strip of black over orange on the greatcoat.

The most significant motorized unit was the 10th Mechanized Brigade and its members were known as the Black Brigade on account of a pattern of black leather coats issued to personnel – mostly to officers and NCOs, with other ranks adopting overalls or standard greatcoats. This three-quarter length coat was issued in 1936. It had a black cloth collar, buttoned to the wearer's right (buttons were concealed) and rank was worn on cloth shoulder straps. The coat had buckled cuffs (known as Raglan cuffs) that allowed them to be secured over leather gloves. This coat was also used by the Polish Air Force.

Motorized troops often wore older German and Austrian helmets, but the French tankers' helmet (from 1919) was also issued to tank crews (as many of the tanks in Polish service originated from France). Instead of side caps, tankers wore black berets (with eagle badges and rank stars or bars). Breeches and boots were commonly worn and equipment was usually restricted to a belt, gas mask, pistol, gloves and goggles.

Air Force

The rank system of the Polish Air Force closely followed that of the Army. The uniform was in khaki in 1936, but in 1938 a new dark blue colour was introduced; this closely followed the cut of the uniform used by ground forces. A particular distinction was the eagle used on caps. This device, adopted in 1936, consisted of a flying eagle within a laurel wreath. It was worn on a peaked cap, in the English style, and was later worn in France and in Britain by exiled pilots. These caps had black peaks with one band of silver braid for officers up to captain, and two for majors, lieutenant colonels and colonels. Flying equipment came from a variety of suppliers and flying suits were often single-piece items from France.

The Home Army

This resistance movement was extensive, but poorly equipped – relying on old stockpiles, limited drops of Allied equipment and captured items. It wore Polish uniform items mixed in with civilian clothes and captured German helmets and uniform items. Armbands were worn and, in the Warsaw Rising (a failed resistance attempt to liberate Warsaw from the Nazis in August–October 1944), brassards and bands in national colours were worn around helmets, to distinguish friend from foe.

▶ **Lieutenant, 8th Light Artillery Regiment, 1939** *The 1936-pattern three-quarter length black leather coat was a popular item with officers. Although mainly used by the armoured troops, it was also adopted by other technical branches such as the artillery.*

YUGOSLAVIA

The uniform of the Royal Yugoslav Army was based on traditional elements and reflected uniforms worn by the Serbian Army in 1918.

Members of the infantry were issued with a new tunic in 1922. This tunic, known as the kaporan, was of a grey-green colour with a fly front set to one side, plain shoulder straps and a standing collar with rectangular collar patches in branch-of-service colours; the collar patches were repeated on the greatcoat. The kaporan was still common in 1941, although a new style was issued in 1939 with a fly front down the centre, stand and fall collar and four pockets with scalloped pocket flaps. Officers retained a standing collar on their tunics and had shoulder boards. The regiment of Guard infantry wore identical uniforms, but with buttons bearing the double-headed eagle and a royal monogram on the shoulder straps; officers had gilt shoulder boards, piped red, with the royal cypher and aiguillettes. Two regiments of mountain infantry wore similar uniforms, but with long socks, baggy trousers and a distinctive badge on the breast pocket; officers wore a hunting horn on the shoulder boards.

Yugoslav greatcoats were double-breasted, had shoulder straps that ended in a roll to prevent equipment sliding off, and had coloured collar patches. Officers wore elegant greatcoats first issued in 1922, but these had shoulder boards and branch-of-service patches in the form of a spearhead (with a silver button at the head). Senior officers had a red reverse to their lapel that could be folded down.

▼ **Major, 1st Assault Battalion, 1941**
Yugoslavia's assault battalions were called chetniks, and modelled themselves on the stormtroopers of World War I. This included the use of a skull as distinctive insignia.

▲ **Private, 2nd Infantry Regiment, 1941**
Yugoslav troops either wore their traditional cap, the sajkaca, or the Adrian helmet. However a number of units around Belgrade received the cacak helmet, which was based on the Czech design.

Headgear

Some Yugoslav units wore the Czechoslovak 1932 model helmet; manufactured in Yugoslavia and known as the cacak after the town of that name where it was produced. The French Adrian helmet was still common. It bore the Yugoslav royal arms: in models manufactured after 1926, this was set within an oval disk. Yugoslav troops most commonly wore the traditional Serbian side cap or sajkaca. Headgear for officers was in a state of flux. Officers not wearing a helmet would either have a peaked sajkaca with cockade or a peaked cap resembling that worn by British officers and with a golden double-headed eagle on a red oval by way of insignia. A simple pillbox style cap, with eagle badge, was also common.

Officers of the mountain regiments could also wear a black busby with tassel, a form of headgear also used by personnel in the assault battalions.

Insignia

Infantry wore scarlet collar patches, officers had golden shoulder boards piped scarlet and, for officers below the rank of major, a scarlet stripe down the centre. These shoulder boards bore pips according to rank and a monogram for those regiments with royal patrons (such as the 2nd Regiment, Prince Mihailo) or a number.

Officers of the 2nd Infantry Regiment had established a training school for special warfare in 1932. By 1940 some six small battalions of assault troops (know confusingly as chetniks, but not related to the royalist partisans of that name) had been raised and equipped. They were uniformed and equipped as the two mountain regiments, but with their own distinctive insignia. This included black collar patches and black piping to the officers' gilt shoulder boards. Officers and men tended to prefer the black busby with a tassel and an eagle badge in gold on a black cloth background. A skull and crossed bones silver badge was worn on the collar patches. The men carried hand grenades, a rifle (the short rifle, VZ-24, from Czechoslovakia) and a dagger.

Cavalry officers had silver shoulder boards. Piping had been yellow before 1924, but after that date it was switched to dark blue – the same for the two Guard cavalry regiments, although they had royal cyphers on their shoulder straps and shoulder boards. Cavalry wore breeches and boots and carried sabres and carbines.

Artillery had black collar patches, with officers having gold shoulder boards piped black. Silver badges on the shoulder board distinguished different kinds of artillery: mortar batteries had crossed cannon barrels under an exploding grenade; fortress artillery had crossed barrels over a tower; anti-aircraft artillery had crossed barrels beneath an eagle; horse artillery had a gun barrel crossed with a sabre; and coastal artillery had an anchor and crossed barrels.

Signals troops had violet distinctions, with officers having two entwined bolts of lightning on their shoulder boards.

Communist partisans wore a great variety of uniforms and civilian items, but usually wore a red star cap badge. Chetnik or royal partisans also wore a variety of items, but many wore their old Yugoslav uniform and sported royal insignia such as the eagle.

Mechanized troops

The Yugoslavs had purchased Renault tanks in 1929, and by 1940 had raised two tank battalions. A squadron with light tanks was also created to support the cavalry. Tank troops wore infantry uniforms, but officers featured a tank badge on their shoulder boards; officers from other kinds of mechanized units had a winged wheel device.

◀ **Sergeant Major, 20th Infantry Regiment, 1941** *This sergeant has the Adrian helmet with the 1921 coat of arms. A newer model, with the double-headed eagle and shield within an oval, was adopted in 1926.*

▶ **Gunner, 114th Heavy Artillery Regiment, 1941** *The double-breasted greatcoat was the most commonly seen item amongst Yugoslavian troops when the Axis forces invaded. It had patches in branch-of-service colours – black, in this case, for artillery, and red for infantry.*

OTHER AXIS POWERS

The alliance of countries supporting Hitler's Germany and the empire of Japan was partly created by force of circumstance. Some countries, such as Mussolini's Italy, were natural partners of Hitler's Fascist regime. Others, such as Bulgaria and Hungary, had been wooed by very effective German diplomacy in the 1930s. Others, such as Romania, fought to restore lost territory, committing forces to win back regions deemed important and to right past wrongs. Some nations such as Slovakia and Croatia were created from the territory of defeated nations and calculated that providing the Axis with troops and resources guaranteed the existence of their new status. Furthermore, some nations found themselves accidently at war: Finland, for example, had come under attack from the Soviet Union and then resumed the struggle, but now in the context of a general war on the Eastern Front. This made for a mixed and rather unwieldy alliance.

▲ *Finnish infantry take up positions during manouevres in the summer of 1939, a few months before the Winter War against the Soviet Union.*

◄ *Hitler and Mussolini meet at Munich on 18 June 1940. Just eight days earlier Italy had entered the conflict on Germany's side and declared war against France and Britain.*

GERMANY'S ALLIES

Nazi Germany had initially been isolated. Early moves towards an alliance with China had been cast aside when Japanese ambition in the east seemed to make Japan a more promising ally, especially given the outspoken anti-communism of its ruling class. Japan and Germany concluded a pact in November 1936 and from then on conducted a close but, because of strategic and geographic differences, badly coordinated alliance, with Germany waging wars in Europe and Japan seeking to extend its rule over the whole of Asia. Japan would continue to fight after the German surrender and it was only the combination of the atomic attacks on Hiroshima and Nagasaki and the Soviet campaign in Manchuria that forced Japan's unconditional surrender in August 1945.

Tripartite Pact

Italy had joined the Japanese-German alliance in 1937, forming the Tripartite Pact in September 1940. Before that the German and Italian relationship had been fraught, especially after the German occupation of Austria.

▲ *Japanese Prime Minister Hideki Tojo, in his general's uniform, with his cabinet, in 1941.*

German support for Italian ambitions in Africa had, however, finally wooed Mussolini. Italy would fight in the Balkans, Africa and the Mediterranean. It also annexed part of France and sent an expeditionary force into the Soviet Union. This force, periodically reinforced, suffered heavily and was eventually withdrawn in early 1943.

The Axis alliance was seemingly improvized, with each power pursuing its own war aims and remaining uncertain as to those of its allies. Germany and Japan failed to co-ordinate an attack on the USSR. Italy repeatedly launched campaigns, and then asked for German assistance.

▼ *General Ion Antonescu, leader of Romania, joins the Tripartite Pact in Berlin in November 1940. This brought Romania and Slovakia into the Axis.*

Other supporters

The Axis was supported by a number of nations who provided troops, supplies and assistance. Bulgaria fought a strange war as an ally of Germany. Its troops participated in the attack against Yugoslavia and Greece, a traditional enemy, but were not deployed against the Soviet Union. Bulgarians fought a counter-insurgency war and a battle against Allied aircraft, before switching sides in 1944.

Hungary had been humiliated by the Treaty of Versailles of 1919 and so was a natural German ally – more so, after Austria was absorbed by the German Reich. Its officers and ruling class were pro-German and there were large and vociferous right-wing organizations in total sympathy with Fascism, the Arrow Cross being the most significant. Hungarians would only fight in the Balkans and on the Eastern Front, where they met with some success. Even so, an abiding hostility towards Romania made them a prickly member of the Axis. Hungary attempted to withdraw from the alliance in 1944 but was occupied and the Arrow Cross assumed control. That government then fought to the bitter end as a German ally.

Romania was a latecomer to the Axis. The country had gained significantly in the Treaty of Versailles, but found itself isolated by crafty German diplomacy in the 1930s. Despite the importance of the Romanian oil fields, British chiefs of staff had concluded in March 1939 that Britain could not intervene to support Romania if an alliance was concluded with that country: Romania was left to shift for itself and attempted neutrality. It was to be punished for its tardiness by loss of territory to its neighbours, Bessarabia being occupied by the Soviets in 1940 and other slithers of territory going to Bulgaria and Hungary. This led to a coup: King Carol abdicated (and left for Mexico), being replaced by young King Michael and General Antonescu's right-wing government. Romania threw herself into an alliance with Nazi Germany, seeing such an agreement as the only way it might recover its lost territory. Romania took part in the war against the Soviet Union in 1941; Britain declared war against Romania in December 1941. The country switched sides in late August 1944.

Then came the countries that joined with Germany as a result of the defeat of other nations.

Axis allies after defeat

Croatia emerged as a loyal German ally from the defeat of Yugoslavia. Slovakia did the same from the destruction of Czechoslovakia. The situation in France was a little different, with the right-wing establishing the Vichy regime as a loyal, if junior, partner. Its

▲ *German officers, standing alongside a French policeman, raise a flag on the Arc de Triomphe in Paris in June 1940.*

troops would defend Madagascar, Syria and Senegal from the Allies before Germany grew distrustful of the French and occupied the rest of the country.

Finland put up a brave fight when attacked by the Soviet Union in November 1939. France and Britain even prepared troops to send out as an expeditionary force in support of the Finns. English-speaking volunteers, enthusiastically applauded by Winston Churchill, were formed up under the command of Kermit Roosevelt, son of US President Theodore Roosevelt. What the wary Joseph Stalin, leader of the Soviet Union, made of this early Churchill-Roosevelt alliance is not clear. But the expedition did not sail, and the volunteers did not make it, although plenty of Swedes and Balts did. Finland was to take part in the 1941 campaign against the Soviet Union. This was known as the Continuation War, as Finland set itself the task of overturning Soviet gains from the Winter War of 1939–40. The Finns were heavily involved around Leningrad, but dropped out of the war in September 1944.

Smaller states allied to the Axis cause are not covered here. Iraq was briefly a German ally, and Thailand was allied to the Japanese. In addition to collaborators in France, the Axis also had (limited) support from client regimes in Montenegro, Serbia and the Czech lands (Bohemia and Moravia).

Volunteers

Finally, a number of volunteers fought alongside the Axis, often drawn from occupied countries, but there were also individuals from neutral countries who fought for Germany for adventure or ideology. In addition, a large force of Spaniards fought alongside the Germans on the Eastern Front.

▼ *Colonel General Von Falkenhorst, right, and Field Marshall Baron Mannerheim, left, review Finland's armed forces, 1941.*

BULGARIA

The Treaty of Neuilly-sur-Seine of 1920 imposed onerous terms on Bulgaria. Conscription was abolished, the Army restricted to 20,000 men and they were not permitted tanks, armoured cars or military aircraft. Territory was lost; Western Thrace went to Greece, the Dobruja to Romania and parts of Macedonia to the Yugoslavs, and it was obliged to pay 2,250,000,000 French francs in reparations. By the 1930s, Bulgaria was challenging these clauses, and with the support of Germany was enlarging and modernizing its armed forces. The country had 24 infantry regiments in 1928 and 32 in 1940, and four artillery regiments in 1928 and 10 in 1940. There were two motorized regiments and a tank battalion (which became a regiment in 1941 and a brigade in 1943) and technical troops. An Air Force was officially re-established in 1937 and a battalion of paratroopers was activated in 1943.

As part of the modernization process, Bulgaria's uniforms were brought up to date. A new uniform was issued in 1936, overseen by the minister of war, General Lukov. The winter uniform was in a shade of brown in a lighter tone than the previous uniform, which had been chocolate brown, a style that persisted until these tunics wore out. The tunic now had a stand and fall collar (previous versions had standing collars, which were uncomfortable), six buttons (bearing the lion for infantry, crossed cannon barrels for the artillery), four pockets, pointed cuffs, shoulder straps and collar tabs in branch-of-service colours. Summer uniform consisted of a sand-green collarless shirt, with officers wearing tunics in this colour. Officers wore tailored tunics in olive green, made from better material, gabardine; they had closed velvet collars or open collars and were worn with shirts and ties. These collars bore litzen as a distinguishing mark, and the tunics had shoulder boards.

Service insignia

Personnel wore collar patches in branch-of-service colours. This was red for infantry, green for frontier troops, black for artillery and engineers, red piped white for cavalry, light blue for aviation and dark blue for medical staff. Personnel serving the armoured brigade had a complicated

◀ **Sergeant, 39th Infantry Regiment, 1941**
The Bulgarian infantry went into combat dressed either in the older style tunic, with standing collar, or a newer version with a more comfortable stand and fall collar. The traditional brown cloth was used for the uniforms of other ranks.

▶ **Private, 15th Infantry Regiment, 1942**
Bulgaria attempted to modernize its armed forces in the late 1930s with a new helmet. This often bore the Bulgarian national colours on a shield badge. This was dropped later in the war.

◀ **Captain, Armoured Brigade, 1943**
Bulgaria's armoured personnel modelled their uniforms on those of the Wehrmacht. The officers' tunic was often worn with a peaked cap in the same colour, but black tankers' overalls and caps were also popular.

▶ **Private, 48th Infantry Regiment, 1945**
In September 1944 Bulgaria changed sides and raised new units. These often wore uniforms provided by the Soviets such as the famous telogreika padded jacket.

system, but the standard tab was red piped yellow. These colours were also reflected on the officers' litzen. Shoulder straps had traditionally carried the regimental numeral on them or a royal cypher of the regimental patron. These were removed on campaign and a simple strap, piped in service colours, was worn. Officers still had these signifiers on their shoulder boards which were in the tunic colour on campaign, piped (this was really the underlay showing through) in the service colour (the armoured brigade had yellow) and with red (for the infantry, tank and artillery) or blue (for the medical staff) lines and metallic pips to designate rank. Parade boards had been gold for most services, but silver with a zigzag pattern for cavalry and for engineers; these boards were sometimes transferred to field uniforms. NCOs had shoulder straps piped in the service colours with bars across the strap according to rank (three yellow bars for a sergeant) and gilt edging to the strap.

Winter uniform also included a practical grey greatcoat. It was double-breasted, with metallic buttons for officers and brown for other ranks. The officers' collars were initially of green velvet but wartime items lacked this. A collar tab with button distinguished branch of service. It was red for infantry, black piped red for artillery, red piped yellow for armoured troops and red piped white for cavalry; piping also continued around the collar.

Helmets

Headgear consisted of a simple side cap for NCOs and privates, and a peaked cap with leather visor for officers. The side cap resembled the Italian bustina, with fold down ear flaps. It had the Bulgarian lion on the front and, on the wearer's right, a shield in Bulgarian colours (white, green and red). Officers wore this cap, too, but also the more traditional peaked cap with a cap band piped in service colours and with piping around the crown. It had a cockade with a gilt surround; the surround was white for NCOs. A peaked cloth cap was introduced in 1943.

Helmets consisted of three versions of the same Bulgarian-designed model: all were commissioned in 1936 and all were similar, with the C-type being lightest. The design was based on the German steel helmet, but had a slight ridge on the dome and swept-back sides. A Bulgarian shield was affixed to the right side.

Specialists

Tankers wore overalls and, from 1942, seem to have adopted German-style panzer uniforms with red collar tabs and skulls and black berets or peaked caps. Italian leather helmets were worn inside the vehicle. Paratroopers wore German paratroop helmets or Bulgarian caps with paratroop wings and Italian or German gear. The Guard cavalry regiment had a service dress as for the regular cavalry, but with white or silver trefoil lace on the collar and lace shoulder straps.

CROATIA

▲ *Nazi propaganda shows a tank of the German SS during the occupation of Split, Croatia, in the fight against the Italian Badoglio government in September 1943.*

An independent Croat state had been declared even before the German, Hungarian and Italian invasion of Yugoslavia of 6–18 April 1941 was over. The plan was to create a kingdom ruled by a scion of the House of Savoy that would act as an Italian puppet state. Instead a band of political extremists led by Ante Paveli , who styled himself the Poglavnik or leader, concentrated power in their own hands. This movement, the Ustaša (whose members were the Ustaše) set about settling old scores against the Serbs and creating a Greater Croat state. The Ustaša formed an army, known as the Domobranstvo (or Home Defence), and this was increasingly supplemented by a shadow army of Ustaše paramilitaries and armed units. The two were merged in 1943.

Home defence

Some 15 infantry regiments were raised, along with a cavalry regiment (the Zagreb Regiment), two motorized battalions, engineers and artillery. These were supported by local militias. Uniforms were initially based on the old Yugoslav model, with light grey tunics with stand and fall collars, light grey trousers and sajkaca caps or the Czech-style cacak helmet. German peaked caps and German helmets began to replace these items. Caps bore badges bearing the initials 'NDH'. Croat units began to wear the red and white chequered shield emblem from late 1941, usually on the helmet but also on the tunic sleeve.

◀ **Private, 11th Infantry Regiment, 1942**
Early Croatian uniforms resembled those worn by the troops of the Austro-Hungarian empire. This individual has, however, obtained a German helmet and attached a Croatian shield badge.

The collar patch on the tunic and greatcoat showed branch-of-service colours, and, again, there was little change from the Yugoslav system. Infantry had crimson patches, mountain infantry green, cavalry had yellow, engineers dark green, artillery red and mechanized troops had black. The insignia on the NCOs and officers' collar patches and shoulder straps also reflected the pre-war Yugoslav design, with mechanized troops adopting a silver tank symbol, and engineers crossed spades and a shovel. Rank was shown by means of silver stars on the collar patch, with officers having trefoils on the shoulder strap (NCOs initially had stripes on their shoulder straps before switching to smaller trefoils). After reforms in 1943, red or red and silver embroidered lace underlay this trefoil system for officers, but the project was theoretical rather than put into practice. As the tide turned against the Croat regime, attempts were made to group reliable personnel into elite formations, including the Croat Storm Division

▲ CAPTAIN, 1ST USTAŠA REGIMENT, 1941
The Ustaša units were raised and uniformed in a hurry. Those who had been in exile in Italy returned in mostly Italian dress. This officer has a German helmet and has simply added the letter 'U' to denote his membership of this organization.

and a battalion of paratroopers. These were kitted out with German or Italian equipment, including the distinctive German steel helmet, with the Croat shield badge on the sleeve.

The Croat air force wore uniforms modelled closely on those of the Luftwaffe, with grey-blue uniforms and for pilots light blue piping to the silver or white shoulder strap and collar patches (which bore birds within a wreath of linden leaves) or for air force artillery red piping. A pilot's badge of an eagle clutching a Croat shield, all beneath 'NDH', was worn above the right breast pocket.

The Ustaša

Among the first organized members of the Ustaša were 200 followers of Paveli who entered the country in the wake of the Axis invasion in April 1940. These men were initially uniformed in Italian uniforms with a distinctive red, white and blue collar patch. The Ustaša fought back against the insurgency (commanded by the Croat Josip Broz Tito), raising a volunteer regiment in Sarajevo in September. Known as the Black Legion (Crna Legija), this was dressed – initially, at least – in black tunics of Italian cut, black breeches and jackboots. Its members also wore a black cap. Insignia consisted of a cap badge letter 'U' containing within it a grenade embossed with the Croat colours of red and white, and a red collar patch bearing the same device, worn on the upper lapel. Officers wore embroidered shoulder straps and a distinctive belt buckle. The distinctive black uniforms rapidly gave way to grey or light grey replacement items.

In addition to this unit, there were dozens of battalions of Ustaša troops, the armed paramilitaries of the movement. They sported various uniforms, all with the movement's 'U' and grenade emblem. An elite unit of bodyguards, the Poglavnik Bodyguard Battalion, had been raised in 1942, becoming a regiment (Poglavnikov Tjelesni Sdrug) and then two regiments by 1943, along with an armoured battalion equipped with German panzers. The Poglavnik Bodyguard Battalion wore the red, white and blue insignia of the men who had first accompanied Paveli , with the blue closest to the wearer's neck, but with the 'U' and grenade symbol imposed. They seem to have maintained Italian-style green uniforms for some time before largely opting for German-style grey uniforms. The Poglavnik Bodyguard regiments had distinctive rank insignia, with red circles and half circles worn on the upper sleeve. A corporal, for example, had two circles, a sergeant two above a bar. Officers had the same style, although red on a gilt background, and these were on the lower sleeve and on a German-style peaked cap or side cap.

► LEGIONARY, BLACK LEGION, 1944 *While the Black Legion received its name from the black tunic and breeches, not all members of the unit were dressed in black. Some made do with grey tunics and grey shirts, in the style of Italian Fascists.*

FINLAND

Finland was involved in the so-called Winter War (November 1939 to March 1940), in which the country faced Soviet invasion, and the Continuation War (June 1941 to September 1944), in which the Finns supported the German invasion of the USSR.

▼ **Sergeant, 4th Jäger Battalion, 1940** *The Finnish Jägers were considered an elite and bore the distinctive badge of the crossed skis and wheel. Peaked caps generally bore a Finnish national cockade or officers' cockade.*

Finnish infantry

The Finnish Army had imposed some uniformity on its armed forces adopting a heavy brownish green tunic in 1927 that was replaced in 1936 with a new grey tunic. It had six buttons, four pockets with buttoned scalloped flaps, shoulder straps, straight cuffs and a falling collar. Collar patches, sometimes attached to a grey cloth patch, sometimes sewn directly to the collar, showed branch of service. This was green edged in white for infantry, and green edged in yellow for Jägers.

Rank was shown by chevrons within the collar patch for NCOs, and by gilt roses (or a lion, in the case of general officers) and decorative edging to the patch for officers. Branch of service was also indicated on the shoulder strap in gilt insignia, crossed rifles above the regiment name or unit number for infantry and a peculiar combination of crossed skis laid over a bicycle wheel (skis in winter, bicycles in summer) for Jägers. Collar patches were often abandoned as the war continued and shortages became acute (at the same time metallic buttons were replaced by plastic or Bakelite versions), but the branch-of-service insignia continued to be worn on the straps, the collar or the greatcoat.

The double-breasted greatcoat was of thick wool and reached down to the calves. It could be unbuttoned at the back to ease movement. Officers could have rank stripes attached to the lower sleeve.

Civic Guards wore an arm badge that showed different combinations of colours for different regions and bore the letter 'S' (standing for Suoljeluskunta).

Headgear consisted of the grey peaked cap that had ear flaps secured by two buttons on the front of the cap when not in use and a Finnish cockade (edged in gold for NCOs). From 1939 officers wore a red cockade bearing a golden lion.

▲ **Second Lieutenant, 26th Infantry Regiment 1940** *Finnish officers could use the German steel helmet, or the peaked cap of the Finnish infantry. In winter they often adopted the comfortable fur cap. The insignia on this second lieutenant's shoulder strap is the crossed rifles of the infantry.*

The peaked cap was often piped in branch-of-service colours. A number of styles of fur cap were worn in winter months, the older version having a notch in the front, the 1939 pattern being rounder and fuller. Helmets were in short supply. Finland issued its own helmet in 1940, based on a Swedish model, but it was rare and German helmets predominated in the years before 1944. A small number of Finns painted a skull device on their helmet, but this seems to have been confined to Jägers and light artillery. The helmet was painted matt or sometimes white.

Trousers were grey and worn either with puttees and ankle boots or more frequently with leather boots. Felt or fur boots were popular in winter, ski troops preferring Laplander boots. Equipment consisted of cartridge pouches for the standard Russian Mosin Nagant rifle (or pouches for the Mauser adapted to fit Mosin Nagant ammunition) suspended from a buckled belt that was usually brown leather. Finland had been part of Russia before 1918 and so had a stock of Moisin Nagant rifles, but also purchased more so they could have a standard issue rifle. Rank and file carried a rucksack, bread bags, a canteen, mess tin and entrenching tool. Most of these items were of German manufacture and dating from World War I. Some infantry were armed with Finnish-made Suomi sub-machine guns. Officers mostly carried German Luger pistols.

Foreign volunteers were equipped in a haphazard manner, but the Swedes at least formed units with insignia of a crossbow, moose head and crossed swords within a disk. These were worn on the shoulder strap beneath crossed rifles (and later on the tunic and greatcoat collar). A device featuring four clenched hands was also worn.

Cavalry and technical troops

The cavalry was uniformed as per the infantry, but armed with carbines and more lightly equipped – for example, they often just had straps or braces in a Y-shape over the shoulders, pouches and a belt. They wore yellow collar patches bordered with red for the cavalry regiment and blue for the dragon regiment. They wore a regimental insignia on the shoulder patch and crossed swords on the greatcoat collar.

Artillery had red collar patches and an exploding grenade insignia on the shoulder strap with regimental number below. Troops in heavy artillery were distinguished by a crossed shell device. Armoured troops had black collar patches bordered initially with grey and from 1941 with orange. Tank personnel often wore a black leather tunic, issued in small numbers in 1936 and worn over a cotton or wool tunic, as well as leather trousers and a leather tankers' helmet. Tank personnel bore a unit insignia on their shoulder straps that consisted of two armoured arms clasping a rose. Aviation personnel and pilots had blue facings bordered in black. Pilots wore a pilot's badge on the tunic pocket and when in the air German-made leather equipment.

◀ **Sergeant, 10th Field Artillery Regiment, 1939** *Winter camouflage clothing gave the Finns a real advantage in the Winter War of 1939–40. This hooded smock had matching gloves and trousers as well as a hood that could be worn over the steel helmet.*

▶ **Tank Radio Operator, 1943** *Finnish armour developed during the conflict and, by 1943, was largely equipped with German material. Some of the improvised early war leather items of uniform continued, and the distinctive arrow badge showed membership of an armoured unit.*

FRANCE – VICHY

After France signed an armistice in June 1940, the country was divided into a German zone of occupation in the north and west, a small Italian zone by the Alps and a zone ruled by collaborationists led by Marshal Philippe Pétain. This collaborationist government also maintained civil rule over the occupied zone.

The Pétain regime dropped the title of 'republic', styling itself the État Français. Known as the Vichy regime after its headquarters in the town of that name in south-central France, it maintained some armed forces and crafted itself into a neutral power, which nevertheless worked closely with the Axis. Those opposing the regime either joined the French Resistance or went into exile, frequently joining the Free French forces of General de Gaulle. In November 1942 the Germans and Italians added the Vichy zone to the occupied zone, dismantling Vichy's armed forces. The French retained just one metropolitan unit, the Premier Régiment de France.

Vichy troops

The Vichy Army was a miniature version of the French Army of 1940. It numbered around 90,000 men, was supposed to be voluntary, but was in part based on a kind of national service. There were 18 infantry regiments (the 1st, 5th, 8th, 18th, 23rd, 26th, 27th, 32nd, 41st, 43rd, 51st, 65th, 92nd, 150th, 151st, 152nd, 153rd and 159th, representing the regions of France), 15 battalions of chasseurs, 12 cavalry regiments (four cuirassiers, four dragoons, two chasseurs and two hussars) and eight artillery regiments. Most of these units went into garrison along France's frontiers, which included the line of demarcation that divided the German-occupied territory from the Vichy zone. In addition, there were colonial troops in North and West Africa, Syria and Indochina – where Vichy France fought a short war against Thailand and allowed the Japanese bases in French territory.

Uniforms were initially based on those worn in 1940. Insignia was sometimes replaced, with helmets

◀ **Trooper, 7th Legion, Gardes Republicaines Mobiles, 1942** *Vichy France relied on paramilitary police and gendarmes to keep order because its own armed forces were severely restricted. This member of the GRM wears the standard Adrian helmet painted the blue of the gendarmes, with the double-headed axe badge.*

▶ **Trooper, Tcherkesse squadron, 1941** *France had a number of Circassian squadrons in Syria. They were uniformed in service tunics with standing collars (white in summer, black in winter) and field uniforms in khaki. French officer had kepis in the colour of their original unit.*

having the 'RF' on the bursting grenade scratched off. Regiments, as before, often wore regiment badges on their tunics. Tricolour armbands were worn initially, until regulations could come into effect and specify what the new insignia should be. Then in 1941 a new uniform was drawn up and began to be issued in 1942. The most notable change was that a helmet in the style worn by armoured units in 1940 was supposed to be adopted. In addition, a new tunic was introduced. It had an elegant cut, with an open collar, four pockets (scalloped flaps and pleats on the upper pockets) and four brown buttons down the front. Insignia consisted of crimson cords above the regimental number, also in crimson. In addition, the tunic was worn (a khaki or olive shirt, often white for officers) with a khaki tie (black for officers). Trousers matched the tunic and puttees (or cream gaiters that resembled spats) and ankle boots were worn; officers preferred riding boots. A variety of greatcoats, parkas and civilian coats were worn in cold weather. The Army was abolished in 1942 and some troops went on to serve in paramilitary or police units.

Colonies

The situation for troops in the colonies was similar, where old uniforms continued to be worn, but many French personnel returned to France – and were replaced by native levies who were raised to supplement the defence of the colonies. Units such as the Circassians in Syria, the Tonkinese Tirailleurs in Indochina and the Malgache regiments in Madagascar therefore became the backbone of Vichy France's colonial army.

Collaboration

Vichy France had a number of paramilitary organizations. One was the notorious Milice Française: active members of this corps were known as Francs Gardes, were armed and were uniformed in dark blue tunics with black shoulder straps. They wore navy blue berets or Adrian helmets pained dark blue. The beret had a silver shield

▶ **Corporal, Foreign Legion, 5th Regiment, 1941** *Although the French Foreign Legion is most famous for its white covered kepi, many legionnaires adopted the French version of the sun helmet for use in Africa and the Far East. This unit, stationed in Indochina, wore the helmet with bursting grenade badge.*

▲ **Badges** *Top left: lapel badge of Tcherkese squadrons; Top right: sleeve badge of the GMR; Above left: helmet badge of the GRM; Above right: lapel badge of the 6th Legion of the GRM.*

bearing the Greek letter gamma Γ γ, silver on a black disk.

Another armed police unit was the GMR, or Groupe Mobile de Réserve, formed in May 1941. These men were uniformed in dark blue chasseur-style tunics with nine buttons and shoulder straps with a silver button by the collar. Silver unit numbers were embroidered on the collar and the insignia of a silver lion's head was worn on the sleeve. They wore berets, police kepis or Adrian helmets with French police badges on the front. In addition, there was the Garde Républicaine Mobile (GRM) or after February 1941 just simply the Garde, belonging to the gendarmerie; these found themselves formed into legions – initially six in France and three in north Africa, later 14. The Garde had badges on their berets that consisted of a knight's crested helmet above a blue and black shield. They also had their own distinctive badges – variations of a Napoleonic-style eagle on a red and blue shield, with the regimental numeral.

Marshal Petain's own bodyguard, the Garde Personnelle, wore gendarme uniform on service. Service dress was blue tunics with black collar lozenges bearing insignia of a double-headed axe on an exploding grenade. Headgear consisted of the armoured troops' helmet, a fatigue cap or a peaked kepi. In 1943 the Groupe Spécial de Protection was also formed to protect President Pierre Laval; most of these were motorcycle riders and had black leather coats and white equipment with a badge consisting of a map of France, a knight and the letters 'GSP' in red, white and blue.

HUNGARY

The defeat of the Austro-Hungarian empire in 1918 devastated Hungary. The country was plunged into revolution and lost territory to neighbours and to the newly independent states. It emerged as a rump and a kingdom: its monarch was the absent King Charles IV, whom the Allies had spirited away to Madeira; Admiral Horthy ruled in his place as regent. The Treaty of Trianon in 1920, which settled the fate of the country, imposed punitive reparations and sanctions and limited the armed forces to an Army of 35,000 men. Hungary resented the treaty, and found ways to circumvent it with help from Italy and Germany. It had reintroduced conscription in the 1920s and began to re-arm (quite intensely in 1938). Hungarians fought the Slovaks in 1938, the Yugoslavs in 1941 and the Soviets from 1941 to 1945.

▼ **CAPTAIN, 20TH INFANTRY REGIMENT, 1944**
The 1938-pattern tent canvas was usually adapted into a poncho by Hungarian infantry. It provided waterproofing with some camouflage.

Strength of armed forces

The bulk of the Army was made up of infantry regiments: there were 56 of these, plus 27 battalions of border rifles. In addition, two mountain regiments were formed in 1939 to serve in the Carpathians and a parachute battalion became operational in 1941; paratroopers later formed the Szent László Division, named after St Laszlo (also known as Ladislaus), King of Hungary in 1077-95 and patron saint of the military. Cavalry consisted of four regiments, whose members still maintained the traditions of hussars and some cavalry companies mostly attached as divisional reconnaissance.

In 1939 Hungary was in the process of mechanizing her armed forces and the 1st Hussars were switching to armoured cars. There were also tank battalions and reconnaissance companies, 16 battalions of cyclists and mechanized infantry. Artillery included horse artillery and later mountain and assault (or self-propelled) artillery. The Air Force had five regiments – two of fighters and two of bombers, with one reconnaissance regiment.

The profile of the Hungarian soldier very much resembled that of Austro-Hungarian troops of 1918. Paucity of funds made this inevitable and yet in the late 1930s some changes were ushered in.

▲ **PRIVATE, 44TH INFANTRY REGIMENT, 1943**
Hungarian infantry generally wore their chocolate brown winter uniform although a lighter summer cotton uniform was sometimes made available (in light green).

Infantry

The standard uniform colour of Hungarian troops was brown, which had a tendency to fade to a sand-brown colour over time. The tunic had a generous waist and breast pockets that had scalloped, buttoned flaps, a stand and fall collar and shoulder straps. It was closed by five buttons, usually of plastic, horn or wood. Officers and NCOs retained gilt buttons bearing the Hungarian St Stephen's crown. A summer version, in light green cotton, was worn. Officers had the option of wearing a rather incongruous white version.

The collar of the tunic had decorative collar patches that ended in a point. By 1944 these patches had been replaced by a strip of lace in service colours, but in 1939 they were conspicuous. The infantry had dark green patches and this applied to the border rifles and mountain troops. Rank was shown on these patches, with NCOs having brown soutache lace at the end of the patch, silver stars at the front (two for a corporal) and with senior NCOs adding a gilt chevron at the end of the patch. Career NCOs later adopted a triangular badge, worn on the sleeve and backed in service colours. Officers had bronzed stars, and senior officers had decorative golden lace patches imposed on the service-colour patch.

These rank distinctions were partially carried over to the brown double-breasted greatcoat. A coloured patch was worn in the shape of an arrowhead on each collar (this was often discarded on campaign). Officers had dark velvet collars (generals had scarlet lining that showed when the lapel was turned back), with the same kind of patch. Greatcoats initially had shoulder boards in service colours, but in 1941 these were discontinued and replaced by gilt bars of lace on the greatcoat sleeve (three for a captain, for example). The Hungarians also adopted a reversible hooded parka in 1942: green on the outside and white inside, this was padded, warm and very popular. Camouflage sheets were also converted into ponchos.

Trousers were of the same colour as the tunics. In the early years of the war they tended to be of a traditional design. They were buttoned at the fly; baggy above the knee, the lower legs buttoned at the calf with four small buttons. A band was slipped under the foot to keep the trousers from riding up. The trousers were mostly tucked into buckled brown leather gaiters or puttees (in brown cloth). Ankle boots were worn, with officers, cavalrymen and mounted artillery generally preferring leather riding boots or the popular lace-up boots (known as Bilgeri boots).

Hungary had relied on the 1916 steel helmet or the Berndorfer helmet until 1935. Then, having been impressed by the German 1935 model, the Hungarians began production of this type in Hungary. It was issued in numbers in 1938 and so was known as the 35/38 model. It was mostly issued in apple green, but some civil defence forces received a grey-blue version and, of course, the helmet was sometimes

◀ **Private, 6th Infantry Regiment, 1941** *Hungarian infantry marching into the Soviet Union resembled the infantry of the Austro-Hungarian empire. The helmet was usually replaced with a simple khaki side cap while on march.*

▶ **Lance Corporal, 22nd Infantry Regiment, 1942** *Rank, for NCOs, was shown on the collar by means of white stars on the collar patch or, later, by stars on the collar with braid in service colours behind.*

◀ **Lieutenant, 3rd Hussar Regiment, 1942** *The traditional hussar-style Attila jacket seen here was worn in winter by Hungarian cavalry officers. Alternatively, cavalry personnel could make use of the brown cavalry greatcoat, which was shorter than that worn by the infantry.*

▶ **Corporal, 24th Artillery Regiment, 1942** *The red stripes denoting the rank of corporal were also worn on the tunic. Gunners were awarded scarlet lanyards if they excelled at aiming.*

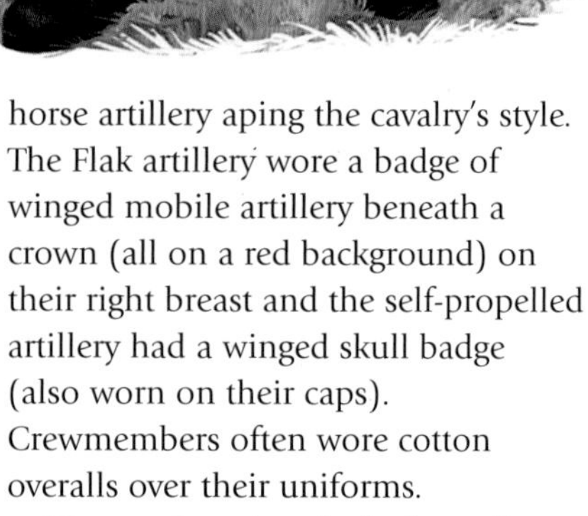

painted on campaign. Issued in six sizes and weighing 1.3kg (2.9lb), it was very robust with a well-made leather chinstrap and a ring on the back rim so that the helmet could be carried by straps.

When the helmet was not being worn, a side cap was used. The most common was the 1920 (or Bocskai) version in brown, with service colour triangular flash on the side (partially covered by three bands of lace) and a Hungarian cockade on the front (with service-colour lace stripes below). It had flaps that could be fastened down with the two buttons on the front or worn to keep the ears warm. In 1944 it was replaced by a peaked cap.

Equipment normally consisted of the 1935 cowhide backpack with rain cape, greatcoat and blanket attached. A belt with simple buckle supported cartridge pouches, entrenching tool and bayonet (with a sword knot for NCOs). A gasmask in a canvas (or after 1942 metal) case was carried. Marksmen wore green lanyards; artillery aimers had red lanyards.

Specialist infantry

The frontier rifles also had green collar tabs but they wore a distinctive eagle and oak-leaf badge on their right breast and the sleeve of the greatcoat. They also had a hunting horn badge (containing the battalion number) on their caps. Mountain troops adopted an edelweiss badge for their caps and as a badge on their breast, and had long socks and ski boots as well as ski suits and gear.

Cavalry

The branch-of-service colour for cavalry, motorized troops and cyclists was cornflower blue. Cavalry wore shorter greatcoats and leather boots. In some cases hussar pelisses (in brown with brown lace) were retained. Cavalry carried carbines in a strap on their belts, and NCOs and officers often retained swords and pistols.

Artillery and technical troops

These troops often preferred the carbine, too. Artillery had red as a distinguishing colour. They generally followed the infantry uniform, with horse artillery aping the cavalry's style. The Flak artillery wore a badge of winged mobile artillery beneath a crown (all on a red background) on their right breast and the self-propelled artillery had a winged skull badge (also worn on their caps). Crewmembers often wore cotton overalls over their uniforms.

Hungary's tank units had cornflower blue patches and a winged tank badge on blue backing. A leather tank suit had been adopted as early as 1936, and a leather helmet was designed in 1939. Italian and German items were also used. Motorized infantry also had cornflower blue distinctions, but they had no distinctive badge.

Signals troops had dark blue collar patches and train personnel had purple. Engineers had steel-grey and medical staff had black. The small river fleet had naval uniforms (sailors' hats and collars), with dark blue distinctions and an officers' badge that had an anchor in wreath. Rank was worn initially on shoulder straps, but from 1942 onwards on the cuff.

Air Force

The Royal Hungarian Air Force was relatively small, but included fighters, bombers, reconnaissance and transport units. While flying equipment was predominantly German, uniforms were Hungarian with some distinctive attributes. The branch-of-service colour was black and this was shown on shoulder straps and shoulder boards. There were no collar patches; personnel instead wore a propeller badge on the collars of their 1930 tunics. Other ranks wore a brown beret or side cap with eagle badge (backed with black), while officers had a peaked cap with black peak and eagle badge. Pilots wore pilots' badges on the breast and the shoulder board moved to the cuff on flying jackets.

The paratroops were nominally part of the Air Force, but they wore the green collar patches of the infantry and infantry uniform. They did, however, have an impressive winged skull beneath a parachute badge for their caps and tunics. It was first issued in 1940 to personnel who had made four successful jumps. The Szent László Division, which consisted of paratroopers and assorted elite units, was formed in 1944 and personnel wore a silver axe in a wreath badge on tunic pockets.

▲ *Hungarian infantrymen participated in the partition of Czechoslovakia in 1938, initially seizing Carpathia and then annexing Carpatho-Ukraine in 1939.*

◄ **Tank Crew Member, 30th Tank Regiment, 1943** *The tankers' uniform owed much to designs being tested by the Italians. The 1936-pattern leather jacket was useful because it offered protection, but regulations had it tucked into the leather trousers and this made the wearer uncomfortable.*

Final days

Hungarian regent Admiral Horthy asked for an armistice with the Soviets when they crossed the border, but was deposed and a German-backed regime formed of leaders of the Arrow Cross movement attempted to stave off a Soviet, Bulgarian and Romanian invasion. The regular Army formed the bulk of Hungary's defences, but Arrow Cross stormtroopers and volunteers were also deployed. They wore a variety of uniforms but all with the brassard bearing the movement's green four arrow emblem set on red and white stripes. Called the Hungaria Movement from 1944 (and so adding an 'H'to their emblem), they defended Budapest in late 1944.

ITALY

Italy was a monarchy, but one ruled by a Fascist government from the time in October 1922 that Mussolini marched into Rome and staged his decisive coup. On the eve of war in 1939 Italy's armed forces were impressive.

Infantry

The core consisted of infantry. There were 106 infantry regiments (with more being raised subsequently), four motorized regiments, six tank-borne regiments, three of grenadiers, 12 regiments of elite light infantry (known as the bersaglieri) and 10 regiments of mountain troops (the Alpini). There were also carabinieri and frontier guards.

The cavalry was in the process of converting into mechanized units, but during the war many of the 30 regiments of cavalry – nominally divided into dragoons, lancers and light cavalry – fought on horseback. There were also mechanized or mounted independent squadrons and combat groups. Then there were the light tank and tank regiments (dating from 1926).

The artillery had 54 regiments of field artillery, an increasing number of mechanized and anti-tank units, five mountain artillery regiments and five anti-aircraft regiments. The technical branches consisted of 18 engineer regiments, a railway regiment, chemical troops, two bridging regiments and two regiments of miners. There were attendant train troops, medical and veterinary services. In addition, Italy could also field a large number of Fascist militiamen and volunteers.

Overseas, Italy had Albanian troops and a large number of colonial units containing natives commanded by Italian officers. These were mostly Askari infantry and tribal cavalry. (The Askari were native Africans fighting in the armies of European colonial powers.)

Italy had pioneered aerial warfare. The Air Force, split between a Naval Air Force (Regia Marina) and the Royal Air Force (Regia Aeronautica), was small but well equipped by the standards of the 1930s – although many of its aircraft were obsolete by the 1940s. In 1941 it began to raise and equip paratroop infantry regiments, organized into the Folgore Division and later the Nembo Division; the Ciclone Division was planned, but did not form. The 80th and 151st

◀ **Captain, 3rd Infantry Regiment, 1940**
The Italian bustina, or side cap, was a practical piece of headgear. It usually bore a branch-of-service badge, in this case the crossed-rifles badge of the infantry. This could be in black thread or machine-woven onto a patch and then attached.

▶ **Private, 38th Infantry Regiment, 1942**
Much of the Italian infantryman's personal equipment was modernized in the 1930s. The water bottle seen here is the 1935 pattern, which also came in a khaki cover for tropical use.

▲ **Private, 11th Infantry Regiment, 1940** *Soldiers of the Italian armed forces still wore the star of Savoy on their collar tabs – Italy was a monarchy ruled by the House of Savoy. Only Fascist organizations tended to drop this distinction.*

infantry divisions (La Spezia and Perugia) were also trained for air-assault operations.

Italian armed forces were divided between operations in Europe, where a grey-green colour for uniforms predominated, and the overseas empire (North Africa and East Africa), where olive green or light khaki was the rule.

The tunic worn by Italian infantryman had been through a number of modifications in the 1930s. A significant change (an open-collared tunic with a coloured collar) had been introduced in 1933, and further adjustments were made in 1934, but the 1937 reform was more far-reaching. This uniform, which came into effect in early 1938, was the outfit worn by the bulk of Italian troops when the war began (for Italy, this was in June 1940, although Italian troops had occupied Albania in April 1939). The 1937 uniform was modern, elegant, relatively practical and comfortable – it came in 21 different sizes; it was destined to be copied by armies in central and eastern Europe.

Tunics

The 1937 ordnance (number 900) called for a new tunic in grey-green. It would have an open collar and lapels, the collar in black wool or velvet with coloured lining (previous patterns had had collars in black, blue or red according to branch of service). The tunic also had three plain buttons (for officers, four gilt buttons showing the branch-of-service insignia), two chest pockets pleated with scalloped flaps and two larger pockets at the waist. The collar bore distinctive collar patches (mostrine) and could be turned up and buttoned that way to keep the neck warm. The tunic could be tightened at the waist with a cloth belt. The cuffs were straight with branch-of-service piping often retained (scarlet for grenadiers, red for infantry) and the shoulder straps were buttoned by the collar.

A jacket was introduced in 1940. This was simpler: it lost the black collar, which was now in the same material as the rest of the jacket, had grey-green buttons and smaller collar patches.

Infantry collar patches were coloured rectangular strips with a star of Savoy (gilt for officers). The patch denoted the division (each of which was composed of two regiments) and was of a traditional design – the 210th and 211th regiments even wore collar patches used in World War I. Specialists wore their special branch-of-service colour under the star but over the divisional patch; divisional artillery, for example, would have a black flame over the patch.

Tunics were to be worn with grey or grey-green flannel shirts. These were either in the 1935 pattern, which abolished the old detachable collar, or

▼ **Private, 10th Granatieri Regiment, 1941** *The bursting grenade was the symbol of Italy's grenadiers – some of whom were sent to China in the 1930s. It was worn within a cockade on the sun helmet, as a metal badge on the officers' peaked cap or as a patch on the side cap.*

◀ **Private, 5th Alpini Regiment, 1942** *Feathers were attached to pompoms in white, red, green and blue to designate particular battalions.*

▶ **Sergeant, 11th Bersaglieri Regiment, 1943** *The Bersaglieri were distinguished by a plume of cockerel feathers. These were attached to the helmet by means of a detachable holder that could be screwed onto the helmet rim.*

Italian greatcoats were mostly the 1937 pattern. These were knee-length and single-breasted in the same colour of cloth as the tunic. The greatcoat had four pockets (including unusual horizontal breast pockets), was fastened with four buttons and had a collar that could be turned up and buttoned in place. The greatcoat collars each bore a star of Savoy.

a modified 1939 pattern. Jumpers were authorized for wearing over the shirt in cold weather. Woollen ties in black – later grey-green – were worn by all ranks, the only exceptions being the Re Division, and the 34th Artillery, which were allowed red ties, and the Lombardia Division and the 57th Artillery, which were authorized to wear blue ties.

Trousers were mostly the 1935 grey-green pattern. In a baggy cut, they were gathered and tied under the knee and worn with puttees 1.28 metres (4 feet) long and a variety of ankle boots. These were mostly blackened leather laced boots with hobnails, although the Alpini had natural leather.

Other infantry units

Bersaglieri were elite infantry. They had crossed rifles with a hunting horn and bursting grenade as an emblem. Their collar patches were crimson (two flames) and they sported traditional cockerel feathers on their helmets. (The round hats traditionally worn by these units had fallen out of fashion.)

Mountain troops, or Alpini, had green collar patches in the form of two flames. They wore a distinctive brimmed hat dating from 1910 with eagle feather or a helmet with feather and pompom according to battalion: the first battalion had a white pompom; the second, red; the third, green; and the fourth, blue. As an insignia they had an eagle over a hunting horn over crossed rifles, with the regimental number in the centre below the eagle; this was worn on caps or stencilled onto helmets. Alpini wore capes rather than greatcoats.

Carabinieri had lace on their collar patches and insignia of bursting grenades with a 'C' in the body of the grenade, worn with a tricolour rosette on colonial helmets. Grenadiers had bursting grenade badges on their caps or helmets and lace on their collar patches. Commandos, or Arditi, were formed into provisional units and given a badge that carried a bursting grenade superimposed over crossed Roman swords.

Helmets

Italian soldiers wore helmets or peakless field caps. Officers had peaked caps. Branch-of-service badges were worn on the front of field caps and peaked caps, and black stencils of this device were often painted onto steel helmets and tropical helmets. For infantry, the device consisted of two crossed rifles below a crown and with a disk containing the regiment's number superimposed on the rifles. Italian troops had fought in a derivative of the

French Adrian helmet in World War I (the 1916 model), but attempts to find and produce a distinctively Italian design began in the 1920s. A prototype was developed in 1931, but in tests by the Granatieri di Sardegna Regiment it proved to be uncomfortable and to offer poor protection. The design was modified and the result – the 1933 model or the trentatre – was remarkably innovative and comfortable: it proved a success when issued in 1934. This helmet was domed, with a small peak and sides that were swept down to protect the side of the head. The lining was of leather, fixed to a frame and also connected the ventilation vents. Rivets secured the leather chinstrap (grey-green for the army, black for the blackshirts); some units in North Africa used a canvas strap. The helmet was generally painted grey-green, although blackshirts painted theirs black and troops in the desert used khaki paint. The Bersaglieri also soldered a clasp to the right of their helmet in order to secure a feather; the Alpini did the same, but on the left.

Italian troops in the colonies wore a domed tropical helmet bound in khaki cloth with branch insignia worn or stencilled in black paint onto the front. In 1936 a flatter helmet, known as the Aden helmet, was introduced.

▶ **Private, Motorcyclist Battalion, 8th Bersaglieri Regiment, 1941** *This motorcyclist, still sporting the cockerel feathers in his sun helmet, would have undertaken reconnaissance and scouting duties for the Ariete Division in North Africa.*

Caps

The most popular form of headgear for Italian troops was the side cap, or bustina. Of an ingenious design, with fold-down peak and with ear flaps that folded over the crown of the cap, it was issued in large numbers in 1934 and after modification in 1935; another version of 1940 split the peak into two pieces of cloth. The cap received a cloth version of the branch-of-service badge and appropriate rank insignia.

Officers continued to wear the peaked cap, too, and, by 1940, this was flatter with a wide crown and black lacquered visor. It had branch insignia and displayed rank as appropriate.

Rank

Officer rank was shown on the tunic cuff, and consisted of gold braid bars with a loop above. A second lieutenant had one such bar with loop, a lieutenant two bars and a captain had three bars. A major had a thicker gold

▼ **Captain, Carabinieri, 1941** *Troops operating in the colonies had the option of wearing long khaki trousers or shorts. Most wore the sun helmet with the habitual colonial cockade and service badge to the fore.*

bar and a thinner bar with a loop, while a colonel had a thicker bar, three bars and loop. Officers with more than 12 years of service wore a gold star below this cuff insignia. Cadets had black insignia piped in gold, warrant officers wore braid on their shoulder straps. NCOs had inverted chevrons on the upper sleeve, in red for corporals (a thick chevron with thinner one below), gold for sergeants and sergeant majors.

▼ **Gunner, 4th Artillery Regiment, 1940**
This gunner is wearing the modified cartridge pouches adopted in 1936. These were lighter in colour than the grey-green leather of the earlier pattern and had an improved opening and securing strap.

Rank insignia was also displayed on the officers' peaked cap. This took the form of bands of braid just above the peak and in principle followed the number and kind of braid on the cuff. Rank was also shown on the peakless field cap, initially in the form of rectangular bands of lace (again following the cuff insignia) on the side of the cap. However, the style of insignia had been modified by 1935 and stars were used instead. A second lieutenant had one gold star, a captain had three and a major had one star in a rectangle edged in gold. Officers with more than 12 years of service had a bar of braid below their stars. Alpini did not follow this system on their distinctive caps, preferring chevrons of gold piped in green: one for a second lieutenant, three for a captain.

Other distinctions

Italian infantry had originally worn a metal arm badge indicating their division, but these were abolished in June 1940 (although examples persisted). Units of the Toscana Division wore a metal badge of two wolf heads above their tunic pockets, those of the Venezia Division had a winged lion badge, those of the Sabauda had a knot and the Torino had a bull. Wound badges, in the form of a strip of gold or silver bar, were worn on the sleeve.

Tropical uniforms

Italian uniforms in Africa (and in some parts of southern Europe) followed the styles set out above, but the cloth was in light khaki (olive green jackets were also common). In many cases, the officer's uniform tunic was replaced by the popular Sahariana, a shirt-style tunic with collar patches; rank insignia were either on the cuff, as bars above the breast pocket or on black shoulder boards, an earlier style retained by many officers in the African theatre. The Sahariana had a detachable cape. Other ranks were issued a simpler shirt version of this item. Many troops wore simple khaki shirts and shorts, baggy trousers, borrowed German items or captured Allied supplies.

▲ **Lieutenant, 31st Tank Regiment, 1942**
This officer wears the practical leather jacket but underneath he would have his standard grey-green officers' tunic with black flames on light blue rectangular collar tabs. Upon moving to Africa later that year, the tunic and breeches would have been khaki.

Equipment

Italian equipment consisted of a leather belt supporting two ammunition pouches (modified in 1936), an aluminium canteen and

▲ **Private, 183rd Parachute Regiment, 1942** *Many Italian troops adapted the 1929-pattern camouflaged tent canvas for use as a cloak. Italian paratroopers went further, creating smocks from similar material.*

flask (1930 pattern), a gas mask (the M-31) and a knapsack made from stiffened canvas. (Mountain troops had the 1939-pattern canvas rucksack.)

Cavalry

Italy's cavalry had been distinguished by branch insignia on their helmets and caps (light cavalry had a hunting horn below a crown, lancers had crossed lances and dragoons had bursting grenades), but in 1935 a simple cross was authorized. A more significant distinction was the three-flamed collar patch, with each regiment having its own distinctive colour – the light cavalry had the flame patch on a rectangular patch of a different colour. Riding boots and breeches were worn. Equipment consisted of the 1927 grey-green ammunition bandolier, with 91/38 cavalry carbine ammunition.

Artillery and tanks

Italian artillery followed the infantry or cavalry pattern of uniform. Branch insignia on caps and helmets consisted of crossed cannon barrels – placed beneath a grenade for field artillery, combined with crossed swords for horse artillery and together with a hunting horn and eagle for mountain artillery. They wore a single flamed collar patch in black piped yellow (blue piped yellow for motorized artillery) superimposed over green for mountain artillery. Engineers had similar patches, but piped red, and variations of lightning bolts below a grenade as a cap badge; miners added crossed axes and hammers, while bridging engineers added crossed anchors and ropes. Chemical troops had a cross within a grenade as a cap badge and an unusual flaming mortar on their collar patch. Signals troops had simpler blue-piped red patches. Tank troops had a two flame red patch (black for motorized personnel) on a blue background, with branch insignia of a bursting brigade over a crossed gun and machine gun barrel. Tank crews often wore berets and the distinctive leather cushioned helmet. The knee-length black leather coat was preferred.

Blackshirts

Commonly known as the blackshirts, the Fascist militia were a significant military presence. The MVSN (the Milizia Volontaria Sicurezza Nazionale) was something of an army within an army, with its own ranks and rank insignia. They had adopted black shirts and black fezzes in the 1920s and these were generally retained by the legions formed for military service abroad, although the black shirt was usually worn beneath the standard army tunic and helmets often replaced fezzes. The MVSN initially issued the bustina side cap to officers only, with the rank and file wearing the traditional fez. By 1940 the cap was mostly in grey-green, but black

▼ **Captain, 14th Cavalry Regiment (Alessandria), 1941** *Italian light cavalry wore a flaming grenades badge on their caps, but also had collar tabs in distinctive regimental colours. These were flames on a coloured patch; lancers would have flames without the rectangular backing.*

examples were also seen especially in the elite M battalions (formed in the autumn of 1941). The cap carried the MVSN insignia of fasces below a star and within a laurel wreath, with the legion number below in a disk. It was mostly on a patch of red cloth, or sewn directly to the cap.

The collar patches worn by the blackshirt legions were inevitably black, but the Savoy star was dropped in favour of the fasces in gilt metal. The M Battalions wore a stylized red 'M' wrapped around the fasces. Most of the blackshirts wore daggers as well as standard army equipment.

Colonial troops

Troops from the colonies wore khaki tunics and baggy trouser and most had Takia headgear (a short fez or round cap) or fezzes. Coloured scarves were worn. Officers wore Italian uniforms, with the scarves.

Foreign units

Italy not only sponsored and supported units composed of foreign personnel, but also raised and equipped a number of foreign units of its own. Many of these were formed into Milizia Volontaria Anti-Comunista (MVAC) or blackshirt detachments, uniformed like Italian blackshirts but with distinctive badges and some local variations – for example, Montenegrin round hats with a macabre badge of a skull clenching a dagger between its teeth. Albania was a separate case because it was annexed by Italy: a small army was retained, with 14 battalions of Albanian volunteer militias. They had blackshirt uniforms with a white qeleshe felt hat or fez and a distinctive round badge on the sleeve: a red circle with black Albanian eagle with fasces.

Slightly different was the Croatian Legion, raised to serve in Russia. It wore Italian Alpini uniforms and equipment and had a distinctive badge with 'Croatian Legion' in Italian and Croat above an Italian cross and Croat checkerboard shield, divided by entwined ropes, topped by an eagle.

In 1942 Italian forces in the Soviet Union raised a squadron of Cossacks, operating as part of the Savoia Cavalry Regiment. They initially wore the regimental uniform, but following expansion in 1943 wore Kuban busbies, carried Cossack swords and wore a distinctive sleeve badge – white over blue over red chevrons. The Italians also raised Arab and Indian units for service in Africa and even had a unit of German volunteers (the Compagnia Autocarrate Tedesca). They wore Italian olive green uniforms with white collar patches, piped red, with a swastika on an Italian rosette on tropical helmets and on armbands on their left sleeves.

◀ **Sergeant, 81st CCNN Battalion 'M', 1942** *The 'M' battalions were blackshirt units that were awarded honorary status for good conduct. The collar patch bears a stylized 'M' over fasces.*

▶ **Lieutenant, 3rd Infantry Regiment, 1944** *By 1944 the new Salo Republic adopted the Roman gladius sword within a wreath insignia, dropping the monarchy's star symbol. The bersaglieri, however, used a skull device.*

Air Force

The Regia Aeronautica was uniformed 0in dark blue and with some particular distinctions. The blue tunic was without

▲ **Legionary, 132nd CCNN Battalion, 1941** *The blackshirts had been key to Mussolini's success. They went on to form armed militias and eventually were the basis for the armed forces of the new Fascist republic in northern Italy from 1943.*

collar tabs (although the traditional star was retained on the collar) and had Air Force buttons, with an eagle below a crown device or plain on the pocket; rank was indicated by means of rectangular shoulder tabs in gilt thread and on the cuffs. This cuff insignia consisted of stripes below a diamond. On the flying jacket the cuff rank device was often placed above the breast pocket, as were pilots' wings. NCOs had chevrons, as for their army counterparts. Air Force personnel tended to wear straight trousers with their service uniform, but preferred breeches in the field.

In the tropics the blue uniform was often replaced by light khaki or white uniform. The Sahariana jacket was popular. This and other tropical-issue tunics took a distinctive shoulder strap in dark blue or khaki with gold piping and insignia – a crown above a combination of stars.

Flying gear usually consisted of the zipped Marus flying jacket with fur collar and brown overall trousers, leather boots and a distinctive leather flying helmet; pilots in Africa often wore white cotton flying overalls rather than the leather jackets. Pilots with different specialisms – for example, dive bombers, bombers and torpedo bombers – wore distinctive badges on their tunic pockets.

Paratroop units were quickly pulled together, so there were variations in uniform with troops in colonial helmets, shorts or baggy zouave-style trousers. They wore light blue collar patches if they wore the tunic or a distinctive shirt-tunic (similar to the Sahariana), but most wore camouflage smocks in the field with the distinctive 1941 paratroop helmet.

Repubblica Sociale Italiana (RSI)

The RSI, formed in northern Italy by the Fascists when Italy surrendered in 1943, received German support. Its troops continued with Italian uniforms, dropping the crown and the star of Savoy and soon developing their own three-flamed collar patches that replaced the star with a Roman Gladio in a wreath. Bersaglieri and Alpini often continued with the old two-flamed patch. Infantry had a red patch, artillery had orange, tankers had blue and blackshirts had black. The Milizia Volontaria Sicurezza Nazionale became the Guardia Nazional Repubblicana (GNR). Paratroopers had winged Gladio on a blue patch. Officers had shoulder straps piped in these colours. A shield in Italian colours was worn on the side of the helmet and troops raised in Germany had a distinctive design of crossed swords with fasces and a swastika. Italian troops who fought with the Allies retained Italian distinctions but were often given British battledress.

▼ **Legionary, 1st Legion of Albanian Fascist Militia, 1943** *Italy sponsored a number of Fascist militias in the Balkans. This Albanian retains his traditional white headgear, with a Fascist badge; the fasces over Albanian eagle is also worn on the sleeve to emphasise political sympathies.*

JAPAN

Imperial Japan was a significant military power in Asia and contributed a great deal to early Axis success. Japan had been a closed country until the 1850s and then embarked upon a period of rapid modernization. That process was soon accompanied by expansion: an expedition went to Taiwan in 1874, and Japan occupied the island in 1895; by 1910, Japan had annexed Korea. Intervention in China and in the Russian Civil War of 1917-22 bolstered Japan's standing as a regional power, but the occupation of Manchuria in 1931 and invasion of China in 1937 started a new phase of Japanese imperialism, leading to the occupation of most of South-East Asia and the Pacific War.

Military expansion

Japanese troops would fight in the cold of Manchuria, where the Kwantung group of armies operated, and the tropical jungles of Borneo. They were required both to wage huge land-based operations against large Chinese or Soviet forces and to conduct amphibious assaults against small islands and archipelagos. To do this, Japan required a huge Army – as well as an effective Air Force and Navy. The Army was expanded rapidly in the 1930s, going from 17 divisions in 1931 to 51 divisions ten years later. It consisted of: Imperial Guards – infantry, cavalry, engineers and artillery regiments; conscripted infantry organized into infantry regiments – and fortress infantry and independent infantry battalions; cavalry regiments; reconnaissance and tank regiments; and artillery regiments. These were supported by engineers, train, railway and medical personnel. The Japanese Army Air Service (supported by its Navy equivalent) provided air cover. It was composed of regiments of bombers and fighters, independent companies and air intelligence units. Ground support included airfield battalions, signal and repair companies. There were also a large number of auxiliary units recruited from subject peoples, including Koreans and Chinese, and various

◄ **Private, 18th Infantry Regiment, 1936**
On campaign, the Japanese infantryman proved himself to be a master of survival. The standard issue tent canvas has been adapted here to act as a poncho, loops and buttons were added to secure it as needed, making it a versatile piece of kit.

► **Private, 6th Infantry Regiment, 1937**
The Japanese had adopted the French Adrian helmet in the 1920s but began developing their own types in the 1930s. This offered better protection than the simple peaked cap worn in World War I.

collaborators in occupied territories – the most significant being the Manchukuo Imperial Army, which was based in Manchuria.

Infantry

Japanese troops had worn khaki since as early as 1886. There were a great variety of hues and shades, but generally summer cotton uniforms were sand-coloured khaki and wool winter uniforms were a shade greener.

The Japanese went to war against China in 1937 dressed in the 1930-pattern tunic. This was known as the M90, which relates to the Japanese calendar, or the M5, because it was issued in the fifth year of the reign of Emperor Hirohito (r.1926-89). Its most prominent feature was a standing collar closed with two hooks and lined with a white cloth to protect the neck. The tunic had two breast pockets with rectangular flaps and was fastened with five leather buttons. There was a buttonable flap to keep the bayonet in place. There were no shoulder straps, but cloth tabs (passants) on the shoulder denoted rank. These were often removed on campaign. The standing collar bore a collar patch in swallowtail form in the branch-of-service colour (red for infantry). A regimental numeral usually featured on the front of the collar but this was often removed on campaign. The undershirt was usually collarless. Imperial Guard infantry had tunics in finer cloth, a kind of gabardine, when on duty in Japan but wore campaign dress overseas – for example, in Malaya.

Officers wore a similar version of their tunic, but it was privately tailored and in better cloth with metallic buttons. It also had additional pockets at the waist.

Red shoulder tabs displayed rank. Privates had a single star device, senior privates had two and veteran senior privates, three. NCOs added a gold strip down the centre and had combinations of stars. Officers had tabs with a central gold stripe and gold edging. Silver stars designated exact rank: a second lieutenant had one, a lieutenant had two and a captain, three. Majors had a tab with three red lines on a gold background and one silver star, lieutenants had two stars and colonels three. Generals had gold tabs and two red stripes with silver stars set within.

Headgear

The most common headgear in 1937 was the wide-crowned service cap with black peak and star badge. Officers had a stiffer version with a black lacquered peak and rim. Both versions had red piping along the crown and a red headband (often removed on campaign). The Imperial Guard units were distinguished by having a star within a wreath badge rather than just the yellow or gilt star. Japan had not adopted a helmet during World War I, being involved only on the margins of that conflict, but – carefully noting developments in Europe – it attempted to test helmets by issuing them to troops sent into Siberia following the Russian Revolution of 1917. Japan began working on a prototype of its own (which resembled the German helmet) in 1917 and also bought quantities of the French Adrian helmet. The prototype was issued in limited numbers and two other forms were also tested in the 1920s: firstly, the star-vent helmet with 14 ventilation holes formed into a star device; and then the cherry-blossom helmet, in which the vents were concealed by a decorative blossom on

◀ **SERGEANT, 11TH INFANTRY REGIMENT, 1939** *The sword was a symbol of status in the Japanese military. Swords passed down from generation to generation were common, but so, too, were standard issue items such as this NCO's blade.*

▼ **JAPANESE INFANTRY KIT** *Japanese equipment grew progressively less complex as the conflict wore on. This set of equipment was quite typical for 1941 and came complete with metal canteen, water bottle and reserve ammunition pouch in leather.*

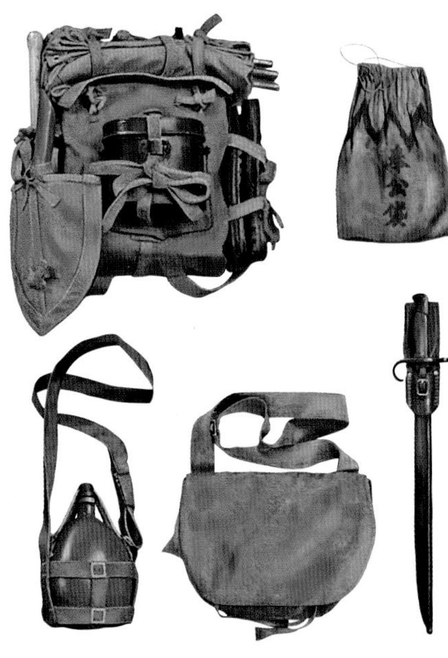

◀ **Private, 41st Infantry Regiment, 1941**
Infantry usually carried the 1938-pattern haversack in khaki cotton. The metal canteen was usually strapped to the back and tucked underneath the whole ensemble was the leather cartridge pouch containing a further 60 rounds of ammunition.

▶ **Private, 55th Infantry Regiment, 1941**
Japan made considerable use of the Type 11 light machine gun despite the fact that it had been issued in 1922 and was superseded in 1936 by the more powerful Type 96.

the top of the helmet dome. Both helmets were round with a slight visor and a rim that flared out to protect the sides of the head. Conclusive trials lead to the adoption in 1930 of a steel helmet known as the M90, which went into production – 5 million copies were produced – and was issued in large numbers from 1932. It bore the Japanese star on the front and had an unusual cotton chinstrap that was often tied in an elaborate knot under the chin. In fact, the helmet offered poor protection and the thickness of the core was increased in 1938 in the M98 helmet. Helmets were often camouflaged with netting, but a helmet cover in leather or canvas was also issued and this could be tightened with drawstrings.

Japan also produced a large variety of tropical helmets, usually matching the outline of the M90 helmet or with a more domed look. They were manufactured from a variety of materials, for example cork covered in canvas.

Footwear

Infantry wore straight trousers, with officers preferring breeches. A kind of pantaloon, bound with straps below the knee and fuller on the leg, was also common from 1937. Most soldiers wore puttees in criss-cross pattern but older-style gaiters were not uncommon before 1941. Ankle boots in natural leather and hobnailed soles were worn by other ranks. Officers often wore riding boots, especially in China.

Winter adaptations

The greatcoat issued with the 1930 uniform was double-breasted. It had two rows of six metallic buttons. It had a simple collar, with five buttonholes where a detachable hood could be fitted behind and no shoulder straps. It was generally free of insignia for other ranks. A winter version with comfortable lining, fur collar and adjustable sleeves to provide a good fit for individual soldiers was also sometimes worn in northern China and Manchuria; in these regions, it was excessively cold in winter and some Japanese units posted there carried ski shoes and skis. Woollen sleeveless jerkins were also sometime used in China. Officers wore a better quality overcoat made from fine wool, which for generals could show rank insignia (brown rings of braid) around the cuff or as appropriate on the collar.

Equipment

Personal equipment consisted of a leather belt (usually in natural leather with a single-pronged buckle) that supported three ammunition pouches. The two forward pouches were usually fastened with studs and contained 30 rounds each, while the pouch worn at the rear (fastened with a buckle) had

60 rounds and cleaning items. The bayonet was worn with a leather frog. A leather knapsack was carried and this had additional straps so that the entrenching tool (with detachable head) could be attached, and so the helmet and spare boots could also be secured. A greatcoat, tent canvas or poncho was strapped over the top in a U shape. Japanese troops carried an aluminium canteen (the 1933 pattern, usually painted khaki) and a mess tin. A haversack was used to carry food or personal items and a gas mask in canvas bag was also worn (on the chest in assault order). It was usually the M95 version with khaki canister, tube and facemask with circular eye pieces or the M99 with rubberized facemask.

▼ PRIVATE 1ST CLASS, 4TH INFANTRY REGIMENT, 1942 *To provide additional support to infantry the Japanese made great use of portable mortars and grenade launchers. This mortar came in a canvas cover with additional ammunition being carried in two canvas and leather pouches worn with shoulder braces.*

Officers carried pistols and swords (as did NCOs). Japanese swords were a sign of authority and were carried in action. The Shin Gunto was the most common design: this sword had come into fashion in the 1930s, when a more traditional Japanese design ousted western-style sabres.

New uniforms

A new uniform began to be issued in 1938 shortly after the start of the war with China and as the old 1930-pattern items needed replacing. Again there were two versions: a thicker wool version and a lighter cotton version. Officers continued with privately tailored items.

The tunic now had a more comfortable stand and fall collar and four pockets, with the lower ones now slanting towards the rear. It was still closed with five buttons but these were no longer metallic, most commonly being produced in bone or plastic. The shoulder tabs had now disappeared, but the new tunic was still without shoulder straps. In the tropics the lightweight cotton tunic was very effective, but additional slits for extra ventilation were sometimes cut into the cloth under the arms. The shirt worn under the tunic was usually without a collar, but a tropical sleeveless shirt with a pointed collar was issued. Officers had collared shirts and an open-necked tunic with lapels and in superior cloth or converted their standing-collar older tunics into tunics with falling collars.

Rank was now moved from shoulder tabs to collar patches, and sometimes moved to the wearer's breast, especially if the troops were in shirt order or because shirt collars obscured patches. The patches followed the same system of red and gold designs as the previous tabs, although generals' patches were now gold. Cadets added a star to their collars. Unit numerals were worn behind the patch: Arabic numerals were used for numbered regiments and Roman numerals for independent or detached units. The collar patches were now red for all branches of service, a specific arm was indicated by a zigzag on the right breast pocket. This was red for infantry. NCOs had a system of rank chevrons on their sleeves, but this was rarely worn on campaign.

The service cap continued to be worn, but the field cap, issued in wool or cotton versions, was now more

▲ CAPTAIN, 214TH INFANTRY REGIMENT, 1942 *It was common for Japanese troops to use sun curtains to cover their necks in the conflict. These could be tied to the peaked cap or attached to the helmet liner or the cap could even be worn under the helmet.*

common – often with sun curtains in the tropics. There were a great number of designs: the one introduced in 1938 had a string-pull that could tighten the hat. All carried a cloth yellow star, mostly on a cloth pentagon. The field cap also came in an officers' version with a lacquered chinstrap and stiffer peak and an other-ranks' version that was less stiff and had a simple natural leather strap.

In colder climes, a fur-lined hat with canvas exterior was issued. It bore the star device and had ear flaps that would button up over the crown when not in use.

▲ *Japanese artillery is hurried forward as Japanese troops pursue a defeated Chinese unit towards the Yangtze.*

◄ **Trooper, 24th Cavalry Regiment, 1937**
Japan made use of cavalry in China and Manchuria. They were distinguished by green collar tabs; unit numerals were often worn on those tabs on parade, but these were usually removed on campaign when plain tabs were worn.

Trousers were in the same style as with the 1930-pattern uniform. It was not uncommon, in the tropics, for troops to wear shorts and shirts despite the risk of mosquitoes. Footwear often consisted of tabi (split-toed) boots or just traditional sandals.

The 1938-pattern greatcoat was now simplified to a single-breasted garment, which was made of inferior cloth. It had a loop to support the bayonet and the front of the coat could be buttoned up in the French style to free the legs when marching. The officers' overcoat did not differ significantly from previous patterns. The greatcoat was relatively useless in the Pacific theatre or in the tropics; instead, a raincoat in rainproofed cotton was issued. It was a buttonable cloak with detachable hood. Officers preferred capes with hoods and slits for the arms. A mix of ponchos or cloaks made from tent canvas were also improvised when re-supply was not possible.

Little by way of new personal equipment was issued after 1938, when a new canvas knapsack was brought in to replace the older leather pattern. In general the quality of all equipment began to decline after 1941. Machetes and axes were, however, issued in large numbers to troops in the tropics and gas masks largely discarded. Portable mortars and grenade-launchers (the M89) were also common. Japanese flame throwers (most commonly the Type 100, which had three tanks) were sometimes used against US troops and in China, but they were unreliable.

Rank and insignia changes

From 1943 rank was also to be shown on the cuff – and the stars on the collar patch were moved closer to the front end of the patch. In some cases the old insignia on the collar was also retained and the two were seen together. Generals were to have three rings and three stars; colonels, two rings and three stars; lieutenant colonels, two rings and two stars; majors, two rings and one star; first lieutenants, one ring and two stars; and second lieutenants, one ring and one star.

Branch-of-service colours were also brought back to the collar patch, but only as a single strip along the base and only for certain support services.

Staff officers wore gold aiguillettes and aides-de-camp wore silver aiguillettes when on duty. Coloured scarves often designated duty officers

▲ CORPORAL, 13TH TANK REGIMENT, 1943 *Tank units were to wear insignia consisting of a tank badge on the collar of their tunics, but such insignia was not usually worn in combat – and overalls were largely devoid of insignia (although this NCO has his rank displayed on his breast).*

on campaign, and white armbands or scarves were worn during night assault operations. Good conduct stripes were displayed as red chevrons on the upper right sleeve of the wearer. A variety of special collar insignia was worn, often in the form of small brass badges above the collar patch. Musicians, for example, wore a harp device and signals troops a rectangular badge or a square with two arms.

Badges for distinctions were worn on the tunic. A badge for NCOs was produced in aluminium. Crossed rifles over a chrysanthemum denoted a marksman, crossed machine gun barrels were for a machine gun specialist and crossed swords and kendo helmet denoted a swordsman. In 1938 red cloth sleeve badges were introduced on the left arm and indicated certain special functions – carpenters had a saw, tailors had scissors and buglers had a bugle.

Cavalry

The cavalry were initially distinguished by green collar patches on their standing collars, then from 1938 by a green zigzag on the right breast. Cavalry wore breeches and boots or leather gaiters and were armed with carbines. Guard cavalry wore the superior officer-style overcoat.

Military police (Kempeitai) wore cavalry uniforms, but with black distinctions and a sunburst insignia worn as a metal badge behind the collar patch. NCOs also wore armbands.

Artillery

Japan's artillery were distinguished by yellow collar patches on their standing collars, then from 1938 by a yellow zigzag on the right breast. Particular branches within the artillery were distinguished by badges on the collar. Heavy artillery had a cannon barrel, mountain gunners had crossed barrels and anti-aircraft units added a cannon barrel with propeller.

Tanks and technical troops

Japanese observers had seen tanks in action on the Western Front in World War I. The Japanese established experimental tank companies in 1925 and produced their first prototype in 1929 – the 89 Model. A tank brigade was formed in 1933, but it was only after the Soviets had trounced the Japanese in 1939 that serious reforms led to the establishment of two (later three) divisions. Independent tank companies also operated, but armour did not play a significant role in Japanese military thinking.

▼ PRIVATE, 2ND PARACHUTE REGIMENT, 1943 *Japanese paratroopers made do with equipment that would have shocked their European counterparts. There were no jump boots and helmets were relatively flimsy affairs in leather. Some sources indicate that Japan obtained some German paratroop helmets, but most used the indigenous version seen here.*

Tankers generally adopted infantry uniforms, but with the addition of a tank collar badge. There was a tankers overall, in khaki, but it was not issued in large numbers. The tankers had a protective helmet first issued in 1932. It was lightweight – weighing just 390 grams (13.8 ounces) – and initially made from leather, although this was quickly changed to padded cloth. The helmet had ear holes and drawstrings beneath these holes to tighten or loosen the crown; a wide chinstrap had holes for the ears and a yellow star was emblazoned on the front.

▼ **Private, 39th Field Artillery Regiment, 1945** *Artillerymen had worn a yellow strip of zigzag lace above their right pockets in the early years of the war to distinguish themselves from the infantry, but this had been dropped by 1943 and most artillery wore uniforms in infantry style.*

Engineers had brown as their branch-of-service colour. This changed to yellow after 1943, when it was worn as a single strip on the collar patch. Train troops had dark blue as their branch-of-service colour, while medical staff had forest green.

Air Force

Japan's Army Air Force wore infantry uniforms. Their branch-of-service colour was light blue (shown on the older standing collars and later as a zigzag on the breast or as a strip under the collar patch). They also wore a propeller badge on their collars. Pilots wore a yellow star in wreath with wings badge (piped in light blue) on their tunic, and observers an eagle in bullion lace (piped blue). Various unit or proficiency badges were worn on the tunic.

Special forces

Japan had lavished attention on her Navy and so it is perhaps not surprising that the most significant of her elite forces were drawn from naval personnel. The Special Naval Landing Force (SNLF), composed of naval personnel acting as infantry, had greener uniforms in the cut of the IJA (Imperial Japanese Army), anchor badges on their helmets (rather than the star), and the helmets were sometimes painted grey-blue; they used naval ranks. Officers wore an open jacket with shirt and tie. Rank was initially shown on shoulder boards before being shifted to collar tabs in 1940, when a new tunic was introduced for naval personnel. These tabs were similar to those in use by the Army but were for officers and in blue (or blue and gold) and had chrysanthemums rather than stars. For NCOs and ratings, a dark green oval patch on the sleeve with red insignia was later replaced by a blue patch and then in 1943 by a shield badge showing an anchor, chrysanthemum and bars. SNLF officers carried swords but naval daggers were also common.

▲ **Private, 5th Fortress Engineer Regiment, 1945** *Japanese troops excelled at camouflage, improvising booby traps and ambushes. Fortress engineers performed much of the preparation for this kind of fighting. They were charged with improving the defences of Pacific islands.*

Japanese paratroopers were split between the Army's raiding regiments and the Navy's SNLF. The Army's paratroopers wore standard infantry

▲ **PRIVATE, 1ST MIXED BRIGADE, MANCHUKUO ARMY, 1936** *The armed forces of Manchukuo included an Army and an Air Force. Personnel adopted Japanese dress, but wore a distinctive five-colour cap badge. These troops saw action in China and against the Soviet Union in 1945.*

uniforms under specially produced one-piece suits that later bore an Army paratroop badge, with rank insignia worn on the arm. The marine paratroops followed the SNLF uniform. They wore a green jump tunic with green pantaloons, again with rank on the sleeve. Ammunition was carried in a special bandolier. Both Army and Navy units wore a distinctive helmet, the dome of which was higher and the rim less flared than the M90 helmet worn by the regular infantry. It was usually worn over a cloth field cap and often with a cloth cover and netting.

Manchukuo

A puppet Army was formed by the Japanese in the Manchurian territories that in 1934-45 were gathered into an empire under the rule of former Chinese emperor Puyi. By 1935 a more formal organization led to the establishment of an Army uniformed in Japanese dress and with largely Japanese equipment. It consisted of a small Imperial Guard, infantry, supporting cavalry, armoured cars and artillery and an Air Force (issued with Japanese aircraft and one German Messerschmitt Bf 109). Troops wore Japanese caps (there were few helmets), stiff peaked caps or fur hats with a distinctive five-colour star insignia, and khaki tunics with shoulder tabs and collar patches in branch-of-service colours: infantry (red), cavalry (green), artillery (yellow), engineers (brown) and train (dark blue).

The Air Force had light blue distinctions. Rank was shown on the shoulder, so that a captain would have a red shoulder tab with gold edging and a central gold stripe with three stars. All the shoulder tabs became red in 1937 or were discarded altogether. A number of White Russian émigrés (opponents of the Bolsheviks in the Russian Civil War of 1917-22 were formed into auxiliary units (the Assano Brigade): they wore the above uniform, although officers seem to have preferred Russian caps of the old imperial army, with the five-coloured star. Mongolians formed the Isono Brigade.

Collaborators

The Japanese formed some units from Chinese collaborators. They also used Mongolian troops – mostly cavalry, in a mix of Japanese uniforms with no insignia and traditional Mongolian caps and coats. Taiwanese troops wore Japanese uniforms, but with the addition of a chrysanthemum to the collar. The Indian National Army (INA) and a Burmese National Army were formed and equipped by the Japanese. The INA wore mostly British items of uniform (with insignia removed), with Japanese helmets, equipment and armbands. Some officers seem to have worn tiger insignia on their sleeves.

▼ **LIEUTENANT, 2ND SPECIAL NAVAL LANDING FORCE, 1942** *These special forces troops were part of the navy and wore naval rank insignia as well as the distinctive yellow anchor badge seen here on the helmet.*

ROMANIA

Romania joined the Axis in November 1940. Its military participated in the war against the Soviet Union, and its Air Force was employed in protecting valuable oil fields around Ploesti.

In 1940 the core of the Army was based on the regular infantry regiments and the ten regiments of Vanatori (chasseurs or light infantry). Two of these (the 3rd and 4th) were mechanized. There were also mountain infantry, the Vanatori de munte. Cavalry was still important (there were 25 line regiments of cavalry, and they were either mechanized, broken up and used for reconnaissance, or used as mounted infantry.

Guard units

There were ceremonial foot and Horse Guards, and also a small Guards division. This consisted of infantry (the 6th Infantry Regiment), Vanatori, a unit of frontier guards and artillery. These units initially wore white collar patches and whitened leather belts, royal monograms on their shoulder straps and crowns on their belt plates, and officers wore decorative embroidery on collar patches and cuffs as well as white and gold aiguillettes. A bodyguard for Marshal Ion Antonescu was created in 1943 and it was uniformed in Guard style with berets.

Infantry

Romania's uniforms had been modernized in the 1930s, the most significant development being the introduction of a Dutch helmet in 1939. Some 628,000 helmets were supplied by the Dutch, largely replacing the French Adrian helmet with a Romanian badge that had been purchased in vast numbers during World War I. The helmet was painted green, was lined and had a cloth or leather chinstrap. Some had a royal cipher, but most were unadorned.

When not wearing the helmet, infantry wore a field cap, which in 1940 was largely replaced by the traditional pointed Capela hat.

The tunic was khaki, single-breasted and had two pockets closed with rectangular flaps. A summer version, manufactured from cotton and lighter in colour, was also available. Buttons had initially been metallic, but from 1941 onwards were either leather or dark plastic. The tunic had shoulder straps, round cuffs and

◀ **Private, 85th Infantry Regiment, 1942**
The Romanian helmet was a licensed version of the Dutch helmet and was sometimes still seen with the cypher of King Carol II. Here it is camouflaged for use in the Russian summer.

▶ **Sergeant, 10th Infantry Regiment, 1941**
When they were not wearing the helmet, Romanian troops opted for the capela cap with its distinctive point. The cap was usually devoid of insignia but had a single button on the front that held the side flaps in place.

◀ **Colonel, 39th Artillery Regiment, 1941** *Officers could chose between the helmet and a peaked cap with high and round crown. This would have had a black band for the artillery and a royal badge beneath a crown. Off-duty wear would have consisted of a simple envelope-shaped side cap.*

▶ **Private, 91st Infantry Regiment, 1942** *An alternative in winter was the wool domed cap, an adaptation of the kind of headgear which had been worn for centuries in rural Romania.*

plain fall collars. Trousers were khaki, as were puttees. Some infantry preferred to wear gaiters or long boots, and most officers wore boots. Winter wear included grey or khaki greatcoats (the 1941 version was closer to being brown) and tall fur caps.

NCO rank was shown on the shoulder strap, with either yellow stripes for corporals or a gold stripe for sergeants or two gold stripes for sergeant majors being displayed. Officers wore a more tailored tunic of British cut with shoulder straps (and bars according to rank), open collar and blue collar patches (infantry belonging to the frontier guards had light green distinctions), a khaki or olive shirt and tie, breeches and boots. They either wore the helmet or from 1940 a broad peaked cap with a cap band in blue, a leather visor (embroidered according to rank) and branch-of-service insignia (crossed rifles) below a crown. In the field this cap was often replaced by a simpler khaki peaked cap, which had rank insignia (in the form of yellow chevrons) above the cloth peak.

The Vanatori had similar uniforms, but their officers had green collar patches with a hunting horn insignia. The Vanatori de munte, who were regarded as elite troops, wore 'VM' on their berets; this insignia was also worn on the shoulder strap. They wore distinctive hooded capes rather than greatcoats and had black leather equipment, long white socks and black boots. The Vanatori, including the mechanized units, often opted for berets or the Capela, and baggy trousers known as golf trousers.

Cavalry

Although cavalry uniforms were similar to those of the infantry, the men wore boots and breeches and far less by way of equipment. Officers wore red collar patches and often wore breeches piped in this colour too. Mechanized cavalry often retained the red distinction, rather than switching to the official grey for mechanized personnel.

Artillery and technical troops

Uniforms worn by artillery and technical troops very much resembled those worn by infantry, although officers had cap bands and collar patches in the branch-of-service colour. This was black for artillery, black piped red for engineers, yellow for chemical troops and grey for armoured units. Anti-aircraft artillery wore a grey version of the artillery uniform; Air Force ground personnel wore a similar uniform, but with light blue patches and cap bands and a winged insignia. This branch colour and winged insignia was also worn by officers of Romania's paratroopers; all paratroopers wore berets and were equipped and supplied with German or Italian equipment. Incidentally, fighter pilots had dark green patches while bomber pilots used red on their field uniforms.

SLOVAKIA

Slovakia declared independence in March 1939, while the Czech lands, now known as the Protectorate of Bohemia and Moravia, remained under German occupation.

The new Slovak state was led by the priest Josef Tiso (known as the Leader, or Vodca, after 1942). It found itself at war with Hungary before changing into a loyal German ally. Slovakia's armed forces consisted of an Army, a small Air Force and the Hlinka Guard (Fascist paramilitaries).

The Slovak Army made use of modified Czechoslovak uniforms. Initially these had been French in style, but in 1930 they were modernized. Khaki tunics and trousers predominated and these were given distinctly Slovak insignia by early 1940. The khaki tunic received buttons showing a two-barred cross on three mountain peaks, and this device was also used on the cap badge and the belt buckle. The tunic itself was of a standard design, closed by five blackened buttons (silver for NCOs) and with four pockets and straight cuffs. The stand and fall collar bore a collar tab in branch-of-service colours. Officers had a khaki jacket with gilt buttons and an open collar and wore khaki shirts and black or brown ties. The distinctive collar tab was worn on the upper lapel.

Equipment was in brown leather with ammunition pouches for the Czechoslovak Vz. 24 short rifle and the Lehký Kulomet Vz. 26 or the German MP 40 (both submachine guns).

Headgear consisted of a soft side cap bearing a Slovak badge or a Czechoslovak Vz. 32 helmet. This was a comparatively heavy helmet, but it offered good protection and was well regarded. It was usually painted olive or brown, had a high dome and a flat base; the lining was attached to the helmet by five rivets. Slovak units being sent into the Soviet Union in 1941 painted a Slovak cross on the side of their helmet and had a blue line painted around the rim of the helmet. This was because the Czech helmet had a similar profile to the Soviet 1940-pattern helmet, and so troops needed a distinguishing mark. Officers wore a peaked cap that bore a winged eagle with a Slovak shield on its breast.

Rank and distinctions

Marks of rank was shown on the collar tab. For infantry this was cherry red. A single silver star on the patch

◀ **Private, 2nd Infantry Regiment, 1941** *Slovaks used a good deal of Czech equipment, including the highly regarded 1932 model helmet. Troops sent into the Soviet Union in 1941 had a blue band painted on the rim to distinguish them from Soviet soldiers who had similar helmets.*

▶ **Lieutenant, 1st Infantry Regiment, 1942** *Slovakia designed its own heraldic devices and began to issue them in 1941. The distinctive cap badge, worn on the simple side cap, showed the Slovak device and it was also displayed on the belt and initially on buttons.*

▲ **Corporal, 1st Cavalry Reconnaissance Group, 1941** *Cavalrymen were used as reconnaissance troops in the campaign against the Soviet Union – note the blue band on the helmet rim.*

denoted a senior private, a corporal had two and a sergeant, three. Veteran NCOs could add a silver flash to the rear of the collar tab. More senior NCOs had silver piping to the collar tab and also added a red stripe to their shoulder strap. Officers followed a similar pattern, but with gold insignia: a second lieutenant had one gold star, a lieutenant had two and a captain, three. A major had one star but gold piping, a lieutenant colonel had two and a colonel, three. The style of rank insignia changed in 1941, with NCOs adding a red and white litzen beneath the star. Officers added gold piping and, for majors upwards, a decorative ribbon insignia beneath the stars.

Artillery units had red collar tabs, pioneers and engineers had black, signals troops had brown and armoured personnel wore pink. Armoured personnel were drawn from all arms and formed composite mechanized units. Tank and armoured car personnel often wore overalls or leather jackets, mostly of German or Italian manufacture.

The cavalry had yellow distinctions and wore uniforms that resembled the infantry, but with shorter greatcoats, breeches and cavalry boots (the infantry preferring puttees and hobnail boots). Air Force personnel had sky blue distinctions, with pilots wearing a winged eagle pilots' badge over their right breast pocket.

Hlinka Guard

This fascist militia's armed battalions – termed the Pohotovostna Oddiely Hlinkovej Gardy (POHG) – numbered 5,000 men in 1944. The POHG either wore black uniforms in infantry style with red collar patches or Italian-style uniforms in dark green with black collar patches. Armbands were used initially and these had the Slovak two-barred cross in red on a white circle on a blue background. Later an SS-style black cuff title was adopted with the words 'Hlinkova Garda' embroidered in white thread. Headgear consisted of either a black side cap with tassel (in imitation of the Italian Fascists) and a badge showing a gold eagle on a red background or, for officers, a black peaked cap. The standard army helmet was also worn after 1944.

Bohemia and Moravia

The army of the Protectorate of Bohemia and Moravia was small and impotent. It adopted a uniform with khaki tunics in 1939. Until 1940, these had a collar patch in yellow (the pre-war colour for Czech light infantry); afterwards, the collar was piped in light yellow with rank stars towards the collar points. The tunics also had yellow-piped khaki straps bearing the battalion number. Troops wore Czech helmets bearing a silver lion on red shield insignia. They also had a badge above their right breast pocket showing the arms of Bohemia and Moravia.

Private Hlinka Guard Assault Unit (POHG), 1945 *The final days of the Slovak state were chaotic. The Hlinka Guard were mobilized to defend the regime and although some units wore black tunics under greatcoats like this, most would have had grey-green open-necked tunics, in Italian style, with black collar tabs.*

GLOSSARY

Aiguillettes: cord or braid worn in loops at the shoulder and with pointed ends. Usually worn as a distinction by officers
Bandolier: leather belt with pouches worn across the chest
Bluse: German term for loose-fitting tunic
Brassards: cloth arms bands bearing unit or specialist designations
Breeches: leg garments worn tight around the knee but baggy around the thighs for ease of movement. Usually worn by officers.
Busbies: wool or fur caps worn predominantly by light cavalry
Bush jacket: a thick cotton shirt with pockets worn long as an unofficial item in the tropics and North Africa
Bustina: Italian side cap with folding ear flaps and peak
Cacak: Yugoslav derivative of the Czechoslovak helmet
Canteen: a wooden or metal container to hold liquid
Capote: French term for the infantryman's greatcoat
Carbine: a shortened rifle or firearm often issued to technical troops
Carabinieri: armed police in Italy, equivalent to the French gendarme
Carabiniers: elite light infantry in French-speaking armies
Chasseur: French term meaning hunter, applied to light infantrymen or, originally, light cavalry
Chechia: soft fez-like cap worn in North Africa
Chevrons: v-shaped strips of cloth or braid worn to denote rank or as awards for service or wounds
Colpack: a wool round hat with a cloth crown
Farrier: a specialist who shod horses
Feldbluse: term used for the German field tunic
Feldgrau: German for the many shades of field grey
Fez: a round or conical cap without a peak but usually with cords worn on the crown

▼ *French helmet badges.*

Flash: a cloth or painted insignia usually worn on sleeves
Fourragère: a decorative length of cord worn at the shoulder, usually in colours commemorating a medal or award
Frogging: decorative lace knots and braid
Gimp: a cord or braid decoration worn on collars or gorget patches
Gorget patch: a patch or tab of coloured cloth worn on either side of the collar by British officers, usually denoting rank or branch of service
Gymnastiorka: a wool or cotton shirt or tunic worn by soldiers in the Soviet Union
Haversack: a canvas bag usually containing food or rations
Howitzer: a short-barrelled artillery piece used to fire munitions at high trajectories
Jäger: a German term for light infantry or riflemen originally used as skirmishers.
Kepi: a round cloth cap with peak
Khaki: dust or mud-coloured cloth initially worn by the British in India
Kitel: a dress tunic worn by Russian officers
Landwehr: a German term for reservist or militia units
Lanyard: lace or cord worn at the shoulder either as a mark of distinction, or, for mounted soldiers, as a practical way to secure equipment
Litzen: decorative strips of lace worn on the collar predominantly by Germans
Mostrine: rectangular or flamed collar patches, worn in specific colours, on Italian uniforms
NCO: non-commissioned officer
Pagoni: Russian for rigid shoulderboards. These showed reg. numerals, branch of service and rank of wearer. They were reintroduced in 1943 after falling out of favour in 1917
Pagri: a turban cloth
Papakha: a fur or lambs' wool cap worn by Soviet soldiers in winter
Pennon: a small flag traditionally attached to the end of the lance to frighten enemy horses, often used on vehicles
Pilotka: Russian fatigue cap, peakless and worn on the side of the head.
Pip: the unofficial term for a brass star or crown worn on the cuff or shoulder strap of British officers to denote rank
Piping: a narrow band of cord or braid cloth which edged a collar, cuff, cuff flap, lapel, or shoulder strap, usually in a contrasting colour to the main uniform fabric
Puggaree: coloured cloth band worn wrapped around slouch hats or round hats

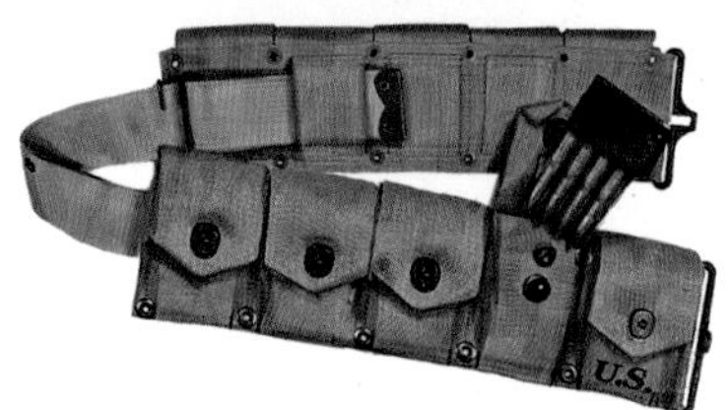

▲ *United States infantry equipment, kit bag, above, and ammunition pouch below.*

Puttees: cloth wrapped around the leg to bind trousers to the leg and keep feet dry
Sahariana: long and practical Italian tropical shirt much in demand in North Africa
Sam Browne belt: a wide leather belt supported by a strap worn over the shoulder service stripes, a strip of lace awarded for length of active service
Shashka: a guardless sword traditionally used by Cossacks
Schützen: German collective noun (meaning 'shooter') used to designate a type of military unit of infantrymen, originally armed with a rifled musket
Shoulderboard: a stiffened piece of cloth worn on the shoulder and carrying insignia or decorative lace denoting rank
Shoulder strap: a piece of unstiffened cloth worn on the shoulder and bearing insignia or lace
Slouch hat: round, brimmed soft hats often preferred by Australian soldiers
Soutache: a decorative strip of lace, usually found on tunic collars
Telogreika: padded and lined jacket popular in the red Army
Topee: *see* Tropical helmet
Trews: trousers cut from tartan cloth
Tropical helmet: helmet made of cork, covered in khaki cloth, with a peak that ran all the way around
Worsted lace: wool material used in the making of rank insignia

INDEX

A
aiguillettes 252
Albania, troops in foreign service 120, 238
America *see* United States
Australia 21, 52–3
  uniform illustrations, private, infantry 52, 53
see also British Empire

B
bandoliers 252
Belgium
  cavalry 183
  trooper, transport battalion 183
  troops in British Empire service 48
  troops in German service 120
  uniform illustrations
    captain, 1st Chasseurs Ardennais 182
    private, 7th Infantry Reg. 182
    second lieutenant, 12th Artillery Reg. 183
bluse 252
brassards 252
breeches 252
British Empire
  air defence 39
  armoured troops 40–1
  cavalry 36–7
  Chindits 43
  commandos 42–3
  foreign troops 48–9
  generals/general staff 24–5
  infantry 26–35
  insignia 25, 27–8, 40, 42–3, 45, 46–7, 256
  LRDG (Long Range Desert Group) 43
  paratroops 44–5, 256
  Royal Air Force 46–7
  Royal Artillery 38
  SAS (Special Air Service) 43
  technical troops 39
  uniform illustrations
    brigadier 24
    captain, East Kent Reg. 27
    captain, Gordon Highlanders 31
    captain, LRDG (Long Range Desert Group) 42
    captain, Worcestershire Reg. 35
    corporal, Highland Light Infantry 30
    corporal, Royal Armoured Corps 41
    gunner, 10th Field Reg. 39
    gunner, 80th Field Reg. 38
    infantry kit 28
    lieutenant, airlanding artillery 45
    lieutenant, Durham Light Infantry 33
    lieutenant, Somerset Light Infantry 29
    major general 24
    major, REME 39
    private, Border Reg. 26
    private, Coldstream Guards 30
    private, commando 42
    private, Gloucestershire Reg. 35
    private, King's Royal Rifle Corps 26
    private, Lancashire Fusiliers 32
    private, North Staffordshire Reg. 29
    private, paratrooper 44
    private, SAS 43
    private, Scots Guards 34
    private, York and Lancaster Reg. 31
    sergeant, Chindits 43
    sergeant, Irish Guards 32
    sergeant, Lancashire Fusiliers 43
    sergeant, RAF pilot 46
    sergeant, Royal Ulster Rifles 28
    sergeant, Trans Jordanian Frontier Force 36
    sergeant, WAAF 47
    squadron leader, RAF 47
    staff sergeant, glider pilot 45
    staff sergeant, Intelligence Corps 25
    tanker, 7th Royal Tank Reg. 41
    tanker, 8th Hussars 40
    trooper, Household Cavalry 36
    trooper, Warwickshire Yeomanry 36
British Free Corps 121
Bulgaria 220–1
  troops in German service 121
  uniform illustrations
    captain, Armoured Brigade 221
    private, 15th Infantry Reg. 220
    private, 48th Infantry Reg. 221
    sergeant, 39th Infantry Reg. 220
busbies 252
bush jackets 252
bustinas 252

C
cacaks 252
Canada 21, 50–1
  uniform illustrations
    gunner, Royal Canadian Artillery 51
    private, Nova Scotia Highlanders 50
    sergeant, Royal 22nd Reg. 51
  see also British Empire
canteens 252
capotes 252
carabiniers 252
carbines 252
chasseurs 252
chechias 252
chevrons 252
China 184–7
  German-trained divisions 187
  troops in Japanese service 247
  uniform illustrations
    captain, 3rd Artillery Reg. 186
    female partisan, Communist Forces 187
    gunner, 3rd Artillery Reg. 186
    private, 303rd Reg. 184
    private, 524th Reg. 185
    private, Big Sword Company 184
    private, Communist Forces 187
colpacks 252
Croatia 222–3
  troops in German service 122
  troops in Italian service 238
  uniform illustrations
    captain, 1st Ustassa Reg. 223
    legionary, Black Legion 223
    private, 11th Infantry Reg. 222
Czechoslovakia
  troops in British Empire service 48
  troops in Soviet service 160
  uniform illustrations, captain, Czechoslovak infantry 48

D
Denmark 188–9
  troops in German service 121
  uniform illustrations
    lieutenant, 3rd Foot Artillery Reg. 189
    private, 4th Infantry Reg. 189
    trooper, Jutland Dragoon Reg. 188

E
equipment *see* individual countries
Estonia, troops in German service 120

F
farriers 252
feldbluse 252
feldgrau 252
fez 252
Finland 224–5
  troops in German service 121
  uniform illustrations
    sergeant, 4th Jager Battalion 224
    sergeant, 10th Field Artillery Reg. 225
    second lieutenant, 26th Infantry Reg. 224
    tank radio operator 225
flashes 252
fourragère 252
France 190–201, 226–7
  colonial units 191, 197–9, 227
  Foreign Legion 199–200
  North African troops 197–8
  Polish troops 200
  troops in British Empire service 49
  troops in German service 121, 122
  troops in Soviet service 160
  uniform illustrations
    captain, 1st Reg. Chasseurs D'Afrique 201
    captain, 12th Artillery Reg. 196
    captain, 13th Battalion of Combat Tanks 196
    captain, 99th Infantry Reg. 192
    chasseur, 7th Battalion of Chasseurs Alpins 193
    corporal, 9th Zouaves 198
    general of brigade 190
    legionary, 2nd Reg. of the Foreign Legion 199
    lieutenant, 2nd Battalion of Chasseurs a Pied 193
    paratrooper, 1st Reg. of Chasseurs Parachutistes 200
    private, 4th Reg. of Tirailleurs Senegalais 198
    private, 5th Infantry Reg. 192
    private, 91st Battalion Alpin De Forteresse 194
    private, 95th Infantry Reg. 191
    private, 255th Infantry Reg. 190
    private, Fusilier-Marin 49
    scout, 24th Group de Reconnaisance 197
    second lieutenant, 4th Reg. of Tiralleurs Marocains 201
    trooper, 1st Motorized Dragoons 195
    trooper, 4th Hussars 195
  Vichy 226–7
    uniform illustrations

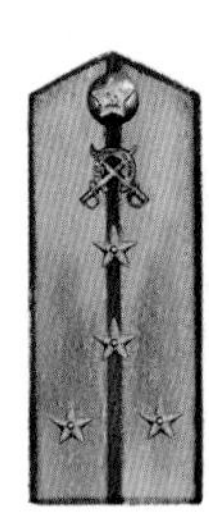
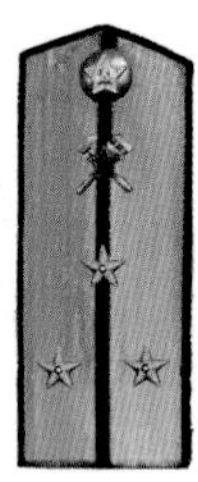
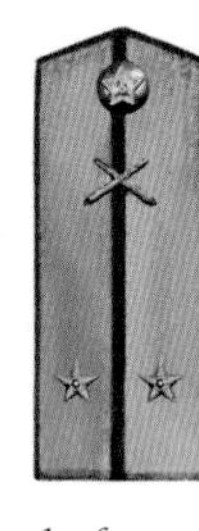

▲ *Russian shoulderboards, from left to right; captain (cavalry), lieutenant (topographical staff), lieutenant (artillery).*

corporal, Foreign Legion 227
trooper, 7th Legion Gardes Republicaines Mobiles 226
trooper, Tcherkesse Squadron 226
frogging 252

G
Germany
Africa Corps 114–15
artillery 126–7
Cavalry 124–5
communications 127
foreign troops 120–3
Army 122–3
SS 120–1
generals/general staff 104–5
infantry 106–13
insignia 105, 108–9, 109–10, 110–11, 117, 119, 129, 137
Luftwaffe 136–7
Luftwaffe field divisions 134–5
mountain troops 130–1
panzer grenadiers 129
panzer troops 128–9
paratroops 132–3
Sondverband 288 115
SS 116–19
uniform illustrations
captain, 3rd Kuban Cossacks 122
captain, Skijager-Reg. 131
corporal, 5th Fallschirmjager Reg. 133
corporal, 35th SS-Panzergrenadier Reg. 116
fusilier, 43rd Luftwaffe Jager Reg. 134
grenadier, 1st Panzergrenadier Reg. 135
grenadier, 916th Grenadier Reg. 111
grenadier, 1053rd Grenadier Reg. 112
infantry general 105
infantry kit 109
infantryman, 347th Infantry Reg. 114
infantry sniper, 58th Grenadier Reg. 113
lieutenant, 1st Horse Artillery 126
lieutenant, 7th Panzergrenadier Reg. 129
lieutenant, 116th Infantry Reg. 109
lieutenant, 242nd Sturmgeschutz Brigade 126
lieutenant, 291st Artillery Reg. 127
lieutenant, British Legion 121
lieutenant, Nord Cavalry Reg. 124
machine gunner, 16th Machine Gun Battalion 107
major general 104, 105
medic, 88th Infantry Reg. 112
officer, 19th Infantry Reg. 106
panzer trooper, 15th Panzer Reg. 115
paratrooper, 2nd Fallschirmjager Reg. 132
pilot, 27th Fighter Squadron 137
pilot, 52nd fighter squadron 136
pilot, 106th Kampfgruppe 137
pioneer, 11th Pioneer Reg. 127
private, 11th Panzergrenadier Reg. 129
private, 12th Mountain Infantry 130
private, 13th Mountain Infantry 131
private, 26th SS-Panzergrenadier Reg. 116
private, 105th Cavalry Reg. 124
private, Spanish Adul Division 123
private, SS Charlemagne Division 121
private, SS Galicia Division 120
private, SS Handschar Division 120
rifleman, 60th Infantry Reg. 107
rifleman, 504th Infantry Reg. 109
senior corporal, 62nd Infantry Reg. 108
senior corporal, 64th Flak Reg. 135
sergeant, 2nd Infantry Reg. 110
sergeant, 3rd Aufklarungs Detachment 115
sergeant, 3rd Totenkopf Infantry Reg. 117
sergeant, 6th Panzer Reg. 128
sergeant, 21st Cavalry Reg. 124
sergeant, 33rd Panzer Reg. 128
sergeant, 638th (French) Infantry Reg. 122
sergeant, Free Arab Legion 123
sergeant, Grossdeutschland Reg. 110
sergeant-major, 3rd Fallschirmjager Reg. 133
SS female auxiliary 118
SS private, 1st Cavalry Reg. 119
SS second lieutenant, SS Aufklarungs Abteilung 118
SS adjutant, 2nd SS Panzer Reg. 117
Waffen SS 116
gimps 252
gorget patch 252
Greece 202–3
troops in British Empire service 49
uniform illustrations
corporal, 6th Infantry Reg. 202
private, 1st Evzone Reg. 203
private, 18th Infantry Reg. 202
second lieutenant, 1st Artillery Reg. 203
gymnastiorka 252

H
haversacks 252
howitzers 252
Hungary 228–31
troops in German service 121
uniform illustrations
captain, 20th Infantry Reg. 228
corporal, 24th Artillery Reg. 230
infantry kit 241
lance corporal, 22nd Infantry Reg. 229
lieutenant, 3rd Hussar Reg. 230
private, 6th Infantry Reg. 229
private, 44th Infantry Reg. 228
tank crew, 30th Tank Reg. 231

I
India 56–7
Gurkhas 57
troops in German service 121, 122
troops in Japanese service 247
uniform illustrations
private, Ghurka Rifles 56
private, Punjab Reg. 56
sergeant, Mahratta Reg. 56
see also British Empire
insignia *see* individual countries
Italy 232–9
colonial troops 238
foreign troops 238
troops in German service 121
uniform illustrations
captain, 3rd Infantry Reg. 232
captain, 14th Cavalry Reg. 237
captain, Carabinieri 235
gunner, 4th Artillery Reg. 236
legionary, 1st Legion of Albanian Fascist Militia 239
legionary, 132nd CCNN Battalion 239
lieutenant, 3rd Infantry Reg. 238
lieutenant, 31st Tank Reg. 236
private, 5th Alpini Reg. 234
private, 8th Bersaglieri Reg. 235
private, 10th Granatieri Reg. 233
private, 11th Infantry Reg. 233
private, 38th Infantry Reg. 232
private, 183rd Parachute Reg. 237
sergeant, 11th Bersaglieri Reg. 234
sergeant, 81st CCNN Battalion 238

J
jägers 252
Japan 240–7
foreign troops 247
Manchukuo Army 247
uniform illustrations
captain, 214th Infantry Reg. 243
corporal, 13th Tank Reg. 245
lieutenant, 2nd Special Naval Landing Force 247
private 1st class, 4th Infantry Reg. 243
private, 1st Mixed Brigade, Manchukuo Army 247
private, 2nd Parachute Reg. 245
private, 5th Fortress Engineer Reg. 246
private, 6th Infantry Reg. 240
private, 18th Infantry Reg. 240
private, 39th Field Artillery Reg. 246
private, 41st Infantry Reg. 242
private, 55th Infantry Reg. 242
sergeant, 11th Infantry Reg. 241
trooper, 24th Cavalry Reg. 244

K
kepis 252
khaki 252
King's African Rifles 55
kitels 252

L
landwehr 252
lanyard 252
Latvia, troops in German service 120
litzen 252

M
mostrine 252

N
Netherlands 204–5
colonial troops 205
troops in British Empire service 49
troops in German service 121
uniform illustrations
captain, 37th Infantry Reg. 205
private, 9th Infantry Reg. 204
private, 42nd Infantry Reg. 204
private, Prinses Irene Independent Brigade 49
trooper, 1st Hussars 205
New Zealand 53
uniform illustrations, second lieutenant, LRDG (Long Range Desert Group) 53
see also British Empire
NKVD see Soviet Union
Norway 206–7
troops in German service 121, 207
uniform illustrations
lieutenant, 3rd Mountain Artillery Battalions 207
private, 12th Infantry Reg. 206
private, 15th Infantry Reg. 206
private, Alta Battalion ski troops 207

P
pagoni 252
pagri 252
papakha 252
pennon 252
pilotka 252
piping 252
pips 252
Poland 208–13
troops in British Empire service 49
troops in French service 200
troops in Soviet service 160
uniform illustrations
captain, 5th Infantry Reg. 208
corporal, 1st Light Horse Reg. 211
insurgent, Warsaw Uprising 212

▼ *The Russian 1939-pattern campaign bag.*

lancer, 2nd Lancer Reg. 210
lieutenant, 8th Light Artillery Reg. 213
lieutenant, 9th Lancer Reg. 2
private, 2nd Mountain Rifles 209
private, 7th Infantry Reg. 209
private, 31st Infantry Reg. 208
trooper, Polish Dragoons 4810
partisan, Eastern Poland 213
puggarees 252
puttees 252

R
Rhodesian units 55
Romania 248–9
troops in German service 121
troops in Soviet service 160
uniform illustrations
colonel, 39th Artillery Reg. 249
private, 85th Infantry Reg. 248
private, 91st Infantry Reg. 249
sergeant, 10th Infantry Reg. 248

S
sahariana 252
Sam Browne belt 252
schützen 252
shashka 252
shoulderboards 155, 252
shoulder strap 252
slouch hat 252
Slovakia 250–1
Bohemia and Moravia 251
uniform illustrations
corporal, 1st Cavalry Reconnaissance Group 251
lieutenant, 1st Infantry Reg. 250
private, 2nd Infantry Reg. 250
private, Hunka Guard Assault Unit 251
soutache 252
South Africa 21, 54–5
uniform illustrations
private, Botha Reg. 55
sergeant, Natal Mounted Rifles 54
see also British Empire
Soviet Union 138–77
armoured troops 170–1
artillery 166–7
cavalry 162–3
Cossacks 164–5
engineers 168–9
equipment 168–9
female flyers 177
female soldiers 159
foreign troops 160–1
generals 144–5
Guards divisions 156–7
infantry 148–59
insignia 144–5, 149–50, 155, 173, 254
marine infantry 172–3
medics 158–9
militia 159
mountain detachments 158
mounted infantry 162
NKVD 146–7
paratroops 174–5
penal units 159
ranks (1940) 149
scouts 157–8
snipers 157–8
Soviet Air Force 176–7
specialists 148, 168–9
technical troops 169
troops in German service 121, 122–3
uniform illustrations
captain, 7th Marine Infantry Brigade 172
captain, 65th Cavalry Reg. 162
captain, 151st Rifle Reg. 154
captain, Tadeusz Kosciuszko Infantry Division 160
Cossack, 39th Guards Cavalry Reg. 164
Cossack, 40th Guards Cavalry Reg. 165
guard, 141st Guards Rifle Reg. 158
gunner, 248th Light Artillery Reg. 166
infantry kit 151
lieutenant, 46th Guards Night Bomber Reg. 177
lieutenant, 142nd Transport Reg. 176
lieutenant general 144, 145
major, 24th Cavalry Reg. 165
major, 242nd Rifle Reg. 156
major, 290th NKVD Rifle Reg. 147
marine, 5th Marine Infantry Brigade 173
marine, 143rd Marine Infantry Brigade 172
marshal 144
medic, 467th Rifle Reg. 159
NCO, 12th Rifle Reg. 151
NCO, 42nd Rifle Reg. 153
officer, 77th Rifle Reg. 149
officer, 642nd Artillery Reg. 166
paratrooper, 1st Parachute Battalion 175
paratrooper, 8th Airborne Brigade 174
paratrooper, 214th Airborne Brigade 175
pilot, 22nd Fighter Reg. 176
pilot, Normandie-Niemen Squadron 161

▲ *German gas mask and cannister, and belt buckle.*

politruk, 638th Rifle Reg. 150
private, 1st Czech Independent Battalion 161
private, 1st Special Mountain Detachment 159
private, 4th Rifle Reg. 155
private, 8th Guards Sapper Battalion 169
private, 29th Engineer Reg. 169
private, 37th Rifle Reg. 148
private, 72nd Replacement Reg. 154
private, 95th Signal Battalion 168
private, 132nd Border Guard 146
private, 244th Rifle Reg. 156
private, 253rd Rifle Reg. 152
private, 321st Rifle Reg. 150
private, 365th Rifle Reg. 153
private, 609th Rifle Reg. 148
private, 902nd Rifle Reg. 158
scout, 188th Guards Rifle Reg. 157
second lieutenant, 210th Tank Reg. 170
sergeant, 2nd Guards Cavalry Reg. 162
sergeant, 14th NKVD Rifle Reg. 147
sergeant, 989th Howitzer Reg. 167
sniper, rifle reg. 157
tank commander, 36th Tank Reg. 171
tanker, 47th Tank Reg. 170
tanker, 75th Separate Tank Battalion 171
trooper, 134th Cavalry Reg. 163
wartime uniform changes 155–6
Spain, troops in foreign service 121, 123, 160
SS see Germany

T
telogreika 252
topee 252
trews 252
tropical helmet 252

U
Ukraine, troops serving Germany 120

uniform development 6–7
uniform illustrations *see* individual countries
United Kingdom *see* British Empire
United States 58–97
  armoured troops 86–7
  artillery 82–3
  cavalry 80–1
  engineers/technical troops 84–5
  General Staff Corps 65
  generals/general staff 64–5
  infantry 66–79
  insignia 64–5, 68–70, 68–71, 71, 73, 81, 82, 86, 92–3, 94–5, 96
  Lend-Lease 20
  Marine Corps (USMC) 90–3
  medics 79
  Merrill's Marauders 88
  military police 79
  mountain warfare 79
  Navy troops 90
  paratroops 94–5
  Ranger battalions 88–9
  Signals Corps 85
  Special Service Force 89
  stars of rank 64–5
  Tank Destroyer Force 82–3
  troops in British Empire service 49
  uniform illustrations
    brigadier general 65
    captain, 2nd Marine Parachute Battalion 93
    captain, 3rd Combat Engineer Battalion 85
    captain, 350th Fighter Group 97
    infantry kit 67, 252
    lieutenant, 10th Infantry Reg. 66
    lieutenant, 21st Marine Reg. 93
    lieutenant, 32nd Armoured Reg. 87
    lieutenant, 157th Field Artillery Battalion 82
    lieutenant, 346th Infantry Reg. 72
    lieutenant colonel 65
    major, 115th Infantry Reg. 70
    major general 64
    marine, 1st Marine Reg. 91
    marine, 4th Marine Reg. 90
    marine, 5th Marine Reg. 91
    marine, 6th Marine Reg. 90
    mechanic, 66th Armoured Reg. 86
    medic, 386th Infantry Reg. 78
    medic first aid kit 78
    military policeman, 3rd Infantry Division 79
    officer, 9th Cavalry Reg. 80
    pilot, 373rd Fighter Group 96
    private, 1st Special Service Force 89
    private, 4th Ranger Battalion 89
    private, 18th Tank Battalion 86
    private, 19th Infantry Reg. 74
    private, 34th Infantry Reg. 75
    private, 36th Combat Engineer Battalion 84
    private, 41st Infantry Reg. 72
    private, 45th Infantry Reg. 77
    private, 60th Infantry Reg. 68
    private, 85th Infantry Reg. 79
    private, 133rd Infantry Reg. 66
    private, 165th Infantry Reg. 76
    private, 263rd Infantry Reg. 69
    private, 317th Infantry Reg. 71
    private, 325th Glider Infantry 95
    private, 357th Infantry Reg. 70
    private, 359th Infantry Reg. 73
    private, 423rd Infantry Reg. 69
    private, 517th Parachute Infantry 94
    private, 599th Field Artillery Battalion 83
    private, Merrill's Marauders 88
    second lieutenant, 120th Field Artillery Battalion 83
    sergeant, 26th Cavalry Reg. 81
    sergeant, 56th Signal Battalion 85
    sergeant, 105th Infantry Reg. 75
    sergeant, 168th Infantry Reg. 67
    sergeant, 506th Parachute Infantry 95
    sniper, 103rd Infantry Division 77
    trooper, 113th Cavalry Group 80
    WAAC, Eighth Air Force 97

▲ *British paratroop insignia.*

United States Air Force (USAAF) 96–7

W
West Africa 55
  uniform illustrations, private, Nigeria Reg. 55
World War II
  aftermath period 14–15
  coming of war 8–9
  timeline of 16–17
  war in the east 12–13
  war in the west 10–11
  worsted lace 252

Y
Yugoslavia 214–15
  troops in British Empire service 49
  uniform illustrations
    gunner, 114th Heavy Artillery Reg. 215
    private, 2nd Infantry Reg. 214
    sergeant major, 20th Infantry Reg. 215
    major, 1st Assault Battalion 214

ACKNOWLEDGEMENTS

Thanks are due to the very professional team at Anness, especially to Joanne Rippin. I would also like to thank Digby Smith, Kevin Kiley, Bair Irincheev, and Donald Sommerville for his helpful comments and sharp eye.

I am grateful to the editorial team at the French-language *Militaria* Magazine for providing astute and original articles on all aspects of this vast subject and to those in Russia responsible for the RKKA.RU website.

The artists who illustrated this volume, Simon Smith and Matt Vince, were patient and talented in equal measure. Any faults in the artwork are my responsibility and not theirs.

This edition is published by Lorenz Books, an imprint of Anness Publishing Ltd, 108 Great Russell Street, London WC1B 3NA; info@anness.com

www.lorenzbooks.com; www.annesspublishing.com

If you like the images in this book and would like to investigate using them for publishing, promotions or advertising, please visit our website for more information www.practicalpictures.com

Publisher: Joanna Lorenz
Project Editor: Joanne Rippin
Artists: Simon Smith and Matthew Vince
Designer: Nigel Partridge

A CIP catalogue record for this book is available from the British Library.

PUBLISHER'S NOTE
Although the information in this book is believed to be accurate and true at the time of going to press, neither the author nor the publisher accept legal responsibility or liability for errors or omissions that may have been made.

The publisher would like to thank the following agencies for permission to reproduce their images: Alamy: pp 6b, 6t, 7t, 8t, 13, 14t, 17 (all). Corbis: pp 2, 7t, 7b, 8b, 9t, 9b, 11t, 11b, 13b, 14b, 15, 16 (all), 18, 19, 20t, 20b, 21b, 21t, 22t, 22b, 23t, 23b, 25, 33, 34, 46, 50, 54, 57, 58, 59, 60t, 60b, 61t, 61b, 62, 63r, 63l, 64, 67, 68, 74, 76, 77, 78, 87, 88, 91, 92, 95, 96, 98, 99, 100t, 100b, 101t, 101b, 102t, 102b, 103t, 103b, 104, 106, 108, 113, 114, 133, 134, 136, 138, 139, 140t, 140b, 141, 142, 143t, 143b, 145, 146, 152, 160, 165, 173, 174, 177, 178, 179, 180t, 180b, 181t, 181b, 185, 194, 199, 200, 212, 216, 217, 218t, 218b, 219t, 219b, 222, 231, 244.